Praise for
The Invention *of* Yesterday

"A beautifully written world history focused on the stories different civilizations have told about who we are. It ends with a fundamental question: In today's extraordinary world, can we build new narratives that are inclusive and global enough to encourage worldwide cooperation in the task of building a better future for humanity?"
—David Christian, distinguished professor, Macquarie University, Sydney, Australia, and author of *Maps of Time: An Introduction to Big History* and *Origin Story: A Big History of Everything*

"Brimming with essential insights and yet always approachable, this is the global history we need now."
—Lynn Hunt, author of *Writing History in the Global Era*

"Tamim Ansary has done it again, writing an expansive, wonderfully readable account of our present world. With deft examples drawn from across history, he skewers the idea that there's anything pure about culture or race. Ideas have blended and meshed across space and time to make the modern world what it is. Ansary is a charming guide to this Blesh of Civilizations, and to the world's permanent—and hopeful—capacity for change."
—Raj Patel, author of *Stuffed and Starved: The Hidden Battle for the World Food System*

"Weaving together multiple complex strands of the human experience into a single compelling storyline, Ansary delivers—in his usual down-to-earth yet erudite style—an engaging global 'narrative of narratives' informed by decades of critical study, reflection, and personal transcultural experience. A deeply enriching, highly relevant read from an important, unique voice of our day."
—R. Charles Weller, Central Eurasian and Islamic world history, Washington State and Kazakh National universities

"*The Invention of Yesterday* is an insightful guide into human civilization packed with information that shows how we have been connected globally since the beginning of history. Tamim Ansary unpacks complicated theories to make sense of how we became who we are today."　—Fariba Nawa, author of *Opium Nation: Child Brides, Drug Lords and One Woman's Journey through Afghanistan*

The Invention
of Yesterday

ALSO BY TAMIM ANSARY

West of Kabul, East of New York

*Destiny Disrupted: A History of the World
through Islamic Eyes*

The Widow's Husband

*Games without Rules: The Often-Interrupted
History of Afghanistan*

*Road Trips: Becoming an American in the
Vapor Trail of the Sixties*

The Invention
of Yesterday

A 50,000-YEAR HISTORY
of HUMAN CULTURE,
CONFLICT, *and* CONNECTION

Tamim Ansary

PUBLICAFFAIRS
New York

I dedicate this book to my friends in all the

many worlds I have passed through over the years.

PublicAffairs
Hachette Book Group
1290 Avenue of the Americas, New York, NY 10104
www.publicaffairsbooks.com
@Public_Affairs

Printed in the United States of America

First Edition: October 2019

Published by PublicAffairs, an imprint of Perseus Books, LLC, a subsidiary of Hachette Book Group, Inc. The PublicAffairs name and logo is a trademark of the Hachette Book Group.

The Hachette Speakers Bureau provides a wide range of authors for speaking events. To find out more, go to www.hachettespeakersbureau.com or call (866) 376-6591.

The publisher is not responsible for websites (or their content) that are not owned by the publisher.

Library of Congress Cataloging-in-Publication Data
Names: Ansary, Mir Tamim, author.
Title: The invention of yesterday : a 50,000-year history of human culture, conflict, and
    connection / Tamim Ansary.
Description: First edition. | New York : PublicAffairs, 2019. | Includes bibliographical
    references and index.
Identifiers: LCCN 2019014273 (print) | LCCN 2019018925 (ebook) | ISBN
    9781610397971 (ebook) | ISBN 9781610397964 (hardcover)
Subjects: LCSH: Civilization—History. | World history. | Culture.
Classification: LCC CB69 (ebook) | LCC CB69 .A57 2019 (print) | DDC 909—dc23
LC record available at https://lccn.loc.gov/2019014273

ISBNs: 978-1-61039-796-4 (hardcover), 978-1-61039-797-1 (ebook)

LSC-C

10 9 8 7 6 5 4 3 2 1

Contents

Introduction

This book was born some years ago when I happened to be reading three seemingly unrelated works of history at the same time. One was about the First Emperor of China, who put a million peasants to work building that Great Wall. Another was about Central Asian nomadic life in the centuries before the Mongol conquests. The third one was about barbarian warriors such as Attila the Hun attacking Rome in its later days.

Because I was reading all three books concurrently, I noticed something that probably would not have occurred to me otherwise. The Great Wall of China going up had something to do with the Roman Empire coming down. A provocative thought. China and Rome were two entirely different worlds and knew almost nothing of each other back then, but between them stretched the Central Asian grasslands of the nomads whence the Huns came riding out. When something big happened in China—like the construction of a wall that blocked invading nomads—it sent ripple effects through the nomadic world, which eventually reached Rome. And, of course, big events in Rome sent ripple effects the other way.

What intrigued me was not the Rome-China connection per se but interconnectedness itself as an aspect of human history. I went looking for other examples, and they weren't hard to find. The religious practices prescribed by the Prophet Muhammad, it turned out, had something to do with Europeans acquiring the magnetic compass. The twelfth-century conquest of Jerusalem by the Seljuk Turks had subtle roots going back to crop failures in Scandinavia centuries earlier. The policies of the Ming dynasty in China contributed to the American Revolution. The

nineteenth-century invention of the cotton gin in the United States devastated family life in sub-Saharan Africa—the list goes on endlessly.

Even tens of thousands of years ago, it seems, when we were isolated
bands of hunter-gatherers ignorant of the many other bands of humans
roaming Earth, we were, somehow, some single far-flung network of
interconnected peoples. The globalized tangle that we are today is only
the latest chapter of a story that goes back at least forty thousand years
and perhaps as many as sixty thousand.

This book takes interconnectedness as one of the through lines of world
history but acknowledges another side to the story. Even as we grow ever
more intertwined, we stay ever more resolutely distinct from one another
as groups. We live on the same planet but in many different worlds. What
any of us humans see as the whole world is just the world as we see it, whoever "we" might be. What we know as the history of the world is actually
a socially constructed somebody-centric world historical narrative. There's a
Euro-centric one, an Islamo-centric one, a Sino-centric one, and many more.
How many more depends on how many collections of people on Earth think
of themselves as a "we" distinct from "others." Any two world historical narratives might have the same events and yet be different stories because the
shape of the narrative depends on the teller of the tale. To say that one of
the many possible somebody-centric world histories is the *real* history of the
world is like saying that one of these maps depicts the world as it *really* is.

The shape of the narrative is what it all comes down to in the end.
History deals in facts, of course, but in history, those facts fundamentally
serve a narrative. When we construct our story, we are inventing ourselves.
That's what we were doing in those caves, long ago, gathered around the
fire, passing on to our children what we remembered about our grand-
parents and reminiscing about life-changing adventures we'd shared and
arguing about which of us really killed the bear and drawing conclusions
about the meaning of life from the stars we saw above—for when ancient
folks looked up at the night sky, they didn't just see stars, they saw constellations. They said, "There's a bear," and they said, "Hey look, a mighty
hunter," and their companions nodded, and as long as everybody in the
group saw the bear and the mighty hunter, there they were.

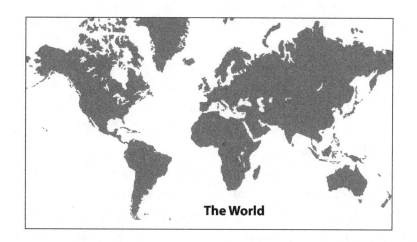

The World

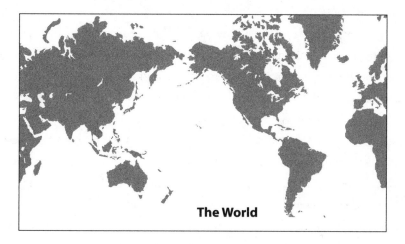

The World

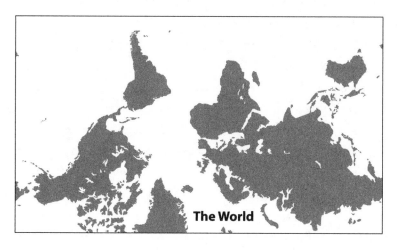

The World

It's all too easy for us modern folks to say the constellations weren't really there. Yes, it's true that those constellations existed only in the minds of the people looking, but then, everything we see and know as human beings is in some sense a constellation: it's there because we see it. We exist as constellations of people. We're immersed in constellations of ideas. We live in a universe of constellations, which are themselves made up of constellations. In the social universe, constellations are as real as it gets.

Social constellations form intentions and set the agendas of history: countries, families, empires, nations, clans, corporations, tribes, clubs, political parties, societies, neighborhood groups, social movements, mobs, civilizations, high school cliques—they're all constellations. They do not exist outside culture. The mighty hunter dissolves upon closer examination into random individual stars. The same is true of social constellations. Clan, country, movement, mob—get up close to any of these and all you see are individual human beings and their ideas.

Culture is a world we invented and keep inventing, a world that would disappear without us. Social constellations are not like rivers or rocks, they do not exist in the physical universe, and yet they have an existence as real as floods or landslides. They must, for they do things in the physical world: build bridges, make wars, invent cars, send rockets to the moon. Any individual human who is part of such a constellation can drop out without the constellation winking out of existence. All the individuals in a social whole can be replaced by other persons without the constellation losing its identity and continuity. Every American who existed one hundred fifty years ago is dead and gone, yet America still exerts clout. Every Muslim alive in 1900 is dead now, but a palpable Islamic entity still influences real events. When we talk about history, we're talking about events that happened only in the cultural universe, and in that universe, social constellations enact the drama; they're the characters strutting the stage.

Forty thousand years ago, such social constellations were imagined into existence by small groups of people who knew each other personally and what they saw together was who they were together. We're not fifty people in a cave anymore; we're eight billion people spread all over the world. None of us can have the perspective of all eight billion. Each of us is part of some smaller social world and bound to the perspective of our own world. We don't see the same stars, and even if we did, we wouldn't see the same constellations: what we see up there reflects who we are down here, and down here we're not all one group. History keeps happening because of that fact: we're not all one group.

When I was in high school, I ran across the word *defenestration*. I had to consult a dictionary to learn that this odd word meant "throwing someone out of a window," and it puzzled me that such a word even existed. After all, there is no term for throwing someone off a balcony or through a doorway or out of a moving car, so why defenestration?

The answer (I discovered) goes back to something that happened in Central Europe four centuries ago. In 1618, one fine day, a group of Catholic lords came to the city of Prague, where most of the people were Lutherans. The Catholic lords had come to deliver a message from the Holy Roman Emperor: Lutherans, the emperor said, must stop building churches on royal land. The Lutherans listened, and then hauled two of those Catholic lords to the window and threw them out. The meeting room was on the third story of the building, so the drop from there to the ground was seventy feet. This was the famous Defenestration of Prague.

Amazingly enough, both lords survived. The stage was then set for interpretation. What did their survival mean? Well, it depended on who you were. Catholics saw the event as a miracle, proof that God was on their side. Lutherans focused on the reason why the lords survived: they landed in a deep heap of dung. The Catholics and Lutherans were both Christians, but when they met, they didn't see fellow Christians or fellow Germans or fellow anything. When they looked at the same event, they didn't see the same event. Even sitting in the same room, they were living in different worlds, and those worlds existed only in culture.

It wasn't just Catholics and Lutherans. Back then Europe was teeming with diverse groups of Christians who saw themselves as "us" and other European Christian groups as "them." Lutherans and Calvinists were both Protestants, but Protestants themselves consisted of many mutually exclusive groups, each with its own worldview. In the tinderbox of us and them that was seventeenth-century Europe, the Defenestration of Prague kicked off the Thirty Years' War, a horrific struggle in which some eight million people were killed or died of starvation, many of them noncombatants. But the contenders weren't individual people, ultimately; they were social constellations.

Could groups involved in such savagery ever reconcile? Could their descendants ever look upon one another as anything but the other? It must have seemed unthinkable four hundred years ago. And yet today, a Lutheran family descended from Germans might live next door to a Presbyterian family descended from Scots, in some small town in Minnesota, without either of them necessarily even *knowing* what kind of Christian their neighbors are, much less caring. A Catholic and a Protestant might join the same book club without worrying about defenestration and have lively conversations in which religion never comes up.

It's not that differences between these groups have evaporated. Their doctrines remain as different as ever. It's just that somehow, over time, they've become different parts of the same culture, some single, amorphous, larger, shared us. Examples like this abound in every civilization. Small worlds *sometimes* do merge into larger worlds; or small worlds intermesh to become distinct parts of single larger wholes, and how this happens is a riddle that can be unraveled only in the cultural universe. Maybe someday two families who live on the same street and send their children to the same kindergarten won't know or care whether their neighbors are Lutheran Christians or Wahhabi Muslims.

Or maybe not, because even though, yes, we're getting ever more interconnected, let's not overlook the way we're doing it: by coalescing relentlessly as social clusters, clumps, and constellations. Ideas and information don't just ripple through the human sea; they travel from culture to culture, and when they cross such borders, some things change. And some things don't. And sometimes borders blur and a bigger cultural something comes into existence, in which parts of both cultures are included, and in which the ghosts of earlier, smaller cultural constellations still live and breathe.

Consider one small example. Chess is played all over the world today, but in the sixth century, it was played only in India, where it was invented. Back then, according to legend, there was a king who fervently believed in free will. Dice games irked him; he wanted a game in which players controlled their own destiny. A savant named Sissa rose to the challenge by inventing a game that depended entirely on strategic thinking, the kind of thinking that makes for success in war. The king was so delighted he offered the inventor gold, but humble Sissa only wanted wheat as his reward: one grain for the first square on his game board, two for the next, four for the next, and so on. The game was played on a board divided into sixty-four squares, and when the king tried to comply with Sissa's request, he discovered that doubling the amount of wheat for each of the sixty-four squares added up to more wheat than the kingdom produced in a year—as Sissa well knew, for he was a mathematician, and mathematics was one of the glories of Indian culture at that time.

Sissa's creation reflected his cultural context in many ways, big and small. It was a game for four players, each of whom had eight pieces. One represented the king and one his top general. The rest of the pieces stood for the four divisions typical of Indian armies at that time: chariots, cavalry, elephants, and, of course, foot soldiers. The game was called *chaturanga*, which means "four branches or limbs." In politically fragmented India, a simultaneous war among four combatants struck a chord.

From India, however, the game moved to Persia, a monolithic society locked into an epic struggle with an equally monolithic Rome. Persia was permeated by a worldview that saw polarity as the fundamental principle of reality: light versus dark, night versus day, good versus evil, life versus death—that's what the world was all about, said the Persians, and the world they were thinking about existed only in culture, that socially constructed realm.

Sure enough, there in Persia, chaturanga turned into a game for just two players, each of whom had sixteen pieces. The board was redesigned to feature alternating squares of light and dark. And the game picked up numerous bits of local color. The very name chaturanga changed into the similar-sounding Persian word *satranj*, "a hundred worries." The general became the vizier, a chief political adviser—every Persian monarch had one of those. Chariots were no longer used in war, so the chariot of the Indian game became a *rukh*, a gigantic, ferocious bird of Persian folklore.

By medieval times, the game had found its way through Spain into Western Europe. And look what happened there. The vizier became the queen. The cavalry turned into knights. The elephants became bishops. Europe had no folkloric bird like the Persian rukh, but rukh sounded like *roq*, which was French for stone, so the pieces formerly known as rukhs now became stone castles.

Yet even as surface features were changing, the internal structure of the game endured: the order among its parts, the template, you might say. The number of pieces remained constant, and they moved the same way. Elephants were bishops now, but there were still two of them, and they could only move diagonally. Chariots became castles, but chariots moved, and therefore so did castles. The king remained the most precious piece on the board, and the whole game was still about protecting one dude who hardly did anything. Check was still check, and checkmate, checkmate. The pawns remained pawns because, apparently, every society has lots of those. And the strategies that worked in India worked just as well in Persia and in Europe. Sissa is long gone (beheaded, perhaps, after trying to claim the kingdom's entire annual output of wheat), but the mathematical ideas of sixth-century India remain solid planks in the edifice of human knowledge today.

What happened to chess happens to pretty much everything in human culture. We're all one humanity, but we never stop creating whirlpools of exclusion. As we interact, ripple effects pass from one human whirlpool to another, and in the process some things change, some things don't, and sometimes, something new comes into being—in general, something bigger.

Forty thousand years ago, we existed only as countless small autonomous bands of hunter-gatherers, widely distributed throughout the wilderness, roaming a world almost entirely unaltered by our existence. Hardly anyone ever met anyone they didn't already know, except at birth—and yet somehow, even then, with no awareness of the fact that we were all interconnected. Today, every habitable inch of the planet is inhabited by humans; no place on the planet remains unaltered by our activity, no life can unfold in isolation from the general flux and flow of human activity, any human action anywhere can have consequences for any other human anywhere—yet somehow, interconnected though we be, we're still grouped into many different socially constructed microcosms that stand in for the unknowable totality of the world itself.

From the bird's-eye perspective, we might consider human history as the story generated by the expansion of these microcosms in the cultural realm and the interactions that occur when they intersect or overlap—interactions that produce everything from psychological confusion, social chaos, and war to cultural efflorescence, religious awakenings, and intellectual breakthroughs. Most significantly, however, even amidst the conquests and enslavements, the rapes and murders, ideas mingle and interleaf until new and more comprehensive conceptual frameworks emerge. We see this in social and economic developments, in warfare, in technology and invention, in religion, art, philosophy, and science. We see it in the course of empires and the spread of ideas. We see it in the occasional overthrow of one global paradigm by another.

The human web has been thickening for tens of thousands of years and will surely go on doing so. In one year, ten years, a hundred years, if we are still around, our lives will not have become less intertwined but more so. More so is the trend, the relentless trend. There does *seem* to be some single human enterprise going on, but it's too big to see. Or at least, we cannot see it yet, any more than the ancient Chinese could see how they were affecting ancient Rome or vice versa. We all want to be part of something bigger than ourselves, but the something bigger has never yet been humanity as a whole. The trajectory looks like it's moving from many to one, but trajectory alone cannot tell us if that's really where this story is headed, especially since we certainly aren't one big happy family yet—or one big anything for that matter.

To get any inkling of the road ahead, we have to look at the road that stretches behind us. How did we get from where we were to where we are? If ever-increasing interconnectedness is the through line, what is the shape of the narrative so far? What are its themes and turning points? What have been its chapters and stages and key events? In short, if history is a story that we're telling one another, what is its plot?

That's the story I went looking for all those years ago when it first occurred to me that the rise of China had something to do with the fall of Rome. And this book is the story that I found.

PART I

Tools, Language, and Environment

Alone among the creatures of Earth, we humans use tools and language to deal with our environment effectively as groups. Language makes stories possible, and mythic stories are what knit human groups together. In our earliest days, our mythic narratives were spawned by geography. We formed webs of meaning with people in our immediate environment. Where we lived was who we were. Through constant intercommunication, we built up shared assumptions about deep matters such as time and space, life and death, good and evil. We lived and died in symbolic landscapes woven of our ideas, and as far as we knew, those landscapes were the world itself. Meanwhile in some other environment, perhaps only a few hundred miles away, people who were clustered around some other great geographical fact and were working as one to wring their nourishment out of that environment were living in a different symbolic landscape, one that they had built collectively.

I

The Physical Stage
(15 billion BCE to 50,000 BCE)

One day in the fall of 1940, four French teenagers were roaming the woods near their home in southwestern France, searching for a legendary buried treasure they'd heard about, when their dog, Robot, suddenly scurried into a depression formed by an uprooted tree and began pawing at something. The teenagers rushed over hoping—but no: it wasn't an old treasure chest; it was only a small dark opening in the ground.

So, they did what teenagers do, what I might certainly have done: they squeezed through the opening to see where it led. They had flashlights with them, which was a good thing, because the hole went down a long way before opening at last into a cavernous room; and there, flashing their lights around, they saw, on the walls and even on the ceiling fifteen or twenty feet above their wonderstruck eyes, bigger-than-life paintings of buffaloes and deer and other animals, rendered gracefully and realistically in black and red and ocher and yellow. They'd found one of the world's most spectacular galleries of Paleolithic art: Lascaux cave.

Spectacular but not unique. Cave paintings like this have been found all over the world since 1868, and they are still being found in hundreds of sites, from Spain to Libya to Indonesia. In many cases, the paintings in a given cave were made over the course of thousands of years; people were coming there to paint, generation after generation. But the oldest of them were made about forty thousand years ago, and the odd thing is, those earliest paintings were already quite sophisticated. What hasn't turned up are transitional products. It's not like Stone Age painters spent a few hundred generations learning to doodle and then a few hundred making blotches vaguely suggestive of animal shapes and then finally figuring out how to make recognizable horses and hunters. Instead, it seems that around thirty-five to forty-five millennia ago, people rather suddenly started making sophisticated art. And it wasn't just paintings. In Asia Minor, paleoanthropologists have dug up complex jewelry made around the same time as the cave paintings. In southern Africa, they found decorative stone knives polished to an elegance still unmatched. In Germany, an amulet-sized bone sculpture of a woman turned up with spindly arms and legs but huge breasts, buttocks, and vulva.

Why did human beings achieve artistic prowess so abruptly? There were other tool-making primates living at the same time as our *Homo sapien* ancestors, and they made the same range of tools, more or less, but theirs didn't change much over thousands of years, whereas ours took a sudden dramatic uptick. *Something* must have happened around forty-five thousand years ago, but what was it? What could it have been?

Coiled inside the answer to that question is our human story.

Every story has a setting, and in our case the setting is the physical universe, so let's start there. Physicists tell us that the physical universe was born about 13.32 billion years ago, which may sound like a long time until you consider that if all those years were dollars, there wouldn't be enough of them to build three modern aircraft carriers, so in some ways, even according to physicists, the universe is rather young.

It all began, they say, with an explosion from a point without dimension. Incidentally, many religious scriptures say something similar. Until this big bang, there was no space, so it would be meaningless to say this point was small. Also, with this explosion, time itself was born, so it would be meaningless to begin any sentence with the words "just before the big bang." There was no such thing as before; there was only after.

In the aftermath of the big bang, the expanding mass of simple matter congealed into countless trillions of stars, all moving away from all the others, though not away from some central point, for *everything*, including space itself, was expanding (and still is). From our perspective, the universe began to get interesting roughly 4.54 billion years ago, when Earth came into existence, one of eight clouds of astral dust coalescing in this region of space around a local star. Due to the gravitational attraction of every particle to every other, each cloud gradually pulled together, spinning like an ice skater, closer and tighter, until it compacted into a round body turning on its own axis and revolving, like its seven sister planets, around the sun.*

In its youth, our own dear Earth was a hot ball of lava. Over the course of a billion years or so, its outer layer cooled into a crust of rock. Then the rains started, and the rains went on until the whole planet was covered with water.

Mixed into this water were a few simple molecules, such as methane, carbon dioxide, and ammonia, molecules with a chemical propensity to link up if they bumped together. When this happened, they formed more complex single units. It's true that only a limited number of new combinations could form randomly out of those first few types of molecules, but as new combinations came into existence, the number of next possible combinations increased as well. Thanks to the ever-expanding set of "adjacent possibles,"** the material universe kept growing in variety and complexity. There was no chance that those first few simple molecules bumping together could accidentally form a frog or a bird. Frogs and birds weren't adjacent possibles. But bump together to form slightly more complex substances such as amino acids? Lipids? Nucleotides? Sure. Not only possible, but inevitable.

---

*Incidentally, when I was young, we were told there were nine planets, but the outermost one has recently been demoted. Poor Pluto, out there in the coldest, darkest part of the solar system, isn't even considered a planet anymore, only a dwarf planet—scarcely better than an asteroid! Even more recently, however, astronomers think they have detected a huge, dark, icy ball of matter ten times the size of our Earth, out beyond Pluto. It's too far from the sun to reflect much light, which is why it has taken so long to discover it. Astronomers have been calling it (cue the ominous music) Planet Nine.

**The term comes from science writer Steven Johnson's book *Where Good Ideas Come From*.

In any closed system (physicists tell us) the amount of disorder tends to increase. Apparently, that's the law. Books shelved randomly by random people don't accidentally end up in alphabetical order; that's just not the default direction of physical reality. Overall, the current is always flowing downhill, from more order to less order until there is no more "down" to go, at which point the current pools up as pond and ceases to exist at all. That's called entropy. But the laws of physics also declare that entropy can be held at bay or even reversed for a while within a closed system—if some outside energy can be tapped. Water always flows downhill—unless a pump comes into the picture. Fire always dies out—unless fresh wood is fed into it. A neat room gets messier—unless someone puts a little effort into tidying things up. Presumably, this cannot happen in the universe as a whole. Why? Because, by definition, nothing lies outside the universe as a whole. To paraphrase the philosopher Ludwig Wittgenstein, "The universe is everything that is the case." Since there's no outside from which the energy could come, entropy can be held at bay only in a small closed system situated *within* that larger environment.

Some four billion years ago, small closed systems of just this sort began to appear on planet Earth. They developed in places where minute cracks in the ocean floor let in heat from Earth's still-molten core. There (or maybe elsewhere) molecules such as amino acids, lipids, and nucleotides connected up to form coherent environments wherein the laws of entropy did not apply: wherein water *could* (metaphorically speaking) run up hill, wherein fires *could* (metaphorically speaking) keep burning. These little clots of molecules were the forerunners of the first simple cells, the fundamental units of life.

Life, then, is a closed system within a surrounding environment: it has an internal order among its parts, which transforms its many molecules into a single whole. This is true of every life-form. A cell. A frog. A human being. You name it.

Life is like a constellation, then, the stars of which are molecules. The constellation is not any of its stars but the order among them all. A life-form, any life-form, must consume energy to maintain its internal structure, and the energy has to come from the outside world. Cells, to put it bluntly, gotta eat. If they don't tap enough energy to hold together, they lose coherence. If the incoherence keeps increasing, a time comes when the constellation is no more. Its material parts, its molecules, are still out there somewhere, but the constellation isn't anywhere. Life has given way to death.

The first traces of life appeared in the global ocean nearly four billion years ago—or maybe even earlier. Whatever the time frame, one thing is certain: life is nearly as old as Earth itself. And while any particular unit of living matter was bound to die, life as a whole proliferated and, by means of reproduction, expanded its capacity to resist entropy. That's the story of life in a nutshell: individuals live, reproduce, and die, but life as a whole expands, branches out, and gains complexity. At least, so far, it always has.

Over the course of billions of years, single-cell life-forms evolved into countless different multicellular ones. Meanwhile, the physical stage kept shifting. Land rose out of the water and formed one big continent. That one big continent broke in two. The two big pieces drifted apart. Those two big pieces fragmented further and kept on drifting until they reached a configuration much like the one that exists today: massive Eurasia over here, gigantic Africa just to the south of it, little Australia to the east, the Americas way off on the other side of the planet, and Antarctica in the farthest south, plus scattered islands here and there, some of them so big they were nearly continent sized. There were no humans on the planet, but the physical stage for the human story was now in place.

About fifty-five million years ago, an island so big that it was practically a continent crashed into the Eurasian landmass. I say "crashed" because I am still caught up in the geologic time scale. On our time scale, there would have been nothing to notice in this period except an occasional earthquake and perhaps a volcanic eruption or two every century or so.

But on the *geological* time scale, this subcontinent s-l-o-w-l-y crashing into Eurasia caused Earth to crumple where they met, and that crumpled ridge became the Himalayas, the world's tallest mountains. The birth of those mountains is significant for human history because of the effect they had on the climate patterns of this region. Winds blowing inland from the seas dropped their moisture when they hit these high slopes, and all that heavy rain created dense forests in Southeast Asia and in the subcontinent called India. Drained of moisture, the winds kept blowing south into Africa, warming up as they moved along. The warm dry air altered the vegetation of northeastern Africa. Dense forests had developed there in wetter times; now as the dry winds came blowing in, those forests began to recede.

The African forest was inhabited at that point by numerous species of animals, including primates of many sorts. Some of the primates retreated with the shrinking jungles, opting to stay in the environment they were best equipped to handle. Others, however, carved out a new way of life at the edge of the forest, where thinning brush left open spaces between the trees. Here, some primates began to live as much on the ground as in the trees. They probably got around in part like kids do on a jungle gym, by holding onto branches and walking along underneath. Meanwhile, the thickets kept shrinking. What had been forest dotted with clearings turned into savannah: grassy countryside dotted with stands of trees.

TOOLS

The savannah is where it all began for us. Those tree-dwelling (but already somewhat bipedal) apes living just where the forest bordered on the savannah developed the ability to walk on two legs without holding onto branches, a good skill to have in their environment because it meant they could scuttle across open grassland to the nearest stand of trees and then run back to the safety of the forest if they had to. Being bipedal, they didn't need their front legs for running; they could do other stuff with those appendages, and so legs turned into arms, and paws turned into hands, and then along came the opposable thumb, and the dexterous ability to make tools, and the bigger and smarter brains appropriate to all the new things these creatures could do.

But wait: the savannah was only one part of the story. Another factor proved just as crucial to our emergence. Northeastern Africa was geologically unstable at this time, which caused extreme climate fluctuations. Around two or two-and-a-half million years ago, this region started going back and forth between hot and cool, wet and dry. Monsoon seasons gave way to long droughts gave way to monsoons. Grasslands turned into deserts turned into swamps. These fluctuations took place over thousands of years, not millions. And thousands isn't much. Creatures that fit their environment as perfectly as keys fit locks were in trouble. The changes were too rapid for biological evolution to come to their rescue. Erratic conditions such as these favored generalists over specialists. It was better to be adaptable than adapted.

In a world where creatures had to keep changing their survival strategies, thumbs, hands, arms, and bipedalism made all the difference. Primates with those features could do an end run around biological adaptation by fashioning tools to make up for their biological deficiencies. At first, they no doubt merely used bits of their environment as tools: with heavy stones they broke nuts, with rough rocks ground seeds, with sharp rocks brought down prey. But then—significantly—they started using the tools they found to *make* tools: using rocks to chip other rocks into knives, using rocks to sharpen sticks into spears. In short, they began inventing.

It wasn't just one kind of primate doing this. Quite a number of different bipedal tool-making primates lived on this planet over the course of several million years. Some died out, others evolved into new, more capable creatures, and their tool kits kept growing. They learned to build and nurse and control fire (yes, fire is a tool). They learned to hunt as coordinated groups, which made them fearsome predators, especially because they equipped themselves with spears and clubs and nets—in short, with tools. They didn't just kill and eat other creatures; they skinned some of them and wore those creatures' skins over their own. Imagine how frightening they must have seemed to their contemporaries.

These new types of bipedal primates used their excellent walking skills to roam all around Africa and across Eurasia. Unlike other animals, they could establish themselves in every sort of environment because they had tools. They moved into forests, deserts, marshes, plains, mountain slopes, river valleys—and these diverse environments shaped who they were and how they lived. If history is a braid, environment is one of its three major strands. Tools are a closely related second one. There is a third strand, but it came later. Who we are and what we've been has, from the start, been intricately related to where we've been and what we've made and done to deal with nature in those places.

None of the creatures roaming the planet a million years ago would have qualified as human. None could have passed unnoticed in a shopping mall today. Biologically, these were not yet human beings. But the constant metamorphosis of life on Earth went on until, about one hundred thousand years ago, give or take a few dozen millennia, some bipedal primates in the world were anatomically indistinguishable from modern human beings. Scientists call these creatures *Homo sapiens sapiens*—Latin for "wise, wise men" (which is a rather egotistical term, come to think of it, since it was invented by us humans to designate us humans).

Was this it, then? A hundred thousand years ago? Was the curtain going up, was the human drama about to begin? I'll venture to say no, not quite yet. The setting was in place, but the characters weren't onstage yet. Those early *Homo sapiens* still lacked one thing that we modern humans take for granted, which brings us back to our starting point. Around forty-five thousand years ago, we humans began painting pictures and playing flutes and dancing. In the race for good stuff to eat, we began beating all the other bipedal primates to the scene. Something must have happened right about that time, something that triggered the rise of human beings to dominance. What was it?

The answer seems to be: true language came into being.

2

History Begins with Language
(50,000 BCE to 30,000 BCE)

Neanderthals had the physical equipment to form words, but words are not language. Crows make sounds that correspond to various items in their environment. You might say they have a word for human and another for dog. They can even create new sounds to denote particular humans. They can caw a sound that tells their fellow crows, "Farmer Brown!" but that's just another word. Words are not language. Along the same lines, animal researchers once taught a gorilla named Koko sign language, and she learned to sign for more than a thousand specific things such as ice cream. But Koko only had vocabulary. She could name things, which is really just a form of pointing. That's not enough.

True language begins when words can join with other words to form an infinite variety of meaningful combinations. Language is vocabulary embedded in grammar and syntax. In true language, while some words do have a direct relationship with an item or event out there in the world, such as:

Chair

Eat

Kill

—other words, not so much, like:

Not

So

Much

In fact, the meaning of many words is not their relationship to something in the physical world; it's their relationship to other words. Developing language meant we could start using words as if they *were* the objects named. Words could then separate from things and have an existence of their own. Once that happened, a whole world of words could form, parallel to the world of things, related to the world of things, but not identical to the world of things. Two language users could enter *that* world and interact within it as if it were the world itself.

Picture two guys talking. One says, "Let's meet for lunch tomorrow at that taco place on Cortland," and the other says, "I'm game. What time? About noon?" Nothing in their physical setting corresponds to any of the words these two guys have spoken. Tomorrow? Lunch? Noon? What could they point to? Nothing. And those are not even the most distinctively linguistic of their utterances. Consider *let* and *at* and *that* and *on* and *about:* those words don't point to anything anywhere. They exist *only* in the linguistic universe they share with *tomorrow* and *lunch* and *noon*.

When we acquired true language, we graduated beyond merely making sounds that triggered our buddies to run or fight or salivate. We elevated our game to making sounds that conjured up, in our fellow humans' imagination, a simulacrum of the whole world. When two guys talk about getting tacos tomorrow at noon, they're not only interacting in a world they're each imagining; they're imagining the same world. If they weren't, they wouldn't both show up at the same place and time tomorrow. That's the truly incredible thing: they're imagining the same world.

Language is what we acquired just before we started making paintings and playing flutes. It's not something we invented. It's a biological trait that developed, like the opposable thumb. We don't "learn" it the way we learn to make risotto. Whatever our group is speaking, that's what we start speaking too. A baby interacts with whoever's around in any way it can: crying, laughing, flailing—until gradually its interactions take on a meaningful quality. What's happening at that point is that the kid is entering the same symbolic world as the group—waking up, you might say, into a reality that his or her group has created and is maintaining.

In the symbolic interaction model of language, meaning isn't situated within each person. Meaning is the web of interactions within a human constellation. We don't "have" meanings that we send to other people through language. We "have" language that we use to *create* meaning with others of our network. When two guys arrange to meet for lunch, they don't invent the words *taco* or *tomorrow* or *lunch*. If both guys die tonight, both the words and the concepts will continue to exist in the social field of which they were parts. Stars can give way to other stars while the constellation remains intact.

At some point, tens of thousands of years ago, creatures who had language gained a crucial advantage over creatures who didn't. Evolution kept selecting for the trait until we humans were full-blown language users: the only ones on Earth. Thereupon, we outcompeted all the other tool-making bipedal primates to extinction. Language is the third strand in the "trialectic" of world history (to coin a term).*

To be clear, we weren't the only animals who could function as coordinated groups. Wolves, to cite an obvious example, operate as packs to bring down prey. Neanderthals probably did at least as much coordinating as wolves. But other social animals had to be together to carry out a plan. They coordinated with one another by sending physical signals back and forth. Their signals triggered responses in one another. Language gave humans the power to work toward some single goal even when separated in space and time. Knit together by language, numerous humans could operate as if they were a single social organism. They could stay in sync even when they were dispersed and couldn't signal one another, even when some of them had to deal with unexpected circumstances that the others didn't know about. They could do this because they were operating within an imaginary world they shared with their whole group. The fact is, we humans don't live directly in the physical universe. We live in a model of the world we have created collectively through language and which we maintain communally. That model was

---

*If a dialectic is a push and pull between two opposing sides, which constantly generates new combinations, a trialectic is the same process but with three lines of interacting forces—which in the case of human history would be environment, tools, and language.

already in existence when we were born; we merely made our way into it as we matured. Becoming an adult meant gaining the ability to imagine the same world as everyone else.

Our stomachs may growl for food regardless of what society we're born into, but our social selves—ah, that's another matter. Our social selves are determined by who we're among. The biological self is a body: it has a brain, a cluster of nerve cells contained within a bowl of bone. But the social self is a person: it has a *mind*, a constellation of ideas, attitudes, thoughts, information, and beliefs drawn from the vast cloud of such elements it shares (and has created) with others. That constellation is anchored to the brain and body, but it is situated outside the body, in the social web of which each person is a plexus. And the web of meaning we create with language—that is what links biology to history. Human groups exist as social constellations, which interact with their environment as if those whole collections of individuals were cells of single entities. Once we started forming such group selves—one and all of which were constellations, webs of meaning that existed only in the minds of their members and not in the physical world as such—that's when the story of humankind truly began.

Always, however, the awesome powers conferred upon us by language posed a problem. The world models that held us together had to fit what was actually out there. And what was out there was an intractable otherness, an ever-changing great unknown. To stay in sync with *that*, we had to keep modifying our models as new information came in. But a whole society can't change its mind the way a biological creature can. It might behave as if it were a social organism, but it doesn't have a brain; it exists only as a web of symbolic interactions among its members. It's those individuals who have to do the changing, and rarely can many minds change at once because telepathy doesn't exist. We inhabit imaginary worlds we share with others, but we come to those worlds privately, each with our own unique constellation of information, ideas, and beliefs.

And if some members of a society alter their perceptions and beliefs and others don't, the model they all share starts to lose coherence. If the model gets muddy, our ability to deal with the environment as single wholes gets weaker. The fact is, we can't afford to get out of sync with the material world, but we can't afford to get out of sync with one another either, and these two imperatives can be at odds—in fact, they often are. The tension between staying connected to one another and staying relevant to the outside world was coded into human life from the moment language was born. That tension keeps triggering dramatic events, and that's why language stands with environment and tools as the third strand in the trialectic of human history.

Before we had language, we probably lived pretty much the way other higher-level primates did. Like them, we roamed our environment as small bands, foraging for plants and hunting animals for meat. Like them, we sheltered near water, dispersed by day, and came together at night around a fire we deemed precious. With rare exceptions, all the members of a given human band were related by blood. The same was no doubt true of other higher-level primates. We did cross paths with kindred bands in our locale from time to time, and sometimes we came together with other bands for ritualized festive gatherings from which at least a few females no doubt came away pregnant. On rare occasions, in circumstances we cannot now know, those pregnancies resulted from sex between humans and Neanderthals: we were that close.

Once we had language, however, we parted ways with all those other primates. It was then that some of us went spelunking down into caves to put magnificent paintings on the walls and ceilings, art that no one would ever see except in flickering torchlight. Music was born in those millennia, as we know by ancient flutes found in some of those caves. We must also have been dancing to the music by then, as evidenced by stick figures depicted in the paintings. The fact that we were making jewelry suggests that fashion had come into existence. And the sophistication of our tools soared dramatically. We weren't limited to stone anymore; we made things out of bones and shells and antlers and probably wood as well, though that hasn't lasted. And it wasn't just grinders and choppers we were making, but fishing hooks and needles. And if we were making needles, we were making clothes. And if we were cooking food, we were surely trading recipes.

Tool making flourished once we had language because we no longer had to watch somebody making something in order to make the same thing. People could describe what they'd done, and others could then duplicate those steps. After all, people now lived in a world that included lots of things they themselves had never physically seen. If someone in a group had seen it, everyone else had as good as seen it, for it was now part of the furniture in the symbolic world that others of this person's group inhabited. Skills and knowledge could accumulate in that symbolic world, as each generation built on what was known in the past to make the tools of the future.

If this sudden blossoming involved the use of language, then this was probably when storytelling began. And if that's the case, then this was probably when humans first had any sense of history, when they first began to invent their own yesterday. Lots of things happened in the billions of years following the birth of the universe, but you can't have a narrative until you have "yesterday" and "tomorrow" and "when I was your age" and "in my grandfather's great-grandfather's time." Storytelling and history imply that the roots of all mythologies go back to this era. For me, this thought—of language blooming and right behind it stories, art, religion, technology—produces a chill. I can almost feel myself there, huddled with a group of folks, all of us related, all of us a single—something. At that point, and from that point forward, humans were definitely on the planet. They dressed differently and didn't bathe as much as we do, but they were us. Definitely us.

3

Civilization Begins with Geography
(30,000 BCE to 1500 BCE)

T ools and language. Armed with these advantages, humankind could spread to environments we had previously found uninhabitable. We could go to places too cold for comfort by wearing the skins of animals we'd killed and lighting fires inside shelters we'd built of their bones. By forty thousand years ago, we were migrating out of Africa into Southwest Asia and from there to Europe and East Asia and then on into the icy north. We went wherever the eating was good, and for hunters the eating was mighty good up there where the big beasts such as mammoths roamed.

As it happens, we developed our killer advantages just when Earth was going into a last glacial period, when the temperature of the planet dropped precipitously. In that period, so much water was locked up in ice that the sea levels were much lower. Places between Siberia and North America that are now open ocean were dry land back then or were covered with a sheet of ice so thick people didn't even know they were walking on water when they wandered over. Following the meat, some humans walked into the Americas. Then the temperatures warmed up, the ice melted, sea levels rose, and the land bridge between the continents vanished. Anyone who had not gone over could not now go; anyone who was over there already could not now come back. Something huge had happened for humanity—one planet had essentially split in half; but of course, no one living at the time was aware of this global event: they were just experiencing the dramas of their many small individual interwoven lives, their social constellation.

By then, however, at least three waves of migration had come into the Americas from Asia and spread all the way to Nova Scotia and Tierra del Fuego. Humans had already been language-using animals for millennia at that point, so people of the Americas no doubt shared many ancestral myths and traditions with their cousins in the Eastern Hemisphere. But after the continents separated, human culture evolved separately for the next eleven thousand years or so, a separation that would have profound consequences down the road.

The environment determines what we do to survive, which in turn determines how we hang together as groups. Environmental differences therefore generate consequential cultural differences. In the world's biggest landmass, which includes Eurasia and Africa, environmental variations generated at least three distinct ways of life. About ten thousand years ago, some people abandoned hunting and foraging and settled in fixed locations to make a go of it as full-time farmers. Tiny villages sprouted in Asia Minor (now called Turkey), in the Levant (now called Israel, Syria, Lebanon, etc.), and in parts of Europe. This happened, and could only happen, in places where the soil was fertile enough and the rain sufficient: environment begets lifestyle.

But even in these areas, some people opted for a different survival strategy. Instead of settling down and staking their survival on farming, they domesticated the animals they hunted and became nomadic herders. Farmers versus herders, settlers versus nomads—this was a crucial divergence. Where herders impinged on settled farmers, they might form a symbiotic relationship. One side was good at producing grains, fruits, and vegetables; the other had meat, hides, and milk products. They exploited one another's expertise by swapping goods.

Sometimes, however, the nomads raided the villages and took what they wanted. In some areas, these tribes may even have traced their ancestry back to common roots. Their divergence could end up as tribal myths told and retold on both sides as epic tales of treachery and triumph. The Old Testament tale of Cain and Abel has the feel of such a myth. Where this story emerged, the environment supported both farming and herding. In this region, the two ways of life were bound to bump against each other.

Finally, along many lakes and seas, people took to seafaring and sought their sustenance in the waters. This was not necessarily a late development. Boats existed before people: the first ones were built by earlier hominids in our ancestral line. From the start, therefore, people found that they could survive on fishing just as viably as on farming and herding—wherever geography permitted.

RIVER VALLEY CIVILIZATIONS

Then, about six thousand years ago, some people found a phenomenally productive type of environment for farming: river valleys that flooded annually and deposited a fresh layer of fertile soil each year. There may have been many such rivers, but four stand out because the first major urban civilizations that we still know about germinated there: the Nile River, the Tigris-Euphrates complex, the Indus River, and the Huang He. They gave birth respectively to the Egyptian, Mesopotamian, Indian, and Chinese civilizations.

If environment begets civilization, why did these civilizations, which were all spawned by rivers, turn out so different? The answer is simple: the four rivers weren't all that similar. In fact, they had key geographical differences, and in shaping their lives to these very different rivers, humans formed different constellations of customs, traditions, and ideas: different world stories.

The Nile

The Nile was a fabulous, two-way artery of communication, but only for the last six hundred miles or so. The river is over four thousand miles long, beginning as several streams in Central Africa, but it passes through gorges and waterfalls and rough waters for the first three-thousand-plus miles. The last of these rough passages are the Cataracts, white-water shallows strewn with boulders and whipped by nasty winds. It is impossible to sail a boat down this stretch of the river and difficult to get through even on foot. Beyond the Cataracts is, however, the Nile valley, which cradled a civilization. In that last stretch, the river is broad and deep and calm. Its current flows steadily north, but over those friendly waters, a breeze blows constantly south. People who put a boat into the water could raise a sail to go south and take the sail down to go north. As a result, people settled all along the river instead of bunching up into isolated towns. Out of this constant interaction, a cultural uniformity emerged, as if the whole valley were, in a sense, a single enormous social constellation.

That's one striking feature of the Nile valley. The other is the protection the very landscape itself afforded. Marauders couldn't get into the valley easily from the south: they'd have to make it through the Cataracts. There were no big threats coming from the east: the terrain over there was too rocky and dry to support much habitation. There were no big threats coming from the west, either: that way lay the Sahara Desert. Egyptians had only to defend the mouth of their shoestring world, the delta. In the rest of the valley, they could pour their energies into building up their bounty.

The cultural homogeneity nourished by this environment enabled people to cooperate on building massive infrastructure with which to manage their river. When the Nile flooded, the waters lapped all the way to the hills on either side. By constructing dams, dikes, and canals, farmers could store the water at its height and release it in measured amounts throughout the year to keep their fields irrigated. Coordinating this project spawned a command structure with many levels of overseers converging to a single godlike decision-maker at the top.

The Nile flooded with great *but not unfailing* regularity, and in years when the floods were weak, people naturally tended to wonder if they were to blame: Was it something they had done? Or failed to do? A society with a powerful central authority coupled with a concern and need to understand and influence nature created a distinctive figure of Egyptian civilization: the pharaoh, a ruler whom the masses believed to be a god.

The pharaoh, apparently, concurred with the masses: he looked down at himself and saw a god. My modern sensibilities can't help but wonder what he thought when he came down with a cold—what kind of god wakes up feeling lousy? but I recognize that no such question could have entered the mind of any individual Egyptian of that time. Individual minds are forged by society, and Egyptians needed to believe that when the pharaoh's needs, wishes, and whims were met, the floods happened exactly as they should. Since no human's every whim and wish is ever met, this connection could never be disproved. Egyptians needed the belief that could never be disproved in order to carry out projects requiring the coordinated efforts of thousands. A doubter would have threatened the security of everyone. Hardly anyone wants to be *that* guy—the guy who threatens the security of everybody. Doubt threatens the social constellation's internal order. Societies tend to frown on doubt.

Building, manning, and maintaining irrigation systems kept countless laborers busy part of the year, but the rest of the time they had little to do, and society could ill afford to leave them idle, for organized but idle workers get restless. Here, then, was a huge workforce in need of something to do and a divine pharaoh whose wishes must be met. Add them up and what do you get?

You get pyramids. You get human effort massively mustered to ensure a pleasant postdeath experience for one man. You get monumental temples and sculptures the size of hills. Irrigation works, pharaohs, bureaucracy, pyramids—all these distinctive elements of ancient Egyptian civilization were generated by the heartbeat of that civilization, the Nile River.

The Tigris and Euphrates

The Tigris and Euphrates empty into the Persian Gulf about 1,350 miles due east of the Nile delta, but they come down from the mountains of Turkey and flow south, roughly parallel to each other, through present-day Iraq, separated by an average of 50 miles, until, just before reaching the Gulf, they join up. This river complex had no cataracts neatly dividing upstream from downstream. Some stretches were navigable, some not. The breeze was inconstant, and the lower reaches swampy. Instead of one continuous culture forming along the valley, Mesopotamia saw the emergence of many separate networks of villages associated with disparate temples and their priesthoods.

Geography provided no protection to these folks, and protection they did need, for although the farming was good near the river, the environment supported pastoral nomadism as well. Villagers had to be ready to fend off raiders coming from any direction, so they built the walls that geography did not provide. It wasn't just towns that emerged in Mesopotamia, but walled towns, which morphed into tough little city-states, such as Uruk, Akkad, Lagash, and Kish, each with its own army of trained soldiers.

The Egyptian constellation discovered that once construction workers exist, they have to be constructing something. Mesopotamians found that once armies exist, they need to be fighting someone. If they're idle they just make internal trouble; so when Mesopotamian rulers weren't fighting off marauders, they were marching their armies upstream or downstream to conquer their neighbors. Egyptians built pyramids; Mesopotamians built empires. Successful conquerors ruling a network of city-states could tap a wider range of resources, which required bigger armies to defend, which led to more military campaigns. About forty-three centuries ago, Sargon of Akkad, the king of Kish, conquered most of the Mesopotamian city-states and founded history's first real empire.

Life in Mesopotamia may sound dreary, brutish, and short, but in fact it was vibrant, firecracker lively, and creative—more so, to my mind, than the serene, inward-looking civilization of the Nile valley. While the Egyptians were building monumental sculptures and graves, the Sumerians of Mesopotamia were *busy, busy, busy* making stuff, inventing stuff, interacting, cutting deals, buying and selling, cooking up laws, breaking laws, spouting songs, making love, stealing, gossiping, quarreling. Mesopotamia's many little city-states spawned an entrepreneurial individualism and a competitive pluralism that came to characterize both Islamic and European civilizations—and how could it not, given the geography of its twin rivers?

The Indus

The Indus River fostered one of the first great urban civilizations on Earth and one of the last to be excavated. At the dawn of the twentieth century, few knew that a civilization had even existed in this valley five thousand years earlier, peaking in two vanished cities, Harappa and Mohenjo Daro. The British had even used bricks baked by those ancients to build a railroad here in the nineteenth century, never suspecting how old the bricks were. Harappan civilization was at its height when the pyramids were going up in Egypt, and its height was high: some five million people inhabited the valley then, living in one-thousand-plus towns spread across many thousands of square miles.

The key to this staggering phenomenon was water. The Indus begins as a multitude of streams, which eventually join to form five rivers, which combine into a single river only a few miles north of the Arabian Sea. The whole area is ribboned with running water. Irrigation was not a problem; farming was easy. This lush abundance generated plenty of leisure: Harappans luxuriated in arts and crafts and engineering. Their biggest urban centers were laid out in regular rows like modern cities. Water being neither precious nor problematic, they equipped their towns prolifically with baths, plumbing, and sewage systems.

But these streams and rivers had a disturbing propensity to change course over time for no apparent reason (rivers do this when they're running through soft soil that has little in the way of rocks and gullies to steer the flow). In Harappan times, the Indus was actually six rivers, not five, but the biggest one vanished at some point back then. Life was good in the fertile valley, but it must also have been haunted by a deep sense of impermanence.

There was also another geographical feature putting its stamp on civilization here. Gigantic spurs of the Himalaya Mountains loomed next to the valley, and on the other side were high grasslands ideally suited for pastoral nomadism. Repeatedly over the ages, nomadic bands came down through those mountain passes and drifted into the valley, where they raided towns or traded with townspeople, setting up where they could. They could not be ignored; they were part of the ongoing story in this region.

A wave of such migrations swelled some thirty-five hundred years ago, just when Harappan civilization was in decline. The newcomers' sense of the world had formed in the vast, dry, open spaces of the steppes. They were coming into a valley densely inhabited by people whose ideas, diet, customs, and lifestyle took shape in a world inundated with water.

These groups didn't blend so much as interleaf. The Harappans were an urban people; these newcomers were rural. The Harappans built big houses and granaries using baked bricks of uniform size. The newcomers built small huts of mud, bamboo, and grass. The ancient people had been agrarian on a grand scale. The later people were herders and small farmers. These newcomers rode horses, drove chariots, and made tools and weapons out of iron. They burned forests and jungle to create pastures and little farms. The Harappans had worshipped fertility deities, many of them female. These later people worshipped deities tracing back to their pastoral nomadic past, predominantly male gods embodying forces of nature, such as wind, thunder, sun, and fire.

The newcomers had no fixed place of origin coded into mythic memory and no impulse to go home, only to go on. They spread east, building villages, from which some of them moved on to build more villages very like the ones they had left behind. They reached the Ganges River valley and flowed right over another older and perhaps already extinct civilization whose traces archaeologists can detect as a layer of yellow pottery beneath a later layer of gray pottery. Those folks may have spoken Dravidian languages, which is a whole other linguistic family, unrelated to the Indo-European ones. The Dravidian-speaking people probably originated in Africa, reached southern India by boat, and spread north from there.

Today we call those migrants from the northwest the Vedic people, because they had a body of religious hymns called the Vedas, thousands of which have come down to modern times. Priests called Brahmins memorized the hymns and passed them down orally, word for word, from one generation to the next. The Vedas give a rich picture of the lives of these ancients: from the Vedic hymns, for example, we know of ancient rituals centered around a mysterious drink called *soma*, made from some now unknown plant. Preparing and administering the drink was a skill performed exclusively by the priests, and they deemed this ritual so important to their way of life that Soma was among their major gods. Where this culture met the one expanding from the south, the seeds of Indian civilization began to sprout.

The Huang He

Moving way, way east, we come to the Huang He or Yellow River, the mother of Chinese civilization. The word *huang*, which means "yellow," refers to loess, a fine yellow dust that gives this valley a layer of topsoil richer and thicker than any other on Earth. The dust comes off distant mountains in the west and is blown here by the wind. The region is otherwise arid, so would-be farmers of ancient times *had* to depend on the river for irrigation. The slopes were so steep, however, that people often had to carve terraces into the hills to grow crops, which is to say, they had to reshape the very earth they lived upon: a monumental undertaking. But the soil was so deep and so fertile that people girded their loins and settled here anyway.

This river was the opposite of a highway. It had virtually no navigable stretches. Boaters putting into this rough current were risking suicide. Settlements sprouted in habitable patches, but instead of interacting continuously by river with other settlements to form a single homogenous culture, each community of farmers in this valley was somewhat on its own.

And all of them lived in constant jeopardy. The silt that gives the Huang He its name and makes it the world's muddiest river has a tendency to cake on the riverbed, raising the level of the water. Settlers had to build dikes to keep the ever-rising river under control; but when the river flooded more than usual, water overflowed the dikes, which was bad, or broke the dikes, which was worse.

In short, life along the Huang He was overshadowed by emergency. Like a bipolar parent, the river that was the source of all abundance also unleashed sudden catastrophe from time to time. Villagers had to be ready to respond. When a dike broke or a storm surge came downstream, there was no time to negotiate who should obey whom. A structure of authority had to be already in place. And in the Huang He valley, given the intimate scale of the communities, the discipline, hierarchy, and obedience needed for survival began, perforce, in the family, with the eldest members commanding the most authority. In fact, when the oldest members died, they didn't leave the scene. As the people of this valley saw it, deceased elders joined the ancestors, lingering on as a supernatural presence in daily life. The structure of authority within the family and the central place of the family within society became defining features of a civilization whose first seeds sprouted along the Huang He.

Early Chinese settlements in this valley tended to follow a pattern. Typically, there would be a ring of eighteen to twenty villages surrounding a market core and surrounded by fields. Each village housed some several dozen households of interrelated families organized around patriarchal figures. Villagers lived near their fields and within walking distance of a central market, where they met with others from their cluster of villages, to socialize, iron out conflicts, and plan big projects. Successful settlements probably extended their reach until they achieved the stature of little kingdoms. Many such kingdoms probably formed, but Chinese legend conflated them into a single empire ruled by a dynasty called the Xia.

The Xia dynasty may have been as legendary as Camelot: no traces of it have ever been found. But that doesn't mean it never existed. The Xia gave way to another dynasty called the Shang, who were also considered mythical until the early twentieth century, when archaeologists stumbled across the remnants of their last capital, the city of Yin. There, archaeologists found thousands of sophisticated artifacts including oracle bones: turtle shells that had been heated and cooled until they cracked. The oracle bones were apparently used for divination. Questions were asked, and experts read the answers from the cracks, just as fortune-tellers read tea leaves. Fortunately for historians, the questions and answers were inscribed on the bones in a script so similar to modern Chinese that scholars could decipher them, proving that Chinese civilization has a continuous history tracing back at least thirty-seven hundred years.

PASTORAL NOMADIC CIVILIZATION

But what of that other path taken by human culture? What about the pastoral nomads? Agrarian life took off spectacularly in a few propitious locations, but the same was true of pastoral nomadism: certain environments fit that way of life as glove fits hand. The main seedbed for pastoral nomadism stretched across the grasslands of northern Eurasia. If you draw a line from the Nile delta to the Huang He delta and then go north from anywhere along that line, you get to the historic heartland of pastoral nomadism.

It would be inaccurate to think of the farmers as the sophisticates who got it right and pastoral nomads as the dumb losers who got left behind. The pastoral nomads developed a way of life splendidly molded to their environment. In that sense, they were no less sophisticated than the city folks. They, too, had civilizations.

Technically, "pastoral nomadic civilization" may be something of an oxymoron; the word *civilization* derives from the same Latin root as the word *city*, and pastoral nomads were the ones who eschewed city life. Indeed, all through history, pastoral nomads were often considered and called barbarians (originally a Greek word meaning "foreign"). But it's been the city folks doing the labeling, and the connotations of "civilized" and "barbarian" reflect their prejudices. Here, therefore, I will borrow the term *civilization* to describe any cultural entity spread across a vast territory and encompassing an immense number of people who, despite myriad particular differences, share an overarching framework of cultural assumptions, aesthetics, and values.

Since the pastoral nomads didn't settle, they didn't form up as kingdoms or empires. Instead, they merged and clashed and came apart as fluid tribal confederations. Their world stretched thousands of miles across Central Asia, through the gap between the Caspian Sea and the

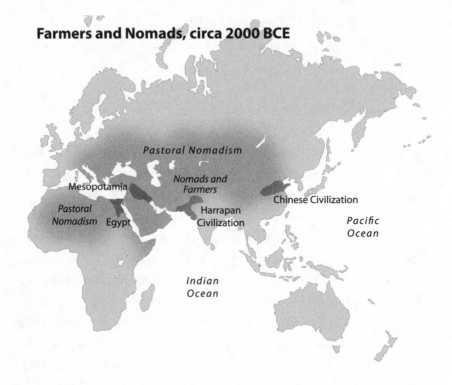

Farmers and Nomads, circa 2000 BCE

Pastoral Nomadism

Mesopotamia

Nomads and Farmers

Pastoral Nomadism   Egypt

Harrapan Civilization

Chinese Civilization

Pacific Ocean

Indian Ocean

Ural Mountains, across the northern shores of the Black Sea, above the mountains of the Baltics, and into the plains of Central Europe. The river valley civilizations were isolated from one another like separate spots of mold. The pastoral nomadic world was a single immense interconnected zone in the north, and it extended down through Arabia and across Africa to the Atlantic Ocean. It formed a sort of lymphatic fluid between the settled civilizations expanding out of the river valleys.

This is not to say that any single person or tribe traveled from Mongolia to Poland. But ideas rippled from tribe to tribe as neighbors dealt with neighbors who then dealt with farther neighbors. When some momentous development disrupted life in one part of a pastoral nomadic zone such as the one in central Eurasia, the ripple effects were apt to lap to both ends of the zone and seep down through its whole southern perimeter.

Early on, some of history's key technological breakthroughs occurred in this world. Somewhere between Ukraine and Kyrgyzstan, for example, nomads first domesticated the horse. We don't commonly think of the horse as a tool, but let's not be so narrow-minded: horses, like stones, are something that existed in the environment and that we reconfigured (in this case through domestication and training) to help us deal with our environment. The nomads completed their achievement by inventing stirrups and saddles. Nomadic women meanwhile invented key items we don't usually think of as inventions: trousers, a garment with separate sheaths for each leg, and later shirts and shirt sleeves, all of which made it possible for nomadic men to ride horses.

On horseback, nomads could travel faster and farther, manage bigger herds, eat better, and live bigger lives. Horses not only *enabled* them to range farther but *obliged* them to, for horses crop grass closer than cows do: any group that had a lot of horses used up pasture more quickly and had to move more frequently.

What's more, increasing productivity meant their population grew. But nomadic groups can't grow past a certain size. Simple logistics won't allow it: moving hundreds of people is one thing, moving thousands quite another. Groups that grew too big were bound to split, some members heading off to pursue their own destinies. In urban civilizations, a growing population meant bigger, denser cities. In pastoral nomadic cultures, it meant ever wider dispersal.

Pastoral nomads came up with two more pivotal inventions, tools by anyone's definition. One was the chariot, which is a cart with two wheels instead of four. The wheel was probably invented in Egypt or Mesopotamia and so was the cart, and the cart was a good tool for moving heavy blocks of stone. But carts are difficult to turn, and they work poorly on random, bumpy surfaces. If you have carts, you'll soon be building roads: one breakthrough leads to another.

Chariots, by contrast, having two wheels, can not only turn but pivot. Just as carts implied roads, chariots implied improved wheels. Chariot wheels became hoops held together by spokes, springy and light. A chariot wasn't much good for building pyramids, and it couldn't carry more than two or three people at the most, but if that chariot was hitched to a horse and the three people were a driver, an archer, and a guy with an ax, it was an awesome instrument of war.

Which brings us to the composite bow, a weapon invented in the steppes. Older bows had been made of single flexible branches, and they had to be almost as tall as a man because a short branch made for a weak bow. The nomads of the Central Asian steppes figured out how to make a bow by gluing together several strips of wood planed to a uniform thickness. They could do this because they had strong glue. Why did they have strong glue? Because they were the first to domesticate the horse. The glue they used was made from horses' hooves: one breakthrough leads to another. Though much shorter than earlier bows, composite bows were far more powerful. People on horseback could pack them into their saddlebags and use them to fight while riding. In fact, these bows made cavalry even more dangerous than charioteers.

The mobility of pastoral nomads, their long webs of intercommunication, their propensity to spread widely instead of clumping densely, and their military prowess accounts for some of the impact they had in early history. Around four to five thousand years ago, out of the Pontic steppe—the region between and above the Caspian and Black Seas—a wave of cultural influence emanated east and west and eventually south across the vast homeland of pastoral nomadism. The people in the Pontic steppe spoke some language that no longer exists because it morphed as it traveled, branching apart as the people branched apart, and changing over time as languages do. Descendants of that protolanguage include Sanskrit and Hindi, Latin and Italian, Persian, Russian, German, Greek, and English. Because this linguistic family extends from India to Western Europe, its original speakers have commonly been called the Indo-Europeans, and it's a convenient term to use so long as one keeps in mind that the Indo-Europeans were neither Indians nor Europeans. They were something else, and they were not necessarily (or even probably) some single people. This was, however, almost surely a cultural wave that emanated from the heart of the pastoral nomadic world.

4

Trade Weaves the Networks
(1500 BCE to 500 BCE)

Geography generated a third branch of human culture as well—a third flavor of civilization, if you will. Resources were distributed unevenly around the planet, so people could create value merely by moving stuff from one place to another. The farther they moved it, the more value it gained. As soon as beasts of burden were domesticated, therefore, some people embarked on long-distance trading as a way of life.

There is a distinction to be made between local trade and long-distance trade. In every group of humans, people no doubt traded with others of their group. There was also, always, a trade thing going on between farmers and local nomads as soon as these two ways of life came into being.

Long-distance trade, however, is a different animal. It wasn't somebody's breakthrough idea. It didn't develop at some time and place. As soon as there was farming, herding, and fishing, there was also long-distance trade. It was no doubt a particularly prominent thread in the fabric of everyday life for nomads. Because they were already living on the move, they knew what goods were available where. They could pick up a few items where they were cheap and trade them where they fetched a good price, and if the trading proved lucrative enough, some might get rid of all those pesky goats and make trade their stand-alone occupation.

Nomads did not wander randomly. Hunters went where they knew the game would be. Herders made their way to pastures they already knew about. Traders traveled from one hot spot of commercial opportunity to

another. Itinerant folks found the most efficient routes among their destinations and used them routinely. For the most part, geography determined
where these routes would be. Predictable webs of roads and pathways
formed, therefore, wherever trading was heavy. Villages situated near the
nexus of many such trade routes inevitably bloomed into towns, and some
of those towns eventually grew into cities whose chief business was vend-
ing amenities to traders—hot meals, warm beds, dry shelter, intoxicants
to drink or smoke, a little sex perhaps—and, of course, providing places
for traders to mingle and tangle with others: markets and bazaars.

Take the city of Petra, for example, in present-day Jordan. It was
situated in an environment too harsh to support farming or even herding. Yet Petra became a wealthy city of storied vitality purely because it
was built into the rocky cliffs of a narrow gorge that traders had to pass
through in their travels between the Red Sea, the Levantine coast, and
the ports on the Persian Gulf.

Big bodies of water nourished long-distance trade as well because
trade goods from many different environments funneled down to their
rims. Wherever people were set up to fish, they might add long-distance
trading to their kit of skills. Wherever boats could dock, trading towns
were apt to sprout. Boats had one great advantage over beasts of burden:
they didn't have to be fed.

As urban hubs increased in numbers, so did the networks of traders'
routes. By 2000 BCE, several overlapping trade networks were emerging
in Eurasia, and each was its own galaxy of cultural constellations.

MIDDLE WORLD

One of the busiest trade webs of ancient times emerged in what
might be called the Middle World: the region stretching from
Asia Minor across the Iranian highlands down through what is now Afghanistan. This region is situated right between the two great river civilizations of the West (Egypt and Mesopotamia) and the two great river
civilizations of the East (India and China). Much of this Middle World

is rugged and rather arid, but numerous streams run through it. Along these streams, villages of subsistence farmers sprang up early on. Pastoral nomads roamed the land as well, and this mixture of villages and nomads in a territory flanked by sophisticated urban centers was exactly the combination that favored the development of long-distance trade.

Not only did the Middle World have rich urban societies at each end, it had ports all along its rim, for this region is ringed by large bodies of navigable water: the Amu River (aka the Oxus), the Aral Sea, the Caspian Sea, the Black Sea, the Sea of Marmara, the Aegean Sea, the Mediterranean Sea, the Red Sea, the Persian Gulf, and the Indus River, and if you boat upstream about halfway to the sources of that last river, you're just about back to where you started.

Huge caravans moved across the Middle World in ancient times, hundreds of beasts sometimes, but they didn't necessarily traverse the

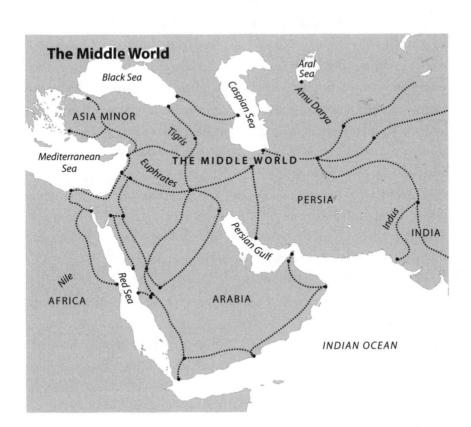

The Middle World

Black Sea

Aral Sea

Caspian Sea

Amu Darya

ASIA MINOR

Tigris

Mediterranean Sea

Euphrates

THE MIDDLE WORLD

PERSIA

Indus

INDIA

Persian Gulf

Nile

Red Sea

AFRICA

ARABIA

INDIAN OCEAN

whole distance. They didn't have to. As trade routes proliferated, so did the number of hubs where trade routes crisscrossed, cities where traders could make deals with traders. There was, for example, the city the Greeks later called Hecatompylos, located about halfway between the markets of China and those of Mesopotamia (roughly where Teheran is located now). Hecatompylos is Greek for "hundred gated," fancifully suggesting the number of roads converging there. Hecatompylos has vanished, but it was at one time the capital of the mighty Parthian Empire, one of a series of empires that rose and fell, here at the core of what emerged into history as Persian civilization.

MEDITERRANEAN WORLD

West of the Middle World was another trade network of global scale: a web of sea routes linking ports all around the Mediterranean. The Mediterranean is so big it nearly qualifies as an ocean, and it opens into the Black Sea, and almost into the Red Sea, to form altogether one truly huge world of water. Getting from one Mediterranean port to another was easy because this sea was friendly to sailors: it didn't have the storms of the Atlantic, it didn't have the waterfalls and swamps of many rivers, and the waters were so calm that if the winds died, sailors could usually just row to shore.

Best of all, the Mediterranean lies entirely within the temperate zone, the world's most habitable environment. Its coastline fronts on many different landscapes. Into its ports, therefore, flowed products from many environments. Traders could load up with grain in Egypt, cedar at Levantine ports, salt in cities on the north African coast, amber at the ports of southern Europe, tin from the Iberian ports in the extreme west, and so much more.

You might assume that the mighty Egyptians dominated this trade network early on, but no: the Egyptians had plenty to trade but little incentive to go a-trading. They were so rich, the world came to them. In fact, the first great Mediterranean civilization emerged on the island of

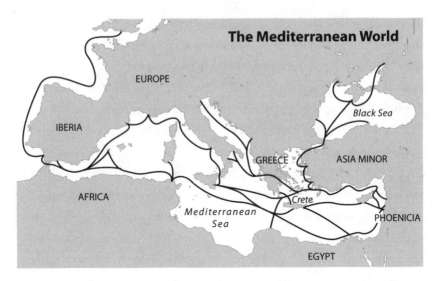

Crete, whose key resource was location: it was smack-dab in the middle of the sea, with excellent access to all the northeastern ports of the Mediterranean. The Phoenicians soon emerged as a rival sea power, and they had a different strategy. They hopscotched from homes in the Levant along the whole southern Mediterranean coast, planting colonies.

Then came the Greeks, whom geography favored as it had few others. Greece is a peninsula that strings out into the Mediterranean as hundreds of islands. The Greek interior is arid and rocky, ill-suited for growing anything except grapes and olives, from which the Greeks made wine and oil. Unfortunately, man cannot live on wine and oil alone, but fortunately (for the Greeks), their lands had countless rocky gulches that ran down to coves along the water, most of them good harbors. Harbors were the key resource of the early Greeks. Their interior being so rugged, they tended to live along their shores and interact even with adjacent neighbors by sea rather than by land. They were oriented less toward their own hinterland and more toward the open waters, the lands they faced looking out.

The first great Greek powers were the Mycenaeans who were basically pirates at first: they sacked Phoenician boats, rammed Cretan ships, and soon had enough goods to go into business for themselves. Around 1500 BCE, they destroyed the Minoan civilization on Crete. Their stories describe this as a war with an evil king Minos who kept demanding that the Greeks deliver virgins to him every year until finally the great Greek hero Theseus went over and crushed the bastard and, just to salt the wound, made off with his (virgin) daughter. The Cretan version of this event would probably be different, if we but knew it.

Around 1200 BCE, a wave of thuggish raiders known as the People of the Sea raked through the Mediterranean world pillaging the whole region. The Mycenaeans essentially disappeared from history at that point. Into their lands and towns moved poorer Greeks from farther north: the Dorians. The next six centuries or so were a dark ages for the region. Scant record remains of the period, but the Dorians must have felt related to the Mycenaeans, for the stories they told about their legendary past featured Mycenaean heroes, and for later Greeks, two such stories acquired a prestige comparable to that of scriptures in other cultures: the Iliad and the Odyssey recounted episodes from a long war between the Greeks and a city in Asia. When Greek civilization again came into the light of recorded history, as many small, maritime city-states, these epics were a part of its mythic memory.

MONSOON WORLD

Then there was a third trade civilization spawned by geography. Asia being so huge, the whole continent functions as a kind of bellows, creating a weather pattern of immense scope. The center of the continent—the steppes, the plains, the taiga—gets extremely cold in the winter, but most of it gets extremely hot in the summer. Cold air is heavy, so in winter it sinks, blowing wind across the land and out over the oceans. In the summer, however, the heart of the continent heats up, and hot air rises, creating a vacuum that sucks wind in from the edges. The outgoing winter winds are cool and dry; the incoming summer winds are warm and wet. These are the monsoons.

The Himalaya mountain range complicates the monsoons by splitting the winds, sending some across China and over the Pacific Ocean and others across Arabia and out over the Indian Ocean. The monsoons of the Pacific

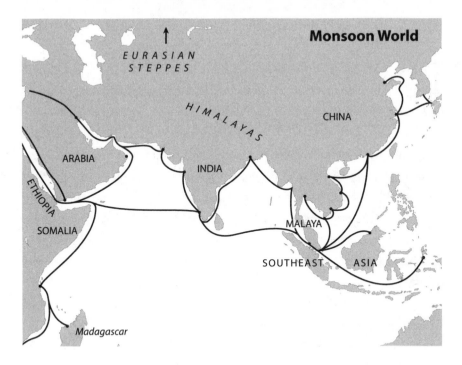

and Indian Oceans overlap in Southeast Asia. So ancient peoples living any-where upon the shores of the Indian or Pacific Oceans could put to sea in sailboats and ride the winds to Southeast Asia in winter. There they'd have to wait a few months for the winds to switch direction, which they always did. Then, the sailors could all sail home to China, India, Arabia, and Africa.

The monsoons generated a world of maritime trade rivaling those of the Mediterranean and the Middle World. This vast network linked East Africa to Arabia to India to Malaya and Indonesia and from there, indirectly, to China. That is why today a language spoken primarily in Indonesia is also spoken in Madagascar and why, millennia ago, African products could be found in Chinese markets.

The monsoons made Southeast Asia a place where sailors from several worlds languished for months, rubbing shoulders and bumping back ends as they waited for the winds to change. This consequently became one of the world's great pots of culture stew, a region where elements from India, China, East Africa, and Arabia sloshed together, resulting in a complicated fusion.

SUB-SAHARAN AFRICA

In 500 BCE, most of the world's fifty million people lived in Eurasia, and most of them lived in the belt of territory stretching from China to Iberia. When people traveled, they tended to go east or west more readily than north or south because the temperature is roughly the same along any given latitude. Along any given longitude, by contrast, travelers eventually go from the steaming equator to one or another of the frigid poles. Add to this, one of the great intractable features of the planet: the Sahara Desert runs across the whole width of Africa, dividing the world's second biggest continent into a southern part and northern part and ensuring that civilization would emerge independently in these two parts.

Geography worked to keep sub-Saharan Africa lightly populated. A dense equatorial jungle made the center of the continent difficult to inhabit. Here, heavy rain leaches nutrients out of the soil, making farming laborious and unrewarding. The jungle also harbored two deadly creatures, mosquitoes and tsetse flies. Mosquitos spread malaria; tsetse flies carry sleeping sickness. Tsetse flies find horse blood especially tasty, so they eliminated the horse factor from sub-Saharan history. And farther south, below the jungle, situated midway between the coasts, is another unforgiving desert: the Kalahari. Early on, then, because of these environmental factors, Africans tended to settle along the coast. In 500 BCE, they totaled about 6 percent of the world's population.

The Sahara was not always the barrier it is today. Fairly recently on the planetary time scale, perhaps as little as ten thousand years ago, this region was fairly lush. Then as arid patches began to appear, people migrated to greener climes. Some went east and mingled with or perhaps became the Egyptians. Some went north and joined the Mediterranean world. Others migrated south along the two coasts. After the Sahara morphed into a waterless wasteland, they pretty much set their own course through history.

About the time Socrates was irritating the elite of Athens, a sophisticated culture had emerged in West Africa, between the two biggest rivers of what is now Nigeria. Historians call these people the Nok because the first traces of their existence were discovered near a modern-day town called Nok. What they called themselves is anybody's guess. The Nok tilled fields immediately surrounding their villages and kept cattle on the outskirts. They learned to smelt copper independently of cultures in the north. Around 1000 BCE, they entered the so-called Iron Age. By 500 BCE, they were making expressive terra-cotta sculptures of animals and of people clad in diverse attire, clothes and ornaments, which hints at social and political complexities, the details of which cannot now be unraveled.

They can't be unraveled because few traces of the Nok remain. They had no written language. They made their homes and public buildings out of wood and other materials derived from plants, which don't last the way stone and sunbaked cob do (cob being a mixture of clay, sand, and straw). Even the Nok sculptures found so far are broken and have been reconstructed from fragments.

The patterns of later cultures in Africa suggest, however, that in the Nok world, the unit of life was the village, the central authorities were the elders, and the inhabitants of a village were an extended clan. Larger political structures were networks of villages. Nok society was not layered like Vedic culture but deeply communal. People within a village could form close family-like links with even distant relatives. An older and younger person might form a parent-child bond, even if genetically they were third cousins twice removed. The village was family writ large.

Speculation based on later cultures also suggests that the Nok envisioned a god of light reifying down through spirits who permeated nature and who included their own ancestors. The spirit world was not distinctly separate from everyday life. Through music and expressive movements people could make actual connections with the spirits. The Vedic people had also sought to connect with the supernatural through sound, but their sacred sounds were precisely memorized hymns administered by religious experts. For the Nok, the medium of connection was music, and the rites were communal: everybody participated in them through call-and-response, choral singing, and the like. In the Greek world, the mystery religions centered around achieving a trance state, which was thought to open a channel to the gods, but only one person, the oracle or seer at the heart of it all, achieved the trance state. In West African culture, it seems, the ecstatic trance was achieved communally, opening a current of connection among members of the whole kinship cluster and the invisible spirit world within which they lived. Culturally, in Nok times, sub-Saharan West Africa may have been one large social constellation, but the individual stars that comprised it are not now knowable.

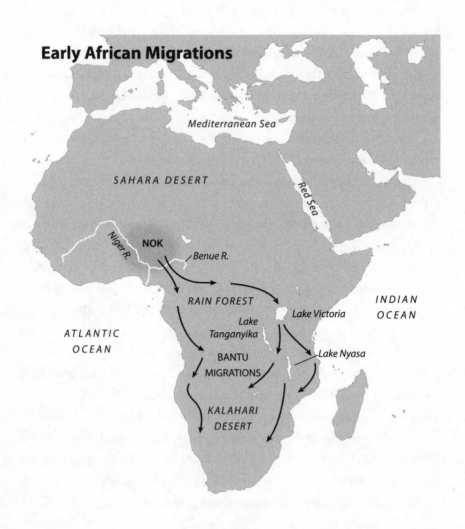

Sometime after 500 BCE, the Noks faded out of history. No one knows exactly why. Some environmental shift may have been involved. Perhaps the area got too wet or too dry or too hot or too something. Or perhaps, the people of this area simply achieved a technological superiority that enabled them to forge into territories previously deemed uninhabitable. Whatever the reason, people started migrating out of areas that are now Cameroon, Nigeria, and Benin. We know of these migrations in much the same way we know of the Indo-European migrations. Virtually all the languages of sub-Saharan Africa belong to one linguistic group: the Bantu family. This points back to some single ancient proto-language, which branched into many languages as the Bantu-speaking people spread out.

The Bantu speakers could move across the equatorial forest because they could use their iron implements to chop down trees, cut through brush, and till root-riddled soil. With their iron weapons, they could push aside the scattered tribes of hunter-gatherers already inhabiting these lands. Like the analogous people of India, the earlier tribes receded deeper into the forest as the Bantu people came through.

The Bantu migrations were not some sudden, sweeping movement. Bantu speakers may have taken a thousand years to reach the east coast of Africa. Their migrations were slow because they were mostly a side effect of their environment. In this tropical climate, heavy rainfall impoverished the soil, and no annual flooding replenished it, so farmers employed the slash-and-burn method of growing crops: they burned brush to create a layer of ash, which enriched the soil. Once the brush was reduced to ash, however, there was no more brush to burn. The ash made the soil fertile for a few years, but after that, people had to move on to a new brush-covered area and do the slash-and-burn thing again. In any given generation, they did not think of themselves as migrating. They were just farming, but their way of farming ensured that over time they would keep moving on to the places where they had not yet been.

The slow migrations eventually brought Bantu-speaking people to the shores of the Indian Ocean. There, many people settled by streams and around lakes and took up fishing as well as farming and cattle herding.

Others turned south and continued migrating, eventually converging with the migrants coming down the west coast. All brought with them their ancestral village-based culture, but webs of trade formed among the villages, and interconnected villages became networks within which some tribal elders acquired king-like status.

In East Africa, Bantu-speaking people interacted with traders coming down the coast or across the ocean. Africans became part of the monsoon network, in which Arabs played a major role. In East Africa, millions of people speak Swahili, a Bantu language blended with Arabic. The name comes from the Arabic word *sahel*, which means "border." Swahili emerged in areas where Bantu-speaking people interacted with Arab raiders and traders. Wherever one culture overlapped with another, ripple effects passed through.

5

The Birth of Belief Systems

(1000 BCE to 350 BCE)

Conventional wisdom says that no more than six degrees of separation exist between any two people on Earth. Supposedly, then, you and I both know someone who knows someone who (repeat four times) knows the pope, the actor Kevin Bacon, and any currently active serial killer. Could be, I suppose. But there's another deep-seated pattern of human interaction that cuts across the six-degrees phenomenon. Call it the clique effect. People living in the same environment tend to interact more frequently with one another than they do with people of other environments.

In ancient times, for example, people who lived in the same river valley and worked on the same great infrastructure project were part of a network of communication that constituted, you might say, an *intercommunicative zone*. Stories they told tended to circulate throughout their zone. They didn't necessarily talk to all the others in their network or even know most of them, but they knew people who knew people who knew those people. Word got around.

News came from other places too, of course. Long distance traders brought snippets of gossip, adventurers turned up, the odd tourist stumbled in—but information from other places was intermittent. The stories that circulated within an intercommunicative zone were continuous and self-reinforcing. They deepened into myths as each person who retold a story dropped the parts that felt unimportant and emphasized the parts they themselves found powerful. The four ancestral river valleys were obvious examples of such intercommunicative zones, but the great trade networks were intercommunicative zones, too, because people who trekked those paths crossed paths with other folks who trekked those paths, and in the nodes of any given trade network, in cities like Hecatompylos, Petra, Minos, and Carthage, they exchanged gossip with hardened travelers from many cultures. So, the Middle World developed its own distinctive body of myths, as did the Mediterranean world. Each became a gigantic social constellation knit together by countless threads of narrative.

In the case of any given people, countless threads of narrative can weave together until they form some single greater whole—a master narrative, if you will: a complex constellation of stories and ideas that fit together to form some sort of coherent whole. A master narrative isn't merely a series of events. To have resonance, a story must unfold in a world that feels real, that feels credible. A master narrative therefore includes a sense of time and space, of who matters in history and what matters in life and of how it all started, where the universe has been and where it's all going. By master narrative, I mean, in fact, a world model, that imagined totality we construct communally and inhabit individually, without which we could not deal with our environment as humans, given that we exist fundamentally as social constellations, not just as individuals.

The primeval master narratives of humankind grew out of the soil of particular environments. They were shaped by geography, that intractable factor. But once a master narrative forms, it can disconnect from geography and take on a life of its own because it filters what feels true, what feels false, and what feels irrelevant. Information that fits with everything else we know has a leg up on feeling true. Just as stories deepen into myths, master narratives gain definition as they grow. People who share such a narrative resist ideas and information that undermine their framework and welcome ones that enrich and confirm it. The narrative becomes ever sturdier, ever more defined. It becomes a structure within which a person can live a life of meaning. And unbeknownst to us who are living those lives of meaning, our master narrative is a mechanism by which a social constellation is perpetuating itself.

Some twenty-five hundred years ago, a number of charismatic individuals distilled concrete belief systems out of the master narratives of their quite various social contexts. I say belief system because I hesitate to use the term *religion* here. Religion means something so specific to most of us that we are apt to understand other religions within the framework of our own. But since every religion *is* a frame of reference, situating one framework inside another is bound to distort both. *Belief system*, therefore, is the term I prefer, generic though it be.

CHINA

The Chinese, it seems, early in their history, began to think of the world as concentric and of history as cyclical. The heart of the world was the empire; the empire was surrounded by tributaries: humbler states that looked to the empire for protection. The tributaries were surrounded by barbarians, and around the barbarians was a world too far away to deserve description.

The empire was ruled by a family dynasty, which went through a predictable cycle. At first, the dynasty had a mandate to govern, a mandate that came from a vast, impersonal, supernatural force, which the Chinese knew as Tian. When the mandate was in place, harmony prevailed and all was right with the world. But as time went on, the dynasty made mistakes and squandered its mandate, and the empire unraveled. Chaos then replaced order—until another individual received the mandate to rule "all under heaven." He established a new ruling dynasty; whereupon, the world entered a new period of order and harmony. And so it went, on and on, round and round.

It's important to realize that in this schema the empire did not mean "our empire" as opposed to "other empires." It was not one among many; it was *the* empire, a metaphysical fact about the world. The barbarians were always trying to get into *the* empire, and sometimes they did advance but only because the empire was going into a period of fragmentation. The real problem was never the barbarians; it was fundamentally internal. Barbarian victories, as well as droughts, famines, floods, rebellions, street crime, and other such troubles, were just symptoms of a dynasty in the process of losing its mandate. They indicated that something was wrong in the heart of the world, as a result of which entropy was gaining ground.

A dynasty lost its mandate because it failed to carry out the ceremonies and conduct that kept the world in harmony. In this view, the material world had an underlying order connecting all the visible facts of existence. There were hidden correspondences laced throughout material reality: among colors, seasons, numbers, days of the week, directions, foods, moods, and so on. Coincidences had meaning. Luck was not random. The connections and correspondences woven through material life added up to a pattern that experts could discern. Living in sync with the hidden pattern brought good luck; living at cross-purposes with it brought trouble—just as moving through a minefield works out better if you have a map showing where the mines are hidden; running across it blindly gets you blown apart.

The empire was the intermediary between mortals and that endless overarching supernatural reality called Tian. Although this term is often translated as "heaven," Tian wasn't a place where good people went after they died. It wasn't a place at all. Nor was it "the Chinese word for God," for it wasn't a supernatural will or a will at all: the Chinese took no interest in personifying Tian by creating images of "him." There was no "him." Tian reflected an impersonal pattern that simply *was* the actual ubiquitous reality of a seemingly chaotic universe.

Around 500 BCE, a man known as Kongfuzi (more familiarly, Confucius) distilled the rituals and observances of Chinese culture into a belief system that served as both an explanation of life and a manual for conduct. Confucius made no claim to prophetic originality, only to scholarship. He had studied ancient divination texts and other such Chinese classics, and he was only conveying correctly what they said. He focused mainly on everyday conduct, especially within the family. He noted that family members had different roles to play and therefore had different standards to meet. Children owed obedience to elders; elders owed loving warmth to children. The family owed obedience to the father; the father had a duty to take care of the family. Everybody owed, and everybody was owed. Life was a web of social debt.

The master's disciples compiled his wisdom into a book called the Analects, which included pithy comments he had made as well as details they had noticed about his everyday conduct. They reported, for example, that the master always straightened his mat before he sat down. It doesn't sound like much until you regard this act as one thread in a fabric of countless threads. Confucius had much to say about etiquette and social rituals but not by way of constructing a cage of empty rules. He taught that people could develop a moral intuition by behaving gracefully in all specific circumstances, and he was providing instruction for such behavior. By fitting harmoniously into the great social project, they could achieve a life of meaning and purpose. His recommendations added up to a prescription for an ideal society, in which empire and family were reflections of each other. The father was emperor within the family; the emperor, called the Son of Heaven, was father within the empire. When everything was working as it should, empire and family comprised a single coherent whole.

Confucius didn't talk about the gods, but his idea system had the power of a religion. Even thinkers who laid out alternatives to the Confucian system (as many did) made their argument within the framework he established. One partial exception was the sage Laozi (also known as Lao-tze and Lao-tzu), author of the Tao Te Ching, who didn't so much argue with Confucius as start a whole other conversation: he distilled a parallel idea system out of the same master narrative as Confucius. Laozi wasn't a public figure, so no one knows exactly when he lived, only that his book was circulating vigorously by 300 BCE. He fastened on the Chinese idea of an underlying pattern to the universe, which he called the Tao ("the way"). Laozi identified human intention as the source of all trouble. He advised that people drop resistance to adversity, stop trying to make things happen, abandon agenda, and let the current carry them. Only by letting go could they get aligned with the Tao.

INDIA

Two thousand miles away, southwest of China, quite a different master narrative was taking shape. Here, the world was not seen as having a single core: nothing in local history supported such a vision. India was a world of villages proliferating across an endless landscape. Kingdoms emerged here and there, but none had metaphysical significance. To people living here, the world wasn't concentric; it consisted of layers. Every village had the same four layers of people, a layering derived primevally from occupation—*varnas*, they were called, and later castes. There were priests called Brahmins, there were warriors and kings, there were farmers and traders, and finally there were artisans and laborers. And below all these layers were people who did the work no one else would touch, like washing corpses.

These layers were not contained by human borders. They ran across political boundaries. They ignored geography as well. For example, marriage between people of different layers? That was a problem, even if they lived in the same village. Marriage between people of different villages? That was OK, if they belonged to the same layer. Cities formed in the subcontinent, but the layering of life manifested in the cities as in the villages.

For Indians, time was not cyclical but illusory. Things happened, and then more things happened, and in the end, things were much the same. Lives differed in superficial ways, but all lives went through the same four stages—again, that vision of a layered world: people were born, they matured, they got old, they died. It happened to beggars, and it happened to kings. Whatever might be going on in society, the most important drama was the one each person had to face alone: birth, growth, decrepitude, death.

The gods were numerous in India, but they were not some hidden pattern of impersonal abstractions. They were dynamic forces with faces and bodies and stories of their own, and they, too, existed at many levels. Some were incarnations of higher gods at lower levels. Some gods incarnated right down into material reality and passed as humans for a while. The material level though most palpable was the most illusory. Higher levels were successively more real until, at last, somewhere high above all layers, multiplicity dissolved into a single, timeless, featureless eternal reality.

Around 900 BCE a series of deep thinkers known to their society as sadhus emerged around the Ganges River valley, men who walked away from families and occupations and retired to the forest to think deep thoughts. Out of the Vedic master narrative, they distilled the seeds of a post-Vedic belief system now known as Hinduism. In sacred songs called the Upanishads, they finalized a vision of the world as illusion and of reality as a single, seamless whole. They sang that people didn't *have* souls but *were* souls. They sang that all souls yearned to rise upward but mostly couldn't because they were trapped in bodies, and when bodies died, the souls suffered reincarnation into new bodies.

The Upanishads introduced the idea of karma as the iron law of the universe: every action triggered a matching reaction. If you did some good, you'd reap some good. If you hurt somebody, you'd get hurt. By somebody. It wasn't necessarily going to happen in the same lifetime. Karma followed the soul through its reincarnations, dictating whether a soul moved up or down in each next birth. Souls that accumulated enough good karma could rise over the course of many lives, through the layers of this stratified universe, to escape at last the endless iterations of the same gloomy story, the one that began joyously with birth and ended gloomily with decrepitude and death.

Here as in China, some thinkers distilled slightly different idea systems out of the same master narrative. Mahavira, the founding figure of Jainism, declared that people could escape from reincarnation by avoiding sex, violence, and possessions. Another seminal thinker, Siddhartha Gautama, known as the Buddha ("the awoken one") offered not so much a philosophy as a practical method for breaking out of the endless cycle in this very lifetime. The Buddha did not advise his followers to renounce the world and sleep on beds of nails; he told them to tread the world lightly, practice moderation, and perform certain techniques of meditation. This practice would loosen the grip of desire, the cause of all suffering, and release them into nirvana, enlightenment—liberation. Like Confucius, Buddha didn't speak of gods. When students asked about supernatural matters, he replied that the question did not contribute to enlightenment. He likened himself to a doctor: the world was suffering, and he was offering medicine.

PERSIA

At the height of Harappan civilization, tribes of herders and small farmers lived in the grasslands north of the Oxus River—a region known as Transoxiana. These tribes called themselves the Aryans, which in their language just meant "noble ones." Around four thousand years ago, out of Transoxiana, people began to migrate south and west. Those who went south entered the Indus River valley. They absorbed the remains of Harappan civilization and became the Vedic people. Those who went west migrated into Iran—a cognate of Aryan. As the Vedic people and the Iranians moved apart geographically, they also diverged culturally. The original language of these people became Sanskrit in the south and Avestan in the west. The hymns they sang became the Vedas in India and the Avesta in Iran.* The Vedic people had rituals involving a now unknown plant called soma. The Avestans had similar rituals involving a now unknown plant called *haoma*. Among the Vedic people, a corps of religious specialists called Brahmins conducted the rituals. Among the Avestans, a corps of religious specialists called *Magi* conducted the rituals.**

The Vedic gallery of gods included one group of beings called *devas* and another group called *asuras*. The devas were angelic; the asuras demonic. The Avestans also recognized two groups of deities. Theirs were called the *daevas* and the *ahuras*. Surely these started out as the same gods. Curiously enough, however, Avestan culture reversed the identities of these two sets of gods. In Iran, the daevas became demonic, the ahuras became angels.

The Aryans who went south were migrating into a lush environment marked by natural abundance. Their gods branched into thousands of distinct personalities, corresponding to the growing subtleties of Indian

---

*Very few Avestan hymns survive, but those few are almost identical to particular hymns in the much larger Vedic canon.
**From magi comes the word *magician*. The three magi who brought gifts to the infant Jesus in the Christian narrative were Avestan priests.

thought. If you had to pick one word to describe the Indian pantheon, you might settle on *multiplicity*.

In Iran, by contrast, the original Aryan gods drifted into alliances associated with ever starker polarities until at last they had formed up as just two sets of deities. *Every* god was either an ahura or a dev, every god was either angelic or demonic. When the Iranians looked at the world around them, they didn't see multiplicity, they saw polarity. Theirs was a world of light and darkness, life and death, truth and falsehood, good and evil.

Some of the ancient Aryan gods lost importance in India but gained stature in Iran, immense stature sometimes. Agni, for example, the Aryan god of fire, became the Avestans' Ahura Mazda, the creator god, the deity of light and life. And then there was Mitra. Among the Vedic people he barely hung on as a minor deva; in Iran, however, he developed into Mithra, second only to Ahura Mazda in majesty and might.

And what sort of god was Mithra? He was the god of contracts. At first blush, this might seem odd. How could contracts rank right up there with creation and destruction as a principle of the universe? The answer lies, I think, in context. What a fertility deity was to an agrarian world, a god of contracts was in a world built on long-distance trade. Here in these Iranian highlands, a landscape of urban hubs sewn together by caravan traffic, society was a skein of agreements among strangers. Folks were constantly dealing with people they might never see again. All was well when both sides were telling the truth and both kept their promises. Lies and broken promises threatened the order of the universe just as surely as droughts and crop failures did in a world of farmers. Small wonder that a god emerged to preside over truth telling and promise keeping and that he ranked among the greatest gods of all.

As the Avestan gods drifted into their binary alliances, a cosmic story emerged in this social constellation to explain the world. In this story, the daevas were the parent gods. They gave birth to the ahuras but then felt threatened by their own children and tried to kill them. The ahuras fought back, and thus began an epic struggle. The meaning of life lay in that struggle. The world was not some bloodless concentric pattern, nor was it organized as strata. The world was fundamentally dramatic. It was a stage on which some single apocalyptic drama was unfolding. Time was neither cyclical nor illusory but linear. Like every story, it had a beginning, a middle, and an end. Right now, we were in the middle of the story, but the end was coming. Yes, the end was coming.

A prophet named Zoroaster condensed these themes into an idea system, just as surely as Confucius had done with the Chinese narrative and the sadhus had done in India. No one really knows when Zoroaster lived. It might have been as early as 1200 BCE or as late as 600 BCE. His legends say he was a cobbler until he was thirty, but maybe he was a blacksmith or some such: no one knows. Then one day he received a supernatural summons to climb a certain mountain for an audience with the god of fire and creation. There, Ahura Mazda gave Zoroaster a message to deliver to humanity. He was to tell everyone that Ahura Mazda ranked so far above all other gods that he *alone* was worthy of worship. He, however, was locked into a struggle with the equally powerful Ahriman, god of darkness. Humankind was situated on the line of scrimmage in this cosmic battle between good and evil. Every action a person took helped one side or the other. Every decision had cosmic stakes.

Most importantly, however, humans had free will. They could make moral choices, and in those choices lay the meaning of life. At the end of time, when Ahura Mazda won the final victory, all who had sided with him would proceed to an everlasting afterlife in a lush walled garden like the ones that dotted the Middle World and were treasured so highly in this arid land. The Avestan term for such a garden was *pairidaeza* (meaning "enclosure or park"). Derived from it is the modern Persian word *firdaws*. The more familiar English pronunciation of the word is *paradise*.

THE FERTILE CRESCENT

What historians commonly call the Fertile Crescent is the territory that arcs from Mesopotamia to Egypt, from the Nile valley to the Tigris and Euphrates Rivers, from one to the other of the world's two oldest urban civilizations. The territory between those two great intercommunicative zones was conducive to both farming and pastoral nomadism, so a lot of traffic moved through the Fertile Crescent, and dense networks of trade developed naturally throughout that region. The Nile valley and Mesopotamia each had a master narrative of its own, but all that traffic moving through the Fertile Crescent generated a third narrative framework, which included themes from each.

Mesopotamia

Mesopotamia, as we've seen, was a world of walled city-states in constant competition. Kingdoms rose and fell, empires formed and dissolved, nomads invaded cities and seized power and then became city folks, only to be conquered in turn by new waves of tribal nomads. How could the Indian notion of a changeless universe feel true here? Pivotal changes were happening all the time! Almost anyone could recite the stories. Many had been caught up in the tumult themselves.

The various Semitic-speaking inhabitants of the Mesopotamian valley—Sumerians, Akkadians, Assyrians, Chaldeans, and others—had been jostling and clashing among themselves for a thousand years before the Shang built their first capital in China. Meanwhile, from Asia Minor and the eastern highlands, people speaking various non-Semitic languages kept coming into the crowded field: Hittites, Hurrians, Mittani, Kassites, Elamites.

New empires were always forming, each one bigger than the last, but they were not the same empire forming and unraveling again and again as in China, or at least, no one thought that way. Here, to all appearances, the locus of power kept shifting. Now these guys were on top, now those guys. Amid this clamor of cities and tribes, people were resolutely *henotheistic*: they believed in many gods but considered one god to be *their* god. Every city had its patron deity, and all these deities were persons: they had physical form, willful intentions, quirks, and agendas. Every city had its central temple in which its god or goddess literally lived, inhabiting some sculpture or token. The priests fed, groomed, bathed, and pleasured their deity and took him or her around the city on occasion to meet the people.

Here, too, the fundamental quality of history was drama: but the petty dramas of this earthly realm were mere reflections of supernatural dramas in which the protagonists and antagonists were the gods. When one city conquered another, it was really one city's god beating the other city's god.

And where did people fit into all this? Why, as servants. The gods created people to bring them food and run their errands. Individual humans could achieve lives of meaning and purpose by fulfilling their roles, not in their own petty worldly dramas but in the dramas of the gods. This required that people figure out what their god needed and wanted so that they could play their roles well. The domination of some cities by others didn't disprove the existence of many gods. It didn't even discredit one's own. It merely revealed that some gods were bigger and stronger than other gods—or that one had lost the protection of one's own god by doing or failing to do something.

Egypt

At the other end of the Fertile Crescent, as we have seen, environment had spawned a more or less homogenous world of intercommunicating people strung along a mighty river for hundreds of miles. The people of the Nile saw a world populated by an array of gods associated with different forces and ideas, but these deities were all related to one another: the gods formed one big (dysfunctional) family.

The world framework consisted of an austere family drama that happened again and again. There was a parent god far away somewhere, eternally keeping chaos at bay. That parent's two sons and daughters paired up as married couples, one good, the other evil. Osiris, the good son, governed the world until his evil brother Set killed him, chopped him up, and scattered his parts. But Osiris's sister-wife Isis gathered his parts and put him together just long enough to get her pregnant. Their child Horus then inhabited the god-like pharaoh and kept the life-giving Nile flowing properly. Every year, like the river that kept flooding and subsiding, this drama was reenacted.

For Egyptians, death was not a final fact. It was a door between two realms. They believed in an afterlife that a few, a very few, might enter. The life that came after death was sweeter by far than the one before. People were bodies now and would still be bodies in the afterlife, but the Egyptian narrative included the idea of a bird-like entity called the *ka*, which lived inside the body. Without a healthy ka, no one could get past the many hurdles between this life and the next. The ka evoked the notion many people have today of the soul. Perhaps some of these ideas are starting to sound familiar.

Could it be a coincidence that the idea of a single god appeared for the first time in this monolithic culture? Around 1350 BCE, it seems, a pharaoh named Amenhotep decided that Aten, the god he worshipped, was the only god. The pharaoh changed his own name to Akhenaten, meaning "Aten-supporter," and shut all the other temples. This put a lot of temple priests out of business, and the moment Akhenaten died, the Egyptian religious establishment restored their traditional system and suppressed his cult.

The Hebrews

Then there was that third civilization-sized narrative, which emerged between the great river civilizations of the Nile and Mesopotamia and incorporated themes from each. The Hebrews (later Israelites) started out in southern Mesopotamia, but led by the patriarch Abraham, they migrated north toward the headwaters of those rivers, turned west, reached the shores of the Mediterranean, headed south along the Levantine coast, took up farming for a while in a land called Canaan, and finally ended up in Egypt for a spell. Historically, this may not have been a single dramatic journey but the migratory range of a seminomadic people.

The Hebrews started out as full participants in the Mesopotamian narrative. They had a tribal god called Yahweh, seen variously as a god of fire and fertility. He was their patron deity, just as Moloch was the god of Babylon. Individual Hebrew families had their own household gods as well, in the form of sacred stones. Being seminomadic, the Israelites had no temple but carried their god with them in a portable container called an ark. Unlike the other Mesopotamian deities, however, their Yahweh was unseen and unseeable: he had no physical form.

Like urban Mesopotamians, the Hebrews conceived of themselves as created by their god to serve his needs. Hard times drove them to Egypt looking for work, but like many another poor immigrant group throughout history, they ended up as slave laborers. They arrived in Egypt less than a century after the traumatic upheavals occasioned by Akhenaten's shocking cult of Aten. The one-god idea was very probably still thrumming in the cultural air. According to the stories of Abraham's tribal descendants, however, during their escape from Egypt, their leader Moses climbed a mountain, just as Zoroaster had done, for an audience with their god. Yahweh revealed himself to Moses there as the only god and announced that what he wanted of his people wasn't blood sacrifices or sensual pleasures like all those false gods. What he wanted from his people was moral conduct. Moses returned from the mountaintop with a succinct list of rules: the Ten Commandments.

Back in the Levant the Hebrews established two tough little kingdoms, Israel and Judah. In Jerusalem, the capital of Judah, they built a temple of their own at last. But they were squeezed precariously between mightier empires, and in 587 BCE, the Babylonians conquered Judah, razed the temple in Jerusalem, and dragged most of the Judeans to Babylon, where they languished for some fifty years.

Those years proved crucial. In Babylon, the captive Hebrews had only their traditions, memories, and scrolls. The word therefore took the place of the temple. From this time forward, one can speak of Hebrews, Judeans, Israelites (and their descendants) as the Jews. Prophets such as Ezekiel and Isaiah formulated a narrative that explained their suffering: they had broken their covenant with Yahweh.

It was then that in Babylon, a city with a thousand pagan temples, this small captive tribe gave birth to the world's first fully formed, enduring monotheism: the Jews declared that their god was not only the best god but the only god. He wasn't in the temple, he was everywhere. He had no physical form and was not to be conflated with any such form: creating an image of him, any image, was sacrilege.

Out of their own tribal history, the Jews forged a religious narrative capable of incorporating not just past historical events but current (and future) ones. In this narrative, God had made a pact with Abraham: the tribe would get its own land in exchange for worshipping no other god. During the exodus from Egypt, He renewed the covenant with those ten laws he gave to Moses. The Jews thereafter acknowledged their obligation to keep the human side of the bargain, which required moral conduct as defined by scriptures delivered to humanity through prophets. Learned scholars called rabbis, who were able to interpret this law, became community leaders rivaling (and eventually superseding) priests.

The Jewish narrative fit right into the linear view of time characteristic of this region, and it mirrored the apocalyptic vision of the Zoroastrians, who were rife in Babylon during the Babylonian captivity. In the Jewish narrative, the world began with a moment of creation and would end with a day of judgment. Zoroaster had posited two gods, one good, one evil. The Jews insisted on the singleness of God. The evil principle survived as Satan, but he was demoted to one of God's creations. Satan did serve a crucial purpose, however. His role was to tempt the righteous to go astray. People made themselves worthy of heaven by resisting him. Without Satan, getting to heaven would have been (as Robert Frost said of free verse) like playing tennis without a net.

GREECE

The Greeks had connections going back to the Pontic steppe. They spoke an Indo-European language. They worshipped deities similar to those of the Iranians and the early Vedic people: they had storm gods and sky gods and earth goddesses and all the rest. In Greece, these deities developed into characters in stories, each one a distinct personality.

But the Greeks didn't see a single story running from a flash bang beginning to an apocalyptic end-time. To the Greeks, the world looked more like an anthology of countless stories, big and small.

What's more, the Greeks' gods were born at various material times and places. The sun god Apollo, for example, was born in Delphi. The gods, though powerful, were not all-powerful. Vague, vast forces circumscribed even their existence. Zeus was the king of gods, but that didn't free him from the dictates of the three mysterious Fates.

The world story went back to a beginning. In this the Greeks agreed with the Iranians: parent gods gave birth to children gods and then unwisely tried to kill them, whereupon the children fought back. But that wasn't the story happening now. That story was over: the parents had lost the war. The victorious young deities were the gods and goddesses of Mount Olympus. Yes, for the Greeks, the gods were headquartered at a particular place in the same world humans inhabited. One could hike to the foot of Mount Olympus and look up and see where they lived. The Greek deities were so much like characters in a drama that the Greeks relished imagining what they looked like, the way someone who enjoys a work of fiction might get caught up trying to picture actors to play the various characters. In fact, the Greeks almost compulsively created sculptures and images of their deities, and it turned out these deities looked pretty much like humans.

The Greeks in short drifted toward a view of gods and goddesses as a parallel race of beings far superior to humans but inhabiting the same world as humans. They had the same sorts of motives and emotions as we do: love, lust, envy, greed, pity, and the rest. They differed from us only in that they were immortal and immensely more powerful. The gods were largely caught up in their own dramas with one another, but since they occupied the same universe as we—indeed the world was ominously crowded with gods—they impinged relentlessly on human life. They were so vast and we so trivial that they might step on us the way we step on ants. And although they didn't ultimately care what happened to us, they might whimsically manipulate our human dramas the way children use dolls to enact imaginary stories for their own amusement.

The gods were neither particularly good nor particularly bad. They were complicated, like people. They issued no moral code for humans to follow—they really didn't care that much. A human could form a personal relationship with a god in the same way one might with another human, but the superiority of the god must go unquestioned and the element of worship must never be missing. Sometimes, and not infrequently (to be quite frank), deities had sex with humans, resulting in offspring who were semidivine. By nurturing their relationships with various gods, people could maximize the chance that particular gods would befriend them, but there was no magic that worked: the gods were not mechanisms but willful beings—like humans. People also had to be really careful not to favor one god over others, for the gods were easily offended. Kind of like humans. Monotheism had no allure here, quite the opposite. Monotheism felt like sacrilege.

In positing a world that contained both humans and gods, the Greek master narrative implied a framework bigger than the gods, a natural world that existed irrespective of the gods. Here lay the basis for a secular world view analogous to the religious views of other civilizations. We humans might take steps to gain help from this or that deity, but fundamentally we were on our own, as were the gods. Kings gained power not because of some mandate from above but because they were tough and smart, qualities they contained internally. The highest human virtue was excellence—at whatever you were good at. Excellence was something different for a poet than, say, a warrior. People had to be well informed about the oh-so-easily-offended gods, but if they wanted to survive and prosper, people also needed to attend to the natural world within which both gods and people dwelt.

To the Greeks, the world was not just dramatic; it was a particular kind of drama. It was a tragedy. The highest virtue was excellence, but the highest sin was too much excellence—confusing oneself with a god. The Greek way of dealing with the vicissitudes of being merely human was to take the initiative, set goals, and try to achieve them, knowing that in the end it would all come to nothing, for people were not gods and if they overstepped that line—and what was immense success but an overstepping of that line?—they'd crash and burn. Daring to strive while accepting the inevitability of fate: these were the keys to a life of meaning and purpose. Where the Indians developed rituals geared toward giving people an experience of timelessness and selflessness, the Greek developed ritualized plays calculated to produce the emotion of catharsis—not a circumventing of suffering but an embrace of suffering as a source of nobility that enabled one to transcend the tragedy that is life.

On the stage set by secular paganism, Greek philosophy emerged as an idea system parallel to the religions emerging farther east. The Greek philosophers were analogous to Confucius, Zoroaster, the Indian sadhus, and the Jewish prophets. One of the first of these, Thales of Miletus, was born around 625 BCE, around the same time as Confucius. About him, we know one striking biographical detail: people were constantly asking him how come, if he was so smart, he wasn't rich. Thales shut them up by cornering the market in olive oil presses and becoming a millionaire. Then he went back to his studies. Like Zoroaster and the others, Thales was no doubt swimming in a sea of ideas that were the content of his society's master narrative. His thinking resonated with his contemporaries because they were no doubt swimming in the same sea.

Thales is hugely important because of one seminal question that he posed: What was the one material thing of which everything was made? He decided it was water, for he noticed that everything was either solid, liquid, or gaseous and that water could take any of those forms. Philosophers who came after him didn't agree on his answer, but they agreed on his question. What was the *one* thing of which *everything* was made? Anaximander said air; Democritus said indivisible bits of featureless matter; Pythagoras said mathematical relationships. There were many answers, but the questioning took place within the framework set by Thales and his ilk, and those questions preoccupy theoretical physicists to this day.

Finally, there were the much-maligned Sophists, who specialized in teaching people how to win arguments. One chief critic of the Sophists (seen by many as a Sophist himself) was an ugly little pest named

Socrates, who hung about in the streets of Athens, asking uncomfortable questions and then arguing about the answers. Socrates established the proposition that people could figure out what was good and true with no intercession from the gods, just by using their brains and engaging in conversation. We know of this man's teachings only from accounts written by his students and admirers, but in this he was no different from Buddha or Zoroaster or many others. By the time Socrates's student Plato, and Plato's student Aristotle, had finished their work, the Greek philosophers had built an architectonic idea system that put people at the center of the universe and framed human life as a quest for goodness and truth through reason and experience.

The Greek philosophers distilled an idea system out of the civilization-sized gestalt they inhabited, and it reflected that gestalt.* Socrates and his ideas could not have gained traction in the Middle Kingdom. Similarly, the Confucian idea system could not have emerged in Greece. What's more, Buddha would not have achieved nirvana in Mesopotamia. And so on and so on and so on. A master narrative is one single whole, and every part of it serves to reinforce every other part of it. Context is all.

---

*The term *gestalt* comes from an early twentieth-century school of German psychologists studying the thresholds of perception. They stumbled across the provocative discovery that once we humans identify a structure made up of many parts, we stop perceiving the parts and simply perceive the whole. This whole becomes a thing in itself, which they termed a gestalt. Show people a hundred dots arranged in a circular pattern, and they'll see a circle. Take away a few dots, and they'll still see the circle. The gestalt has its own identity and continuity, or as psychologist Kurt Koffka put it, "the whole is other than the sum of its parts." (Not greater than, which is a trivial assertion; *other* than.) The gestalt phenomenon explains why we can learn some things and forget some things and yet remain the same social self: the subtraction and addition don't alter the gestalt that is a person's self. It also explains why, in the presence of contradictory information or incompatible beliefs, people experience cognitive dissonance, a discomfort they feel compelled to reduce. A human needs to be a single whole. It also explains why societies have a propensity to screen out ideas that contradict their dominant narrative and embrace ideas that fit: they are social constellations struggling to become themselves.

PART II

One Planet, Many Worlds

As tools extended our reach, our worlds grew bigger. Wheels, chariots, roads, written language, and the like let ever-greater numbers of us intercommunicate across ever-greater distances. Our networks overlapped as they expanded and sometimes merged into bigger networks of people and stories and meanings and ideas. Eventually, political control superseded mere geography in determining who intercommunicated with whom. Empires formed within which money acted as a solvent and military forces kept order. Local narratives merged into master narratives that knit innumerable people together as members of overarching social wholes bigger than any geographical fact, more enduring than any mere tribe or kingdom or empire. Eventually, whole world-scale civilizations came into being, vast, inward-looking networks of people who saw themselves at the center of the human story. Countless threads of connection ran among these various worlds, and they knew of each other, but each saw the others as peripheral players in a universal drama. Where worlds overlapped, conflicting narratives sometimes blended over time, giving rise to new narratives that incorporated some elements of earlier ones and discarded some others in service to a new coherence.

6

Money, Math, Messaging, Management, and Might

(2000 BCE to 500 BCE)

Civilizations are clouds of ideas without centers or borders; they're too big and too vague to form intentions and carry out plans. Kinship clusters, on the other hand—clans and such—are too small to undertake massive projects such as managing the Nile or terracing the Huang He valley. To grapple with environmental challenges at that scale, people needed intermediate social forms built on roles and rules. Political states emerged to plug this gap.

States reinforced the clique effect by turning social clouds into something more like social cells. Just as a cell has a nucleus and a membrane, a political state has a governing authority and a border—a fuzzy border, perhaps, but some perimeter zone demarcating an inside world from the outside world. To operate effectively, states needed certain material mechanisms. From the start, for example, the coherence of a state depended on material mechanisms for such functions as messaging. By messaging, I mean everything people do to communicate their thoughts and wishes and intentions to one another. The clout and size of a political state was limited by the speed and efficiency with which its members could trade messages.

Back when every human was a member of a small band of hunter-foragers, people could exchange all their necessary messages face-to-face. The group might disperse by day, but everyone came back together at night. If you needed to tell someone something, you could do it next time you saw them, which would be between one sunrise and the next.

But as social webs expanded, whole groups grew too big for everyone to know everyone. No single person could have had direct contact with every other person living in the Nile valley. The messages that knit a state together had to go through a chain of transmission. One person conveyed a message to another, who conveyed it to another.

It took the coordinated labor of thousands, however, to build and operate something like the irrigation systems of the Nile. Each of those thousands had to contribute their own small bit to one larger plan. If the bits didn't fit together, the larger plan was doomed. There had to be some central decision-maker communicating back and forth with the thousands working on the project. Those thousands had to function like the limbs of a single decision-making brain. At that scale, it couldn't simply be a case of one person telling another to tell another. One person had to tell *many* others, who each told *many* others. Only thus could messages issuing from one central source—pharaoh, king, chieftain, head priest, council of elders, whatever—reach all the thousands involved in the common enterprise. No wonder many early civilizations built pyramids: the Egyptians built them as mausoleums for their nobility, the Mesopotamians as temples for their gods, the Maya as raised platforms for religious rites. But I dare say people gravitated toward the pyramid as a form in part because of its metaphorical power: it expressed something fundamental about civilized human existence.

When one authority was communicating with people widely dispersed in space, speed became a key consideration. If a message took two days to reach its intended recipient, it took at least two days for the response to come back. That's a four-day lag. A lot can happen in four days. When the governor's next order arrives, it might no longer fit the situation. The speed at which a message could travel determined how big an area one authority could govern.

In 2000 BCE things didn't change as quickly as they do now. An order issued two days ago might still be relevant two days from now. But even in that slow-changing time there had to be some point beyond which decisions from the center would get hopelessly out of sync with real-life circumstances at the peripheries. What was that point? Three days? Four?

For the sake of argument, let's say it's seven days: people living beyond that point are outside the control of the central governing authority, whoever that might be. Out there, if an emergency comes up, people can't wait for orders. Someone closer to the scene has to make a decision.

In this scenario, tools begin to make a crucial difference. In hunting-gathering times, messaging technology was pretty much nonexistent. A message could travel as far in a day as a human could walk. A ruggedly fit human might be able to get a message about eighty miles out and bring an answer back within a week, but that's assuming the messenger maintains a steady pace hour after hour, day after day, which would have been hard to do when the messenger had to ford rivers, climb hills, fend off wild animals, and deal with marauders. In prehistoric times, even the greatest leader's radius of control could not have been much more than thirty miles, tops.

Then horses were domesticated, and they revolutionized political life. A horse can go an average of 8 miles an hour, which translates to 64 miles in an average day, which would make the radius of control about 430 miles. Of course, even on a horse, the ancient traveler would have had to ford rivers, climb hills, and so on, so let's trim the estimate to a conservative 350 miles—that would have been the maximum size of a political state.

But wait: as long-distance trade proliferated, people built roads and bridges, which eliminated thickets and rivers as factors. They gained control over their local environment, which reduced such hazards as animal attacks and marauders. The development of a technological infrastructure slowly maximized the speed of messengers mounted on horses. The potential size of political states expanded.

In Mesopotamia, the first political units of any account were city-states, beginning with Uruk, which emerged around fifty-five hundred years ago. This city was ruled by Gilgamesh, the legendary protagonist of the world's first written epic poem: Gilgamesh was probably based on a real king, and his city of Uruk was surrounded by a six-mile wall, which means he directly dominated about three square miles; but the rulers of Uruk exerted control over much land surrounding their city. In fact, Uruk's control eventually stretched about one hundred fifty miles from north to south, and perhaps fifty miles east to west—about the limit for the technology of the time.

But time passed and technology advanced. A thousand years after Gilgamesh's reign, Sargon of Akkad, another Mesopotamian ruler, cobbled together an empire that stretched almost 1,000 miles, from southeastern tip to northwestern top, and covered about 308,000 square miles. Eight hundred years after that, Egypt's New Kingdom pharaohs controlled an area 20 percent bigger than Sargon ever did. Another eight hundred years after that, the Assyrians and then the Babylonians controlled an empire nearly twice the size of Sargon's. The increasing size of empires correlated to the increasing speed at which messages could be transmitted, which in turn reflected the development of technology and infrastructure.

Speed, however, is only one consideration. Another is message degradation. Messages transmitted down an oral chain can change without anyone knowing it. Think of the party game Telephone, in which one person in a circle whispers something to the next, who whispers it to the next, and so on around. The last person tells the group what he or she heard, and inevitably it differs comically from what was originally said. The more links in a chain of transmission, the greater the message degradation.

Memorization was important in ancient times, but it was reserved mostly for sacred texts. It wasn't practical for keeping track of daily interactions in a complex society. Written scripts therefore came into being as an extension of language.

In Mesopotamia, by 2000 BCE, people were using cuneiform to send and receive messages. Cuneiform consisted of strokes and symbols stamped into wet clay, which were preserved once the clay dried. This script probably emerged out of trade. The earliest inscriptions were found on containers sent by merchants to other merchants. The inscriptions identified what was in the container and how much of it or how many. Such messages let a person receiving the box know he or she had gotten what was sent. Both parties needed this assurance for a business transaction to work. If a box was marked "twelve pearls" the servant who delivered it couldn't claim his master had sent a dozen grapes. Early cuneiform writings included marks for bread, grain, beer, and other goods typically traded in this area.

Cuneiform probably originated as pictures of things, but by the time it came into prolific use, the written symbols didn't match the objects they represented. It wasn't really necessary. In a business network, where goods were going back and forth, only so many items needed to be represented. Everyone involved in the system knew what those were and could memorize the symbols for them. What gave the script its form was not the correspondence between sign and sense but the ease and speed with which the signs could be made. Given that they were being scored into mud with a stylus, lines and wedges won the day.

In Egypt, meanwhile, hieroglyphics were taking shape as a scripting system. These symbols came out of religion. The first hieroglyphic marks were pictures on the walls of temples and the tombs of important people, recording real or mythic events, the kind of wordless storytelling that inventive graphic novels do today. Gradually, the pictures got simplified and stylized until they evolved into glyphs, symbols that stood for whole categories of things. These glyphs were still connected closely enough to the objects they represented that a naïve observer could make out what they meant just by looking. The glyph for sun looked like a sun, the glyph for man, like a man.

Then came the Phoenicians' great conceptual leap. They were maritime traders who were constantly crossing paths with people who spoke different languages. They developed a script associating various marks not to items in the world, of which there are billions, but to sounds humans could make, of which there are only a few dozen. With this tool, the Phoenicians could record how people on some strange shore said hello, and the next time they visited, they could get the interaction off to a good start by saying hello in the local language.

The great thing about the Phoenician system was its simplicity. With the same few phonemes—indivisible units of sound—people could make a virtually infinite number of words. Once this system had emerged, people could mark not just how people in strange places said hello, but what they themselves were thinking at that moment, even if they'd never had that particular thought before. If they could say it out loud, they could record it, and if their handwriting was much better than mine, they and others could later make out what they had recorded. The Phoenician system inspired related script systems all around the Mediterranean world from the Levant to Iberia.

In fact, the phonetic system was so powerful that its logic spread to other scripting systems in the region. Take hieroglyphics, for example: fine for religious uses but too elaborate for daily messaging needs in a busy, bureaucratic society like Egypt. So a parallel system of simplified glyphs evolved called *hieratic*. Hieroglyphics were still used for sacred texts, but letters, contracts, government documents, and the like were written in the quick-and-dirty hieratic script. Then, hieratic glyphs began to be used in the same way as rebus puzzles. In a rebus, as you may know, the symbol for sun can be used to mean son. A guy named Carson can write his name as a picture of a car plus a picture of a sun. Once the simplified picture of a thing became a token that could be combined with other signs just for the sound of its spoken equivalent, pictograms had begun their evolution toward phonics.

Hieratic could be written more quickly than hieroglyphics, but the marks still went back to glyphs, so there were thousands of them, making the system hard to learn. Gradually, therefore, hieratic became the script of choice for sacred texts and an even more simplified, more phonetic script called *demotic* emerged for everyday functions. By the time Rome conquered Egypt in 30 BCE, demotic had devolved into a fully phonetic alphabetic script like the one pioneered by the Phoenicians.

Meanwhile, a whole different scripting strategy had emerged in China, and this one didn't drift toward phonics. Quite the opposite, in fact. Like hieroglyphics, the Chinese script started as pictograms: each mark was a stylized picture of the thing it represented. The written word for tree was a tiny drawing of a tree. Such a system had great utility for the disparate communities up and down the Huang He, which were isolated enough from one another that the spoken languages tended to diverge.

In China, pictograms evolved into ideograms, so that a given symbol might represent not just some material item in the world but an *idea* such as love or justice. These ideograms might be compared to mathematical symbols. When two people see a mark like 3 or 7,432, they'd say it differently, if one was French, say, and the other Russian, but they'd take exactly the same meaning from it. The idea exists quite separately from the sound.

As this script developed, it became possible to express in writing meanings that actually *couldn't* be expressed in speech, which is to say, the script became a language in itself. A script that departed from any given spoken language had its advantages. For one thing, it meant that through the use of documents, one authority could govern people speaking many different languages. This had profound ripple effects down through Chinese history.

The needs of traders and bureaucrats spawned written scripts, and the same needs gave rise to mathematical symbols: written numbers. When a merchant sealed a dozen pearls into a box, the inscription couldn't just say pearls, it had to say how many. Originally, cuneiform made no distinction between mathematical and semantic information. If a drawing of a sheaf of barley meant "barley," three of those marks meant "three sheaves of barley." This gets cumbersome, however, when you're dealing with, say, fifty-six sheaves of barley. So, numbers separated from things and became stand-alone items that could be represented by marks of their own. Thus did mathematics become a language of a sort too, but a language of a very special sort, a language that could cross cultural borders without the meanings changing.

If messaging is comparable to the nervous system of a social organism, written records are its memory cells. But the unity of a social organism doesn't consist merely of one decision-maker sending messages to thousands of subordinates. In a social constellation, just as in the human brain, the center is not in any one place nor in some single human figure but in the coherence of the whole, for it's not just messages that flow through a functional social organism, it's also material goods. Every so-ciety, no matter how primitive, has a system by which people exchange goods and make use of one another's skills for their own benefit.

In the eighteenth century, the Scottish philosopher Adam Smith proposed the cheerful notion that the earliest human communities had barter economies: one guy spent all day fishing and another spent all day making shoes, and when the first guy needed shoes, he took the shoe-maker a fish, and vice versa. Eventually, according to Smith's theory, this grew so unwieldy that people invented money. But how did there even come to *be* a guy who did nothing all day but make shoes? And another who did nothing but fish? This, Smith didn't explain.

Unfortunately for Smith's theory, no society has ever been found that operated on barter in the way that he described, for money is not, in fact, an invention. Like language, it's a spontaneous by-product of hu-man interaction. Money is also not a thing; it's an abstraction. No one trades a cow for a coin because they want the coin. They trade the cow for a coin so they can trade the coin for a wagon. Money is just a way of translating cow to wagon. It brings *value* into existence as a substance separate from all material things that have value, in the same way that mathematical marks bring quantity into existence as an element separate from all things quantified.

Within a human group, when everything can be quantified in terms of a single unit of measurement, any sort of thing can be exchanged for any other sort of thing. If messaging can be compared to the nervous system of a social organism, money can be compared to its circulatory system: it creates a network of links through which value can flow from place to place. A material good available in one place can pop up as a completely different material good in another place; only money can make this happen.

Money emerges in any community where trade exists—which is every community. In prisons, where people generally don't have cash, cigarettes spontaneously turn into currency. Their value as smokeable items gives way to their value as a precise means of measuring what any-thing is worth compared to anything else.

In Mesopotamia, five-thousand-year-old written records show that the temple bureaucracies at the core of every community kept detailed accounts of people's services to the temple, expressed as bushels of barley. But when the workers came to get paid, they didn't necessarily get barley; they got an amount of *something* equivalent in value to a quantity of barley. There was no cash involved in these exchanges, only credit—the record of what one was owed: credit thus came into existence before cash. When money emerged, it didn't replace barter; it replaced calculations of credit and debt.

When ancient kings piled up great stores of gold, they didn't just go out and buy stuff with it. They kept the gold as a measurement of their net worth. When those kings undertook big projects requiring the participation of many people, currency came into existence.

War is a stark example, as David Graeber explains in his book *Debt: The First 5,000 Years.* A king with a big army could bend many others to his will, but the king had to feed, house, and clothe his soldiers. How was a single person to do all that? If he put a large staff in charge of it, how was he to keep and feed and house and clothe all of *them*? It was a logistical conundrum. But there was a clean and simple solution. The king could pay his soldiers (and staff) in units of gold and impose taxes on his subjects payable only in units of gold. The king's subjects had to sell goods and services to the king's soldiers to get the gold they needed to pay the king's taxes, which obliged individuals under the rule of a particular king to use their own initiative, ingenuity, and resources to maintain the army that kept them ruled. The king had only to collect taxes and pay his soldiers, and his net worth never went down, because the gold he paid his soldiers kept flowing back into his treasury.

Whatever the king accepted as payment of taxes became currency, but the power of money to enable transactions extended beyond any kinship cluster, language cluster, or worldview. As early as 2000 BCE, trade goods flowed between places as widely separated as India and Asia Minor. For such transactions to take place, units of currency that worked in one place had to be exchanged for units of currencies that worked in other places. This required that the relative values of *currencies* be calculable.

Calculation is the common denominator here. Money could not have come into existence without mathematics, which emerged in tandem with written scripts, out of the exigencies of messaging, in a world mediated by long-distance trade, which involved interactions of mutual benefit among people in disparate places—which is a long of way of saying that, in the social universe, everything is connected to everything.

As messaging, money, mathematics, management systems, military technology, and, yes, master narratives matured, so did the size of political states. Akkad was bigger than Uruk, and Assyria was bigger than Akkad. But the change was not steady and incremental. The Achaemenid dynasty of Persia exercised imperial control over eight million square miles, more than five times the size of the empire ruled by the Assyrians, and this escalation of scale took place rather suddenly—within half a century. Something must have happened to enable such a striking development, and it must have been happening in a lot of places, for with Achaemenid Persia, an age of superstates began, an age of megaempires. Persia was not unique; it was only the first of the megas. It was followed closely by comparable empires centered in Greece, India, Rome, and China. Persia turned the crucial corner toward its enormous imperial expansion in 533 BCE, when it conquered the largest, most sophisticated Mesopotamian empire of the time, the neo-Babylonian empire of the Chaldeans. But why now? Why Persia? And why the megaempires that followed?

7

Megaempires Take the Stage

(500 BCE to 100 CE)

Today, Babylon registers as a synonym for "sinkhole of corruption." In its day, however, and in its region, Babylon was considered the city of the gods. With its thousand-plus temples, it had for Mesopotamians something of the aura that Mecca has had for Muslims over the centuries, or that the Vatican has had for Catholics. Babylon was the city of learning and libraries, of art, grace, and culture, of splendid buildings and gorgeous gardens. All this has been obscured by the fact that Babylonia was also a merciless imperial power that ruthlessly sacked cities, drove whole populations into exile, and dragged many a hapless wretch back to its capital to live in captivity. Among these captive peoples were the Judeans, who became the Jews during their captivity and wrote the books that made Babylon a synonym for cruelty and corruption, proving that in the long run the pen really is mightier than the sword.

Jewish tradition tells the story of a banquet hosted by Prince Belshazzar of Babylon for about a thousand of his closest friends. The wine was flowing and the merriment growing when suddenly, in a dimly lit corner of the gigantic room, a disembodied finger appeared and on the wall in letters of fire wrote: *Mene Mene Tekkel Upharsan*, which meant "Counted. Counted. Weighed. Divided/Persians." It looked like gibberish, in short, but Belshazzar knew it wasn't prudent to ignore words written in letters of fire by disembodied fingers. So he called in the Jewish dream interpreter Daniel to decode the message. Daniel said the words meant "Your days are numbered. Your deeds have been weighed and found wanting. The Persians are coming to divide your kingdom."

And Daniel was right. Persian armies were descending from the hills at that very moment, led by King Kourosh, known to Western historians as Cyrus the Great. The Persians were an Iranian tribe, and Cyrus belonged to the Persian royal family, the Achaemenids. As soon as he inherited his father's throne, he reduced the other Iranian tribes to junior partners and marched on Croesus, king of Lydia, the richest kingdom of its day—it was, after all, the place where coinage was invented.

Croesus had stout allies ready to crush Cyrus as soon as the fighting season opened, which wasn't till spring, as everyone knew—everyone except Cyrus, that is. He was thinking outside the box. He marched on the Lydian capital in the dead of winter—who *does* that?—and took the undefended city easily.* Cyrus went on to conquer every hill and dale that met his eyes until his rule extended to the borders of Mesopotamia.

In 539 BCE, the Babylonians weren't worried about the Persians. They had three concentric forty-foot-high walls around their city. Babylon was impregnable. But as history has shown, even the impregnable can get pregnant. Babylon got its water from the Euphrates River, and the water came in through culverts under the walls. Cyrus cut some quick canals to drain these culverts and then his soldiers crawled through the empty pipes into the city.

Instead of executing the whole conquered dynasty and selling the people of Babylon into slavery, as was standard practice, Cyrus let the Babylonians restore their temples and permitted their captives to return to their homelands. The Jews went back to Israel at this point and absorbed Cyrus into their religious narrative as the good king. Cyrus's son went on to conquer Egypt, and the next emperor, Darius, consolidated the conquests. During his reign, the Persian Empire of the Achaemenid

---

*After conquering Lydia, Cyrus took an unusual step: instead of exercising the conqueror's right to kill his foe, he made Croesus his consultant on Lydian affairs.

family reached a size no political state had ever come close to equaling: it stretched from the eastern edge of what is now Afghanistan to the northern border of what is now Sudan, and by the time Darius was done, he had this huge empire humming like a well-tuned engine.

How did the Persians do it?

The answer goes back to all those M's: management, messaging, money, and military might. Take management, for starters. Cyrus and his successors accommodated conquered peoples as a political strategy, but they also ran a tight ship: they divided the whole empire into twenty-three provinces, each administered by a *satrap*, a governor appointed directly by and accountable directly to the emperor. Achaemenid Persia had a single, no doubt about it, decision-making authority. That's management.

The single authority could govern this vast realm because the Achaemenid Persians developed a most sophisticated messaging infrastructure. They built a network of roads made of pounded earth that ran throughout the empire. The trunk of this system was the 1,500-mile-long Royal Road, which ran from the capital to the western edge of the empire, a smooth surface on which horses and chariots could move at top speed. Secondary roads branched off at useful points, like nerves off a spinal cord.

Along the roads, at regular intervals, were government-built hostels where travelers could rest and get food and shelter for the night. With this infrastructure in place, the Persians could operate a sort of pony express, a corps of state-paid couriers riding from station to station along state-built roads. At each station, the courier handed off his bag of messages to a new courier with a fresh horse. The couriers stopped to rest, but the messages never did. And when the couriers moved, they moved fast, for they didn't have to worry about wild animals, food, water, or whatever. The state had sorted all that. They could devote themselves purely to their job, and their job was to keep the messages moving. Thanks to this system, a message could travel the length of the empire in seven days or less. If seven is the magic number, the Achaemenid Persians came in under the wire.

What was to stop distant satraps from organizing their own bases of power and eventually declaring themselves independent kings? The Achaemenids met that problem with the "king's eyes and ears," a corps of royal inspectors who roamed the empire, watching for signs of any trouble the emperor might need to know about. This Persian institution was, essentially, an elaborate spy network. So much for the second M—messaging.

Then there was money. The Persian Empire contained within its borders numerous regions wealthy in their own disparate ways: Egypt produced grain; the Scythians of the northern steppes raised horses; Afghanistan had gold and precious gems galore. What joined all these productive regions together was a rational tax system. Victorious kings had long demanded tribute from people they conquered, but there's a difference between tribute and taxation. Tribute paid by conquered people to their conqueror was a method for enriching the conqueror but also for keeping the conquered tamped down. If tribute left the tributaries poor and weak, it was working. A rational tax system was just the opposite: it took only as much out of a region as the region could deliver without a loss of productivity. The more an area flourished, the more a ruler could milk out of it in taxes. A tax system was working when the taxpayers were doing ever-better economically.

The third Persian king, Darius the Great, followed up on the system pioneered in Lydia (now just a province of his empire) by minting two sets of coins: one was the *daric*, made of gold, and the other a silver coin called the *siglos*. The imperial government used these coins to pay for its huge infrastructure projects and its armies. It also made its satraps responsible for collecting taxes from their regions in the form of the king's coin. When the imperial government issued coins to workers, the workers spent them on things they wanted, which put the coins into circulation. Once standardized coins were circulating in abundance, the emperor's subjects could use them to trade anything for anything within the empire. Goods flowed wherever the king's coin had credibility.

If any single area could have all the gold, grain, horses, gems, and other products that were available somewhere in the Persian Empire, it would be incalculably wealthy. With standardized coinage facilitating the flow of goods from anywhere to anywhere within Achaemenid Persia, that empire *was,* in a sense, the one place with all those many products.

The king's coins worked better than plain bits of gold and silver because their weight was absolutely regulated, and their ratio absolutely standardized. This brings us back to mathematics. One daric was worth twenty siglos. Period. The king's coins represented the fruitful intersection of money, math, and trade. You could be sure some slippery-fingered middleman hadn't shaved a little off the edges of a daric because it was stamped with a picture of an archer, and you could be sure it wasn't bronze covered with gilt, because counterfeiting the king's coins was a crime, and the king's eyes and ears were everywhere, and despite a reputation for tolerance, the Persian kings were not Mr. Nice Guys. Ultimately, for money to work in tandem with taxation, it had to be backed by military might.

Of that, the Persians had plenty. They could draft soldiers from an immense territory. Providing the state with soldiers, horses, and military materiel was one of the obligations of every governor. As a result, the Persians could keep a huge standing army. Within that army, they had an elite force of ten thousand warriors known as the Immortals who fought as disciplined units wearing distinctive and identical uniforms so that anyone meeting them on the field of battle could tell immediately who they were up against. A troop of Immortals always had a back-field of reserves dressed exactly like the front-liners. If a front-liner went down, a backbencher instantly took his place. To the people fighting them, the Immortals looked like they could take a sword through the heart and pop right back to life. It wasn't the Persians who called these troops the Immortals. It was the people who faced them in battle.

I dwell on the Achaemenid Empire at some length not because Persia was unique but because it wasn't. Money, math, messaging, management strategies, and military technology were moving forward in many places. Sixth-century Persia was merely the place where these developments first converged to a tipping point. At that moment, Persia had a phonetic written language derived from cuneiform, a state-of-the-art postal system, a world-class spy network, government-issued coins, a rational taxation system, and a standing army spearheaded by an elite corps of warriors. *That's* how come there was a Persian Empire. The Royal Road, the darics and the siglos, the satraps and the Immortals—these were among the countless individual but interrelated features that fit together to comprise the constellation of Persia.

To all these M's, let us add one more: master narrative was a factor here too. The core Persian realm had a coherence deriving from the Zoroastrian worldview, which was so widely shared in this region. Yes, Cyrus and his successors let their subjects worship as they wished, but this dynasty bestowed official favor on the faith that saw the world as a stage and history as a cosmic contest between light and darkness, a belief system woven into the social fabric of the Iranian highlands and quite compatible with the master narratives of the Fertile Crescent. It's probably no coincidence that the political reach of the Persian emperors matched the territory permeated by these narratives. The Persians brought money and might and all the rest of it into the field, but a master narrative made the field a single whole, which gave the Persians something to conquer and hold: it's easier to grip a rock than a pile of pebbles.

The same developments that climaxed with the rise of the Persian Empire were underway elsewhere as well. Road-building technology was advancing in China, Mesopotamia, and Western Europe. The Assyrian Empire had a spy network and the rudiments of a postal system. More and more societies were using written scripts of one form or another. Mathematical learning had spread with the same disregard for cultural factors as diseases. The Lydians happened to invent coinage, but other societies were groping toward some similar way of standardizing hard metals into workable currency.

And, of course, military technology had been advancing on every front. By 1000 BCE, bronze had given way to iron, and iron improved into steel. Catapults and siege machinery had been invented. Chariots now routinely featured sword blades attached to their wheels. Something like the Persian Empire was bound to come into being. Yes, it took a Cyrus to make it happen. He was a remarkable personality, but remarkable personalities are not actually all that rare. Some have entered history because, like Cyrus, they caught a wave just as it was cresting. Others died unknown because their context gave them nothing to work with. No snake ever won a footrace.

Persia grew about as big as it could for the master narrative that held it together and the technology it possessed. Eventually, it overlapped with a social reality expanding from a different center. When the Persians tried to conquer the Greeks, they were so overextended, their cultural and material resources could not stand up to the unified coherence of a people fighting at home.

The Greeks are often seen as plucky little cities minding their own business until the Persian bullies came along, but actually these Greeks were hardly runts. They had been a dominant naval power in their part of the world for centuries. Their reach extended from colonies in Italy to trading posts in the Black Sea. It's true that they had no single ruler, but a single ruler can be overrated as a source of strength. Yes, the Greeks operated as numerous autonomous, self-ruling city-states, each with its own laws, but the people of these many states shared a single network of thought. They shared a language, an ethos, a sense of common history. They knew and revered the same poets. They recognized the same gallery of deities. They visited one another's oracles for advice. They had many institutions in common: the Olympic Games, for example, were already three hundred years old at this point. The Greeks were not just random people scattered across a bunch of islands and peninsulas. They were a self-aware social constellation living in their own collectively constructed world, a world that embodied who they were, an identity that included not-Persian as a feature. Just to clarify, the Greeks were also not Chinese, but not-Chinese was not part of the Greek identity.

In 490 BCE, Darius the Great sent an army into Greece, and the Athenians trounced it in the Battle of Marathon. The Athenians were fighting twenty-five miles from their home base, the Persians eighteen hundred miles from theirs. At that distance from home, beyond the limits of the Persian narrative, Darius was not so great. Ten years later Darius's son Xerxes invaded Greece with the biggest army the world had ever seen and burned down Athens. But the Greeks destroyed his entire navy at the Battle of Salamis, and Xerxes had to slink home in defeat.

The Persian assault accomplished what failed efforts of this sort have often accomplished. It fired up the Greeks, stoked their pride, and fueled a golden age. The Greeks already had a long history of intellectual vigor. Two centuries had passed since Thales posed his seminal question, a century and a half since Pythagoras formulated his famous theorem. Now, in the afterglow of the Greco-Persian Wars, Greek dramatists poured out some of the greatest plays ever written, sculptors carved immortal works of art, and philosophers such as Plato founded seminal schools of thought. At this point, there was no way the Greeks were going to become dim peripheral stars in the constellation that was Persia. They had too much swagger to see themselves as anybody's perimeter. They were a mustered group-self capable of forming an agenda. They didn't just drive the Persians back, they took the fight to Persia. This was inevitable.

Alexander the Great was not so much Greek as Greek-ish. His father ruled Macedonia, a provincial kingdom on the fringes of Greek culture. To the Macedonians, the Greeks were big-city sophisticates. To the Greeks, the Macedonians were country rubes. King Philip of Macedonia hired the great Athenian philosopher Aristotle to tutor his son Alexander. No high-ranking Athenian aristocrat would have dreamed of hiring some Macedonian to tutor *his* children.

Still, when King Philip conquered the Greek cities, his kingdom identified itself as Greek. When his son Alexander took the throne, he looked east and saw Persia with Greek eyes, and the Greeks had a score to settle with Persians. We often hear that, over the next ten years, Alexander the Great "conquered the world." If you compare a map of his empire with the one Darius the Great ruled, you can see that what he actually conquered was the Persian world.

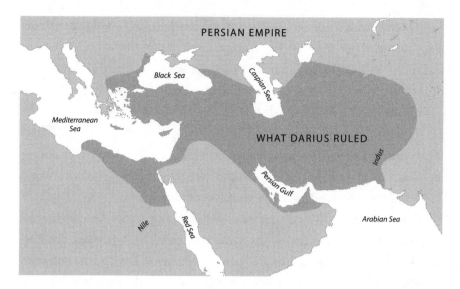

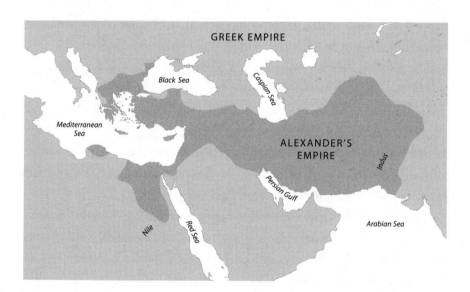

But just as the Persians exceeded the limits of their own coherence when they invaded Greece, the Greeks exceeded theirs when they crossed the Indus River. At that point, Alexander's soldiers had come almost three thousand miles with him, but metaphysically speaking, when they crossed the Indus, they were strangers in a strange land. They had entered India, with its castes and its many-armed goddesses and its trace memories of massive Vedic horse sacrifices and its sense of time as stationary and of the world as illusion—the sheer quantity and intensity of *differentness* must have overwhelmed armies of people steeped in the culture of the Hellenized Middle World. They were no longer at the easternmost edges of a reality they could imagine and understand. They were now at the westernmost edges of reality as somebody else understood it. They were not protagonists here; they were extras in a world historical story expanding from another center far away.

For the fact is, while Alexander was rampaging across Asia, a gigantic empire was forming in India. The same conditions that spawned the Persian Empire had matured to a tipping point here. The Indian colossus, the Cyrus and Alexander of this realm, had already emerged. He was Chandragupta Maurya, a penniless orphan of the merchant caste, whose parents had died young. Legend has it that sometime in his boyhood years, Chandragupta fell asleep under a tree and woke up to find a tiger licking his face. At that moment, he knew he was destined for greatness.

By the time Alexander's troops crossed the Indus River, Chandragupta had taken over Magadha, the kingdom into which he was born. As the Hellenic armies withdrew, Chandragupta Maurya's troops moved into the vacuum. The Maurya Empire ended up bigger than the Persian Empire, bigger even than Alexander's conquests: it stretched from the tip of India to the Khyber Pass and beyond.

How could any emperor control such a vast territory? We're back to all those M's: management, messaging, money, math, military might, and master narrative. The Mauryans, like the Persians, built a network of roads and rest stops to supplement India's countless river highways. They built a postal system much like Persia's. They standardized weights and measures and issued their own coins. They set up a Persian-style administrative structure of villages nested within subdistricts nested within districts nested within provinces, whose governors reported directly to the throne. And like the Persians, the Mauryan emperors had a massive intelligence network. Anyone from a merchant to a Brahmin priest to a prostitute might be a spy, funneling information from his or her corner of the empire to the center.

What's more, Chandragupta's world was steeped in a master narrative that had now fully matured. It wasn't Zoroastrianism here. It was Hinduism-Buddhism-Jainism. Though slightly different from one another, these idea systems coexisted comfortably as distillations out of the same master narrative. Religion generated a cohesion that allowed one king to envision ruling it all because there was an "all" to rule.*

The Persians, Greeks, and Mauryans rose to grandeur within the same few centuries. Following fast on their heels, two more gigantic empires formed, one at each end of the world's most heavily populated belt, the Chinese empire in the east and the Roman Empire in the west, and since these proved to be the most enduring of the first megastates, they are worth a close look.

The Chinese had long spoken of a universal empire synonymous with themselves, but the known empires of the past had not actually encompassed much territory. In the third century BCE, however, the empire of the Chinese mythic imagination came rather suddenly and completely into being in the material world.

It was a two-step process. It began in the climactic days of a long Warring States Period. By 249 BCE, seven culturally Chinese states were vying for supremacy between the Huang He and Yangtze River valleys. One of them was Qin, a militaristic kingdom with a swashbuckling ruler. When that swashbuckler died, he left a thirteen-year-old boy as his heir. The rulers of the rival kingdoms licked their lips and sharpened their swords: Qin looked ripe for the picking. But they underestimated that boy. He struck first, he struck hard, and a twenty-eight-year war

---

*Ashoka, third emperor of the Mauryan dynasty, had a dramatic conversion experience to Buddhism after a particularly bloody battle. He then made Buddhism the favored doctrine of his realm. Ashoka's subjects could still worship who and how they pleased, but the state supported Buddhist teachers and missionaries and arranged for Buddhist teachings to be carved on stones and pillars throughout the empire. Ashoka himself gave up hunting in favor of meditation and developed his own doctrine of the dharma, the principles of conduct leading to a good life. He is remembered to this day as a Buddhist luminary in his own right.

ensued. When the screaming stopped, the rival kingdoms were all mere provinces under the thumb of a king who now gave himself the grandiloquent title of Shi Huang di: the First Emperor.

With this title, he placed himself within a line of iconic figures of history as seen by Chinese historical mythology: first, there had been three supernatural sovereigns, who did things like set the moon and sun on their course; then came the Five Emperors, who did things like invent agriculture and writing and silk; and now came the First Emperor, whose dynasty would rule the Middle Kingdom for ten thousand generations—or so the emperor himself declared and who was going to argue with *him*?

The First Emperor deepened his grip quickly and brutally. To block the nomads of the north, he put some three million conscripts to work connecting defensive walls built by the various kingdoms of yore, into a single Great Wall stretching more than three thousand miles. A million people died building that wall, but the wall got built and China was secured. Shi Huang di adopted an anti-Confucian philosophy called Legalism as the official doctrine of the state. It was as stern and dogmatic as the Confucian idea system was gentle and intuitive. Legalism prescribed exact laws that must be obeyed, and it specified the punishments that must be meted out for disobedience: no gray areas, no fuzzy lines.

The First Emperor also nationalized important industries including iron and salt, minted a round coin with a square hole as the official currency, standardized weights and measures, and imposed a rigorous system of taxation and regulation that specified exactly what each peasant family was to grow on its little plot of land. And like all the other first-generation empires, Shi Huang di's China soon boasted roads, hostels, a massive postal system, a pervasive spy network—the works. Whether the Chinese got the idea for these developments from other social worlds such as Persia or thought of it themselves is unknowable but also immaterial, since both are happening all the time: ripple effects are traveling from world to world, but at the same time, people everywhere are busy looking for advantage on their own. Wherever it came from, if an idea works, it takes root and grows. And for the First Emperor, the administrative mechanisms that worked so well in Persia worked here too.

Then the First Emperor died, and a backlash erupted. His son was swept away by a flood tide of brigandage and senseless violence. It looked like the other side of the cycle described by Chinese historians, who saw flying apart and coming together as equal and opposite forces. This time, however, a second stunning figure suddenly emerged. Liu Bang, a shrewd peasant of chilling resolve, exploited the chaos to rise first to bandit leader, then to warlord, and finally to one of two men fighting for control of the entire empire. When his last competitor captured his father and threatened to boil the old man alive, Liu Bang wrote back: "Send me a cup of the soup." His rival ended up committing suicide, and in 202 BCE, Liu Bang declared himself emperor of a united China and founder of a new dynasty: the Han.

The period of fragmentation had lasted only seven years, almost too short to be called a period. Liu Bang essentially resurrected the Qin dynasty, changing only the name: now it was the Han dynasty. Shi Huang di had done all the dirty work needed to knit a fractious world into an orderly society. When the Han came to power, they didn't have to sacrifice a million lives to secure China's northern border: the wall was there. They didn't have to organize the regulation of the Chinese people down to the last person; the Legalist bureaucrats had already seen to that. The Han could instead curry favor by *reducing* taxes. And having inherited unquestionable military superiority within their borders, they could ease up on the Qin policy of universal conscription. In short, the Han could govern with grace what the First Emperor had built with blood. They established a system of governance that lasted (with one short interruption) for about four centuries, a period of efflorescence in which the constellation known to history as China came entirely into view.

The Han emperors restored the primacy of Confucian thought, the belief system most deeply rooted in the Chinese master narrative. Shi Huang di and his ministers had burned the ancient classics, hoping to create a new world in their own image, but they didn't get all the books. Surviving copies were brought out of hiding and copied and distributed until society once again brimmed with the accumulated wisdom, traditions, ideas, and ethos of the Confucian past. Those classics became the food and fuel, the lifeblood, of a massive bureaucratic state extending from the South China Sea to the edges of Mongolia.

To govern this expanse, the Han dynasty established a mechanism unique to China, a civil service staffed by men who had demonstrated learning in the classics. Everywhere else, kings delegated power to relatives and associates, who in turn delegated power to *their* relatives and associates, who delegated and delegated and so on down. In a sense, in those places, everyone at every level was ruled by a king type. In China, by contrast, mere kinship didn't (necessarily) get you a job in the government: it helped, no doubt, but you had to have studied the classics too. In China, theoretically, everyone at every level was ruled by a scholar-bureaucrat. Thanks to China's ideographic script, officials who spoke different languages and were widely separated in space could work together through written correspondence. They got the same meaning from a written text, no matter how it sounded when read out loud.

But the Chinese script took so much work to master that the scholar-bureaucrats inevitably came to form an intellectual-political elite peculiar to Chinese society. Along with many other elements, this corps of scholars gave China's political cohesion a distinct flavor of its own. A neutral observer would not have confused this constellation with the one in India or the one in the Middle World. The cultural elements of China added up to a coherent Chinese whole.

ROME

Meanwhile, at the other end of Eurasia's most heavily populated belt, a Mediterranean superstate was congealing. The whole time the Macedonian Greeks were swaggering across Asia, Rome was gathering strength. The decline of Greece and the rise of Rome were not exactly consecutive events; they overlapped somewhat. But when Greece was peaking as a cultural and military power, Rome was like a rowdy teenager still looking for itself. In the age of Plato and Aristotle, Pericles the Great, and all those immortal Greek playwrights, Rome was a scrappy little city, tough but not an empire yet.

The Romans turned a significant corner toward their ultimate identity in 509 BCE when they overthrew their king. From that time on, Rome had a political system peculiar for the times, a government run by several hundred men called the senate. These men were elected—but only by the patricians, the landowning elite of Rome. Each year the senate elected two of their ranks as chief executives or consuls. These men functioned in lieu of a king. But there were always two consuls, never just one, and after a year both consuls had to step down and two new men took their place: the Romans were *really* leery of kingship.

At the height of the Greek golden age, a power struggle was raging in Rome, landowners versus peasants, patricians versus plebeians, aristocrats versus commoners. The two social classes negotiated a settlement by creating a new set of magistrates, elected by the plebeians alone. These so-called tribunes had only one power, but it was a mighty power. They could say no: they could veto anything the senate proposed. On the face of it, this system looked like one that could not possibly function in the face of a crisis.

The Romans also drafted a body of laws called the Twelve Tables, which were not directives from a deity, like the Ten Commandments, but an explicitly secular treaty between groups of people angling for a way to function as a social whole. No one said these laws derived from the gods. Everyone took these to be laws based on reason and tradition. In theory they set forth fundamental principles from which all particular laws could henceforth be derived. Some were procedural, like how many days you had to wait for a debt to be repaid before your debtor became your slave. Some were quite specific; for example, if a man sang a song slandering another, he must be clubbed to death. Some were social, like the decree that women could never attain adulthood but must always remain guarded like children.

The laws of the Twelve Tables seem grimly primitive today, but the thing is, the Romans did enshrine an abstraction as the highest authority in the land, higher than the senate, higher than the consuls, higher than any human being. In Rome, theoretically, *no one was above the law*. In practice, of course, this rule was honored more in the breach than in the observance (to quote Shakespeare), but still, the Romans did bring the nobody-above-the-law idea into the world, just as the Chinese had put into play the *idea* of meritocracy.

Rome turned another corner when the powerful Etruscans of the north decided to reinstate Rome's ousted king. The Romans and Etruscans went to war over this. When it ended, Etruscia was just another part of Rome. In 387 BCE, tribal nomads called the Gauls invaded Italy, attacked Rome, and actually got into the city. The Romans battled them bloody and drove them out, and with this they really began to feel their oats. Then along came Pyrrhus, the king of mighty Macedonia, known far and wide as a military genius. He invaded Italy with a huge army and won a series of costly victories until at last he found himself deep inside Italy, out of troops, stranded. Oops. So much for Pyrrhus.

The Romans then went to war with the most formidable maritime power of the Mediterranean world, the Phoenicians of Carthage, on the African coast directly across from Italy. The Carthaginian general Hannibal is remembered as a military genius, one of the greatest in history. He marched over the Alps with scores of elephants to attack Rome from the north! The Romans had no such genius to put in the field. All they had was their ungainly governing system, in which several hundred men made decisions under the guidance of consuls who changed every year. No one remembers much about the colorless generals that this peculiar body sent out to fight Hannibal. Each was more colorless than the last, and every battle seemed to showcase Hannibal's brilliance. Yet somehow the war ended with the Romans seizing Carthage, hunting down Hannibal, hounding him into committing suicide, and finally razing Carthage and killing or enslaving all of its inhabitants. By the time Rome was done, Carthage was no more. Say what you will, something about the Roman system seemed to work.

Rome was a supermilitarized society: all eligible men served in the armed forces. Their armies were disciplined groups of soldiers operating as single units, like chess pieces moved by their commanders. They could build moats at breakneck speed, isolating enemy forces from supplies. No one could stand up to them.

If physical infrastructure was the key to Persian success, it's no wonder the Romans outdid the Achaemenid Persians in size, strength, and longevity. They invented concrete, which hardens best when wet. With this marvel they could bridge any body of water, and their aqueducts could carry fresh water hundreds of miles, so they could put cities anywhere. And with their siege machinery and their engineering prowess, they could take any city that wasn't theirs already. The Romans surrounded the Mediterranean with an unparalleled network of highways built on beds of stone, far better than those of the Persians, some thirty thousand miles of the best roads anyone had ever built (or would build for more than a millennium), and their roads enabled them to get to trouble spots before rebels got their boots on.

Patriotic fervor was like a religion for Romans. They were living in the epic story of Rome itself, from which even the poorest of citizens apparently derived a sense of identity and pride. And the whole society was permeated by the pagan secular humanism that derived from Greece and undergirded Roman law. Indeed, Rome's epics traced their origins back to the Trojan War. It's not just that the Romans had the same array of gods and goddesses as the Greeks except with Latin names. They saw those deities within the same framework as the Greeks: a "natural" world that contained both humans and gods. Rome, in short, was Greece without the subtleties. Minus philosophers but plus engineers—and concrete.

Romans did the bulk of their conquering when they were still a republic. In that era, the senate actually governed, the consuls really were chief executives, and (some) Roman citizens really did elect their leaders. The first Roman emperor, Augustus, didn't finalize his grip on power until 27 BCE, and he took the coy step of titling himself not emperor but *princeps*, or first citizen. For the next two and a half centuries after that, the Mediterranean world was part of a single political superstate, bound together by a singular network of roads and unified by a single monetary system and a single set of laws. These factors enabled an unprecedented flow of goods within an immense territory. Material culture didn't differ much from one end of the Roman Empire to the other.

When the Common Era began—by the year one, that is—eight out of every ten humans lived between the Atlantic coast of Europe and the shores of the South China Sea. Virtually all of them lived within the borders of a political state, and most of them within that handful of superstates or their remains. Some lived in the Roman Empire, some in the Persian Empire, now known as the Parthian Empire, some in the Hindu and Buddhist successor kingdoms to the Mauryans, and some in Han China. Throughout this zone, vast stretches of land were bound together by master narratives, messaging networks, money systems, written laws, and the military might of organized governments.

This is not to say that kings and emperors had much of an actual presence in their subjects' daily lives. Power was everywhere structured like those Russian nesting dolls: people were enmeshed first of all in webs of family and extended family, the shape and texture of which varied from society to society and was governed most directly by a faith-religion-idea system and a local body of history, customs, and traditions. Marriages, meals, childcare, education, recreation, how people engaged in sex and with whom, what toys children played with, what stories they told, what made them laugh, what made them weep—these were shaped not by governments or political machinery but by daily interactions with others of their culture and community. Women played a major role in shaping any given society's distinctive texture in daily life, the feel of real life at the ground level, but their influence cannot now be known in much detail because historians and other writers were mostly men and interested mostly in the dramas among men.

Meanwhile, political states and superstates, controlled almost exclusively by men, created grids. Within those grids, life flowed according to impulses generated organically by custom, tradition, and biology. No one could discount the grids imposed from above or live as if they didn't exist. The areas in which the state impinged most directly on everyday life had to do with taxes, armies, and public works projects. Taxes mattered because everybody had to pay them. Armies mattered because powerful men were constantly trying to enlarge the territories that owed them money. Bystanders got killed in these battles, and ambitious men joined armies to share in the rewards of successful rampage.

Public works mattered because when the might of the state was directed toward building big things, whether monuments, mausoleums, public buildings, dams, bridges, roads, palaces, or what-have-you, some people gained opportunities to make money and some got drafted unwillingly into work they would not otherwise have done, with consequences in either case for every other aspect of the lives people were living.

8

The Lands in Between

(200 BCE to 700 CE)

Political states have borders demarcating one "interior" from another.
Civilizations have frontier zones, where the coherence of one master
narrative gradually dissolves and the power of another fades in. Borders
are porous, however, and frontiers are nebulous. All through history, people have moved from one world civilization to another through the spaces
in between. Merchants, tourists, adventurers, bandits, armies, migrants,
criminals on the lam—all have carried with them trinkets, goods, games,
jokes, recipes, riddles, songs, stories, judgments, rumors, opinions, and
countless other sorts of artifacts, ideas, impulses, and habits. Human cultures may clot into constellations, but connections have threaded among
them forever.

People inhabiting the lands between distinct civilizations have always, therefore, played a vital role in the ever-increasing interconnectedness of humankind. Culture didn't need particular humans to carry
it, so long as there were people living in between. Neighbors influenced
neighbors who influenced neighbors. Disembodied ripples of influence
moved through the social realm as waves through the sea, no particular
molecule going much of anywhere except up and down. Cultural ripples
did not even require peaceful contact between neighbors. Communities
engaged in war also swapped items and ideas—not to mention genes.

The Han dynasty, which ruled China for about four hundred years
(206 BCE to 220 CE), was more or less constantly at war with its northern
neighbors, the nomads of the Eurasian steppes. The Chinese called these

nomads the Xiongnu. China was a long way from Rome, but bands of tribal nomads roamed the lands in between and had webs of interaction among themselves. Descendants of the Xiongnu and related tribes later swept into Western Europe, led by a man named Attila, and they battered Rome. In Europe, these nomadic raiders were known as the Huns. In the east, they were part of Chinese history, and in the west, part of European history; but they were not mere adjuncts to other people's histories. They belonged to a galaxy of social constellations as vast as any other. They had a story of their own.

THE SILK ROAD

From the Chinese point of view, the Xiongnu were the primeval troublemakers. These were the barbarians who had been raiding Chinese villages "forever." They spoke an Altaic language utterly unrelated to any spoken by the Chinese. They followed a way of life that was actually hostile to the bureaucratic fabric of roads, written laws, and postal systems that China had become. They were the reason why earlier Chinese kingdoms had built stretches of wall along their northern frontiers. They were the reason the First Emperor had sacrificed a million lives to join all those short walls into one Great Wall: he did it to block out the Xiongnu. In periods when China had fragmented into warring kingdoms, those kingdoms were like cousins fighting cousins for the family estate—an empire to which they all felt they belonged. When the Chinese fought the Xiongnu, they weren't fighting cousins. They were fighting the absolute *other.*

In the second century BCE, the Chinese emperor and his advisers saw a way to put the squeeze on these particular barbarians. They reached out to *another* confederation of pastoral steppe nomads living farther south and west. The Yuezhi tribes were constantly quarreling with the Xiongnu, probably because both groups were pastoral nomads and their grazing grounds overlapped. Han strategists decided they might lure the Yuezhi into a military alliance and start a useful bit of war among the nomads.

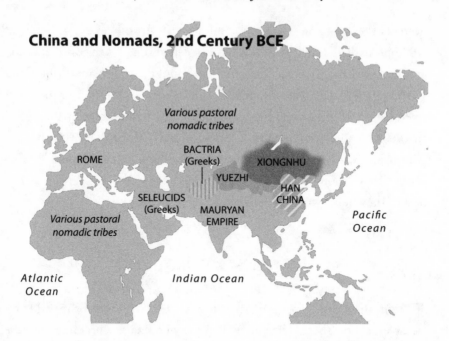

China and Nomads, 2nd Century BCE

But the Xiongnu saw what was coming. In 176 BCE, they launched a deadly preemptive strike. The Yuezhi put one hundred thousand warriors in the field; the Xiongnu countered with three hundred thousand. It was a massacre. So soundly beaten were the Yuezhi that they fled the region and disappeared.

But where did they go? Thirty-eight years after the catastrophe, the Chinese government sent an expedition out to look for them. The expedition was considered too dangerous to risk anyone important, so they put a petty palace official in charge, a man named Zhang Qian. Poor Zhang didn't get far. The Xiongnu captured him and they held him for ten years—not that it was the cruelest form of captivity: he married a Xiongnu maiden, had some children with her, traveled with the tribe, and melted in with them. But one day he spotted an opportunity to bolt, and right then he bolted. The opening, however, wasn't on the Chinese side of Xiongnu turf. Zhang had escaped into the great unknown beyond the nomads' outermost grazing grounds. He was now in lands where "no civilized man" had ever gone before.

And what did he find in this exotic outermost ring of the concentric world? Bats with human faces? Dragons? Savages who feasted on human flesh? No. He found kingdoms as urban and civilized as China itself. Here flourished cities with great public buildings lining broad paved streets. Here stood statues, temples, libraries, and schools. Here were crackling markets full of merchants hawking goods from countless distant lands.

Here in the bazaars of these cities so far from the Middle Kingdom that it had taken Zhang ten years to reach them, including the arduous time he had spent with the Xiongnu, the intrepid Chinese explorer found fabric and bamboo canes made in Szechuan, a province so deep inside the Chinese empire that even the Xiongnu had never heard of it. Goods had traveled from that far corner of the empire, over the Great Wall, across Xiongnu territory, and to these exotic cities presumably without any single human being having made the journey until Zhang Qian.

And where goods had gone, you can bet that ideas had gone, for trade involves conversations, calculation, money of some sort, concepts of relative value, notions about the way contracts should be negotiated, relationships that endure over time, ideas about the gods and the cosmos and human destiny and how men and women should behave and whether it's OK to flirt with strangers and how children should speak to elders.

What Zhang had stumbled upon were Bactrian cities founded by the Greek generals who had inherited this portion of Alexander the Great's conquests. But the Greeks were on their way out now. Historical forces set in motion by the Chinese themselves were washing them away. What forces? Well, when the Yuezhi fled the catastrophic battle the Chinese had manipulated them into, they drifted down to the Indus River valley. There they regrouped. The five tribes that formed the Yuezhi confederation abandoned the pastoral life in favor of farming and trading. One tribe among them came to dominate all the others. From capitals at Peshawar and Kabul, this Kushan tribe extended an empire north, west, and east. Within a few generations, they were no longer beaten dogs fleeing from ferocious nomadic warriors. They were a tough, urban power with well-equipped and well-organized armies of their own.

They had, however, no interest in a military alliance with China. Perhaps they remembered what had happened earlier. Besides, they now had a good trading relationship with the Xiongnu and wanted to keep it that way. As a matter of fact, even before their flight from the steppes, even as the Yuezhi were fighting and killing the Xiongnu and vice versa, these two groups were trading with each other. Curiously enough, one main item the Xiongnu got from that trade was silk, which the Yuezhi got from the Chinese. So even as the Xiongnu were fighting the Chinese tooth and claw, they were developing a taste for the silk their enemy made.

In China, silk was so abundant even peasants wore it, but among the Xiongnu, it was so rare, only the high born could afford it. The men of the Xiongnu tribal elite flaunted their status to one another by dressing their womenfolk in silk. They hosted banquets at which they one-upped their guests by serving food on bronze platters artfully crafted by the Chinese (and the occasional Yuezhi skull, skinned and polished into a drinking goblet).

Meanwhile, the fighting between the Chinese and the Xiongnu never let up. In these battles, the Xiongnu possessed one notable advantage: they had horses. Chinese territory was ill-suited for raising these beasts. They needed horses to fight the nomads, but where could they get horses? Well, they could get some from the Xiongnu—in exchange for silk, jade, and bronze artifacts that the Xiongnu were hungering for. In short, the Chinese used their productive and commercial prowess to acquire from the Xiongnu the horses they needed to fight the Xiongnu. Life is complicated.

The Great Wall had been built to keep the Xiongnu out of China, but over time, it evolved into a market zone where the Chinese and the nomads traded with each other. Don't get me wrong: raids and counterattacks never stopped. The two adversaries never became pals, yet trade between them kept escalating because, as it turned out, the nomads had more than just horses to offer the Chinese. Their territory, like the Mediterranean Sea, bordered on many different environments. These tribes of highly mobile nomads could transport goods from numerous points on their vast perimeter to the wall. They could bring honey, wax, furs, and aromatic woods from the forested far north to China's frontier markets. From the west, they could bring exotic fruits and wines made from grapes, a coveted alternative to the rice wines made in China. Silk was wonderful, but cotton was almost equally wonderful, and at that point cotton was produced mainly in India.

The Han Chinese couldn't expand their empire into the steppes because the nomads were too well adapted to that environment; there the nomads would win any all-out battle. But the Chinese could and did build a chain of garrisons snaking west from the Great Wall. They built these forts to protect traders flowing to and from China.

Eventually this panhandle of the Chinese empire touched up against another protected zone: the empire of the Kushans. And goods that made it that far could flow on safely to India in the southeast or to Persia in the west. From Persian territory, traders could take the goods into kingdoms along the Mediterranean, ruled by heirs of Alexander's generals. And from there the goods could get to Rome.

This network of routes across the central Eurasian steppes was later called the Silk Road because silk was the most glamorous of the many products moving through it. At the time, no one called it the Silk Road because no one realized there was any single thing deserving of a name, for the Silk Road wasn't actually one road but many, and no one really traversed the whole length and breadth of it. People had names for their local branches, and they bought and sold whatever was flowing through those. They didn't know or need to know where those items had originated or how their local market was situated with respect to some planetary pattern.

The Kushan Empire began to coalesce in the first century BCE and eventually stretched from the Indus River to the Aral Sea. It included a chunk of what is now Iran, a belt of what are now the Turkic states of central Asia, all of Afghanistan and Pakistan, and a slice of what is India today. When the Kushans lost their grip and faded out of history, successor kingdoms of various sizes kept emerging in more or less that same area. There was always some sort of state here because this territory

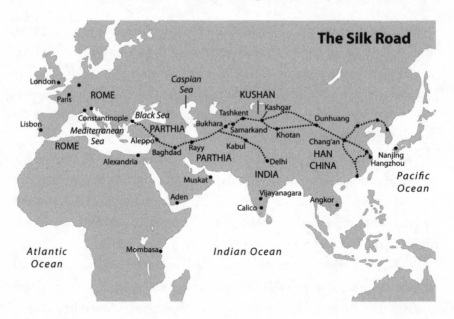

The Silk Road

straddled the Silk Road and included some of its crucial nodes, places where many roads converged and from which many roads branched away.

In supplanting the Central Asian kingdoms planted by Alexander, the Kushans absorbed some of their Hellenic residue. In overrunning the Hindu and Buddhist kingdoms of northern India the Kushans absorbed some of *that* cultural residue. In extending their dominion west, they lapped into the Persian world. And in the east, they encountered the tendrils of an expanding China. This Kushan Empire (and its successors) overlapped with four of the ancient world's major intercommunicative zones. Through this empire, therefore, cultural detritus flowed among the four worlds like corpuscles through a circulatory system.

But funny things happen when cultural detritus from different cultures knock about together in a new context. Ideas don't drift about as single motes, they link together to form structured wholes, constellations of concepts. When they fit snugly as coherent parts of a larger structure, they resist fragmentation. But when such constellations cross cultural borders, they might have to adjust a little to fit in. A few ideas might jar loose in the process and float about as single motes. Constellations that originated in different cultures might bump together in an in-between zone and form new constellations of ideas, constellations that include elements from both originals and exclude ones that do not fit.

The Kushan Empire was an archetypal example of such an in-between zone. Buddhism provides a good example of what sorts of mixings happened there. The Kushans championed Buddhism, so a great many Buddhist missionaries came streaming into their empire from India. Originally Buddhists had frowned on sculptural representations of the master because, the feeling was, you didn't need to know what Buddha looked like, but in the Kushan world, Buddhists were inhaling the fumes of Hellenic culture left behind by Alexander the Great. The Greeks routinely made images of deities as a way of experiencing their spiritual flavors, and in this milieu—what do you know: Buddhists started making sculptures of the Buddha to express, through his features and postures, the spiritual equanimity they sought. These Buddhist sculptures looked sort of...Hellenic.

The Kushan Empire also overlapped with the Persian world, home to the Zoroastrian narrative. This was a world crowded with constellations of ideas descended from Avestan times, one of which was the cult of Mithra. Mithra had originated as the Aryan god of contracts and truth telling; over time, he'd morphed into a supernatural being born of a human mother and a divine father, which situated him right on the line between the everlasting and the temporal. Being both human and divine, Mithra could draw humans away from death and toward everlasting life. He was a savior.

Here in the Kushan world, where Buddhists often encountered followers of Mithra, a new notion was born into Buddhism of certain exalted spiritual luminaries who made it right to the edge of nirvana but instead of crossing over into bliss, paused on that line and reached back to help others. They were saviors. And like Mithra, they straddled a line, in this case between the illusory material world and the timeless reality. These figures were called *bodhisattvas*, and the greatest of them (who was yet to come) was a figure known as—no, not Mithra, but close—Maitreya.

In addition to favoring Buddhism, the Kushans loved and favored long-distance traders. As a result, traders streamed through their empire too, on all the same routes the missionaries were traveling. Inevitably, as people met and conversed, the two currents mingled. In Central Asia, traveling merchants began converting to Buddhism, and Buddhism acquired an ever more commercial flavor.

The tilt toward commerce coincided with some interesting developments in Buddhism. A whole new version of the faith was emerging, built around the bodhisattva idea. It was called Mahayana Buddhism, which means "large vehicle Buddhism." This school held that achieving nirvana was not necessarily a solitary journey undertaken by each individual soul. It was a joint venture led by a bodhisattva steering a boat that was carrying many ordinary folks.

Mahayana Buddhism opened the door to the notion that each person might not have to do all the disciplined living and hard meditation needed to achieve nirvana. A few exceptional devotees could live as monks and do the difficult work for many. Those few could make striving for nirvana their full-time occupation. The ordinary person living an everyday life could inch closer to the ultimate goal just by helping and supporting the monks.

Mahayana Buddhism therefore spawned monasteries that not only housed monks but also served as repositories for donations from people who believed in the Buddhist way but couldn't (or couldn't bring themselves to) quit their day jobs. Such monasteries came to possess much gold and lots of land. The wealth could not be funneled into consumption, for extravagant consumption wasn't the Buddhist way; so instead, monasteries directed their capital into grand enterprises requiring more money than any one individual could afford.

In this time and place, "grand enterprises" typically meant trading expeditions involving large caravans of animals and people, along with way stations and rest stops, plus financial mechanisms to facilitate transactions. All of this came together perfectly, since long-distance traders were increasingly Buddhists, and Buddhists were increasingly traders. Through the monasteries, therefore, ordinary Buddhists could invest their wealth directly in salvation but indirectly in trade.

Commercial goods flowing through the Kushan world went both east and west, but Buddhism flowed only east. What could account for that? Well, travelers heading west found the cultural soil ever less hospitable to Buddhism. The master narratives of Iran and Mesopotamia cast the universe as an apocalyptic drama with a beginning and an end, featuring gods as protagonists and people as their adjuncts. Buddhists saw the universe as a featureless field within which events and materials didn't really exist and each individual soul was moving toward an eternal, formless, impersonal nirvana. The two frameworks were incompatible, and there was no larger framework that could incorporate the ideas of both Buddha and Zoroaster, or of both Buddha and the Jewish prophets, or at least none such could easily form. Buddhism being the newcomer to this region, it was Buddhism that failed to thrive.

Buddhist ideas moving east, however, found richer soil. It's not that the dominant Chinese paradigm digested Buddhism all that readily. Buddha and Confucius were like oil and water. They offered internally consistent but entirely different conceptual gestalts. Buddha was all about the journey of the individual soul; Confucius was all about the individual's social context. Buddha was all about the cosmos; Confucius was all about family and empire. Buddha was all about detaching from this material world. Confucius was all about conducting oneself gracefully in the material world. Buddha was all about merging into the eternal. Confucius was all about behaving properly in the here and now.

In China, however, another idea system had long been percolating as well. The sage Laozi had fielded a philosophy rooted in the same field of cultural ideas and traditions as Confucius but addressing somewhat different questions. Laozi focused on how a person could cope with the chaos and hardships of the world. He said, don't get caught up in the illusion that you control anything; the only thing you really control is whether to cling or let go. A person inspired by Laozi's ideas was apt to seek peaceful solitude in nature, to practice observation and contemplation as virtues, to value stillness. Taoism was just as much a native plant of Chinese civilization as Confucian thought; it tapped equally authentic aspects of a

Chinese worldview spawned by the land itself. When Buddhists drifted into China and bumped into Taoists, they saw (somewhat) kindred spirits.

What's more, unlike the Western world, the Chinese had no tradition of jealous gods demanding exclusive worship. In China the same person could practice Taoist rituals, bow to Confucian values, and burn incense to minor spirits inhabiting some particular place: they didn't have to choose. In the glory days of the Han dynasty, Confucian thought had the full endorsement of the state, but Taoism thrived among common folks. Han officials studied the Confucian classics as preparation for roles in the ever-expanding bureaucracy, but Taoism cooked along as a religion embraced by peasants in the fields and manual laborers in the towns. Since trade was an occupation looked down upon by the Confucians, traders occupied the same lowly stratum as peasants and laborers and therefore knocked about with those folks socially. Traders were the very people converting to Buddhism in ever greater numbers at this time, so Taoists and Buddhists were breathing the same air.

Buddhism made slow headway in China as long as the Han emperors kept a strong grip on social reality, but in the third century, the Han dynasty did what dynasties always eventually do, according to the sages of ancient China. It misbehaved until it had squandered its mandate and the empire began coming apart. Four hundred years of Chinese unity gave way to three-plus centuries of warring kingdoms, centuries in which common folks never knew who was in charge or what tomorrow would bring. In those conditions, Taoism found a growing audience, and as Taoism flourished, cultural space opened up in China for Buddhism too.

Meanwhile, the cult of Mithra continued to spread through the Persian world. The rulers of what was now the Parthian Empire were pushing west at a time when the Romans were pushing east. Asia Minor was the line of scrimmage between the two. In this frontier zone, Roman soldiers encountered the cult of Mithra.

The cult of Mithra had properties similar to mystery religions, a familiar fixture of the Greco-Roman world. A mystery religion revolved around a body of secret knowledge. Adherents of such a religion started out as know-nothing novices, but by absorbing the secret knowledge, they graduated ever closer to the center, until at last they arrived at the heart of the mystery. There, they or a seer operating on their behalf could make direct contact with the supernatural. Because Mithraism echoed these themes, it resonated for Roman soldiers, and a reconfigured cult of Mithra emerged as a new mystery religion in Rome.

The central figure in the Mithraic mysteries was born from a virgin mother named Anahid, a human who had given birth to a god. The birth took place around the winter solstice, which is to say, on or about December 25. During his career on Earth, Mithra was attended by followers corresponding to the signs of the zodiac, of which there are twelve. Virgin birth, savior of humanity, born on December 25, twelve apostles—is any of this starting to sound familiar?

Mithraism flared in the Roman Empire a little before Christianity. Early on, these two movements were in neck-and-neck competition for the soul of the Greco-Roman world. Christianity won in the end, and by the fourth century, Mithraism had died out completely, but not before imparting particles of itself to the Christian narrative that came later.

SPICE ROUTES

In southern India, the Silk Road network overlapped with another circulatory system of great consequence, a world system spawned in part by the monsoons. A key hub of this world was the Arabian Peninsula: a huge desert surrounded on three sides by water and dotted with oases. Around Arabia were several other semiarid landscapes: the Horn of Africa, the Iranian highlands, the edges of the Levantine plains. Inhabiting these lands were various peoples whose languages were related: Hebrew, Arabic, ancient Phoenician, Sumerian, Akkadian, Nabatean—these all belong to the Semitic language family. Their prevalence between the Mediterranean Sea and the Persian Gulf speaks to a long period of historical intertwining among the ancient peoples of this region, whoever

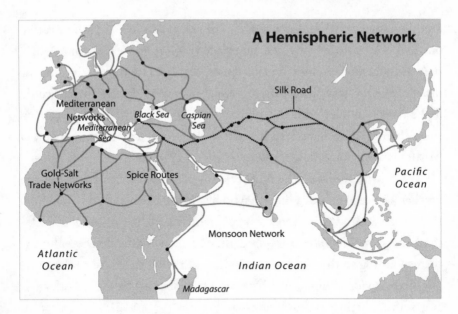

A Hemispheric Network

Silk Road

Mediterranean
Networks   *Black Sea*   *Caspian Sea*
Mediterranean Sea

Pacific Ocean

Gold-Salt
Trade Networks   Spice Routes

Monsoon Network

Atlantic Ocean   *Indian Ocean*

Madagascar

they originally were.* And out of this arid area radiated the glamorous and rather mysterious Spice Routes of the ancient world.

Today, when people say "spice" they mean one of those many substances that give distinctive flavors to food; but that's not exactly what we're talking about here. The ancient spice traders did deal in saffron, pepper, cinnamon, and the like, but they also dealt in myrrh, aloe wood, incense, gems, essential oils, dyes, medicines, exotic bird feathers, healing creams, cosmetics, aphrodisiacs, magical potions, mystical aids, and other things you wouldn't put in food. *Spice*, in this context, is an umbrella term for trade goods that were rare, compact, light, transportable, marketable, and more or less imperishable. Even diamonds counted. Spices were generally things people wanted, not things people needed. They indulged the human urge for pleasure, luxury, recreation,

---

*People who speak the same language don't necessarily share ethnic or genetic roots. Neighboring groups, conquered groups, and even conquering groups sometimes relinquish their own language in favor of someone else's. Immigrants to America mostly end up speaking English, no matter what their original language was. Never, however, does such a transference occur without real-world mingling and interaction.

ecstasy, and orgasm. Spices, in this larger sense, were a dominant factor in the global economy thousands of years ago and they still are today. (Think drug trade.)

Arabia and its surroundings produced some of the earliest spices. In those deserts, less than one hundredth of 1 percent of the land could be used for farming. In the heart of that region, vegetation was so sparse people couldn't survive even on herding. As it happened, however, in and around Arabia Felix ("fortunate Arabia," as Rome's Pliny the Elder called it), there grew a hardy tree whose few leaves could be dried and pounded into a powder that, when mixed with fat and dried, could be sold as aromatic cakes called frankincense.

But to whom could the desert dwellers sell their frankincense? To one another? No. You have to fill your belly before you can indulge in spices, and the primal necessities could only be gotten from the urban-agricultural civilizations of the great river valleys plus the trade entrepots between them. So the desert dwellers took their potions to where the rich folks lived.

Camels, domesticated around thirty-five hundred years ago, quickened the spice trade, for these "ships of the desert" were the archetypal vehicles of transport across wastelands. Camels could go days without water and cope with extremes of temperature. In the same week, the same camel could travel from the Gobi Desert, where temperatures topped 110 degrees Fahrenheit, to high mountain passes, where the snow never melted. Camels could carry heavier loads than horses or mules, and on top of all that, they were cuddly and nice. Actually, I'm kidding about that last part. I grew up with camels parked two blocks from my house, and believe me they are mangy, ill-tempered creatures. But they can be handled by those who know how, and spice traders were the experts with this know-how.

For the most part, these specialists were middlemen, dealing in products they had gotten from someone else. Middlemen have to worry about consumers and producers trading with one another directly, so spice traders tended to keep producers and consumers ignorant of each other. They held their sources, routes, and destinations as closely guarded secrets.

They told fanciful stories about the hardships and dangers of getting the products they were selling. Greek historian Herodotus reported that frankincense was precious in part because flying snakes inhabited the trees that produced this treasure. To harvest frankincense, people had to burn a certain resin, the smoke of which drove the snakes away temporarily, at which point people rushed in and gathered as much as they could before the snakes came back and killed them. Many a good man must have died bringing this spice to market! No wonder it cost so much! Herodotus got this from a reliable source: some spice trader no doubt.

Because the goods typical of the spice trade were light and precious, merchants could carry them great distances, especially once the desert routes connected to the monsoon routes in the east and the Mediterranean networks in the west. Because they were so inherently rootless, spice traders developed cultural styles distinct from those of the sedentary people with whom they traded. They tended to favor portable gods associated more with ideas than places. Spice traders tended toward multilingualism and were apt to develop cosmopolitan views. Eventually, they organized into guilds and networks that ran across cultural and political borders. These constellations existed more in social space than in geographical space, and they had an internal coherence of their own. They were like an alternative universe of shadow states spanning the more palpable universe of political states.

Even as distinct seas of culture formed, influences and ideas trickled from sea to sea through capillaries such as the Spice Routes and the Silk Roads, through areas where intercommunicative zones overlapped and where constellations of ideas bumping against one another intermingled, traded parts, and emerged as whole new conceptual constellations.

9

When Worlds Overlap
(1 CE to 650 CE)

For thousands of years, people have been growing more and more interconnected, but this has never been a smooth and steady process like sugar mixing into sand. Historically, it's been a case of fits and starts and stops and stutters, a case of social constellations forming and expanding and eventually overlapping, and those overlaps generating friction and trauma and confusion until enough threads and themes from each cluster have interwoven to form a single larger whole, a new gestalt—in the course of which, some threads and themes have been added and some others discarded because they no longer fit.

In his 1953 novel *More Than Human*, Theodore Sturgeon combined the words *blending* and *meshing* to coin the new term *bleshing*. He used it to describe what happens to six characters in his story, dysfunctional individuals who clash and quarrel until they discover that their odd abilities fit together because they are actually six parts of a single new organism, *Homo Gestalt*. *Bleshing* is a good term for describing what has happened in history when vast constellations have overlapped and great master narratives have combined into single, larger, new world historical stories. In the first eight hundred years or so of the Common Era, a whole lot of bleshing took place across the world.

ROME

Consider, for example, what happened in the Roman Empire. Historians often describe the decline and fall of this empire as one of history's pivotal events. In general, they date the fall to the fifth century of the Common Era, a period in which Rome was hammered several times and in which the last official emperor was deposed by a "barbarian." Depending on which blow you consider to be the cause of death, Rome "fell" in 410—or 455—or 476—or maybe in 492. Or was it in 395, when the Roman Empire was officially split in two? Or perhaps as early as 378, when a barbarian army decisively beat Rome for the first time and killed the emperor himself in battle?

No matter which date you choose, if you go with Edward Gibbons, the British historian who coined the term *decline and fall*, you blame Christianity. Consider, however, an alternative account that has taken shape in recent decades.

In its days as a republic, Rome expanded across Asia Minor, down the shores of the eastern Mediterranean, through Egypt, and across North

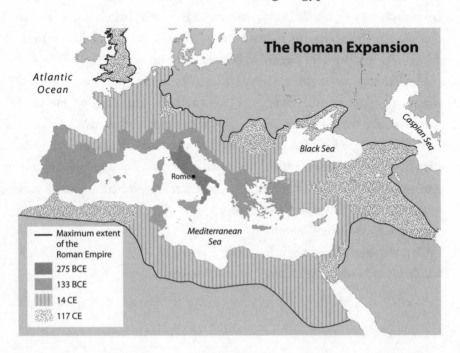

The Roman Expansion

Atlantic Ocean

Caspian Sea

Black Sea

Rome

Mediterranean Sea

Maximum extent of the Roman Empire
275 BCE
133 BCE
14 CE
117 CE

Africa and at the same time expanded northeast to the Danube River, up into what is now France, and west to the Atlantic Ocean. That's a lot of expanding, and most of it happened between 500 BCE and the start of the Common Era.

But if a state is a social version of a cell, its borders are like the cell's membrane. They separate what's inside from what's outside. Currents of information flow more heavily within a cell than between the interiors of two cells. The same is true of states. Once Rome had conquered the Fertile Crescent, all those Fertile Crescent narratives—from the many temple gods of Mesopotamia, to the single God of the Hebrews, to the animal-headed family of Egyptian deities—all those belief systems were now inside the Roman state, sloshing around among the many currents flowing through that Greco-Roman world.

One of those idea systems was Judaism. It shared with other Mesopotamian cults the idea of a tribal god, along with the correlative notion of "my god is better than your god." Of them all, however, only Judaism had formulated the idea that there is but one God.

The Roman conquests ensured that information flowing through their empire flowed through villages and communities inhabited by Jews, which meant that Jews encountered the secular-pagan ideas of the Greco-Roman world on a daily basis. It also meant that Judaic ideas got into the bloodstream of the empire and flowed to other lands ruled by Rome, including places where the secular-pagan narrative held sway.

Jewish ideas did not simply dissolve and disappear into these currents, for the Jewish narrative had a coherence that resisted dissolution—rather like the Vedic culture of ancient India. Jews felt themselves to be a captive nation within the empire, and they experienced tribal nationalism as an expression of their faith. This faith demanded that Jews agitate for a nation of their own because Judaism recognized no separation between the concerns of God and the affairs of humans. God's laws were *about* human interactions with one another, and if God's laws covered matters usually regulated by governments, such as contracts, inheritance, criminal conduct, and criminal punishments, then the religion that bound these tribes together as a people required that they live under their own government, not that of Rome.

As soon as their land was conquered, therefore, Jews began to chafe. The concept of a messiah emerged within their religious narrative, a charismatic figure empowered by God to lead Jews to freedom. In this time of ferment, the Jewish world soon grew rife with fiery agitators railing against Rome and preaching religious renewal like the prophets of yore, and for Jews, any of these *might* be the messiah.

Among them all, one luminary stood out. His name was John, and he inducted his followers into his inner circle with a ritual called baptism. John the Baptist was a Jew, but initiation rituals were a common feature of the mystery religions so common to the Greco-Roman world at this time: the Mithraic mysteries, the Eleusinian mysteries, the Orphic mysteries—all had some sort of initiation ceremony that transformed a person from outsider to insider. These mystery religions typically promised insiders access to secret knowledge that would exalt them spiritually and give them a happy future, possibly even immortality (though, of course, only an outsider could see any mystery religion as typical of anything; each necessarily regarded itself as unique).

Around 29 CE (perhaps a bit earlier, perhaps a bit later), a man named Jesus, son of a carpenter, met John and accepted baptism. Jesus proved to be one of the most charismatic of the possible messiahs in the Jewish nationalist movement. As a result, the local Roman officials arrested him and asked him just one question: "Are you the messiah?" To the Roman officials, that question meant: "Are you leading a rebellion against Rome?" When Jesus said yes, the Roman authorities had him crucified because that's what Rome did to rebels. Nothing personal, just policy: thousands of rebels had been crucified before Jesus, and thousands more would be crucified after him. Most Romans had no idea Jesus had ever lived much less that he'd died. But Jesus had a handful of followers, some of whom, after his crucifixion, began to murmur that he wasn't dead. They said they'd caught glimpses of him here and there, alive as you or me. With these reports, the followers of Jesus began proliferating, and this Jesus movement soon diverged from mainstream Judaism.

Judaism as such could not have spread throughout the Roman world because it was a belief system tied explicitly to a particular group of people. It asserted a covenant between God and the descendants of Abraham. If you weren't descended from Abraham, you weren't part of the covenant. The followers of Jesus, spearheaded especially by the preacher Paul, altered the formulation. Paul had never met Jesus, but he experienced a dramatic conversion one day on his way to Damascus. According to Paul, what Jesus offered was not a covenant between God and any particular tribe but between God and all humanity. Any man or woman of the empire could see themselves included in *that* covenant.

Paul himself was born Jewish and identified the Torah as scripture because in his day, for followers of Christ, there was no other. Only later did the Gospels emerge, written reports of what Jesus had said and done. At that point, Christians recast the Torah as the Old Testament. For Jews, the Torah never became the Old Testament; for them, it remained the Torah.

Mainstream Jews went on waiting for the messiah. Christians believed he'd already come. What they meant by the messiah, however, was not what the Jews had meant. Mainstream Jews considered it the worst form of sacrilege to claim that someone walking around on this Earth in a human body was God. For Christians, by contrast, this became a central article of faith. And according to Christians, God did promise his people a kingdom, but it was not some earthly real estate. It was the Kingdom of Heaven where Christians would dwell forever after death, somewhat like the afterdeath world imagined by the ancient Egyptians. To feel included in the Jewish covenant, you pretty much had to be born to Jewish parents, live by Jewish law, and (for men) get circumcised (ouch). To feel included in the Jesus movement, you just had to get baptized and believe in Jesus. Anyone who wanted to could join.

In the Roman world, the idea of a god who was also a man required no great conceptual leap. The secular-pagan world was rife with such figures. Hercules and Achilles, for example, had supernatural gifts because they were born of human mothers impregnated by gods. At the very time that Jesus Christ was on his path to crucifixion, the Roman elite were declaring that the emperor Augustus had become a god. Christianity was not, then, the exact antithesis of Greco-Roman culture; it was in competition with various other manifestations of that culture. Romans who rejected Christianity agreed that a man could be a god but refused to accept that there was only one God. Jews who rejected Christianity agreed that there was only one God but refused to accept that this (or any) man was he.

Christianity emerged right where these two apparently contradictory narratives overlapped. It represented a synthesis that took some themes from each and rejected some that didn't fit. The new movement took a definitive turn after the events of 74 CE, when some nine hundred Jewish rebels under siege in a fortress called Masada committed mass suicide rather than submit to Roman rule.

By this time, a shrinking number of Christians had been born Jewish; a growing majority were pagan converts. The Jews were rebelling against Rome to secure a nation for their tribes. The new Christian converts had no dog in that fight. They had enough trouble with Roman authorities just for being Christians. Why should they also endure Roman reprisals against the Jews, whom they weren't and never had been? In this context, Christ's advice that Christians "render unto Caesar that which is Caesar's" made new sense, underlining the distinction that was growing between Christians and Jews. For Greco-Roman pagan humanists, the idea of two separate realms, the secular and the supernatural, was quite familiar. In Levantine Judaism, however, "that which is Caesar's" was a meaningless phrase. Nothing was Caesar's. Everything was God's.

Judaism therefore remained a social bubble within the galaxy of social constellations that was the Roman world. Christianity, by contrast, spread like kudzu and could do so for two reasons. First, it fit in well enough with the Greco-Roman idea that the secular and the divine both existed but were separate spheres. Second, Christianity spoke to a vast audience, for it addressed the life most of the empire's inhabitants were really living. When we hear of the grandeur that was Rome, we picture baths and banquets and bowls of peeled grapes—but those grapes weren't peeling themselves. All ancient societies regarded slavery as normal, but Romans depended on slavery more than most. In this empire, slaves were not just servants and sexual chattel but the engines of production. They mined the salt, broke the rocks, rowed the galleys, and tilled the earth on vast farming estates. A free Roman who had fewer than four slaves was considered to be living below the poverty line. Wealthy individuals owned as many as fifty thousand slaves or more. Slavery was an inevitable by-product of Roman militarism, for in their centuries as a republic, Romans were constantly marching off to conquer new places and hauling back captives by the tens of thousands. By the time Christ was crucified, over 25 percent of the empire's population were slaves.

What's more, if you were a free Roman trying to make a living, what wages could you command, given that whatever you were offering to do for money, most employers could have done by slaves for free? It all added up to an empire in which most people were either slaves, wretchedly poor peasants, or huddled masses of unemployed slum dwellers whom the state kept quiescent with free entertainment and just enough bread to stay alive.

For the Roman elite in the glory days of their republic, the pagan framework rang true because it explained what they saw happening all around them every day. They did the rituals and told the stories, and the victories kept piling up, the cities got built, and the rich got richer. It was easy for them to believe that the poor were poor for a reason and that slaves were only getting what losers deserved.

Not so for all those slaves and beggars. For them, by the start of the Common Era, the pagan narrative described a world without meaning. Then Christianity came along and said: this world was a mere test for what would happen after death. The poorest, meekest, and most oppressed were passing the test; they would live on forever in the kingdom of bliss. The Roman elite were mostly failing. For them, getting into heaven would be harder than it was for a camel to pass through the eye of a needle. Framed by the Christian narrative, now everything made sense. Aha! Such is the power of narrative.

The pagan state tried to stamp out Christianity by staging public entertainments in which lions ripped Christians to shreds. It probably didn't happen often, but how often did it have to happen? The spectacle of one lion devouring one hapless human was sure to spark stories that spread like brush fires. Such spectacles were state terrorism, and that's how terrorism works: it's not the physical destruction that does the job, it's the emotions created by the stories and reports. This, too, is the power of narrative.

But in these gladiatorial spectacles, two narratives were intersecting. With its violence, the Roman state was saying, "We can kill you in the most horrible ways." With their chilling equanimity in the face of death, Christian martyrs were saying, "Death is but a gateway to eternal life for Christians." The state could launch horrific stories but could not control what people heard when those stories reached them. When a Christian martyr praised Jesus even as he or she was being devoured, it only made the Christian narrative seem more true. Ratcheting up the horror only made this Christian coda more memorable. The very steps the Roman state took to erase Christianity instead fueled its growth. It's not with physical weapons that one narrative beats another—it's with meaning-making prowess.

As Roman society grew ever more bloated on slavery and inequity, its bureaucratic apparatus lost coherence. Meanwhile, the Christian network kept developing. Christians took care of their own. They communicated efficiently among themselves and mustered as needed to meet their communities' crises. For its own people, the Christian network gradually took on some of the functions of government. As the life force of pagan Rome rotted from within, Christianity flowed into its exoskeleton.

By the fourth century, Christianity had become something like a shadow state mirroring the secular Roman state visible to the public. In the secular state, an emperor governed the entire realm. The realm was divided into provinces; each province had its governor, and each governor had an administrative staff in charge of managing subdistricts. Throughout all the provinces, officials were working from a single, official, written code of laws, which defined how people should behave and interact.

The Christians' realm was also divided into province-like units, but the Christians called their units dioceses. Each diocese was administered by a bishop. The bishops of major cities were called metropolitans, and they enjoyed greater authority than rural bishops who had smaller, more dispersed flocks. All these bishops worked from a growing written body of canon law derived from the Gospels, just as Roman law had supposedly derived from the principles underlying the Twelve Tables. Among all the bishops, one had higher authority than the rest, and he was—who else?—the bishop of Rome. Later this man would inherit the title of *pontifex maximus*, the very title used in pre-Christian times for Rome's top administrator of pagan rites. Later still, this top officer of Christian Rome would be called the pope.

It was fourth century Roman emperor Constantine the Great who finally gave into reality and admitted he could govern his far-flung empire more effectively with the administrative apparatus built by the Christians than with the rusting machinery left over from ancient Rome. In 320, on the eve of a crucial battle, he claimed to have seen a cross in the sky. Inspired by that sign, he entered the battle waving the Christian banner. After victory, he declared Christianity legal, moved his capital to Constantinople, and began transforming the empire into a Christian empire. Without official support, the pagan narrative began to wane. In 395, Emperor Theodosius went that one final step and outlawed paganism. He made Christianity the official religion of the Roman Empire, the only one endorsed by the state.* The Roman narrative inherited from Greece had now bleshed with the Jewish narrative inherited from the Levant.

In converting to Christianity, Constantine not only turned the Christian network into his own Roman bureaucracy, he also made himself, in effect, the head of the Christian church. In 325, when doctrinal disputes threatened the unity of the global Christian community, the emperor himself called a council of bishops and charged them with deciding what Christians believed. Out of that council came the Nicene Creed, which established the doctrine of the trinity. Roman Christians embraced the core belief that God was a single deity but also a trinity of God the Father, Jesus Christ the son, and a spiritual force called the

---

*Judaism remained legal, but the laws were oppressive to Jews. From this time on, for example, Jews could no longer legally own land in the empire.

Holy Ghost. All three were of the same essence, were the single God, were three, were one.

Meanwhile, overlapping narratives were also generating friction elsewhere in the empire. North of Rome lived a multitude of Germanic tribes whom the Romans had been fighting since the days of Julius Caesar. None of them, incidentally, called themselves Germanic. They called themselves by particular names such as Goth, Vandal, or Suevi. Each spoke its own tribal language, similar to but not necessarily identical to those of neighboring tribes. The German language did not yet exist.

German was actually the Roman word for these tribes. It denoted something like "gangs of hooligans up north who are always making trouble." They were to the Romans what the Xiongnu were to the Chinese. The Germans, however, were not pastoral nomads. They were trying to scratch out a living as farmers in heavily forested land where the soil was dense and wet and hard to till—especially for people who didn't have steel-tipped plows. The pastoral nomads of the steppes had perfected a lifestyle dovetailed to their environment: they were herders. The German tribes of northern Europe were not really nomadic, but they weren't settled folk either. They were unsettled poor farmers, moving about restlessly in quest of better land and better conditions, and this quest drew them relentlessly south.

Wherever Germans overlapped with Romans, two incompatible world historical narratives were rubbing against each other. The Germans had no cities, knew nothing of town life. Their society featured war chiefs who ruled small areas from wooden hilltop forts in which lived not just their kinfolk but also their retainers: bands of men bound to them by oaths of mutual loyalty. The Germans took these oaths very seriously.

Common folks lived in villages surrounding the forts. They did the heavy labor of farming under the authority of local war chiefs. Another major figure in this world was the judge. He arbitrated disputes among disparate lordly domains. No one appointed or elected a judge. People simply ended up as judges by accumulating so much respect over time that others looked to them for judgments. Since these tribes had no written script, judges worked from no fixed code. Instead, they based their judgments on tribal traditions and, as best they could, on precedent: if a ruling had gone one way in the past, it should go that way again. Judges had to have broad life experience, prodigious powers of memory, and a deep knowledge of their own people.

Judges could not hand their authority down to their sons. The sons had to earn status of their own. Lords could not necessarily bequeath their retainers to their sons. Oaths of loyalty were between the people swearing. When one party died, the oath was null, and the sons had to earn their own respect anew. The Germans saw a world built on personal connections and networking, personal bargains and promises.

About two centuries into the Common Era, the German migrations picked up pace. Tribes on the frontier pushed aggressively into Roman territory. They pushed because they were being pushed. New waves of migrants were coming out of Central Asia. The Romans called the new migrants *Scythians*, which was really just Roman shorthand for "troublemaking barbarians who aren't Germans."

The Scythians were the westernmost edge of migrations that had begun in the Far East. Their roots went back to the nomadic Xiongnu who had been raiding China since time immemorial. Once the Great Wall was built and the mighty Han dynasty had congealed, the Chinese were able to stop these tribes from raiding *their* world. But pastoral steppe nomads lived almost as much by raiding as herding. If they couldn't raid China, they'd raid someone else. But who? The Asian steppes were full of pastoral nomads, and when nomads raided nomads, they didn't get much they didn't already have. In fact, young bucks of tribes in their path tended to join them instead of fight them. What the pastoral nomadic raiders needed were cities to plunder. One wave of nomads, the Hephthalite Huns, headed south and east, toward India. Down that way, they found the Kushans, stomped them out, and took over their cities. These nomads soon turned into settled city folk themselves.

Other steppe nomads headed west, but in that direction there was a lot farther to go before the raiders came to any substantial urban fleshpots.

Flurries of raiding had time to swell into motley armies. By the time these raiders appeared in Europe, they were a menacing horde. These were the Scythians the Romans spoke of. Their ranks were filled with ragtag remnants of people from all the places they had moved through, which is why one can't really apply any single ethnic or linguistic label to them. Even the Huns who led the mob were a motley crew, but the core of them were people who spoke an Altaic language like the Mongols, like the Turks of modern times, like the Xiongnu who had once troubled China. For all practical purposes, the Huns *were* the Xiongnu. When they began pushing into Europe, they aggravated the migrations of people already in place—the Germans. This is how, by blocking out the raiders of the steppes, the Great Wall of China contributed to the hammering of Rome.

Let's not call it "the fall" of Rome, though. That phrase evokes a picture of screaming savages battering at walls and breaking through and descending finally upon a great and graceful city to pillage and rape. In actuality, not so much. For one thing, unlike China, Rome didn't have a wall (except for a few miles of stonework in Britain). What it had, mostly, were troops stationed in garrisons here and there to keep Germans from straying into Roman territory and trying to settle. On the frontier, Roman troops and German tribes clashed and skirmished but not 24/7. Much of the time, they were nodding curtly at a distance, or shouting insults at one another from closer, or trading a bit of meat for a bit of bread, or flirting with one another's women, or quaffing a brewski together between fistfights.

Over time, Germans on that blurred frontier picked up a little Latin, the better to haggle with Roman troops when necessary. If they could get some Roman clothes, all the better: Roman clothes were nicer than their own. Sometimes, Romans were captured and lived as slaves of Germans, or Germans were captured and lived as slaves in the empire, and then escaped and went home, bringing with them bits of cultural attitude.

One assimilated Goth, a man named Ulfilas, straddled the two worlds. He had grown up Christian and become a bishop. Around 350, Bishop Ulfilas translated the Bible into Gothic, using an alphabet he had invented. But the Gothic language didn't have a word for every word in Latin or Greek. The Goths' vocabulary had emerged out of experiences quite unlike those of the early Christians in the Holy Lands. When Ulfilas used Gothic words to express Christian ideas, he produced a Bible subtly different from the one used by the churches of Rome and Constantinople. Once a Gothic Bible of any sort existed, however, German tribes began converting—to their own brand of Christianity.

Ulfilas rejected the Trinitarian Nicene creed in favor of one propounded by the controversial Bishop Arius of North Africa, who taught that there was only one God, a father God. Jesus Christ resembled God but was not of the same essence; he was only one of God's creations, albeit the most glorious of them all. The Germans gravitated more to this Arian creed than to the Nicene, perhaps because in their world, when a son's stature matched his father's, a power struggle was coming and chaos loomed. Perhaps the Arian creed felt more comforting. Still, conversions to Christianity of whatever creed helped to further blur the distinction between German and Roman. Their clashing idea systems became two different stars in the larger constellation that was Christianity.

And then the bleshing began. The Romans didn't think of the Germans as a serious menace like the Persians on their eastern border. The Germans were just hooligans whose barbarism made them a threat to civil order. But when the Romans were recruiting soldiers, they wanted the toughest guys they could find, and the rowdy Germans often fit that bill. And for penniless Germans, joining the Roman army meant three squares a day and a place to sleep. Germans began to swell the ranks of Roman armies and didn't think of this as betrayal because they didn't think of themselves as "the Germans." Their battles were as much with other "barbarian" tribes as with Romans.

Roman military tradition dictated that generals share the spoils of battle with their troops. On the frontier, when Roman generals (who were sometimes Germans) defeated marauding bands (who were mostly Germans), they distributed any plunder they recovered to their soldiers (who were often Germans). And with the capital so far away, it sometimes made sense for the government to appoint generals on the frontier as civil authorities and have them administer Roman order in their locale. These were called *comes,* which evolved into the title of count. Sometimes, when a German chieftain entered Roman territory and managed to grab some land, it made sense to simply call him the governor of the area he was already controlling and label the tribute he was demanding his salary. These mini-kings were *duces,* from which derives the title of duke.

You can see where this was going. The Roman and German worlds were getting shuffled together. The ever-more Romanized Germans were becoming the human capital of the ever-more Germanized Roman world. The Germans weren't trying to destroy Rome. They were trying to become Romans.

Climbing the social ladder in snobbish Roman society was all but impossible for an outsider but advancing within the Roman army? Very possible. A really good fighter might end up in the Praetorian Guard, a body of crack troops charged with protecting the emperor. Those guards acquired the power to depose and install emperors. Eventually, most of them were Germans, and sometimes they put one of their own on the throne.

In the fourth century, the Roman Empire found itself locked into an epic struggle with a brilliant Gothic king named Alaric. Rome had its own brilliant commander-in-chief, Stilicho, who battled Alaric to a standstill, saving the empire time and again. But Stilicho died at last, and two years later (in 410 CE) Alaric sacked Rome. Historians sometimes say *this* was the year Rome fell.

Ah, but not so fast: Alaric was the son of a Gothic king who made a treaty of friendship with Rome. Alaric was sent to Constantinople at the age of eight to seal the treaty. He grew up in the eastern capital and enjoyed a Roman way of life. He got a Roman education, learned to read and write, and spoke both Latin and Greek fluently—he was hardly anyone's image of "screaming barbarian with an ax."

And Stilicho, the Roman champion? Well, he was actually the son of a Vandal father. The Vandals were another of those Germanic tribes that had originated far to the north. Stilicho had joined the Roman cavalry in his youth and worked his way up the ranks until he ascended high enough to score a marriage with a Roman noblewoman. He was hardly anyone's image of a stiff-lipped Roman blueblood. In fact, Alaric and Stilicho served together in the Roman military in their youth. They were comrades in arms back then: friends, almost!

In the generation after Alaric, the Huns ravaged the edges of the Roman world. Led by the dreaded Atilla, they marched on the city itself, and the Romans couldn't stop them. Was this when Rome fell? Nope. Attila died before the Huns reached the city itself, and without Attila's leadership, his armies dissolved.

A short time later, the Vandals did sack Rome (thereby making their name a synonym for loutish destruction). Was that the real fall of Rome? Naw. The Vandals looted Rome for three days but kept a promise to the pope not to go around killing people or wrecking buildings. After three days, they went home to Carthage, a rebuilt Roman city. From that capital, the Vandals ruled a North African kingdom in a more or less Roman way. They maintained the Roman tax rolls and lived as the Romans had: they patronized theaters and hippodromes, kept libraries open, enjoyed performances by singers and mimes, strolled in well-maintained parks, and no doubt ate peeled grapes while lolling in luscious baths, steeping in sexual pleasures.

The fact is, Rome never fell. It started out as a Latin world. It soaked up Greek themes as it expanded. The Greco-Latin blend then got Christianized. And eventually, the Christianized Greco-Roman world got Germanized. People who lived through the fall of Rome didn't know Rome was falling; they just thought Rome was changing. The Germans were graduating from outsiders to insiders, and as they permeated the Western world, they dissolved the fabric of the ancient empire into a collection of semi-independent forts and villages, of little kings and littler dukes and even littler counts. The people living through these changes did not necessarily see decline. After all, many of them were of German descent. Their tribes had spent many hard centuries longing for decent soil to till, and now at last they had such soil. How was this decline?

Way back in the fourth century, the Roman emperor Diocletian had ruled that free peasants could not leave their land or change the work they did. Laws like this turned European peasants into serfs. Serfs were not slaves. They were assets, inseparable from the land, like the trees and streams, the minerals and wild game. A person who acquired a piece of land acquired the serfs too. Germans didn't introduce serfdom to Europe; they inherited it from the Roman past, but they took to it gladly, for it fit right into the world they were making, of self-sufficient agrarian units ruled by lords. All this was happening within an overarching Christian framework that harked back to the political structure of ancient Rome.

In the East the state retained coherence. Rome morphed into the Byzantine Empire (which went on calling itself Rome). Eastern churches continued to look to the state for protection: they had a state to look to. Eastern Christianity, therefore, became a church within a state.

In the West, however, the state vanished, leaving the bishop of Rome to fend for his people himself. He had to shoulder the responsibilities traditionally handled by governments. He distributed grain from his own estates to keep the people of Rome from starving. He hired soldiers at times to enforce order. He took it upon himself to broker peace among the many little kings and dukes who now ruled material life. He negotiated treaties with warlords such as the Lombards,* the last tribe of Germanic invaders to come drifting down from the north.

In 590 CE, a man named Gregory became the pope. He was the son of a Roman senator. (Yes, deep into the seventh century, the Roman world still had senators.) Pope Gregory declared that he outranked all the other bishops. He was not first among equals; he was head of the whole Christian body. Local bishops in Western Europe fell into line, increasingly ceding spiritual and doctrinal authority to this single central figure, the bishop of Rome. By the time Gregory died, in 604, he had gained something of the stature once enjoyed by Roman emperors. The bleshing of the Greek, Roman, Levantine, and German world historical narratives was now complete.

---

*The Lombards believed that the great god Wodin favored men with long beards. According to their stories, they once tricked Wodin into helping them win a battle by having their women dress as men and tie their hair in front of their faces to look like exceptionally long beards. After their victory this tribe was known as the Langobards, the "long beards," which eventually became Lombards.

DAR-UL-ISLAM

Meanwhile, about two thousand miles southeast of Constantinople, too far away for Romans to know or care about, another monumental drama was unfolding, very different from the one in Europe. At the center of this one was a man named Muhammad ibn Abdullah, an almost exact contemporary of Pope Gregory's. The pope lived from 540 to 604 CE; Muhammad lived from 540 to 632 CE. In the year 610, when Muhammad was already middle-aged, he went into a cave in the Arabian desert and came out imbued with a message. He went back to his hometown of Mecca, a lively little trading town on the Red Sea coast, and started preaching. He didn't just deliver speeches, he poured out exhortations in a lyrical language and incantatory style that departed dramatically from ordinary human speech. He said he was delivering a message from God.

Today, if you saw a guy behaving like this on the streets, you'd probably think he was raving. In Muhammad's cultural environment, no one saw him that way. His behavior fit right into the context of his time and place. Just as Jesus in his lifetime had been one of many Jewish leaders preaching a message of revolutionary renewal, so Muhammad was part of a tradition already ancient in this part of the world. Pagan cults of pre-Islamic times had long featured mystical seers possessed of an eerie ability to communicate with gods in a language unintelligible to ordinary humans. The seer would enter a trance-like state, utter mysterious sounds, and then come out of it and tell people what the deity had said.*

Muhammad's contemporaries included other self-proclaimed messengers from the gods. When Muhammad started preaching, people understood what sort of figure he was claiming to be. They'd seen such fellows before. They only doubted the authenticity of *this* one. Was he *really* channeling the supernatural? Anyone can pretend to be a seer. The people of Mecca found Muhammad's core message suspiciously grandiose and perhaps self-serving. He was claiming that there was only one God and that he was the one and only messenger of this one and only

---

*The apostle Paul tapped into this same tradition when he started "speaking in tongues."

God. In ten years of preaching, the messenger gained only a handful of followers. Then he led his group up the coast to a city called Yathrib, soon renamed Medina ("the city"), and there, having established himself as leader, Muhammad built his following into a massive movement.

Standard accounts often describe Muhammad as an unsophisticated, illiterate herder who lived in an obscure part of the world. This is an image cultivated as much by Muslims as by people outside the faith, for it enhances the sense of his career as a miracle. In actuality, Muhammad's Arabia was an epicenter of the far-flung spice trading network that was already ancient by the seventh century, and Muhammad was not a herder but the executive manager of a successful trading company owned by his wife. The camel caravans of Arabia threaded among all the ancient urban civilizations of the region, carrying goods from the Egyptian world to the Mesopotamian, from the Levant to the Hijaz, from the Mediterranean Sea to the Indian Ocean, and from the Red Sea to the Persian Gulf. Make no mistake, these were cosmopolitan people exposed to a wide array of influences and information.

Judaism and Christianity were like parent and child, for Christianity had branched out of Judaism. Judaism and Islam, on the other hand, were more like cousins; neither had branched out of the other. Both traced their ancestry back to the same root: Abrahamic monotheism. In spirit, they resembled one another more than either of them did Christianity. The Jewish prophets had seen no distinction between the religious and the secular; Muhammad agreed with them on that. For the Jewish tribes, living by God's rules had everything to do with how they fared as a people living in history. Muhammad's idea system followed the same line. Muhammad, however, replaced the idea of tribe with that of community—but not just any community. *The* community. A tribe was something you pretty much had to be born into. The community of Islam was a metatribe that anyone could join by simply embracing its core doctrine: there was only one God, and Muhammad was truly his messenger. Islam didn't even have an initiation ritual, like the baptism of Christianity. If you wanted to join, all you had to do was say the words.

For Arabian Muslims, if Jews were like cousins, Christians were like second cousins. Yes, they, too, had a great prophet, but the followers of Christ had misread the message and fallen back into a sort of paganism, for if God could have a son, why not a father, a mother, an uncle, nephews, aunts? For Muslims, God the father and God the son sounded too much like Zeus the father and Perseus the son. For them, as for the Jews, monotheism was the axiom you couldn't fiddle with: one God was *the* core truth.

From the start, Muslims experienced their religion as political. Islam was a community; Islam was the government of this community; Islam was the law of the community. When Muhammad moved to Medina with his band of followers, he was like a conductor who had finally found an orchestra. If God's commands really were the prescription for an ideal *community*, the only way to prove it was for God's messenger to *govern* a community. If God really was speaking through him, the community would prosper. It was a proposition as concrete as any scientific experiment, and the results of the experiment seemed to confirm the hypothesis dramatically, for within the messenger's lifetime, the community expanded across the whole of the Arabian Peninsula and absorbed all the feuding Arab tribes into a single sociopolitical framework. Within three generations, that community and its constellation of ideas stretched from the Rock of Gibraltar to the foothills of the Himalayas. It was governed by a khalifa or caliph—the title for a man acting not as a king nor as a prophet but as God's administrator, managing the community in accordance with instructions given to the messenger. In practice, the caliphate soon split into two caliphates, and then into three, each claiming to be the only caliphate, and so the single universal Islamic state became more and more theoretical. But as the single-state faded away, the term *Dar-ul-Islam* ("realm of Islam") gained prominence, serving to suggest that even if Islam wasn't a single political state, it was certainly a single *something*.

After the messenger's death, out of the fluid, living example of his life, his followers distilled a formal doctrine that came down to five points. You had to testify to the singleness of God and acknowledge Muhammad as his messenger; perform a certain prayer ritual five times daily; donate a percentage of your income to charity; fast during a certain month of the year; and make a pilgrimage to Mecca at least once in your lifetime if you could afford to (if you couldn't, you were excused). Anyone who fulfilled those five requirements was part of the community. It was easy.

But that simple core soon acquired an elaborate superstructure of rules, generated by the first of the five requirements. If you accepted that Muhammad was the messenger of God, then it might be that your conduct had to conform exactly to the messenger's instructions and examples because those came from God and applied even to areas that other societies might consider secular.

The fact that Muslims conceived of their religious community as a political fact meant that streaming out to conquer their neighbors raised no difficult moral questions. Islam was a state, and conquering the neighbors was simply what states did: Assyria, Persia, Rome, Egypt—all had done it. Muslims felt their campaigns differed from the others' in that they had a noble purpose: to secure the survival of a community living by the laws of Islam, thereby ensuring that God's will could continue to be demonstrated on Earth and provide an example that drew others into the light. With Muslims in control of government, the Muslim way of life could not be obstructed, the inspiration could not be obscured. This sense of mission guaranteed that the Muslim community would keep striving to expand its political borders.

Christianity had started out as the religion of slaves and poor people in a powerful empire. Islam started out as the religion of small but independent groups ruled by no one but themselves. Christianity achieved political power by taking over the apparatus of the state within which it was born. Islam achieved political power by conquering its neighbors and its neighbors' neighbors. Different routes, same result: both ended up huge and powerful.

As Islam expanded, political control swiftly translated into the Islamization of cultures under Muslim rule. Those who lived in areas governed by Muslims were not by any means forced to convert to Islam. "No compulsion in religion," the messenger had said. But for anyone living in these territories, membership in the community did have its benefits, and if you converted, you came in for those benefits. If you didn't, your loss. Literally: your loss. You had to pay a tax for not being Muslim.

Many North African Christians were descended from German tribes that had embraced the Arian creed. Muslim theology said there was only one God, the one God was not a trinity, and the Prophet was merely one of God's creations. That was pretty much what Bishop Arius had said. Switching from Arian Christianity to Islam was therefore not that big a leap. The Church of Constantinople, on the other hand, condemned Arian beliefs. As long as North African Christians were ruled by the Byzantines, they had to fall in line with the Nicene Creed. In Muslim-ruled areas, by contrast, Christians could practice Christianity any way they wanted; the government did not care which form of error they embraced. The Muslims did impose that tax, but then the Byzantines demanded taxes too. North African Christians had no real reason to prefer Byzantine to Muslim rule.

Nor was there much resistance to Arab cultural hegemony. Many people had swept across North Africa over the centuries, leaving it something of a cultural mishmash. Ancient Phoenician, Roman, and Hellenic traces were still sloshing around alongside Germanic, Roman Catholic, and Byzantine ones. When the Arab Muslims came along, they quickly absorbed this hodgepodge into their single coherent story of the world. The Islamic narrative turned a garbled world into a meaningful one. Arabic replaced the various earlier languages. Traders began imitating Arab business practices. Clothes, art, and architecture took on an Arab flavor.

The first Arab conquerors lived in garrisons outside the local towns to inoculate themselves from infidel beliefs; but people gravitate to money-making opportunities, and that's exactly what the business-minded Arabs brought. Old towns spread until their markets surrounded the garrisons, and new towns emerged along the coast as well. Under Muslim rule, urban life quickened in North Africa. Arabic culture and all the traces of earlier cultures bleshed into something new.

Meanwhile, along the southern rim of the Sahara Desert, from east to west across Africa, Bantu-speaking people started interacting with

Arabized Muslims from the north. The Muslims rode across the desert on camels, looking for gold, but the camels that brought them across the desert could not get down into the equatorial jungle where the gold mines were. To get the gold, the Arabs had to trade for it with the local people. Fortunately, they had something to trade that was just as precious as gold, at least to the people of the sweltering south: they had salt.

This configuration gave tribes in the grasslands between the Sahara and the jungle the opportunity to prosper as middlemen. Vigorous cities sprang up in this belt, and a series of rich and powerful empires emerged, right where countries like Senegal, Mali, and Mauretania are now located: first came Ghana, then Mali, and then the Songhai Empire, each one bigger and more powerful than the last. Ghana may have originated as early as 400 CE, but it came to regional prominence around the time Islam was on the rise.

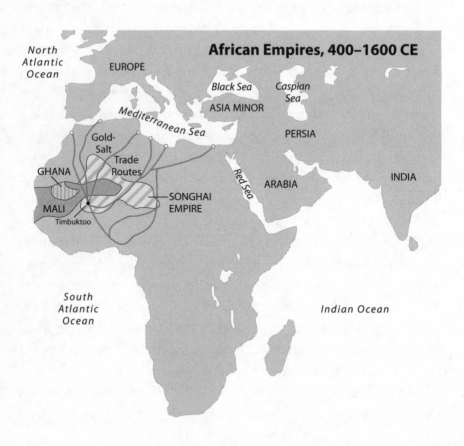

The gold-salt exchange drew the Africans of these empires into a global trading network dominated by Muslims, which opened them up to Islam. Slowly the whole sub-Saharan belt of grasslands, stretching from the Atlantic to the Indian Ocean, got absorbed into the Islamic master narrative. The conversions began in the glory days of the Ghana Empire and gathered momentum in Mali times. First the commoners converted, and then the elite. Threads of earlier, purely African narratives were incorporated into the fabric, however: the oral storytelling tradition, for example, which functioned as the repository of historical memory, and the matrilineal systems that determined the lineage of kings, making for a distinctively African version of Islam.

For Africans involved in the gold-salt trade, converting to Islam meant gaining membership in a fraternal, inward-looking community that must have felt like it had swept the whole world, so overwhelming had been its early expansion. Eventually, Islam spread even to East Africa, where Arabs had long operated as slave traders. The Arabs acquired the slaves from African tribes on the coast in exchange for products from many lands—just as Europeans did much later in West Africa. Race played no part in this slave trade. The coastal tribes felt no more kinship with the inland tribes than they did with the Arabs. There was no guarantee, however, that the Arabs might not decide to capture and enslave the coastal people with whom they were trading—unless those people converted to Islam, for Islam forbids Muslims to enslave Muslims. So, wherever Arabs operated as slave traders, the locals had a strong incentive, shall we say, to convert.

Muslim armies heading east from Arabia entered Persian territory, and here too they scored easy military victories. A plague had recently swept the region, leaving devastation in its wake. The invading Arabs were hardy, healthy desert folks battling haggard souls struggling out of sick-beds. What's more, Persia's ruling (Sassanid) dynasty was old and corrupt and had long been locked in a debilitating war with the Byzantines. Persian governments had levied heavy taxes to fund this fighting, squandered countless lives, and gained no territory whatsoever. Who could feel allegiance to such rulers? When the Arab armies arrived, the Persian elites met them in battle, but common folks opened their gates, hoping the Muslims would lower their taxes and get government off their backs.

What Persia posed was not a military challenge but a cultural one. Bleshing came less easily here than in North Africa because a powerful master narrative was already in place. Recent decay notwithstanding, this Middle World heartland had a deep sense of its distinct Iranian identity going back to Cyrus the Great and before him to Zoroaster.

To be sure, the Islamic narrative didn't feel completely foreign here. The idea of a divine community built on instructions from God; of a struggle against evil by the forces of good; of today's deeds counting on a day of judgment at the end of time; of a garden of bliss where the good would reside for all eternity—this all had some resonance in a Zoroastrian world. The religious credo was acceptable. What Iranians sniffed at was the *culture* of the rude desert dwellers from the western wastelands. They bristled at any notion of Arab cultural superiority. Islam OK, Arabism no.

As the Germans had done with Christianity, therefore, Iranians secured themselves a place in the Islamic world by embracing their own version of Islam. In their version, known as Shiism, Muhammad's divine mission had been hijacked immediately after his death by opponents of the Prophet's divinely ordained successor, his son-in-law Ali. An Arab khalifa had then murdered Ali's divinely ordained successor, his son Hussein. Hussein, as it happens, had married a Persian princess, Shahrbanu. Her son, fathered by Hussein but Persian through his mother, was the next divinely ordained successor to Mohammad's authority. In this way, Persians established a blood connection between themselves and the messenger's intimate circle. Hussein's dramatic martyrdom made him a salvationist figure in Shia Islam: he was permitted to intercede with God on behalf of sinners. Shias commemorate the day of Hussein's death as the holiest occasion in their calendar. The Shias originated in Arabia, but they were a dissident religious minority within the Muslim community, and Persians were a dissident cultural group within the burgeoning Islamic empire, and so the two currents interwove to form another distinct thread in the Islamic fabric: Mesopotamian, Levantine, North African, Hellenic, and Persian themes had now bleshed to form a vast new social constellation known to itself as Dar-ul-Islam.

MEANWHILE, IN CHINA . . .

In the seventh century, just as Dar-ul-Islam was taking shape and Europe was sinking into a feudal twilight, something big was happening in China. Out of the smoky turmoil of warring kingdoms rose a swashbuckling colossus named Wendi, an almost exact contemporary of Prophet Muhammad and Pope Gregory.

The transformations wrought by Wendi, however, produced nothing like Dar-ul-Islam, nor anything like post-Roman Europe either. China was already its own social constellation. A distinctively Chinese master narrative gave it shape and meaning. The universe was a cyclical story, and a new cycle was beginning. Wendi was like an eerie echo of the First (Qin) Emperor. Like that earlier titan, he fused an assortment of warring kingdoms into one single coherent empire: by the time he was done, the Middle Kingdom was back. In 585, Wendi declared himself the first emperor of the Sui dynasty and ruled as such for nineteen years. When he died in 604 (the same year as Pope Gregory and just six years before Muhammad declared himself messenger of God), his son Yangdi took over, and he proved to be an even more ruthlessly ambitious colossus. His assassination brought the dynasty to an end in 618, just two years before Muhammad's migration to Medina, the moment that, for Muslims, marked the beginning of history. The rebirth of the Middle Kingdom and the eruption of Islam were essentially simultaneous events.

Like the First Emperor, Wendi imposed a bureaucratic grid over Chinese society. The First Emperor's regulations had specified what each peasant family must grow. Wendi's equal-field system declared that all land belonged to the emperor, and he allocated parcels of it as he saw fit. Anyone capable of producing value from land got land to work. How much they got depended on how productive they could be. Land was periodically reallocated, so if things weren't working out, the allotments could be corrected.

The First Emperor had built the Great Wall: it cost the lives of a million-plus workers, but it solved the age-old problem of the nomads. The Sui emperors built the Grand Canal. It cost a million-plus lives, but it solved another crucial problem for the Chinese constellation. Prior to the Sui emperors, there were really two Chinas. The north had the bulk of the population. The south grew most of the rice. Cargo transported from south to north mostly went by sea, where fickle currents, storms, and pirates got all too much of it. Very little went by land, because the south was both swampy and hilly, and beasts of burden couldn't cope with it.

The two Sui emperors fixed this problem with an inland waterway connecting north and south. The Grand Canal still exists and still performs the function for which it was built. Calling it a canal, though, sort of trivializes it. What the Sui dynasty emperors did was carve a major artificial river into the earth, connecting their two enormous natural ones, the Huang He and the Yangtse. The Grand Canal provided a safe, placid, entirely defensible, and controllable waterway, up and down which barges loaded with grain could float. It knit the Middle Kingdom together as never before: the bulk of the population now had easy access to the bulk of the food. The two Chinas bleshed, and the empire boomed.

This was not the only bleshing going on. At some point in his life, Wendi met some Buddhist monks and liked what they said. As emperor, he took Buddhism under his wings. Whether he sincerely converted to the faith is hard to say but irrelevant to ask. As did Constantine with Christianity, Wendi had strategic reasons to embrace Buddhism. Buddhists in their quiet way had built an immense trade network and trading expertise. Wendi was running an empire like one big family farm, but farming was not going to produce true prosperity, not by itself. The system needed trade to make it work. Since the entrenched Confucian gentleman-scholars disdained trade, the Sui had a sharp incentive to make Buddhists and their monasteries part of the Chinese constellation.

Even though the Sui dynasty didn't last much longer than the Qin, the next two centuries saw a heavy stream of Chinese seekers traveling to northern India to visit Buddhist shrines, schools, and monasteries. They brought back the scriptures and sacred works of Buddhism and translated them for a Chinese audience. In this, however, they faced one notable challenge. The original works were written in Sanskrit, a highly inflected, polysyllabic language with an alphabetic script. Written Chinese, by contrast, was a monosyllabic, uninflected language employing a script based on ideograms. Sanskrit and its descendants had an exceptional capacity for expressing high-flown abstractions without reference to material realities. The Chinese script, grounded as it was in palpable elements of the real world, tended to render abstractions in terms of terse, observable specifics. The Sanskrit word for *universe* was rendered in the Chinese script by a combination of three characters that mean mountains, rivers, and the earth. The Chinese scripted rendition of *human ego* is a combination of characters that represent wind, light, and one's native place.

The Chinese translators had to render Buddhist texts into Chinese using terms that already existed in the Chinese script. These terms all had established meanings and connotations. How could ideas hitherto unknown to the Chinese experience be expressed in this script? It was the same conundrum Bishop Ulfilas had faced in translating the Bible for a Gothic audience. The Chinese translators ended up leaning heavily on characters used by Taoist sages to express Taoist ideas in their writings. For example, the Chinese Buddhists used the term *Tao* to express what the Indian Buddhists had called *dharma*. They used a Taoist word meaning inaction for the Indians' concept of nirvana.

Inevitably, Chinese Buddhism absorbed some of the flavors of Taoism and imparted various subtle flavors back. Out of this bleshing came Chan Buddhism, a uniquely Chinese version of a faith born in India. The idea of a soul journeying toward a transcendent reality gave way, in Chan Buddhism, to techniques of meditation aimed at achieving harmony in the present, where one was now. Practitioners of Chan Buddhism savored nature and favored contemplative retreat. Chan spiritual life was laced with a strong appreciation of particular locations. This form of Buddhism made its way to Japan (and eventually to California) where it is still known as Zen Buddhism. In Zen, the concept of nirvana—a permanent state one strives to reach—gives pride of place to the slightly different concept of *satori*—a revelatory awakening into each present moment.

The Qin dynasty had lasted just one generation. The Sui dynasty lasted a mere one generation and a half. The First Emperor had built, albeit with blood and brutality, a framework that made China governable. The Sui emperors did almost exactly the same thing. What followed the First Emperor's career was the long-lasting Han dynasty, whose four centuries of dominance established the essence of Chinese culture. What followed the transformative careers of the two Sui emperors was the Tang dynasty, whose three centuries of dominance are commonly considered the heart of China's golden age, a luster that continued long into the succeeding Song dynasty. The Han inherited the structure built by the Qin emperor, the Tang inherited the one built by the Sui. Neither dynasty had to cope with the resentments their predecessors had stoked. When the Tang took over, China's agricultural productivity was peaking, the Grand Canal was working magnificently, and networks of trade were sewing the empire together as never before.

Out of northern China, the Tang emperors extended their control along a panhandle extending west on the Silk Road to border finally on the Islamic caliphate(s). The politically powerful north absorbed the cultures of the Yangtze River basin into an idiosyncratically Chinese

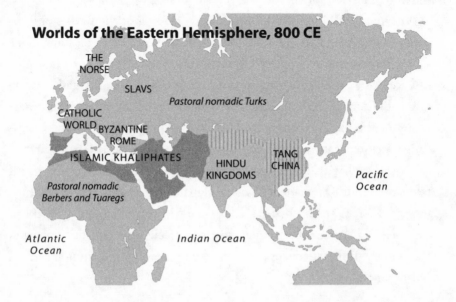

Worlds of the Eastern Hemisphere, 800 CE

THE NORSE

SLAVS

Pastoral nomadic Turks

CATHOLIC WORLD

BYZANTINE ROME

ISLAMIC KHALIPHATES

HINDU KINGDOMS

TANG CHINA

Pacific Ocean

Pastoral nomadic Berbers and Tuaregs

Atlantic Ocean

Indian Ocean

culture blended of Buddhism, Taoism, and Confucian ideals. A powerful, centralized government carried this cloud of culture to the shores of the South China Sea. There the Chinese imperial government reached its limit, but the fruitfully interwoven cultural juggernaut kept expanding east and west and across the waters into Korea and Vietnam, and farther into Japan to some extent. The teachings and spirit of Confucius infused both Korean and Vietnamese cultures and remain visible today. Buddhism seeped into Vietnam and in an altered form into Japan, and those influences, too, remain visible still.

In the end, a mist of Chinese cultural influence extended from the rim of the Eurasian steppes to the archipelagoes of the eastern Pacific. Throughout this region, an east Asian civilization came into being as a single vast social galaxy. Within it, to be sure, earlier social constellations persisted as distinct clouds. Japan was never China; it always embodied a distinct culture of its own. Korea absorbed social and aesthetic themes from China but maintained a stubborn, fragile independence from the Chinese emperors throughout the ages. Vietnam absorbed influences from China into its own Mekong River culture, but this remained a culture shaped by the geography of a hot, wet world living, above all else, on rice; and while Buddhist and Confucian ideas did seep in, the Vietnamese stoutly fended off Chinese political domination for a thousand years. To this day, Vietnam, Korea, Japan, Laos, and Kampuchea retain their own distinctive cultural flavors.

And yet they all do register as parts of some single larger cultural constellation. There is no denying, after all, that Vietnam and China are more like each other than either is like Norway. We'd certainly group both Vietnam and China with Korea more readily than we would with Angola. And all three are more similar to Japan than all four of them are to Cuba. Differences among these societies were real, but they were also situated in a vast conceptual framework inhabited in common by multitudes of social constellations with interconnected narratives.

10

World Historical Monads
(650 CE to 1100 CE)

In the year 800, an omniscient alien flying over planet Earth would, I think, have seen humanity grouped into some number of more or less stable civilizations, each of them a coherent but inward-looking universe unto itself. Each of them was, to coin a term, a world historical monad. I borrow the term *monad* from German philosopher Gottfried Leibniz who defined it as the entire universe from a single point of view. For Liebniz, the universe was made up of monads, and since every monad *was* the whole universe, each contained all the others as parts of itself.

This might be a bit of a mystical stretch for the physical universe, but as a metaphor for the *social* universe, the monad strikes me as dead on. Every world history is really a somebody-centric story framed by a master narrative that puts itself at the center. In the year 800, China was just such a world historical monad, the Islamic world was another, India another, and Western Europe still another. Each of these geographically anchored civilizations was permeated by a world-scale master narrative of its own. Most of the monads knew of the other monads but situated them as peripheral regions of what it saw as the world, which is to say, as peripheral parts of itself.

These were not, of course, the only world historical monads on the planet. The intercommunicating zones of Mesoamerica no doubt comprised another. Something of the sort must also have developed along the northwestern coast of South America. There may have been another considerable world historical monad laced through the Amazon jungle as well, although virtually nothing is known of that one now. And there were surely others, big and small, around the world—in the Russian north, southern Africa, or any inhabited place where an intercommunicative zone could develop. But in the global East, where over 80 percent of humans lived, China, India, the Islamic World, and Western Europe were the dominant monads of the time.

CHINA

In the year 800, China was bursting with vitality. During the three centuries or so of Tang dynasty dominance, Chinese artistic culture peaked. Here, the world's first prose novels were written. Here, painters were creating exquisite landscapes dotted with tiny human figures, the culminating expression of Taoist-Buddhist bleshing. Here, a Tang emperor founded China's first acting and musical academy, which fielded the world's first opera troupe. Remember that, here, the Han dynasty had recruited scholars steeped in the Confucian classics to serve as bureaucrats; now, the Tang took that process one step further by developing a formal set of comprehensive exams to test would-be government officials not just on the Confucian classics but also on law, mathematics, politics, history, calligraphy, mathematics, painting, and poetry—yes, in Tang dynasty China, if you wanted to be a powerful bureaucrat, you had to be good at writing poetry.

In Tang times, on orders from the emperor, a Buddhist monk built the first mechanical clock, a three-story device driven by a water wheel. Woodblock printing, a Chinese invention, made the printed book a commercial product for the first time: the oldest surviving example of such a book is a Chinese translation of the Buddhist classic, the Diamond Sutra, published in 868 CE.

Taoism and Buddhism had done quite a bit of bleshing by this time, but neither had disappeared completely into the other. Both idea systems were still thriving. Taoism persisted as a popular religion slanted toward magic, but dabbling in magic turned Taoist monks into protoscientists.

In looking for ways to turn base metals into gold, they developed the first rudiments of chemistry. In trying to perfect their fortune-telling prowess, they moved astrology toward astronomy. In searching for potions to confer magical powers, they compiled a pharmacopeia identifying over eight hundred medicinal herbs. Ironically, in seeking methods for achieving immortality, Taoist monks accidentally invented gunpowder.

Toward the end of its run, the Tang government turned against Buddhism because Buddhist monasteries had enjoyed exemption from taxation for centuries, and by the ninth century they owned as much as 40 percent of the land in China, tax-free. In 843, the emperor ordered all the monasteries closed, confiscated their lands, and forced some quarter of a million Buddhist monks and nuns out into the world to work for a living. As a stand-alone idea system with political force, Chinese Buddhism never recovered, but Buddhist themes had worked their way so thoroughly into the Chinese aesthetic that they had become invisible.

In the ninth century the Tang "lost their mandate," and a warring kingdoms period ensued, but then the Song emerged, and they were like Tang part two. Chinese culture continued to glitter, though it went through a subtle shift in flavor: it became less lyrical. The focus of society shifted from art to technology. The Chinese had woodblock printing; now they invented movable type. The Chinese had gunpowder; now they started using it in cannons, not just fireworks. In this period, the Chinese invented the magnetic compass. They also invented playing cards, and Song bureaucrats found another novel use for paper—as money. Nowhere else could this have happened, for paper money required a central government with complete jurisdiction over economic activity, and only China had such a system at that time.

Under Song rule, the economy grew so robust that many households began selling items previously produced purely for private family use—fabric, garments, prepared foods, and the like. Household production ratcheted up to an industrial scale. It became a badge of status for families to hire laborers to do work previously done by the householder's wife and children. In fact, it became a badge of noble status for the women of a family to be rendered incapable of working, so the hoi polloi could see how well the household was doing. Upper-class Chinese families increasingly took up the practice of binding young girls' feet in bandages that caused their foot bones to break as they developed. These girls grew into women with abnormally small, dysfunctional feet, incapable of common labor. During Song times, men of the Chinese elite saw these broken feet as beautiful. This was the dark side of cultural power and wealth.

China was unusually open to the world for much of this time. Arab ships docked in Chinese ports. Camel caravans from Persia and Afghanistan came to flourishing markets along the Great Wall. Commercial goods flowed in and out of China from Southeast Asia, the Islamic world, India, and Africa.

It's no wonder, then, that the Chinese thought of their world as *the* world. All this art, commerce, and invention took place within a world historical framework of great coherence. The Chinese still saw the present as part of a cyclical narrative with a momentum no mere human could alter; they still saw the world as a story unfolding in a concentric universe. They still thought of their society as the Middle Kingdom surrounded by barbarians who were gazing in with envious longing. In good times—and these were very good times indeed—an imperial family with a mandate from heaven ruled all the world that mattered, resulting in a harmony so ubiquitous it enabled countless intricate streams of life to mesh as perfectly as threads in a bolt of silk.

"Open," however, did not mean "outgoing." China was open to the world but remained an inward-looking civilization. Arab ships docked at Chinese ports; Chinese ships didn't dock at Arab ports. That would have struck the Chinese as inappropriate. Tributaries and barbarians came to the emperor, not the other way around.

INDIAN SUBCONTINENT

For all its government-regulated creativity and productivity, China was not the world's richest society. In the year 800, that badge probably belonged to India. The Chinese world featured a state-mediated, inward-looking singularity that was quite truly efflorescent. But India achieved an equally vibrant cultural coherence and creativity through multiplicity.

In India, kingdoms came and went, and it didn't make much difference to the social fabric. Semiautonomous villages remained the fundamental unit of daily life everywhere. Castes continued to run right through political boundaries. These factors had defined society under the Mauryans, and they continued to define life in the many smaller empires and kingdoms that emerged after the Mauryans collapsed. In China, the post-Mauryan centuries would have been considered a "warring kingdoms period." In India, that concept had little relevance. Political fragmentation did not mean cultural fragmentation. The first centuries of the Common Era were a fruitful time in India for art and wealth and trade, for social advancement and intellectual achievements.

Some five hundred years after the Mauryans left the stage, another far-flung empire emerged out of the same general area. Oddly enough, even though there was no connection between the two, both were founded by men named Chandragupta. The later empire took its very name from its founder: it was the Gupta Empire.

The Mauryans had favored Buddhism; the Gupta favored Hinduism. But neither dynasty conferred official status on its favored faith. That just wasn't the Indian way. The Guptas merely created conditions friendly to various Hindu sects, just as the Mauryans had done for Buddhism. In the centuries of Gupta dominance, the worship of Vishnu flourished in the north, the worship of Shiva in the south, and the worship of many other gods across the land. These numerous gods reflected numerous meshing social groups. Temples and monasteries dotted the landscape, and the Gupta supported them, perhaps out of political expedience but also, no doubt, because kings and court officials were sincerely devout.

Pilgrimage played a crucial part in Hindu life, no matter who was king. Devotees traveled to distant sacred places such as the Ganges River to seek purification. If they couldn't get to the Ganges, they went someplace closer. There were plenty of choices. Pilgrims, like locals, underscored their devotion with rich donations to favored temples. India's highways and waterways supported a dense flow of traffic. Wealth moved around in the subcontinent—but it also pooled up in countless places, especially where temples spawned trading centers, just as Muslim garrisons had done in North Africa and Buddhist monasteries had done in the Eurasian steppes.

The Indian impulse toward multiplicity quickened over time. Castes subdivided into *jatas*, which were ever more intricate groupings linked to occupations. There was no necessary limit to these. Any occupation could become such a social grouping. Goldsmiths, blacksmiths, potters, weavers—all belonged to their own jatas. No governments ordained this system. No authority figures organized or controlled it. The culture itself generated these interlocking puzzle pieces, which performed somewhat the same function here as guilds later did in other societies. Jatas kept a complex system of production and exchange coordinated with minimal friction.

Under Gupta rule, India hit a classical period. Metallurgy and medicine made great strides. Indian doctors learned to cauterize wounds, perform surgeries, and extract medicines from minerals and metals as well as vegetables. Ayurvedic medicine matured as a system for increasing health and not just curing diseases. Indian mathematicians developed the decimal system of notation and began formulating trigonometry. Dazzling temples and palaces were built, and great plays were produced. Kalidasa, "the Shakespeare of India," was writing at this time. And after centuries of oral transmission, the great Vedic epics, the Ramayana and the Mahabharata, were written down at last. The Mahabharata includes the Bhagavad Gita, a dialogue between the god Krishna and a prince named Arjuna, a text with high scriptural status in the world of Hinduism.

In later Gupta times, the Laws of Manu gained authority. Manu was said to be a towering sage of ancient times, or perhaps more than a sage, perhaps the very creator of the world—accounts varied. What didn't vary was the substance of his message. Manu was, shall we say, a rigid conservative. His text codified rules for Hindu life. It specified what to eat, who to eat with, how to dress, whether women should have various rights

(Manu thought not), whether people of different castes should marry (Manu thought not), and whether they should even eat at the same table (Manu said no). These prescriptions and proscriptions were probably knocking about as part of Hindu oral tradition, but now that they were written down they tended to set caste in concrete as an institution. They also laid the groundwork for *suttee*, the supposed obligation of a woman to set herself on fire if her husband died before she did. Here, again, was the dark side of burgeoning cultural power and soaring wealth.

The Gupta gradually lost their grip. Big chunks of their empire broke away. By the time Muhammad was born in Arabia, they were gone, and India had again fragmented into many kingdoms. But again, political fragmentation did not imply cultural breakdown. All across this vast terrain, wealthy, vigorous, and culturally brilliant societies went on pursuing their destinies.

But as Hindu narratives were gaining ground in the subcontinent, Buddhism was fading out. Buddhists scorned caste distinctions, but caste was too deeply embedded in this region to dissolve easily. Brahmins and Kshatriyas, the two high castes, tended to own land and hold positions of political power at the village level, and they naturally resisted an idea system corrosive to their entitlements. There was, however, no big war between Hinduism and Buddhism. In theory, the two could coexist. Like China, India had no tradition of jealous gods demanding exclusive worship. In this social milieu, a person could worship Buddha, make a nod to Shiva, and honor a multitude of lesser deities. No one saw it as heresy, because heresy had no meaning in a universe defined by multiplicity.

This social milieu, however, put the very coherence of Buddhism at a disadvantage. The Buddhist narrative could not absorb motley Hindu sects and still be Buddhism. Hinduism, by contrast, was big, diverse, adaptive, open, and absorptive. It was not so much a religion as an orientation toward religiosity itself. For Hindus, those who revered Buddha could worship him in their own way and include bits of ritual from their neighbors if they wanted. In fact, Hindus gradually came to include the

Buddha in their pantheon, as an avatar of a higher god, one among many exalted souls worth revering. Some believed that he, like the beloved Krishna, might have been an incarnation of Vishnu. The specifically Buddhist part of the worship thus faded out. Hinduism didn't defeat Buddhism or drive it out so much as digest it: a very Indian way of bleshing.

Buddhism as such did hang on for a while in southern India, where Buddhists called their faith Theravada, which means "the doctrine of the elders." They meant to suggest that, unlike those Mahayana revisionists up north, they were staying true to the original teachings. As they saw it, Buddha had taught that striving for nirvana was an inherently individual quest. No one could get there for someone else; each person had to get there on his or her own or not at all. Theravada Buddhists shaped their practice around this assumption. From the southern tip of India, Theravada Buddhism crossed the waters to Sri Lanka, and there it found a home.

In the ninth century, as the Tang were giving way to the Song in China, India was a dense web of villages stretching across a subcontinent intricately connected by trade, with opulent cities at its nodes and many different kings in power. Tens of millions of people were busy across the land with farming, handicrafts, devotional rituals, commerce, money lending, and artistic work. Not only was this whole world legendarily rich, but the wealth was visible. Anyone passing through could see it, and all that visible wealth drew merchants in like flies to sugar.

Many came through the mountain passes of the northwest, but little traffic flowed the other way. Ancient Vedic doctrines had decreed that going north of the Indus rendered a person ritually impure. Something of this ethos persisted into post-Vedic times, but it didn't crimp the economy. India was vast and varied enough for internal trade to keep the commerce boiling.

Traders also came to southern India by sea. This southern portion of the subcontinent is a thick spit of hot jungle surrounded by some of the world's most navigable waters. Here, as in the north, however, Indian traders did not go west much, and Indian idea systems didn't spread to

Arabia or sink roots in Rome. Mere distance doesn't account for this. Southern India is closer to Arabia than northern India is to the Huang He. Here, as in the steppes, however, the narratives that held sway in the Mediterranean and the Middle World resisted bleshing with those of the subcontinent. It's not that in the year 800 these narratives were hostile to one another. Muslim traders came from Arabia and Persia and, while they didn't blesh with Hindus and Buddhists, they interacted with them peacefully. Arabian merchants sold horses to Indians in exchange for spices and gold. Both sides came away contented.

From India, the currents kept flowing east. In this direction, not only Muslims but also Hindus and Buddhists carried their themes to the peninsulas and 83,000-plus islands of Southeast Asia. The cultural waves emanating from India eventually met and mingled with the waves of influence coming out of China, overlapping finally in the peninsula that is now called (what else?) Indochina.

Indians could tolerate political fragmentation because they derived unity from that vast web of ideas known (only later) as Hinduism. Like the Chinese, they were living at the center of their own world model.

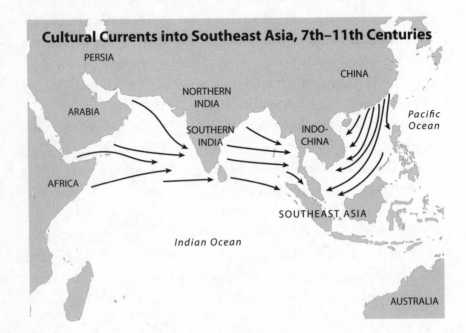

Cultural Currents into Southeast Asia, 7th–11th Centuries

PERSIA

CHINA

NORTHERN INDIA

ARABIA

Pacific Ocean

SOUTHERN INDIA

INDO-CHINA

AFRICA

SOUTHEAST ASIA

Indian Ocean

AUSTRALIA

When they looked beyond their own borders, they saw the peripheries of their own internal model. They traded willingly enough with strangers who came from other climes. They were glad to get exotic goods (such as silk) without having to endure long journeys. They were happy to receive visitors and their merchandise. But they were not curious enough about the western visitors to follow them home. They did not need to follow them home; they were already home.

THE MIDDLE WORLD

The Middle World, the lands stretching from Asia Minor to the Himalaya Mountains, was now the Islamic world, and it, too, had a coherence that made it inward looking and self-sufficient, for in the course of its expansion, Islam had proved to be not just a religion or a religious state but a civilization. The caliphate had given way to a multitude of secular states paying lip service to a caliphate that existed only in the Muslim imagination, but Islamic culture flowed across borders, and Dar-ul-Islam continued to exist as some single social whole.

In all the lands ruled by Muslims, people came to favor a style of clothing reflecting the way of life taught by the messenger. In all these lands, distinctively Islamic styles of architecture evolved. A mosque in Cordoba might differ in details from one in Central Asia, but both expressed the same aesthetic. Everywhere in the Islamic world, the suspicion of representational art came to be reflected in abstract, floral, and geometric designs instead of in the anthropomorphized deities and worshipful humans found in areas permeated by Hinduism, Buddhism, Christianity, or Hellenism.

Islam, like Hinduism, provided an overarching conceptual framework for a wide array of peoples, and not by any means were they all Muslims. Christians and Jews figured prominently in early Islamic governments. Many Persian intellectuals (though seeing themselves as wholeheartedly Muslim) communed with the ghosts of Zoroastrianism still haunting their lands. All, however, inhabited the same world historical monad.

Dar-ul-Islam was just as self-involved as the other monads, yet somehow, in its very self-involvement, it epitomized an outward-looking civilization. For one thing, it *was* the Middle World. The Islamic social galaxy bordered on all the other great world historical monads of its time and place. It stretched across the steppes to northern China, it touched the Indian world both north and south, it ran through Southeast Asia to the southern shores of China, it bordered on the Greek remnants of the Roman world in the eastern Mediterranean, and it stretched the whole length of North Africa to overlap with the black African Islamicized kingdoms in the south while at the same time rubbing up against the emerging Roman Catholic world in the north.

Location only reinforced a key factor here: the Muslim attitude toward commerce. When Islam surged out of Arabia, warriors formed the leading edge, and right behind them came waves of businessmen. The pre-Islamic Arabs had been commercial to their bones. This attitude carried into Islamic times. The messenger himself had been a trader married to a business entrepreneur. He knew all about money and credit and debt. Given these values, wherever Islam took hold, commerce flourished.

Location and trade made translation a core preoccupation for Islamic intellectuals. Muslims learned about printing and paper making from

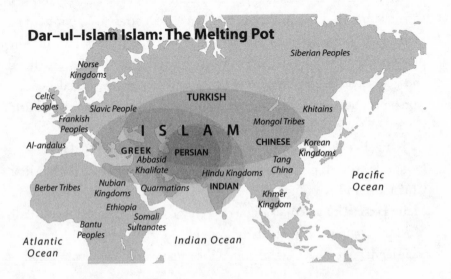

Dar-ul-Islam Islam: The Melting Pot

China, and right away started producing books. They filled great libraries with Arab and Persian translations of works by the seminal thinkers
of other cultures, both earlier and contemporaneous. Western historians
have tended to dismiss the intellectual achievements of Islamic culture
in this period because, they say, it produced no breakthroughs of its own:
Muslims only translated the creative achievements of others. But if ever-
increasing interconnection is an important through line of history, there
is nothing trivial about translation. Thanks to this passion, and to their
geographic location, Muslim intellectuals were the first ones in a position to make direct comparisons among the ideas of the great Chinese,
Indian, Greek, and Persian thinkers. They were uniquely situated, therefore, to start asking the question: How could *all* of these things be true?

Exposure to many systems of thought drew Muslim philosophers
into an obsession with encyclopedic compilation. "Let's get everything
anyone knows about this subject into a single book so we can compare"
was the impulse. The Muslim philosopher Ibn Sina, for example, wrote a
compendium of medical knowledge that became the authoritative text-
book used not only in the Islamic world but in European medical schools
as late as the 1600s.

The same impulse led Muslim thinkers to attempt grand philosophical
syntheses. As they saw it, if God was a singularity, the world must also add
up to a singularity. In Greek philosophy they heard seductive echoes of
their own tenets. Plato had argued that the palpable world is but a shadow
of a real world consisting purely of ideas, and the neoplatonist philosopher
Plotinus had developed this into a radical doctrine of utter, ultimate unity.
If all chairs were but shadows of a single idea of chairness, and if all circles
were but shadows of a single idea of circleness (etc., etc.), then surely *all*
everything must be the shadow of a single reality, a singularity that existed
purely as idea. Plotinus called this ultimate reality the One. To Muslims,
that sounded an awful lot like Allah. (To me it sounds like the highest
constellation of all.)

Muslims were thrilled, therefore, to stumble across Aristotle's logic, a
method for establishing truth through reason. They thought they might
use Aristotle's logic to prove the maxims of religious faith! In addition

to developing logic, Aristotle relentlessly broke the material world down into categories, the better to study and explain it. Following in his footsteps, Muslims inched into fields of natural philosophy that were much later known as science. The Chinese tended to focus on practical and technological innovations at this time: the compass, the clock, the wheelbarrow. Muslim philosophers were more interested in digging out the underlying principles that animated material reality. For example, when different metals melted into a single alloy, what was that all about? The Arabs called their study of material change *al-kimiya*, derived from *kráma*, the Greek word for alloys. The West later called its version of this enterprise alchemy. And today we call it chemistry.

The search for abstract, underlying principles aligned with an interest in mathematics, the purest embodiment of abstract underlying principles. Islamic thinkers absorbed into their framework the mathematics of India: its numerals, its computation by place value, its brilliant idea of treating zero as one of the numerals. And then Islamic mathematicians added one more notation, a mark to stand for "particular unknown quantity." Today, x is the mark that usually denotes this quantity. People had long been able to guess the approximate value of unknown quantities from a given number of known quantities. The mathematicians of the Islamic world asked if there was a systematic way to reduce a range of possible values to a single necessary value. The Arabic word for necessity is *jabr*. The Persian mathematician Al-Khwarizmi ("the man from Khwarezm") codified a system for achieving this calculation, which he called *al-jabr*. (Today, we call it algebra.) Al-Khwarizmi formalized the more general idea of calculations that could be performed as an orderly series of mechanical steps leading inevitably to one correct conclusion. These came to be called *al-khwarizms*, which today we call algorithms. Long division is an algorithm. So is the multiplication of big numbers. So is every computer software program. Many English words that start with the syllable *al* (alcohol, for example) contain the ghost of some long-ago enterprise by some now-forgotten Muslim intellectual. Everything is connected.

Yet for all its energetic curiosity about other people's achievements and ideas, Islamic civilization was just as self-involved as China and

India, for like the others, it was a world historical monad. When Muslims looked at the world outside their own, they saw the Islamic model of reality they had constructed internally. The people out there were, in the Islamic worldview, the ones who had not come around yet but eventually would, just as children eventually grow up and become adults. When Muslim scholars delved into Greek thought, they weren't looking to meet the Greeks halfway: they were studying how Greek thought might help them complete the Islamic model of reality. On that model, they were not prepared to give an inch: they understood their model of the world to be, not some model, but the world itself. That's everyone's understanding of their own model.

Greek and Indian ideas interested Muslim intellectuals only as complements to the central social project of their own world historical monad: building the edifice of immutable laws known as the *sharia*. These were the laws that enabled God's community to function as divinely intended. Muslims thought of the sharia in much the same way that European intellectuals later thought of science: it had an objective existence. It could not be invented; it could only be discovered. It had the immutable certainty of the stars. Once the appropriate religious experts had unearthed every last detail of the sharia, humankind would at last be able to live as a community whose every citizen would earn eternity in paradise just by following the pathways marked by the sharia. Completing this vast scaffolding became, therefore, the central project of Islamic civilization, just as science would later become the central project of Western civilization.

EUROPE

Even as Islam was expanding and Dar-ul-Islam was firming up, a new world was taking shape in Western Europe too. There, in the centuries following Gregory's papacy, political life stabilized into a system of feudal manors, which were essentially postage-stamp kingdoms. Each manor produced more or less everything its inhabitants needed. Each was ruled by a feudal lord. In all secular matters this lord served as lawmaker and judge. Larger structures were defined only by oaths of personal loyalty between little lords and bigger lords. This had been the political system of the Germanic tribes back when they were nomads, eying Rome and hungering for land. This was the system they enshrined once they got the land they'd been craving.

By Gregory's time, Christians already thought of the church as something more than a collection of religious buildings, sacred texts, and shared beliefs. The wise men of the east had long been describing the church as a single mystical whole, the incarnation of Christ on Earth. If you were part of this body of believers, you *might* get into heaven; if you weren't, you absolutely couldn't.

The church secured the authority to decide who was and was not part of the church. It could excommunicate any particular person, which is to say, expel them from the body of all believers and thereby condemn them to hell forever. Saints could intercede for sinners, but only the church could decide who were saints and who were sinners.

Even for devout Christians, entry to heaven wasn't guaranteed. Faith, according to the Catholic constellation of ideas, was not enough. People also needed "works" to their credit. In this context works did not mean good deeds in the boy scout sense; works referred to the rites and rituals prescribed by the church, such as mass, confession, and penance. Only the church could determine what rites were necessary and how exactly to perform them. A person had to be free of sin to achieve eternal bliss. It's hard to avoid committing at least a little sin to survive in this world, but the church had the power to absolve people periodically of such stains and to give their souls one last cleansing just before they died. This all added up to awesome power.

The Catholic Church was not a state. It was Western Europe's alternative to a state. The coherence of its constellation of ideas gave it a dominion rivaling that of any government. The church had its own canon laws, formulated and finalized in Rome. It had its own source of revenues from tithes. It gained the power to levy taxes in some cases. The church had land and kept acquiring more. It possessed the exclusive power to appoint the clergy, who alone could provide absolution from sins. In the centuries after Gregory, the Catholic clergy were ever easier to spot because the garments they wore began to diverge from those of regular folks. They lived under special rules, too. They could not marry or have children, but they had status, for no one else could do what they could do: open the doors to heaven.

The Roman Catholic Church extended and deepened its reach until every village in Western Europe had its own church and each had its own priest. Every locale had its bishop, and everyone recognized the pope in Rome as the top authority on spiritual matters, which was a big deal because "spiritual matters" formed a great portion of all the matters that mattered to the average European Christian. And it was an especially big deal because, by the end of the eighth century, just about everyone in Western Europe *was* a Christian. The only exceptions were a tiny handful of peripatetic Jews, and the pagan barbarians of the far north. The overarching framework offered by the Catholic Church gave Western Europe a cultural unity that offset its political fragmentation.

Monasteries were a key element of this new world historical monad. Born in Africa in the early days of Christianity, monasteries spread throughout Western Europe, not as rivals of the church but as its allies. In a hard, rough time, when the European world was fragmented into feudal fiefs and no authority guaranteed public safety between the fiefdoms, joining a monastery or a nunnery and living out one's life as a monk or a nun, devoted to chastity, religious practice, nonviolence, and, in some cases, intellectual labor was one option for any Christian inhabitant of Europe.

In the year 800, the secular and spiritual realms of Christian Europe entered into an official marriage. That year, on Christmas Day, the pope placed a crown on the head of the major German king, a man named Charlemagne, and declared him emperor of the Holy Roman Empire. This empire endured for centuries to come, although in its later days it was mostly an imaginary entity, not unlike the caliphate of the Muslims. Symbolically, however, it signaled the birth of Europe as a single *something*, distinctly different from the world historical monads of the farther east: Dar-ul-Islam, India, China, the pastoral nomadic world of the

Asian steppes, and the sea nomads of the monsoon network. Western Europeans would later call their realm Christendom.

If Dar-ul-Islam was the archetypal outward-looking civilization, Christendom was the exact opposite. Most citizens of this monad lived and died no more than a few miles from wherever they were born. Hardly anyone went anywhere during his or her lifetime. Most had no reason to wonder about worlds outside their own locale. Most didn't know such worlds existed. Shortly after Islam was born, Western Europe had fallen into a defensive posture that reinforced its closure. In the west, European Christians faced Muslim armies coming out of Africa. In the east, they had to fend off wave after wave of new invaders from the Eurasian steppes: Avars, Magyars, Pechenegs—the list goes on and on. In the north loomed the frightening and ferocious Norse people.

Historians used to speak of this period as the Dark Ages. From the global perspective, there was no such thing. The light was always shining somewhere, and the light was never shining everywhere. For Western Europe, however, this part of the world became an undeniably poorer place in the centuries after Alaric and Attila, Vandals and Visigoths. Even the richest lords of Europe now lived a cruder life than moderately well-to-do Romans at the time of Christ. The level of technology declined, maintenance lapsed, and infrastructure crumbled. Ever fewer people learned to read and write. Ever fewer books were written.

Long-distance trade shrank to a trickle in Europe at this point, in part because Christendom was suspicious of money. Money facilitates interactions among strangers across far-flung territory, and true to their Germanic tribal roots, European Christians of the Dark Ages didn't trust interactions among strangers. They preferred that deals be made among people who knew one another and could depend on oaths and honor to guarantee the outcome. People still went to local markets to exchange goods and services, but from the fifth century onward, European commerce drifted increasingly toward barter. In honest barter, the items traded were presumably of equal value. If a barter exchange left one side richer and the other side poorer, it looked like skullduggery of some kind must have occurred. Anyone who got wealthy from trade was therefore suspect. Honest wealth was derived from land and the fighting skills of armed retainers loyal to the landowner. These values spawned disrespect for trade and sanctified production derived from soil.

The decline of Europe serves as one more illustration of how interconnected the world was even then. The Islamic world honored the very attitudes and values that Germanic Christianity despised, and this had consequences for them both. As Muslims saw it, merchants were doing the same work as God's own messenger, so how could that be bad? Since trade flourished wherever Islam took hold, hard currency flowed into the Muslim world like water flowing downhill.

This was especially true of silver, which stands out among metals for the balance it strikes between abundance and scarcity. From the start, when minted into coins, silver made a perfect currency. Copper was a little too plentiful; people could get it without participating in the system of exchange. Gold was too rare. No society has enough gold to power the multitude of small exchanges in a functional economy: if people have to use gold to buy shirts, pay for haircuts, and eat in restaurants, not very many people will be buying shirts, getting haircuts, or going out to eat. Silver is just abundant enough to have value as a commodity but just scarce enough to function as a working currency for a whole (and complex) society.

Silver inevitably flows to places where currency is powering economic exchanges. It drains away from places where exchanges are not happening. It's not that silver has a brain. The intentions are not supplied by silver; they're supplied by the humans handling silver. In the ninth century those who had some silver took it to a place where they could buy something with it. What else would they do? Whoever got the silver out of those exchanges took it to a place where *they* could buy something with it. Why wouldn't they?

In the centuries immediately after Islam was born, the volume of exchange taking place in the Islamic world outpaced any other. Much of the world's silver, therefore, drained out of Europe, like water flowing downhill, into the Islamic Middle World. This was a self-perpetuating cycle. Less hard currency meant fewer exchanges *could* take place, and fewer exchanges meant more hard currency flowed away. Material circumstances kept reinforcing one way of life in the Islamic world and another way of life in neighboring Christendom. The first was all about long-distance interactions. The second was all about the local: pretty much every Western European's social world consisted of fellow villagers, local priests, the local church, a nearby monastery perhaps, and the "Emerald City," which was distant Rome—wherein presided the wizard at the epicenter of the European world historical monad: the pope.

THE AMERICAS

As for the other side of the globe, we don't really know what was happening there during all this time, at least not in any great detail. In the year 800, traditional estimates say that about 90 percent of our species lived in the temperate belt of Africa and Eurasia, somewhere north of the equator, and another 6 percent lived in sub-Saharan Africa, mostly along the perimeter of the continent. The Americas supposedly had about 3 percent of the world's population, although that number is pretty speculative and much disputed. What written records there may have been are lost to us now. Still, the Western Hemisphere contained about one-third of the world's landmass, and substantial civilizations had been flourishing there as well, so here are some of the cursory details we do know about the Americas of ancient times.

A few people may have come to these continents from Scandinavia; a few may have come across the Pacific from Polynesia. A few may even have come to the Caribbean from West Africa—maybe. But most inhabitants of the Americas at this point were descended from hunter-gatherers who had come in from Siberia during the last glacial period.

Urban civilizations formed later in the Americas than in the global East. Perhaps the human population has to hit a critical mass before cities can form, and the Americas were at first too sparsely inhabited for that. The early migrants were big game hunters, and North America was full of big game. It might be that in these continents, hunting and gathering worked well enough that everyone had plenty to eat so long as tribes spread out, in which case, there would have been no need to exchange the freedom and excitement of the nomadic lifestyle for the grinding tedium of the farmer's life. Or it may simply be that these continents were populated later.

Geographically, the Americas more or less mirror the other great hemispheric landmass. Both have a temperate belt north of the tropics and another one south. Both have vast grasslands flanking these temperate belts. In the Eastern Hemisphere, the grasslands are the steppes of Eurasia and the plains of southern Africa. In the Western Hemisphere, they are the prairies of North America and the pampas of Argentina. Straddling the equator in the global East is the large equatorial jungle of Central Africa. Straddling the equator in the global West is the even more enormous Amazon jungle of Brazil.

Despite these rough similarities, however, human cultures took quite a different course in the two hemispheres. When great urban civilizations formed in the Americas, they didn't spring up along the obvious big rivers. The Mississippi was not the Nile of North America. The Ohio and Missouri were not its Tigris and Euphrates. Curiously enough, American cultures comparable to those of Egypt and Mesopotamia emerged not in the temperate zones but in the tropics. They emerged on the high mountain slopes of Peru and in the jungles and swamplands of Mesoamerica.

Here, as on the other side of the globe, people undertook huge infrastructure projects requiring that many unrelated people work together, which gave rise to bureaucratic societies that built splendid pyramids, produced elaborate art, and made discoveries in mathematics, astronomy, and other fields. But the great collective projects of the Americas were not about managing precious water to irrigate alluvial soil. In the Americas, people collaborated to cope with too much water (and too little level land). The Maya dug canals to drain swamps and build up farmable plateaus of dry soil within the wetlands they called home. In South America, sophisticated agrarian societies terraced their extremely steep hillsides to create level land watered by rain and runoff from streams higher up.

Early urban civilizations of Eurasia relied on irrigation. Early urban civilizations of the Americas depended largely on rainfall. Technology can deal with irregular flooding better than it can with irregular rainfall. Engineers can use tools to store and manage river water; engineers can't use tools to make rain start and stop. They can't cope, as well, with variations in the weather. Perhaps this is why the high cultures of the Americas followed a certain recurrent pattern. They rose to splendor and then, rather abruptly, collapsed.

It happened to the Olmecs who settled along the Gulf of Mexico around 1500 BCE. They are considered the mother culture of Mesoamerica because artistic and cultural symbols and motifs of their civilization show up again in most later cultures of this area. In 900 BCE, the Olmec capital near the modern city of San Lorenzo had a thousand people. Then, for some reason, it was abandoned. The Olmecs built a new capital at modern-day La Venta. Then around 400 BCE, it, too, collapsed, and the Olmecs disappeared. No one knows where they went.

In Oaxaca, the Zapotecs ruled a large area from their capital at Monte Alban. They flourished for well over five hundred years, and then they abandoned their cities. Why? No one really knows. The Maya rose to grandeur in what is now Guatemala, but in the second century their society collapsed. So they migrated a bit north, and by the sixth century they had built cities such as Uxmal and Tikal around enormous pyramids. In the eighth century, for some reason, they abandoned those great cities and moved farther north to the Yucatán Peninsula. There they built Chichén Itzá, one of the most impressive pre-Columbian cities of the Americas; but by the twelfth century that too had fallen into ruins. The Aztec of Central Mexico were still on the rise in the sixteenth century when the Spanish arrived; so there's no telling when or if their cities would have been abandoned too.

Most striking of all was Teotihuacan in Central Mexico, the biggest ancient city of the Americas, born about a century before the Common Era. By the year 400, it had as many as two hundred thousand inhabitants, which made it perhaps the fifth biggest metropolis on the planet in its day. Teotihuacan anchored a trade web extending from the Pacific

Ocean in the west to the Gulf of Mexico in the east to the heart of Central America in the south. Was it an empire in the same sense as Persia? There's no way to know. Did it have a postal system and a civil service, like China? We don't know. Were its rulers tribal chieftains? Kings? Priests? Unknown, unknown. Who built the city, what language did they speak, what did they even look like? None of this is known.

One of the few things we do know for sure about Teotihuacan is that its name was not Teotihuacan. That name means "city of the gods," and it's what the Aztecs called the place centuries later when they stumbled across its deserted ruins—for like so many other great Mesoamerican urban centers, this city was flourishing and then it wasn't. Sometime between 600 and 650 CE—yes, right around the time that Islam was born and the Sui emperors were rebuilding China and Pope Gregory was defining Christendom—the core of Teotihuacan was burned. No one knows why or by whom. Probably it started with a drought followed by famine followed by revolutions, invasions, and wars. At least, that's the accepted theory. The common people went on living in the slums and suburbs of the former metropolis for a while, but eventually they drifted away too.

Cities rose and fell in Mesoamerica, but culture had a remarkable continuity. The Olmecs played a game with a rubber ball in which the losers were decapitated. The Maya played a similar game two thousand years later in the Yucatán Peninsula, hundreds of miles away. Feathered serpents populated Olmec art. Feathered serpents symbolized the god Quetzalcoatl for the Toltecs fifteen hundred years later. The Olmecs pictured their god of the underworld as a jaguar. Jaguars showed up in the art of many later Mesoamerican cultures. Was this because the environment was simply teeming with jaguars? That's not really an explanation. The environment was teeming with many kinds of animals. Why did the jaguar become so iconic?

Whatever the original reason, the jaguar was picked early, and so it held on. That's how it goes with narratives. Once a kernel forms, new kernels adhere to it, because once a framework has coalesced, it shapes the judgments and values of people living within it: once "beautiful" has been established, people strive to make what "everyone knows" to be beautiful, not what "everybody knows" to be ugly, even though beautiful and ugly have no objective existence separate from the humans doing the "knowing." A cultural framework becomes a screening device that allows a narrative to continue inventing itself in its own image. The continuity of culture here suggests that all of Mesoamerica was interlaced with travel and interaction: it must have been one big intercommunicative zone—and thus one big constellation of people and ideas.

In the global East, the friction between pastoral nomads and urban civilizations generated some of history's key dramas. In the Americas, it seems, no such dramas took place. The Americas had grasslands too, but the hunter-gatherers who lived there never developed into pastoral nomadic civilizations capable of taking on the big urban powers. Instead, they continued to refine their hunting-and-gathering way of life. The reason is simple: North America had no animals that could be domesticated. It had no sheep, no goats, no cows, nothing that could be herded. It's true that millions of bison roamed the great plains, but for some reason, these ill-tempered animals can't be tamed, and when you can't domesticate a grouchy two-ton animal with horns, you'd better not try to milk it. Indigenous Americans developed ways to stampede these beasts over cliffs and then swarm in and kill them for their meat, but that's not herding, it's hunting.

Furthermore, the Americas lacked the animals that people of the global East used to transport themselves and their cargo. No horses existed here, which made a huge difference. There were no oxen, donkeys, camels, or mules, either. The Andes area did have lamas, which are in the camel family, but their slender legs make them unfit for carrying or dragging really heavy burdens or loads.

In the global East, the wheel rose to importance because wheels could be fitted to carts, which could be loaded with cargo and then dragged by big, powerful beasts. Once wheels were a crucial part of everyday life, people were moved to explore what other uses could be made of a circular artifact. In the Americas, without animals to pull heavy carts, there was no point in perfecting the wheel. It's not that the wheel was not invented. Americans made things that were round—calendars, for example, and some children's toys—but they didn't develop the potential of circle-shaped things as machine parts.

Information and ideas tend to spread throughout any social pool as people talk to people. The Eastern and Western Hemispheres, however, had been two separate pools ever since the land bridge vanished. For thousands and perhaps tens of thousands of years, cultural ripple effects could spread throughout each one, but not from one to the other. Great world historical monads no doubt existed in the Americas and no doubt affected one another in numerous ways, but east and west knew nothing of each other. That would change, however, a few centuries later. And in those centuries, something happened in the Eastern Hemisphere: the cultural center of gravity shifted in Eurasia, from the worlds east of the Mediterranean Sea to those in the west. The reasons were complex, the results apocalyptic.

PART III

The Table Tilts

By the year 1000, East Asian cultures from the Mediterranean Sea to the Pacific shores of China could look back on centuries of cultural power, creativity, and wealth. Europe was poor but stable and incurious, as it had been for centuries. Then the balance shifted. Ripple effects traveling through Eurasia interwove, until all the worlds of this continent were the various theaters of one big story. In this era, nomad warriors erupted out of the Eurasian steppes, two vast world historical narratives locked horns, and pandemic disease laid waste to vast swaths of humanity. Amid this tumult, ideas, inventions, technologies, and goods went sliding from East Asia into Western Europe. There, a powerful new narrative dissolved the feudal framework of Christendom, gave rise to science, and sent mariners hungrily out to sea in search of precious goods they now knew existed in East Asia. Meanwhile, in the East, an opposite narrative formed, an impulse to resume the interrupted histories of the glorious past. This narrative gave rise to czarist Russia, the gunpowder empires of Islam, and the Ming dynasty of China. The entire Eastern Hemisphere was interconnected now, but this hemisphere still knew nothing of the Americas, where powerful empires had flourished in the past and where new ones were rising now. These many currents were converging toward an apocalyptic moment.

Out of the North

(850 CE to 1200 CE)

For the several centuries flanking the year 800, Europe snuggled in the dark warmth of Catholic feudalism. Everybody knew their neighbors; strangers were rarely seen. Life was sparse, but life was stable: nothing much changed from decade to decade, generation to generation. In that same period, the worlds east of the Mediterranean were living in the bright ages, bursting with vitality, webbed with traffic. There in the east, ideas, inventions, accomplishments, and technologies had been piling up and piling up for centuries.

But then...

Then something happened. As if a great table had tilted, ideas, inventions, artistic inspirations, and technologies, not to mention goods and products, went sliding from East to West. They slid from the Chinese and Indian and Islamic world into Western Europe. Why did this happen? What made the table tilt?

No single answer will do; history is never about single answers, but here is an interesting thing. If you're looking at the world from the Chinese point of view, you find that this was a period of instability for the Middle Kingdom. The Chinese had long been mustered against the pastoral nomads of the north, and in this period the nomads started to make headway. If you switch your focus to India, you know that sometime in this period, Islamic armies began pushing down through Afghanistan, into the subcontinent, launching a dramatic struggle between two great world historical narratives, a struggle that remains unresolved to this day. If your world historical view puts Europe at the center, you find that late in this period, a hugely consequential clash broke out between Christian armies from Europe and Muslim Turks in control of the Levantine coast.

At first glance, these might seem like entirely separate dramas that happened to be happening around the same time. After all they were happening in different theaters, widely separated from one another. China! India! Asia Minor! Palestine! France! How disparate can locations be?

Take a broader look, though. These weren't a bunch of different stories unfolding in a bunch of different worlds. It only looks that way if you think of history as the story of what happened in urban civilizations. If you include the pastoral nomads as part of the single human story, then all these dramas were happening in one region of the world, the long perimeter of the Central Eurasian Steppes. They all involved tribes who had originated as pastoral nomads in those steppes. Clearly, *something* was happening up there, but what was it?

Improbable as it might seem, the roots of this story trace back to Scandinavia, where the pagan Norse people lived. The Norse were distantly

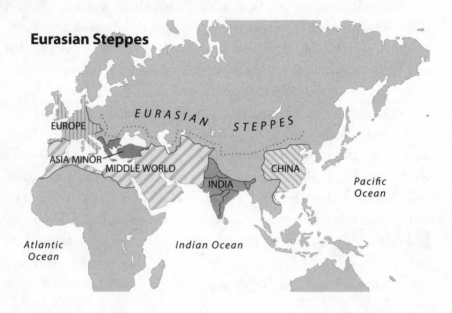

Eurasian Steppes

EUROPE

EURASIAN STEPPES

ASIA MINOR

MIDDLE WORLD

CHINA

INDIA

Pacific Ocean

Atlantic Ocean

Indian Ocean

related to the Germanic tribes infiltrating Rome. They lived in the harsh north because they were among the last to settle in Europe. The hardest land to work was the only land left for latecomers. The Norse scratched out a living as best they could, hunting, fishing, and farming.

Around the time that Christendom was coalescing in the south, the European climate went through some small fluctuations, when the temperature rose or fell by one or two degrees centigrade. These fluctuations weren't enough to make much noticeable difference in the south, but in the far north, at the extreme edges of human habitation, even such slight degree changes had outsized effects: people living *on* the edge went *over* the edge. When temperatures dropped, crop yields shrank, and since older established men monopolized the good farmland, younger men just coming into adulthood formed gangs, built boats, and went out into the great wide world to make a living plundering strangers—and were honored at home for doing this successfully. A slight rise in temperature could cause trouble too, for it melted ice, flooding farmlands, and again the young bucks were inspired to go out a-plundering. From the eighth to the eleventh centuries, the environment worked Scandinavia like a bellows. It let the population grow, then clamped down and blew out boatloads of predatory warriors with nothing to lose. Some two hundred thousand people streamed out of this area over several centuries, mostly in groups of a few dozen at a time. Some headed into Western Europe, some went south toward the Black Sea, returning to Scandinavia between raids.

The Scandinavians who ravaged Western Europe are remembered as the Vikings. The name derives from the old Norse word *vik* meaning "fjord"—they were the people who came from the land of fjords up north. They hit England and the coast of France and rowed far up rivers and sacked castles and looted monasteries. The English called them the Danes, and the French called them the Normands ("north men"). Eventually, the Normands settled on the coast of France, an area that was thenceforth known as Normandy. Some of the Danes established footholds in the British Isles among the Anglo-Saxons already living there. In 1066, the Normans invaded England, and set themselves up as an aristocracy ruling over the Anglo-Saxons. Over time, these groups bleshed to form the England that we know. Other Vikings mingled with the Franks, and where this interaction occurred, France emerged. Others kept going south, into the Mediterranean, and set up kingdoms in southern Italy and on the North African coast.

These Vikings gradually became Catholic Christians. Their values, myths, stories, and ideas bleshed with the Germanized, Christianized Roman-Greek culture already in place. In this process, the Viking ingredients went through some predictable modifications. For example, the people of the north revered certain trees and decorated them in dead of winter as pagan emblems of enduring life. The Catholic world absorbed this as the custom of the Christmas tree. The Norse believed in figures they called elves, man-sized, rather menacing creatures with supernatural powers. These became ever smaller and cuter and more harmless as the Vikings became Christianized.

The chief of the elves sometimes put coal into stockings hung by the fire as a grim warning to people who had transgressed of dire punishment to come. This top elf devolved into a jolly fat man who still put a lump of coal in the occasional stocking in a good-humored way but mostly rewarded good (children) with presents on Christ's birthday. Europe held onto the notion that these elements came from the extreme north. To this day, Santa Claus lives at the North Pole (not far from Superman's Fortress of Solitude, no doubt). With Viking elements kneaded into it, Europe's Germanized, Christianized Greco-Roman civilization became the starter dough for what is now commonly called the West.

THE RUS AND THE TURKS

Meanwhile, another half of the same story was playing out on the other side of Scandinavia, for while some of the warrior bands out of Scandinavia headed west, others headed east. The ones that went east generally called themselves the Rus. They found the headwaters of mighty rivers such as the Dnieper and the Volga and rode them south toward the Black Sea. When they came to rapids or falls, they simply carried their longboats to the next navigable stretch of water and kept going. Along the way, these rough warriors passed through forests inhabited by Slavic tribes, subsistence farmers who lived in small autonomous villages. The Rus sacked their villages, took whatever food and other goods they could find, and kept a-going, just as the Vikings were doing in Western Europe.

The Rus discovered what many another marauder had learned. Marauding was not an efficient way to get anything in particular. If you sacked a castle, you got whatever happened to be in the castle. If the particular thing you wanted was a toothbrush, you might not get one this way. What you had to do was grab anything you could sell for money and then use the money to buy what you wanted in the next good market. Thus did pirates and plunderers morph into traders.

Gold and silver were the best plunder because they were money already. In the west, the Vikings found plenty of those metals in the monasteries and churches in the form of sacred relics and religious artifacts that could be melted down. But the Slavic villagers had no such artifacts and no precious metals. They were subsistence farmers who had only the food they grew and the goods they made. So, the Rus captured and sold the villagers themselves, as slaves, to buyers in the south, thus turning people into money. Indeed, the word *slave* derives from Slav, a gloomy testament to the volume of this commerce after the ninth century or so. Some were sold to the Byzantines, but most were sold to traders from the Islamic world. There, Slavic slaves mostly ended up as household servants and sexual chattel.

The Rus who came down the rivers of eastern Europe were mostly men, and you can bet they kept some of the captured Slavic women for themselves. So the children of the Rus were often born of Slavic mothers and grew up connected to their mothers' culture, speaking Slavic languages. Within a few generations, the Rus had vanished into a Slavic-speaking local aristocracy without much connection to their distant cousins in Scandinavia. These Slavic aristocrats called themselves

Russians, and they were no longer subsistence farmers but well-armed and aggressive warriors.

The Russians aspired to conquer Constantinople, but that was like fleas aspiring to bring down an elephant. Constantinople was the world's most formidably fortified city, protected by water, walls, wealth, and all the weapons gold could buy. So some of the Russians went to work for the Byzantines as elite troops called the Varangian Guard. Thanks to this contact, the Russian elite gradually converted to Christianity. They joined the Greek Orthodox Church, and willingly or not, their subjects followed suit. A Byzantine missionary named Cyril created a script for the Russians, and with the Bible as their gateway book, these former pagans became a literate society, just as the Goths had done earlier, in Western Europe.

The Russians proved to be energetic commercial folks who gladly dealt in cash. The most important form of cash at this point was silver. The richest rivers of silver were flowing through Dar-ul-Islam. The Russians' realm bordered on Muslim markets all along the Black and Caspian Seas. From the Muslim world, therefore, silver streamed up through Russian networks into Scandinavia and from there seeped back into the economic circulatory system of northern Europe—with profound consequences, as we shall see.

Meanwhile, the Russians were continuing to push into the Pontic steppe. They came up against the Khazars, a Turkish tribe whose elite had converted to Judaism. The Russians wiped them out. The Khazars had controlled a rich trade in commodities from the northern forests. The Russians took control of that flow now. And kept going. Soon, they were skirmishing with the nomadic warriors of the Central Asian grasslands. It wasn't a cakewalk. The Russians were tough, but so were the nomads. The frontier between them became a zone of constant friction. The Russian advance slowed to a crawl, but they did keep advancing, and they kept consolidating their rule as they advanced. Russian fiefs hardened into Russian principalities, which eventually coalesced into one single powerful and wealthy Russian kingdom, headquartered at Kiev.

In previous centuries waves of tribal nomads had streamed west from Central Asia, through the gap between the Ural Mountains and the

Ripple Effects Out of Scandinavia, 8th–11th centuries

Black Sea, into Europe. The Avars had come this way, the Magyars, the Scythians, the Huns, and, before them all, the Indo-Europeans, who-ever they were—but the Russian state plugged the corridor. Not only did they block further migrations from the steppes, but they kept pushing their blockade east, crowding the pastoral nomads of Central Asia. The nomads pushed back, but when it was easier to raid in other directions, they weren't picky; they raided in other directions. The rise of Russia compressed the Central Asian grasslands, setting off ripple effects that were felt across thousands of miles of territory.

In the 900s, the jostling in Central Asia led a proto-Mongol people called the Khitans to push against the borders of China. They built themselves a kingdom right there on the frontier. The nerve! The Song were just then consolidating their power internally, and now they had to commit mili-tary resources to their northeastern border. Then, things got even more dicey. Out of the Siberian heartland came the Jurchens. They built a kingdom right next to the Khitans, and they too started chewing their way into Song dynasty China. They, in fact, expanded right into the Huang He valley. They in fact even dared to claim they had received the mandate of heaven and now *were* the Chinese, the legitimate heirs of the Tang and Han dynasties. The Song imperials begged to disagree and tried to block them but failed and had to give ground and then more ground, until at last the Song had relinquished their holdings in the north. They finally regrouped in the Yangtze River valley, and there they built a new capital and went on flourishing for a while as the brilliant Southern Song dynasty. But they had lost the original heartland of Chinese civilization, the Huang He valley where this culture was born, and although they didn't know it, much worse was yet to come.

The heart of the Eurasian steppes bordered on Dar-ul-Islam. By now this had dissolved into many separate Muslim states paying lip service to a "universal" caliphate that existed, for the most part, as an honorific title, nothing more. The rulers of these many kingdoms were constantly battling Turkish nomads crossing their borders to raid villages. When they captured Turkish boys in battle, they hauled the lads back to their capitals to be slaves. Unlike the lowly Slavs, these boys were trained in the arts of war. When they grew up, they were used as elite bodyguards or crack frontline troops against the nomads. Somehow, their royal masters imagined that these boys would be as loyal to them as sons to fathers. Somehow, it never quite worked out that way. Like the Praetorian Guard in Rome, the Turkish slave-soldiers tended to topple their owners and take over.

As soon as they did, they faced the same problem as their former masters: more pastoral nomadic invaders coming out of the steppes. It didn't matter that the new raiders were also Turkish. Rulers had to keep out raiders, or they'd be goners themselves. Strangely enough, the new rulers went about this in the same way as the old rulers. They captured nomad boys in battle and trained them into scary-tough slave-soldiers—who did just what one might expect. They overthrew their masters and seized power. The Turks thus chewed their way into the Muslim world from both within and without.

As they came into the Islamic world, the Turks converted to Islam, just as the Germans had converted to Roman Christianity in the West. But what these new Turkish Muslims favored was a rough-and-ready warriors' version of Islam. The subtle similarities between Greek philosophy and Islamic theology made them yawn. These warlords leaned more toward Islam as a book of rules and a corps of experts to interpret those rules, and a cadre of armed officials to enforce them.

By roughly 1000 CE, Turks had emerged as the military-political elite of the Islamic world. Arabs held onto religious doctrine, theology, law, and education throughout this world. Persian culture still provided most of the philosophers, scholars, scribes, scientists, and administrators. Turkish, Arab, and Persian strands interwove to form a new Islamic fabric, rather different from that of the original Arab-dominated caliphates. The cosmopolitan curiosity of the past, which had led Muslim intellectuals to the edge of science, began to wane. What the disruptions fueled instead was theology, mysticism, poetry—and war.

One of the new Turkish rulers, Sultan Mahmud of Afghanistan, invaded India seventeen times to sack temples and haul treasures back to his capital city of Ghazni. Sultan Mahmud claimed to be serving God with his Indian forays, for he was destroying pagan idols just as Messenger Muhammad and his companions had done. And after Sultan Mahmud's campaigns, Turkish rulers and their Afghan tribal allies made a habit of raiding India. Eventually, some of these invaders established a permanent seat of political power in the city of Delhi, on the banks of the Ganges River, and from there ruled a sultanate that waxed and waned in size but was sometimes bigger than Germany, France, and England combined. The Turks were always, however, a militant Muslim minority trying to rule an overwhelmingly more numerous native Hindu majority. From this time forward, two narratives occupied the same geographical space and stubbornly refused to blesh, perhaps because their core doctrines were mutually exclusive.

Meanwhile, on the heels of the Ghaznavids, out of the steppes came yet another wave of invaders: the Seljuk Turks. These warrior tribes headed west instead of east. They conquered all that is now Iran and swept through Asia Minor. In 1071, at the Battle of Manzikert, they stomped the Byzantine army and marched south to conquer what Christians were calling the Holy Lands, the strip of fertile territory along the eastern shores of the Mediterranean Sea. These conquests triggered the immense event known as the Crusades.

The humbling of the Song, the Turkification of the Islamic world, the Afghan expansion into northern India, the Crusades—these dramas loom large in the world historical narratives of China, India, the Islamic world, and Europe. From the panoramic point of view, however, they look like a single interwoven drama that began in northern Europe, rippled through the Asian steppes, created disruptions in the urban civilizations along the whole perimeter of that region, and resulted finally in that great tilting of the table that shifted the balance of cultural power from the Eurasian east to the Eurasian west. The next five centuries saw this story continue to unfold across a vast swath of planet Earth.

12

Europe on the Rise
(800 CE to 1300 CE)

J ust before that great tilting of the table, Europe was a patchwork quilt of feudal estates sewn together by the Roman Catholic narrative. Back then, most Europeans were peasants, and most of those peasants were serfs. They managed to produce just enough food for themselves, their lords, and the functionaries of the church. They had little time and energy left over for producing a surplus of any kind, whether of food or of manufactured goods.

In the ninth century, however, very slowly, all but imperceptibly, things began to change. Peasants had been making small improvements in their tools and methods, and these accumulated toward a tipping point. The heavy plow came into use: it could sink into the moist clay soil of the forested north and cut through the roots that riddled it. The land up north was harder to till than the sandy soil of the south but more fertile if one could but work it. Peasants added to their plows a side plank that turned the soil as the plowshare cut its furrow, thus combining two arduous steps into one. European peasants also perfected a collar that let them yoke horses to their plows instead of oxen. Since horses move faster, they could plow more land in less time.

Peasants had traditionally left half their land fallow each year to let the soil rest and recover. But they discovered at some point that soil did just fine if it rested every third year. So peasants started planting two-thirds of their land each year instead of half. Do the math and you find that just like that, boom, they had 20 percent more land to farm—with no extra effort or investment!

More land to work, more land plowed in fewer hours—what does it mean? It means better-fed people with more spare time. Peasants could make more of the artifacts they were already making for their own daily use—fabrics, garments, flatware, pots, whatever. They took the surplus to local crossroads on specified occasions to trade with peasants from other manors.

As crossroads markets prospered, some became regular events. Over the centuries, some of those developed into permanent trading hubs, which eventually clotted into towns. And a few of those towns started hosting seasonal fairs that drew plenty of would-be traders. Most were locals, but gradually merchants started coming from farther afield. With many vendors gathered in the same place for one or more weeks, people could make deals with other people at the fair. A merchant might come in with a cartful of linen, make a deal to trade some of it for a quantity of salt, and then trade the salt for a bunch of swords and some bags of barley—during this process, the physical goods didn't have to move with each trade. As the deal makers were all in the same place, they only had to keep track of their agreements. When the fair ended, the merchants could bustle around reconciling their records down to a bottom line and then finally take possession of the goods they had ended up with. A guy who came in with a wagonload of cloth might come out with a wagon-load of grain, even though in the course of the fair he might have traded cloth for shoes, for hats, for God only knows what else.

In fact, these fairs eventually provided a venue where merchants might come with no concrete goods at all, just promises: a load of fertilizer now for ten wagonloads of barley in six months. An agreement by one party to pay another party a set price at some future time for a set quantity of a product that didn't yet exist allowed both parties to do business in accordance with a financially predictable future. And that meant more business got done because business is mostly about the future, not about today.

By the eleventh century, the Viking onslaughts were dying down, and the European world was starting to absorb the Vikings; by then, in their many years of sacking monasteries and melting down treasures, the Vikings had put a lot of gold and silver back into circulation as currency. Meanwhile, their Russian cousins were channeling silver back into Europe from the Islamic world. Hard money greased the wheels of trade. Trade fed rising productivity. The European economy picked up momentum.

Back when virtually all Europeans lived on feudal manors, they almost all lived harsh lives, but at least all had a place to live, a job to do, a social constellation to be a part of and thus a way for their lives to be meaningful. If fewer people could produce all the food needed to keep the whole society fed, some number of people were going to be surplus labor, which is to say: they'd be out of work. And indeed, some feudal lords discovered that it was cheaper to hire seasonal workers and discharge them for the year at the end of each season, when the work was done. That way, they didn't have to support unpaid serfs year-round.

Even as Europe's productivity increased, therefore, so did the number of displaced people. Homeless beggars roamed the landscape, robbing travelers and hunting game on forested manor lands. Think Robin Hood and his merry band, except without the "merry" part. The poor crowded the roads, slept under bushes, and died where they lay down, unmarked and unknown. Even comfortably settled folks were exposed routinely to this uptick of misery.

As one response to these conditions, the Catholic constellation of medieval Europe generated a new religious vocation: mendicant friars. These devouts were associated with monastic orders, but they lived on the road instead of in monasteries; they were itinerant spiritual devotees who depended on Christian charity for survival. This institution sopped up some of the excess beggars while helping steep society even more thoroughly in the Catholic narrative. If the Church of Rome was the heart and lungs of Catholic Europe, and the monasteries were its veins and arteries, the mendicant friars operated as capillaries, channeling a crude salvation to souls at the most local level.

CHRISTENDOM

By 1000 CE, Europeans between the Baltics and the Atlantic were forming a consciousness of themselves as some single entity: the term *Christendom* came increasingly into use, and it didn't just mean all Christians. There were Christians in the world who were not part of Christendom. There were the Nestorian Christians of the Persian world, for example, and the Coptic Christians of Egypt, and many others.

For that matter, even Byzantine Christians were not exactly part of Christendom. The Christians of the west were starting to see those of the east as...well...sort of different. They were Christians, to be sure, but...well...different. Questions had arisen about how the Mass should be said, whether to use religious images in worship, what exact phrase to use during the crucial rite known as the Eucharist, and what exactly happened during that rite. And most of all, Byzantine churches performed the Mass in Greek, Western European churches in Latin.

All of these details added up to a dividing line. In 1054, the arguments came to a head when the bishops of Rome and Constantinople (known respectively as the pope and the patriarch) excommunicated each other. This showdown revealed something crucial: both men could not *possibly* have the authority to excommunicate. It had to be one or the other. Therefore, the churches split, and after that, although Christians on both sides of the line still saw the others as Christians, they also each saw the other as tainted with otherness. The otherness of this other helped reinforce Western Europeans' sense of *their* Christianity as a special bond.

With friars, beggars, peddlers, and traders wandering through all the time, people heard news and stories of distant places. The idea of travel grew less outlandish. Pilgrimage fit right into the dominant narrative as a form of tourism. Visiting a shrine was like going to church, only more so. Certain monasteries possessed items of religious significance that people could see or even touch: a bit of a saint's cloak, a lock of a martyr's hair, a sliver of the true cross.

The worthiest pilgrimage sites were, of course, in the Holy Lands where Christ himself had walked. For a native of Western Europe, however, a pilgrimage to the Holy Lands was an arduous journey fraught with dangers. Getting there might take months. And when they arrived, what did they find? The holy sites were all in the hands of heathens, horrible in their otherness. It was then that a story long gathering force in Europe intersected with another story long gathering force in the Middle World. Muslim Turks expanding out of Central Asia had come to rule an area just beginning to be heavily visited by Western European Christians. The Turks were not so much hostile to the Christians as disdainful. To the Muslim Turks, these folks from Europe were simple brutes clinging to a superseded revelation because they didn't know any better. Someday, they'd wake up and join the community, but until then, why not soak them for all the silver in their pockets? Christian pilgrims found they had to pay exorbitant fees, wait in tedious lines, endure contempt, and sometimes suffer outright abuse—and from whom? Ignorant heathens headed for hell who had the audacity to consider themselves (of all things!) superior. The pilgrims went home with many a resentful horror story to tell.

What they went back to was a world churning with change. The European custom of primogeniture mandated that the entirety of a noble's land be inherited by his eldest son. This meant that Europe had a growing surplus of landless noble younger sons with no outlet for their ambitions. The only honorable vocations for men of this class were owning land and making war. Earlier, when Europe was under siege from every side, younger sons of the nobility had plenty of war to keep them busy and fulfilled. In that age, European culture had spawned a particular technological specimen of warrior: the knight in metal armor. Now, with the invasions waning and peace on the rise, the knights of Europe were all dressed up with nowhere to go. Meanwhile, as big fish swallowed little fish, feudal manors were coalescing into larger, fewer duchies and kingdoms.

In short, European Christendom was a boiling cauldron of mendicant religious fanatics, war-hungry landless knights, ever-more-ambitious dukes and kings, a powerful and monolithic church, and burgeoning quantities of money with which great enterprises could be funded. All Christendom needed now was a great enterprise to fund.

One day in 1095, leading members of all the main sectors of Christian European society came together for a singular event. Pope Urban II, head of the universal church, visited Clermont (in present-day France) where one of Europe's most important monasteries was located. There, he delivered an impassioned message to an audience that included eminent clergymen as well as the highest paragons of Christendom's military aristocracy, the Frankish knights. The pope told his audience of a letter he'd received from Emperor Alexis of Constantinople: the Byzantine Empire was under attack from heathens. The Turks were marching on Constantinople, and if they took that city, they'd be coming for Rome next. Someone had to do something. The pope called on the knights of Christendom to head east as crusaders—warriors for the cross—and take holy Jerusalem back from those heathens.

As the pope delivered his message at Clermont, charismatic friars such as Peter the Hermit and his lieutenant Walter the Penniless were preaching the same message to the masses in nearby towns. A thrill ran through Christendom at the prospect of uniting as one to achieve a single apocalyptic goal: recover the Holy Lands!

The mendicants were the first to attempt it. Walter the Penniless and Peter the Hermit led a motley mob of beggars and unemployed townsfolk east to Asia Minor, where bemused Seljuk warriors casually wiped them out. Later that year, however, the European knights came, the tanks of their time: enormous sword-wielding hunks of metal and meat, hard to kill or even stop. The knights of Europe devastated coastal cities and at last took Jerusalem. They ended up establishing four crusader kingdoms on the eastern Mediterranean seaboard.

From then on, Europeans who went east had places to land, cities ruled by Christians, where they would be safe when they arrived and where they would find inns that welcomed Christians and where increasingly they might make contact with people who knew people who knew their people back home.

Whether they went as pilgrims, crusaders, or mere adventurers, travelers to the east found bazaars brimming with goods that would fetch a fine price back home, especially exotic fabrics and spices, by which I mean "spices" in the larger sense—not just flavor enhancers but preservatives, potions, and all the rest. In Europe, spices had been so rare, people hoarded them like gold. The Venerable Bede, a famous ninth-century scholar, specified in his will how his pepper should be divided among his heirs. Sugar was so precious, the Romans treated it as a medicine, not as a cooking ingredient. As for fabrics, a few noble ladies might have had a garment or two made of silk, but for the herd, silk was the stuff of dreams. And if you've ever worn flax underwear under a suit of armor, you can understand why European knights appreciated cotton. (Not that I myself have, but I can imagine.)

Once the crusader kingdoms were in place, the Levant became the eastern edge of Europe's rising market system. As the Crusades dragged on, western merchants forged prickly business links with Muslim merchants. Cities in the Balkans battened on traffic headed to the holy places by land. Cities on the Italian coast grew rich from ferrying Europeans to those destinations by sea. Merchants, pilgrims, and crusaders streaming to the Levant brushed elbows with other Europeans who, despite some differences, inhabited their same world historical narrative, thereby reinforcing a sense of shared identity.

Most of the ships bound for the Holy Lands embarked from Venice, Genoa, or Pisa. Since these cities were situated right between the bazaars of the east and the buyers of the west, they quickly took control of the growing east-west trade and developed into mighty Mediterranean seafaring powers. And in scrabbling with one another for supremacy, they built up their naval technology, which made them ever mightier and mightier.

The greatest stream of pilgrims, merchants, and crusaders flowed through Venice. These travelers came with all sorts of coins. Venetian goldsmiths found they could make a profit selling people precious metal in exchange for their coins and then selling the local coins back to travelers going the other way in exchange for silver or gold.

The money-exchanging business required calculating the value of one coin versus another: How many of this duke's coin equaled how many of that duke's? And how much of either coin was worth how much gold?

Amateurs could lose their shirts trying to make such calculations. Venetian goldsmiths, however, handled transactions of this type routinely, so they developed the relevant expertise. They set up benches outside their shops to do business. The Italian word for bench is *banque*, so these guys were called banquers. Today, we call them bankers.

As time went on, these businessmen discovered they could make a tidy profit offering safe storage places for precious metal (and gems and such) until such time as the owner returned from wherever. The banker would accept some designated quantity of precious metal and give the person a signed note certifying his deposit. When that person came back later, from the Holy Lands say, he could exchange the signed note for the previously deposited gold—less a fee for the service, of course.

Then again, people with gold on deposit sometimes got in trouble on their journeys and signed their note over to someone else as a form of payment. Honorable bankers paid whoever presented a note that bore their signature, in part because bankers who wouldn't honor their own signatures probably didn't stay in business long. In fact, there was no theoretical limit to how many times a banker's note might change hands before it was presented to the banker for a withdrawal. In fact, a well-regarded banker's note might go on circulating indefinitely as if it *were* the specified quantity of gold. In fact, it might never come back; it might simply turn into money, a new kind of money: a banknote. And so a new factor came into the imaginary world constructed and shared by Western Europeans of Christendom.

Bankers discovered that they could lend gold out for a short term while its owner was gone. As long as the gold came back before its owner, no harm was done, and the banker would make a bit of money by charging a fee for the short-term use of that gold. Busy bankers found they always had so much gold and silver in their vaults, awaiting their owners' return, that the actual gold never had to move. They could make loans by offering signed notes redeemable for some set quantity of gold upon presentation: as long as the loans were repaid on time, the people whose gold was on deposit never suffered any inconvenience. They might not even know that their gold had ever been loaned out—on paper (or, to be scrupulously accurate, on vellum at this point, or on parchment). Thus did a whole new way to earn a living emerge in Crusades-era Italy.

The most consequential contributions to this new field may have come from Leonardo of Pisa, remembered now by the nickname Fibonacci. In his travels around the Mediterranean, this young mathematician encountered business methods common to the Muslim world. In 1202 he published the book *Liber Abaci* (Book of Calculation) about Arabic mathematics (which was, actually, Indian mathematics). It opens with the fateful words: "The nine Indian figures are: 9 8 7 6 5 4 3 2 1. With these nine figures, and with the sign o…any number whatsoever is written." Bankers quickly recognized how much easier it was to multiply 8,976 by 125 using the long division algorithm of the Muslim world than it was to multiply MMMCMLXXVI by CXXIV. Arabic numerals and arithmetical calculations used in Dar-ul-Islam—place value, decimals, long division algorithms, algebra, and much more—quickly spread through Europe, along with various business methods of the east: double-entry bookkeeping, for example, and credit instruments (instead of cash) in business transactions, all of which required sophisticated accounting. European business was never the same.

Pilgrims heading for the Holy Lands faced one knotty problem: What form of money to carry? Local coins would not be accepted far from home. Gold and silver were negotiable everywhere, but for that very reason, they were of interest to bandits and thugs everywhere. Pilgrims could travel in groups and hire mercenaries to protect their precious metal, but what was to stop mercenary bodyguards from killing their clients and pocketing their valuables as soon as they got a few miles from home?

The church created a new institution to help solve this problem: military-religious orders became part of the feudal Catholic constellation. Members of such orders were exempt from taxes and automatically absolved of sin for any violence they might commit in defense of the faith. Being under monastic orders, these warriors took vows of poverty and chastity and lived sparse lives. Two of them, the Hospitallers and the Teutonic Knights, specialized in providing medical services. A third group, the Knights Templar, undertook to safeguard pilgrims and their valuables on the way to and from the Holy Lands. Christians could trust these guys not to kill them for their money because these were holy men—Christian monks.

Eventually, the Templars began moving money back and forth as a stand-alone financial service. Christians in the Holy Lands who needed funds from home or had wealth they wanted to send back called on the Templars. They could trust the Templars because the church itself guaranteed their honesty. The Templars began moving so much money in both directions that they found they didn't have to move any actual money at all. When people gave them money to transmit to some distant spot, they could simply send a note to the other office, specifying a sum to be paid out of the accumulated stockpile of wealth at that end. The money could not be stolen by thieves because nothing was moving except information. The Templars' work put them in a position to realize something that very few Europeans understood at the time: money was not actually a thing. Money was information. It all came down to accounting. Once in possession of this arcane secret, the Knights Templar began to morph into the world's first international bankers.

The First Crusade gained Jerusalem for the Christians. The Second Crusade confirmed the Christian presence in the Levant. The Third Crusade became the stuff of legends, featuring an epic duel between two leaders famous for their supposed generosity and civility. Saladin was the sultan of Egypt, Richard the Lion-hearted was the king of England. These combatants may have been perfect gentlemen, but their duel didn't end in a draw. It ended with a treaty that ceded Jerusalem back to the Muslims, and Jerusalem never came back into Christian hands. Thus ended the first phase of the Crusades.

The loss of Jerusalem stirred up agitation in Europe for a Fourth Crusade, but by this time, the picture had grown muddier. Commercial considerations had started to complicate the religious idealism of the Crusades. And what's more, the Western European knights didn't feel much kinship with the Greek-speaking Orthodox Christians they had (theoretically) come to save.

The Byzantine capital had long been one of the world's most impregnable cities, surrounded on three sides by water and on the fourth by a series of immense walls, but all those impregnable defenses were irrelevant when the knights of the Fourth Crusade came knocking because these guys were not the enemy. These were fellow Christians come to lend aid. Right? For them, surely, the doors could be opened wide. Right?

The members of the Fourth Crusade never made it to the Holy Lands. In 1204, they ran amok in Constantinople, ripped up the city, looted the churches, took whatever silver and gold they could find, deposed the Byzantine emperor, and declared Constantinople the capital of their own (short-lived) Latin Empire. This marked the final schism between the Greek-speaking Christian empire of the east and the successors of the Roman Empire in the west.

13

The Nomads' Last Roar
(1215 CE to 1400 CE)

J ust as the Fourth Crusaders were sacking Constantinople, a whole new force was coalescing on the other side of the Muslim world. Its eruption out of Central Asia represented the climax of a drama that had begun long before the rise of the Xia Dynasty or the fall of Babylon. This drama was the oft-contentious encounter between the pastoral nomads of northern Eurasia and the agrarian-urban civilizations of the Eurasian south, and now this drama was coming to a head.

It was in the thirteenth century that the Mongols led pastoral nomadic civilization to its zenith of power. Their domination lasted a century at most, but in that brief moment, the Mongols had a profound impact on the world and especially in completing that "tilting of the table" under discussion here.

Before their surge, the Mongols had gone pretty much unnoticed by the world at large. They were numerous, motley, autonomous clans, living in tents, riding hardy little ponies, herding huge flocks of sheep and goats, and skirmishing among themselves: typical, old-fashioned pastoral nomads of the central Asian steppes.

Then in 1167 a boy named Temujin was born. Orphaned early, on the run for his life as a teenager, Temujin nonetheless managed to claw his way up to chieftain status. At some point, a rival kidnapped his wife—big mistake: Temujin demolished that rival and absorbed his warriors. And his wives. Now he was a bigger chieftain. He went on picking strategic quarrels and forging political links until he had fused the Mongols into a single, tight confederacy ruled by himself. Just as European barbarians were sacking Constantinople, Temujin made an ominous move: he changed his name to Genghis Khan, which means "lord of the universe."

Now he turned his attentions outward. His Mongol troops attacked both the Jurchen kingdom of what had been north China and the Turkish Muslim kingdom in control of Afghanistan and Iran. The Mongols burned down the ancient Bactrian city of Balkh, known as "the mother of cities." They massacred the people of Herat and Nishapur down to the last man, woman, and child. Sweeping west across central Asia, they mowed down all the Turkic tribal kingdoms and confederations in their way. They crossed the Volga and waded through blood to reach the Russian capital of Kiev, which they razed, whereupon the Russian Empire was no more: the Russians were now just vassals of the Mongols.

Genghis Khan had spent twenty long years fusing the fractious Mongols into a single political unit. It took him only another twenty years to build an empire bigger than Rome's had ever been. When he died, in 1227, his sons and grandsons took up the family business, which was world conquest. They dealt death blows to the upstart kingdoms that had crowded the Song out of northern China. They invaded Korea and reduced Vietnam to vassalage, which the Chinese had never managed. A grandson of Genghis Khan wiped out the Southern Song and brought the two-thousand-year-old Middle Kingdom of China to an end. Meanwhile, in the southwest, another grandson of Genghis burned down Baghdad, where the nominal head of the Islamic world was still holding court. The Muslim caliphate was no more.

When rumors of this storm first reached Europe, many Christians rejoiced. They thought a mighty force was coming to their aid. They thought it was Prestor John, a mythical king of Christian lore. Prestor John was thought to rule a rich kingdom somewhere in the heart of Africa, or maybe somewhere in the heart of India, or maybe—well, anyway, somewhere in the heart of somewhere—and now, he was coming.

Except, he wasn't. By the time the Mongols had eviscerated Russia, Europeans realized that these were not the other Christians. Joy turned to dread. The pope had previously sent envoys to Genghis Khan proposing a grand alliance. Now he sent missives pleading for mercy. In Hungary and in Poland, local kings drilled their troops and welcomed recruits from the two most formidable military-religious orders of the day, the Knights Templar and the Teutonic Knights. All these combined armies sallied out to stop the Mongols—and got annihilated. The Mongols then stood poised to sweep across Europe to the Atlantic Ocean. There is no reason to doubt that, had they kept going, they would have done exactly that.

But they didn't keep going. Europe was saved by a fluke. In 1241, just when the Mongols reached the gates of Europe, Genghis Khan's successor, his son Ogodei Khan, died. The top Mongol leaders put the conquest of Europe on hold while they rushed back to Mongolia to work out which of them would now be the Grand Khan. It took two years to sort out the succession, by which time, from the Mongols' point of view, new fronts had opened up, cities and peoples that called for more immediate sacking. The conquest of Europe was postponed again—indefinitely as it turned out, for in 1260, having just burned down Baghdad, the westward-marching Mongols ran into the Mamluks.

Mamluk means "slave" in Arabic, and the Mamluks were one of those curious slave states that had popped up here and there throughout Dar-ul-Islam over the centuries. Like other slave kings, the Egyptian Mamluks were Turks captured in battle as boys and raised as warriors. They ruled Egypt not as a kinship-based dynasty but as a corporation that constantly replenished its ranks with new slaves captured (or purchased) as boys and trained in the military arts. In 1260, the Mamluks met the Mongols at a place called Ayn Jalut and stopped them in their tracks. That battle marked a watershed: the Mongol Empire never expanded any further. And how could it? Given the technology of the time, it had surely reached its absolute administrative limit. It was the biggest contiguous empire the world had ever seen, and there would never be a bigger one until the rise of the Soviet Union.

It lasted only another fifty years or so, give or take, but during that time, the entire territory from the Pacific Ocean to the Mediterranean Sea, from the Baltic to the South China Sea, was under one political

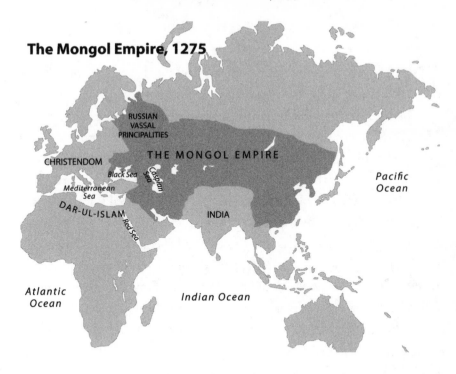

The Mongol Empire, 1275

jurisdiction. This had profound implications for the hemispheric market, for as it turned out, Genghis Khan and his successors were not nearly as bad at managing the lands they had conquered as one might have expected of such brutish warriors. For one thing, they were interested in erasing barriers to the speed and efficiency with which goods and messages could travel. They did this so that pastoral nomads could move freely among good pastures. They did it so that tribute could flow quickly and efficiently from conquered regions to their capitals. They did it to enhance their military control, which depended on moving troops and messages swiftly throughout their empire—but the bottom line is, they did it. They improved old roads, built new ones, established relay stations and hostels and postal networks, removed trade barriers, eliminated bureaucratic obstacles to long-distance trade, and supported credit systems. What had been for centuries a loose collection of regional trade networks now became a single busy web of traffic that spanned much of the Eastern Hemisphere.

THE MONGOL HOLOCAUST AND EUROPE

Europe west of the Balkans took no direct hits from the Mongols. For those Europeans, the biggest consequence of the Mongol eruption was disease. This problem began far away, probably in the foothills of the Himalayas. In any given area, deadly microscopic parasites and their hosts go through a trajectory: initially, the parasites feed on their hosts without restraint, and when they've killed one host, they move on to another. But if they wipe out their whole host species, they've committed suicide. So parasites come to an accommodation with the higher life-forms within which they live. The parasites grow less virulent, and the host species builds up a biological tolerance. One dreadful parasite had reached just such an accommodation with people living in the Himalayan foothills. It went mostly unnoticed there because it no longer killed people very much. This germ infested not only humans but also certain burrowing rodents plentiful in the region. As it happens, vast numbers of similar rodents lived in the forested lands north of the Silk Road. Those rodents, however, had never seen the infection in question: they lived too far away. Fleas carried the germ, but infected fleas died before they got that far north.

Then came the Pax Mongolica. Suddenly, within the web of intercommunication built by the Mongols, there were couriers on horseback going from the Himalayan foothills to the Siberian forests at tremendous speed: the Mongol couriers routinely traveled over a hundred miles a day. An infected flea hitchhiking in the saddlebag of such a horseman could end up a thousand miles away from its point of origin before it died. Infected fleas from the Himalayan foothills thus made it to the northern forests and there found an immense community of burrowing rodents, potential hosts, which had never seen the parasites they carried. The disease turned virulent there, as disease does when it finds new hosts to prey upon. In this state of virulence, it moved from rodents to humans passing through. The bacillus in question was *Yersinia pestis*, responsible for the bubonic plague.

The plague flowed west along the Silk Roads. Perhaps it would have died out in the sparsely inhabited lands along the way except for one startling episode. In 1345, the Mongols who then ruled Russia set siege to a city that was resisting their rule, the city of Caffa on the Black Sea. The siege was stalling, so the Mongols tried one last measure. They gathered the corpses of their own Mongol warriors who had died of some horrible, mysterious illness and hurled them into the city with catapults. Even this failed to force a surrender, so the Mongols gave up and went away.

In the city, life seemingly went back to normal. Merchants loaded ships with cargo and sailed to Italy to ply their normal trade. They docked at a town in Sicily and unloaded their cargo. The rats that inevitably lived on such ships scuttled ashore, bearing fleas that carried the plague. In Europe, the illness found another vast field of biologically vulnerable hosts, and this time the hosts were people. The Black Death swept across Europe like a tsunami, cresting and waning and cresting and waning, new outbreaks happening every ten years or so. Over the course of several decades, the Black Death killed at least a third of all Europeans and maybe more. In the fourteenth century, this monstrous disease must have felt like the end of the world to people in the midst of it.

History was no stranger to plagues. Disease had changed the course of history many times. And it wasn't always the bubonic plague. The biblical plagues might have been typhus. Malaria probably helped weaken Rome. The plague that ravaged Justinian's Byzantium might have been smallpox. An epidemic of some never really identified disease seems to have cleared the way for the Islamic expansion of the seventh century. But the Black Death of Europe was the most devastating and consequential flood of disease the world had seen—up to that point. And it happened because the Mongols had produced such a spike in Eurasian interconnectedness. At the time, however, it's safe to say that no one in Europe made a connection between the Mongols and the plague.

The Black Death killed a lot of people but for many of the survivors, life actually improved. For one thing, unlike a military invasion, an epidemic doesn't damage infrastructure: it kills people but leaves roads, buildings, canals, and such intact. And the loss of people has consequences. Before the Black Death, feudal lords were ramping up their use of wage laborers instead of serfs as a way to save money. But after the Black Death—guess what? Lords found themselves facing a labor shortage. With one-third (or more!) of the continent's population gone, paid workers had unprecedented bargaining power. In the aftermath of the epidemic, wages went up, and peasants hit the roads in search of better opportunities. This sort of mobility had been illegal in Europe since the days of Roman emperor Diocletian, but now, lords were powerless to stop it.

At the height of the plague, when people were dying right and left, some women moved into positions of relatively greater power than before. It didn't last, as patriarchal institutions pushed back. But in the immediate wake of the Black Death, some women inherited their dead husbands' lands. A few even took over their deceased husbands' businesses. If they had any craft skills (and many did, since much of the meaningful production in feudal Europe was actually carried out by women), some could now market what they made for their own benefit. Unprecedented ideas began to be heard among women. Some dared to voice the sentiment that women might be better off *not* marrying, for by remaining single they could retain control of their own destinies. In previous times, unmarried women had no destinies of their own. Men controlled the public world, and men controlled the economy. Ambitious unmarried women were apt to end up as beggars, prostitutes, or corpses.

Europe came out of the pandemic as Earth's most volatile social landscape. During the plague years, tightly organized, self-governing walled towns emerged as a new kind of social unit. Towns were born of trade, and towns now gained a coherence that spelled political power. At this point, Western European warriors, pilgrims, and business entrepreneurs had been streaming to markets at the eastern edge of the Mediterranean for two-plus centuries. Thanks to the Mongols, they now found those markets overflowing more than ever with products from Persia and Afghanistan, from the Eurasian steppes, from India, from the Spice Islands of Southeast Asia, from China. Wherever traders, warriors, and migrants move in great numbers, so do goods, ideas, inventions, and technical innovations. In that sense, the Mongols completed what the Crusades had begun. Among the constellations of culture east of the Mediterranean, there had long been a great deal of interaction, which had generated a far-flung network of interconnections—and now Europe was part of that network.

14

Europe and the Long Crusades
(1100 CE to 1500 CE)

The Crusades traditionally refers to nine distinct military campaigns carried out between 1095 and 1272. Those campaigns were only one part of a much bigger story, however. The Long Crusades, as we might call them, were an encounter between two world historical monads that unfolded over the course of five centuries along a front that extended thousands of miles, from central Spain to the heart of Asia Minor and down the Red Sea to the Indian Ocean. For Europeans, the Mongol eruption was only one event in that historical drama, and since the Mongols didn't hit Europe directly, it was not even a very crucial episode. The great tilting of the Eurasian table that shifted cultural power from east to west occurred during the Long Crusades.

The Short Crusades—those nine distinct military campaigns—can be described pretty starkly as a duel between Saracens and Franks. The Long Crusades were more complicated. Fighting was part of it, yes, but much of the fighting was among the crusaders for control of some resource or trade route that had come into view as a result of the Short Crusades. A lot of the fighting was also among various branches of the ruling Turkish tribes and among various other Muslim powers vying for control of this or that city against their cousins, often to gain an advantage in trade with European Christians; for amidst it all, when they weren't fighting one another, the Christian transplants from Europe were neck deep in commercial dealings with the Muslims.

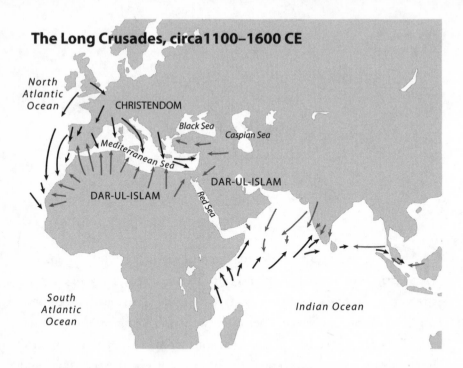

The Long Crusades, circa 1100–1600 CE

The Mongol eruption played a key role in the Long Crusades, even if Europeans didn't know it, because it hammered China, demolished Russia, and laid waste to Dar-ul-Islam but left Christendom virtually untouched. As the Long Crusades wound down, a continent already on the rise at the start of the Short Crusades found itself negotiating from a position of growing strength vis-à-vis the East and in particular with the Islamic world against which it scraped directly.

INVENTIONS

With so much traffic moving back and forth across the long frontier between these two worlds over the course of the Long Crusades, hundreds of consequential ideas, inventions, innovations, and technologies trickled into Western Europe. We've already spoken of banking, business practices, and Indian mathematics, but there was so much more: gunpowder, firearms, paper, printing and publishing, medical knowledge, chemical laboratory equipment, distilling technology, mechanical clocks, geared machine works, the magnetic compass, the astrolabe, the sextant, the bowsprit rudder, the lateen sail—all these technologies had germinated in the east and now came west. The list of inventions, innovations, and ideas that moved the other way during this period is...short.

Many inventions, however, took off dramatically when they got to Europe. Gunpowder, for example, was invented in China in the Tang era, but there it was used for fireworks, mainly. The Tang didn't have any real need for guns; they already governed everything that mattered with bureaucratic and financial mechanisms, and in their confrontations with the nomads, what they needed were horses, not cannons.

Then gunpowder got to Europe, and in this context firearms technology surged. Why here? Because Europe was not a single empire but a multitude of distinct, autonomous, more or less evenly matched political states competing with one another (about five hundred of them in the year 1000). If some weapon gave one state a slight edge, its rivals quickly adopted the same technology to stay even.

Staying even was important because, as the Short Crusades wound down, armed men began coming home from the Holy Lands, many with no job skills outside of violence. Since there were few jobs for such men in Europe now, some returnees formed free companies, independent armed bands who roamed the countryside, looking for "work." They called themselves *free lances*, and the longer they roamed about, the more trouble they made.

Political rulers came up with a solution of sorts. They hired these mercenaries to carry out military campaigns in neighboring states, which got the free lances out of their own yard and into some other guy's. The other guy then drained the infestation of free companies from his turf by hiring them to fight another little war somewhere. Given the number of small political units in Europe, there was plenty of fodder for such wars. Western European history remembers this period as the Hundred Years' War.

All this warfare spurred rapid improvements in military technology. Europe had stone castles, and there's nothing quite like a stone castle to make a cannon look good and a bigger cannon look even better. European warfare featured armored knights impervious to swords but not to bullets and bombs. Guns and cannons made knights in shining armor a romantic relic of a bygone era, like the cowboys of wild west fiction.

Military technology was a social equalizer in a way. Anyone with a finger could pull a trigger. The new weapons made combat a long-distance affair in which numbers made the difference far more than muscles. And if numbers made the difference, then the most powerful military leaders were going to be the ones who could hire the greatest number of soldiers, equip them with the latest weapons, and organize them most effectively. Battles were going to be fought by armies of soldiers not armies of warriors. The military type was going to be someone who followed orders. Military leadership became a business management skill.

And if money made the difference in war, the new elites would be the people most adept at making money. That description fit the top merchants of the towns, that growing new phenomenon. What's more, in this context, countless tinkerers went to work developing better guns, improvements they might sell to some duke or king, for in a world increasingly permeated by market forces, a man could make his fortune by building a better gun.

Clocks were probably just as transformative as guns. The first mechanical clock was probably that three-story mechanical device invented in China by a Buddhist monk. The Chinese clock was a huge building-sized device with a stream running through it, which turned wheels synced to gears, which rotated other gears. As a result, the whole towering structure sounded a bell at regular intervals. But the Chinese didn't appreciate this device's utility as a clock because they took no deep interest in the time of day. They had no reason to care if it was 3:16 or 3:42. They were farmers: they wanted to know how long till the next vernal equinox. In this context, the three-story clock's ability to sound the time of day added nothing to its value as a calendar. So it remained an ingenious toy.

The idea of the mechanical clock made its way into the Muslim world, but it didn't take there either, perhaps because in that social constellation, time of prayer was enshrined as the fundamental marker of time, and scripture ordained that time of prayer be determined by the position of the sun. In that context, mechanical clocks interfered with the function of time in everyday life. And if the clock was competing with time of prayer, the clock was bound to lose.

Then the mechanical clock got to Europe. There, tinkerers got busy making crucial improvements. They figured out how to power clocks with pendulums or slowly uncoiling springs instead of with running water. By severing clocks from natural events, they turned clocks into stand-alone artifacts measuring something that could not be detected by sensory means. Earlier devices for keeping track of time (such as the sundial) linked time to natural phenomena. Time of day ultimately meant "position of sun." A day had no absolute length in that system of measurement: it was shorter in winter and longer in summer. In that system, time was inseparable from place: sunset here was not the same as sunset over there. Time was not the same for everyone. The mechanical clock transformed time into a mysterious, independent current of *something* that was always flowing, always forward, always at an unvarying pace, always the same everywhere. Meanwhile, European clockmakers were figuring how to make clocks smaller, until eventually clocks got so small they could be mounted in the bell towers of churches, where any local could see what time it was. Once that happened, everyone in a given area could be living in the same temporal frame; everyone could be connected to everyone else with a web of clock time.

What fascinated Muslim tinkerers about the Chinese clock was not the time telling per se but the clockworks that made it function. The idea of using cogs and gears to make natural forces do useful work—this was intriguing. Engineers of the Islamic world began exploring what else could be done with clockworks harnessed to forces of nature. They developed sophisticated windmills to grind grain and pump water. Wind-driven machines made it to Muslim Spain and from there into Catholic Europe. Tinkering with improvements to windmills led Muslims to invent such unsung but consequential inventions as crankshafts, camshafts, tie rods, and flywheels, and these too seeped into Europe, with the windmills.

In the Islamic world, these machine works led to no particularly profound social changes. That's probably because no one had an incentive
to apply clockworks to industrial production, for production was already
booming in small but countless workshops, and mechanical enhancements
to artisanal production didn't add enough to make it a worthwhile investment for any particular artisan. What learned Muslims mostly did with
clockworks, therefore, was to construct ingenious toys for their moneyed
elite. One such device operated a mechanical band of five musicians. Another animated a robot waitress who filled one's teacup upon command.
Still another flushed a basin—which, curiously enough, did not lead to
the invention of a flush toilet. Once the idea of machine works reached
Europe, however, they made a tremendous splash, as we shall see later.

Perhaps the most consequential technology transfers of this era had
to do with books. Before the Crusades, most books produced in Europe were written on vellum, a calfskin leather stretched and scraped
and worked into thin sheets. It was difficult and expensive to make, one
reason why so few books were produced in Europe. The Chinese had
long ago invented paper, and Muslims had acquired this technology as
spoils of a ninth-century war, fueling a book industry in Dar-ul-Islam.
Europe, however, was basically bookless until around 1200, when Europeans learned to make paper.

By this time, the Chinese had also invented not just the printing press
but movable type. In China, movable type technology went nowhere because the Chinese script is not alphabetical. Printing a book with movable
type required making thousands of individual characters. Making a hand-
written copy of the book was less bother, really. Moveable type didn't excite
much interest in the Islamic world either because although Arabic script is
alphabetical, it isn't simple. In the Arabic script, some letters connect with
some others and some don't. When they connect, they change form, but
their form depends on whether they're connecting to the previous letter,
the next letter or both, and that depends entirely on the word they're in.

The Latin alphabet used in Europe, by contrast, had twenty-six un-
changing stand-alone letters. (Capitals came later.) In Europe, therefore,
moveable type dramatically simplified the process of copying a book. There

were only twenty-six letters to drop into a frame, and with those twenty-six bits of metal type, a publisher could create any word in the language.

What remained, then, was only the problem of using type to imprint an image on a sheet of paper. Around 1440, the German goldsmith Johannes Gutenberg figured out how to do just that, with an adaptation of a wine press (itself an adaptation of an olive oil press, itself derived from the screw Archimedes invented to lift water in the third century BCE). Gutenberg now had a fully functional press and was ready to print books. He printed only two before his unscrupulous "business partner" Jacob Mentz gained control of the invention and got rich off it, while Gutenberg went blind and died. But the two books Gutenberg printed proved momentous: they were a book of psalms and the Holy Bible.

And let us not forget sailing. A great deal of sophisticated nautical technology originated in China but was adopted and refined in Southeast Asia. There, between China and Australia, stretch several archipelagoes comprising more than twenty-five thousand islands and covering nearly two million square miles of Earth. People could easily cross the short distances from one island to another, but they did have to deal with tricky currents of wind and water. The Malays came up with the idea of tug-bolt sails mounted fore and aft, each one capable of pivoting to catch the wind at any angle the sailor chose. Combinations of such sails enabled Malays to sail in whatever direction they wanted, no matter which way the wind was blowing, by tacking (traveling on a zigzag path).

From far away, the Malay sails looked triangular. Inspired by distant glimpses of this illusion, sailors on either side of the Malays developed fully triangular lateen sails, which accomplished the same thing as the Malay's tug-bolt devices. The Polynesians to the east developed one kind of lateen sail; the Indians, Arabs, and Persians to the west developed another version.

The Chinese also invented the magnetic compass, and from China, the magnetic compass found its way to the seafaring people of maritime Southeast Asia, who passed it on to Muslim and Hindu merchants plying the Indian Ocean and the Red Sea. Muslim scientists wrote treatises about how compasses worked and manuals about how to make them.

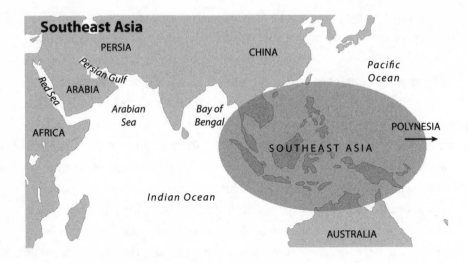

Southeast Asia

PERSIA

CHINA

Pacific Ocean

Persian Gulf

Red Sea

ARABIA

Arabian Sea

Bay of Bengal

AFRICA

SOUTHEAST ASIA

POLYNESIA →

Indian Ocean

AUSTRALIA

From the Red Sea and across the Mediterranean, these devices made their way to Europe's Atlantic coast.

The principals of these devices might have been familiar to Europeans already, but they had not found much purchase because sailing on the Mediterranean didn't require much trickery. If you could see where the sun was setting, you knew which way was west, and if the wind wasn't cooperating, you could row. The Phoenicians, Greeks, and Romans all relied on oars and square sails. The Vikings made it to Iceland and Greenland with nothing more than these, plus sunstones.* In the storm-prone Atlantic, European sailors stayed within sight of land because otherwise they wouldn't know which way was north. Then in the fourteenth century, they added the magnetic compass to their tool kit, and the compass changed everything.

The Islamic world played a key role in the transmission of nautical innovations from China to Europe because Islamic traders took a particular interest in navigation. For one thing, their religion required that five times a day they stop what they were doing, face Mecca, and perform certain ritual prayers. This was a special challenge for long-distance traders moving across deserts and seas. Five times a day, they had to

---

*Sunstones were a certain kind of rock crystal that, when you looked through them, showed you where the sun was, even on cloudy days.

figure out which way lay Mecca. A traveler could not derive the answer from the sun or stars alone because it wasn't like asking which way was north. If one had started in Mecca and gone south, Mecca would lie to the north, but if one had gone west, it lay east. If one had traveled a wandering path, all bets were off. The astrolabe told travelers where they were compared to where they'd been, thus allowing people to determine their exact location on Earth no matter how far or how randomly they'd traveled. Astrolabes, however, don't work well at sea, which made the compass even more vital for traders plying the monsoon routes. You can see why a civilization fascinated with geography embraced the astrolabe, the compass, and all other technologies related to mapmaking.

You can also see why these nautical devices intrigued people on the western seaboard of Europe, for when these people looked west, they saw waters no one had ever crossed, and when they looked south, they saw waters from which no one had ever come back. Europe was now a continent full of restless seadogs who wanted to go places, but these hardy men needed more than courage to head across the waters they lived next to. They needed better tools. And once the Long Crusades ratcheted up the interaction between Dar-ul-Islam and Christendom, Western Europeans could start building just such a toolkit.

THE UNIVERSITY

In the eighth century, Muslims had planted a state in southern Spain, a caliphate, which they claimed was the only caliphate because, by definition, there can only be one. Dynasties had changed since then, but in 1100, the Spanish caliphate still existed, and its capital city of Cordoba was one of the world's three greatest in size, wealth, vitality, learning, intellectual achievement, and manners. Cordoba had libraries loaded with the books of many cultures. Translation being a central preoccupation for Muslim intellectuals, the nearby city of Toledo had become a world capital of translation. There, Muslim scholars churned out Arabic editions of classic texts from every place that Muslims had ever visited, including works written by the ancient Greeks. And there, in Toledo, scholars also translated these translations from Arabic into Latin. Christians were at war with Muslims, but some did visit cities such as Toledo to shop and take in the sights, and some came away with Latin translations of Arabic translations of Greek texts.

In Europe, monasteries had long been the go-to place for intellectuals. Monks generally knew how to read. Copying books was part of their vocation. Local vernaculars were developing, but the monks kept Latin alive because they thought it to be God's language, and they wanted to make sure their prayers were heard. They studied the speeches of Cicero not for the content but because his speeches provided a superb model of Latin grammar.

When travelers from Spain brought along the occasional Latin text translated from Arabic, monks who got a hold of it put it in their library. Literate people traveled long distances to such monasteries to read books they'd heard were there. Some even took up residence nearby so they could study the book more thoroughly. Other people interested in the topic of that book gravitated to the same vicinity not just to read the book but to hear what seasoned scholars had to say about it. Communities of reading and learning and intellectual discussion formed around monasteries with good collections of books.

The whole process resembled the one that had spawned centers of learning in the Muslim constellation. There, men deeply steeped in important religious texts attracted students who became learned and famous in their own right and attracted more students. Muslim centers of scholarship featured a novelty in the world of learning, a university degree. Students were tested by acknowledged scholars, and if deemed learned enough, they got a diploma certifying their authority to issue opinions on theological questions.

Such diplomas were crucial in the Islamic world because the sharia, the edifice of Islamic law, was considered the ultimate basis of society. The fundamental structure of this edifice came from scripture, but every new brick came from a *fatwa*, a ruling issued by a qualified scholar. Each fatwa became part of the canon later scholars had to take into account when they rendered opinions on novel questions. Any new fatwa had to fit in with all previous fatwas, and once it was issued and accepted by scholarly consensus, all future opinions had to fit in with *it*. Scholars issuing fatwas therefore *had* to get it right—civilization depended on it.

But who was to judge? Islam had no formal structure of authority—no bishops, no pope, no one to certify that any particular person had the authority to issue a ruling. This is where Muslim universities stepped in. Each university consisted of a corps of experts, a flock of aspiring scholars, a regular schedule of classes, and a course of study aimed at enabling students to read and comment on important works and carry forward the intellectual traditions of the culture. To enter this program, students had to take a preparatory course that included reading, writing, classical Arabic grammar, history, and the science of hadith—the discipline involved in distinguishing which sayings of the messenger were authentic and which ones bogus.

Christian Europe wasn't building a sharia, but the university was a constellation of ideas that could hold together as it moved across borders. So the concept of the university took root in Europe too, with structural elements borrowed from the Islamic version of the same. In Crusades-era Europe, scholars identified four subjects as worthy of study: theology, philosophy, medicine, and (canon) law. But as in the Islamic world, before aspiring students could start studying one of these fields, they had to prove they were up to doing the work; otherwise, they'd just be wasting some important scholar's time. So in Europe, the preparatory course included seven subjects: grammar, logic, rhetoric, arithmetic, geometry, music, and astronomy. Upon completing this preliminary course, students were issued a certificate called a baccalaureate, which is Latin for "beginner." It meant that now they could *begin* their studies. The baccalaureate still exists. Today, it's called the bachelor of arts degree or BA: the standard generic college degree.

The first universities emerged in Italy, at Naples and Bologna, and at Paris, and then a bit later at Oxford, England. Then a renegade branch of Oxford scholars broke away and started their own university at Cambridge, and soon universities were sprouting all over Europe.

The professors at these universities were called schoolmen or, to use the Latin term, scholastics. The schoolmen were almost all monks. The greatest of them, Thomas Aquinas, was born just as Genghis Khan was dying, and Aquinas died just as the Mongols were declaring themselves emperors of China. In the West, at that moment, the eighth of nine Crusades had just begun to gather force. As Greek, Arab, and Persian thought seeped into Western European universities, prestige accrued to philosophy, which in this context meant deep thinking about religious doctrine. The philosophers of Islam had been down this path already. Taking as axiomatic that the scriptures were true, that God made the world, and that God was rational, Muslim thinkers of Islam's classical age (the age of the caliphates) had labored to work out relationships among the teachings of religion, the phenomena of nature, and the precepts of Aristotelian logic. The scholastics tackled pretty much the same intellectual project, though the precepts they were trying to reconcile with observed phenomena were different.

In this period, when European Christians searched for a past to admire, they were drawn to the centuries before their own traditions. Monastic scholars in the burgeoning universities began to see ancient Greek texts as legitimate objects of study. They weren't suggesting that Zeus ranked right up there with Jesus. Securing an afterlife in heaven remained life's ultimate goal. But the Greeks, they suggested, had some pertinent things to say about the here and now.

Certain aspects of the ancient Greco-Roman narrative had never really vanished from the Catholic conceptual framework. For the Romans and the Greeks, the world contained both secular and supernatural realms, and they were separate. The Catholic world accepted that dichotomy but held that only the supernatural realm mattered, only the afterlife.

With the Greco-Roman narrative stirring back to life, European intellectuals permitted themselves to focus on the other half of the dichotomy. They allowed themselves to ponder nature apart from considerations of salvation. The scholastics started down this road when they imbibed the learning filtering out of Dar-ul-Islam. At the time, they did not see that they were opening the door to secular themes simply by entertaining the premise that reason reflected an attribute of God, that people could therefore use reason to plumb the mysteries of God's creation, and that there was nothing wrong with doing so.

Albertus Magnus, a scholastic monk associated with the University of Paris, took a great interest in alchemy, which he learned about from Muslim sources, and he began laying the foundations for transforming alchemy into chemistry, based on observation: his method meant trying stuff, recording what happened, and then trying more stuff. (Along the way, he wrote an influential treatise on how to make, of all things, better gunpowder.)

His contemporary Roger Bacon, also a monk, also a professor, also a dabbler in magic and alchemical change, asked the groundbreaking question: How could one determine that a given piece of information was true? Hmmm, good question! Never goes stale, that one. Conventional wisdom said: First, check scripture. If it conflicts with that, it's false. If it passes the scripture test, run it at the Aristotle-bar: Does it make rational sense? If it doesn't clear the Aristotle-bar, it's not true. Bacon, however, dared to suggest that what made sense was not always what was true. He suggested that the validity of a proposition be determined by a three-step process: prediction, experiment, and follow-up observation. He thus laid out a method for gaining true information about the world without any reference to God. His argument said nothing *against* God, mind you; it merely didn't mention God. But this omission was in itself revolutionary, for Bacon was tacitly endorsing a central feature of the Greco-Roman narrative: it's not always all about the gods; there's other stuff too.

Magnus's most celebrated student was the towering Thomas Aquinas who gained lasting fame for using Aristotelian logic to prove the existence of God. A couple of centuries earlier, the idea that the existence of God could use some proving would have struck any European Christian as both laughable and blasphemous. Aquinas, Bacon, Magnus, and their contemporaries fully believed that God caused everything and that God trumped all. They weren't doubters; they merely developed a line of enquiry that led from material question to material answer without detouring through scripture. At the time, they saw no problem with carrying out this project within the Catholic framework. They were just adding more stars to the constellation. Filling in the picture, as it were.

The thing is, though, the questions people ask shape the kinds of answers they come up with. When the Egyptians painted humans in profile, it wasn't that they had never seen people from the front. They just didn't ask or care how that could be portrayed: they had other preoccupations. When Byzantine artists made elaborate mosaic portraits of Christ using gold to create flat, shimmering patterns, it wasn't that they couldn't figure out how to achieve the illusion of depth. They weren't interested in that illusion; they were out to represent a spiritual state visible only to the soul. By the same token, the Chinese artists of the Tang era were not asking how to make such an exact copy of what the eye sees that no observer would be able tell if it was real or painted. They were asking how to evoke, with art, the serenity, stillness, and harmony of the mind approaching nirvana.

In fifteenth-century Italy and in Western Europe generally, artists began asking a different question, a question descended from the work of the scholastics. The scholastics had implied an "out there" that wasn't God. European artists got interested in what that out there was "really." Driven by this question, they sought ways to duplicate material reality in an objective way: to create with paint the illusion of depth, to reproduce the play of light and shadow that makes drapery look as it does in real life, to portray the actual proportions of human figures and capture how their muscles bulged when they were straining. In questing for these sorts of answers, they came up with art like Michelangelo's statue of Moses, which made one pope uneasy because he thought it was *too* lifelike and thus, maybe, encroached on a monopoly of God's.

Leonardo da Vinci began dissecting corpses to understand what internal structures made living humans look the way they did. His work was closely linked to the material concerns of his patrons. Prominent among these was war, so Leonardo worked on ways to construct things like better siege engines by understanding the physics of materials. His questions did not *quite* present as heresies because he wasn't offering a different view of how to worship. He was simply acting like there were things to think about other than God. His work implied that an objective world existed and that gaining information about it required interacting directly with material stuff. Want to build a better siege machine? Figure out how far a cannonball will go on a given amount of gunpowder. Want to set a broken bone properly? Cut a body open and see what's in there and how it's put together. Leonardo's curious mind committed him to the sort of analytical observation that we now associate with science.

At first, the church fathers didn't grasp the implications of what Leonardo and his ilk were doing. They didn't realize that talking about something other than God implied that something other than God existed. They didn't realize that conversations unrelated to scripture were the first ripples of a long-buried narrative waking up, that ancient Mediterranean vision of a natural world that contained *both* humans and gods: the narrative that gave meaning to the Greek constellation of long ago. Church fathers had no inkling yet of the threat to the feudal Catholic constellation that was germinating within the bosom of the church itself.

Protoscientists such as Leonardo were a threat because when people fixated on observation they began to spot little things that didn't quite add up. Disturbing anomalies showed up, for example, in the movements of those pinpoints of light in the sky at night. Every culture since time immemorial had studied those lights with religious fervor. A society's ideas about those lights tended to reflect the narrative that gave its world meaning.

The star charts of feudal Europe were created by second-century mathematician Ptolemy of Alexandria, who based his charts on the work of the Greek philosopher Plato. Plato said all those pinpoints of light were heavenly bodies mounted to an invisible crystal dome surrounding Earth. The sphere was rotating, so the stars were moving through the seasons. When they returned to their original position, one year had passed.

This made pretty good sense. The only trouble was, not all the pinpoints of light moved in exactly straight lines. Plato thought this could be explained if one assumed that each erratic star was attached to a smaller (invisible) disc of its own, which was in turn affixed to one great crystal dome rotating around Earth. Each small disk was rotating on its own axis while the great sphere turned. To the human eye, the stars mounted to the edges of those smaller spheres seemed to be moving erratically. The savant who knew enough to take the invisible spheres into account could see that there was nothing erratic about any of it: all the movements embodied perfect mathematical order. All the motions in the sky formed perfect circles. And of course, they did. God would not have made an imperfect universe.

Plato's theories enabled Ptolemy and other early astronomers to not only predict the pathways of the stars but to diagram the invisible spheres that made it all work. The trouble was the system didn't account for *all* the observed motions of *all* the stars. To account for little glitches that showed up, savants had to add more (invisible) discs. They had to explain that some heavenly bodies—not all, but some—were mounted to their own smaller invisible rotating wheels, which were mounted to the larger invisible wheels, which were mounted to the one big sphere. Each time a new glitch was found, another disc was added. The Ptolemaic explanation of the night sky was now a very complicated manual of star charts based on an intricate clockwork of invisible discs and spheres. But it couldn't be disputed because it worked almost perfectly. *Almost* being the key word here.

Europeans committed to the feudal Catholic narrative had no argument with mathematical harmony as one of God's essential features. This had become an article of scholastic faith. Human senses might not be able to discern the hidden order of God's creation, but human reason could get at it. Looking for the principles of nature that explained the tumult of appearances: this was a quest to know the mind of God. Nothing wrong with doing that. Except—this quest was soon to have momentous, unforeseen consequences.

THE CONCEPT OF EUROPE

The first crusaders came from France, so Levantine Muslims called all of them Franks. The crusaders meanwhile called all their adversaries by a single name too: Saracens. For Muslims, steeped in their own importance, coining a single term for the invaders was a way of dismissing them: Why bother differentiating one gnat from another? For the Europeans, giving their adversaries a single name had a different import: it aided the construction of a monolithic other.

In Europe's feudal era, every little area was so sunk in local concerns that no one would have identified themselves as European, just as none of us now living in the Milky Way would identify ourselves as Milky Waysian. The Crusades, however, opened European Christian sensibilities to a sense of common identity, as parts of a single social whole. As Christians streamed to the Holy Lands, they brushed up against people of many backgrounds from many places, and get this: they were all headed to the same place, and they were all on the same side! But "same side" required that there be at least one "other" side. The more binary the two sides, the stronger the identity shared among Europeans. They didn't have to do any actual crusading to feel pride of ownership in the heroic quest, just as one doesn't have to play football to exult when the home team wins. Only a minority actually went east to fight, but everyone knew there was an east to go to and a war to fight. The Crusades thus helped give birth to the concept of Europe. By knowing the single thing they *weren't,* these diverse peoples came to a stronger sense of some single social whole they *were.* A new social constellation was gaining definition now.

An identity shaped by the otherness of the other gains coherence by eliminating all traces of the other from itself. It's no surprise, then, that as Muslims took back the Levant, the Crusades didn't end; they shifted to Europe, and there turned inward. In 1231, the Catholic Church created a judicial organ, the Inquisition, to sniff out heresies within Christendom. The Inquisition spotted two such impurities right away in France: they were the Albigensians and the Waldensians, two movements of religious revivalists who claimed that poverty and self-denial were essential features of Christian life. Any bishop lolling in luxury could see how sacrilegious *that* was. Encouraged by the Inquisition, the French king launched Crusades against both of these heresies, crippling the Waldensians and wiping out the Albigensians utterly.

Later, the Inquisition identified witchcraft as a major contamination. Tens of thousands of witches were found and burned at the stake over several centuries, most of them elderly, husbandless women. The Inquisition pressured people accused of witchcraft to name other witches, thus ensuring that the campaign to wipe out witches would never reduce the supply of witches. It was important that the supply not shrink, for the emerging constellation needed witch hunting to help construct itself. In northern Europe, the Teutonic Knights went on a crusade against pagan tribes near the Baltic Sea and, in cleansing Europe of those heathens, carved a new kingdom for themselves: the state of Prussia.

Another trace of otherness in European society were the Jews, small communities of whom had been scattered throughout Europe since Roman days. Back then, when the legal status of Christians was upgraded, that of Jews was correspondingly downgraded. Among other restrictions, they were forbidden to own land, which boxed them out of the feudal economy that soon formed. Many Jews became itinerant peddlers to earn a living.

During the Crusades, political leaders in Christendom found another use for Jews. Catholic doctrine prohibited Christians from making interest-bearing loans to other Christians; Jewish law placed similar restrictions on Jewish lending to Jews. Both groups, however, could lend to people outside their faith. But in Europe, just about everyone was Christian, so there hardly *was* anyone outside the faith to lend to or borrow from. This opened a niche for Jews to make a living as moneylenders, for almost everyone they met was a potential client.

English monarchs exploited this situation by actually cultivating Jewish moneylenders. A growing economy needs credit, and if Jews were lending money, Christians didn't have to. Then when kings needed money, they could wring it out of the (Jewish) moneylenders as fines for usury. To meet the king's demands, the moneylenders had to call in their loans. In effect, then, English kings were using Jewish moneylenders as an indirect way of taxing their subjects, which channeled the inevitable resentments raised by taxation away from the king and toward a minority conspicuous for its otherness.

The rising enthusiasm for cleansing Europe of the other put Jews in a precarious position. And indeed, in 1290, after populist rumors arose that Jews were eating Christian babies for Passover, all the Jews of England were expelled. Many migrated to Spain or to France where they only faced more persecution.

As the fifteenth century drew to a close, Western Europeans still imagined the world in binary Crusading terms. There was Christendom, and there was the other. The highest enterprise for any Christian king was to push back the other. In this regard, the situation in the east was disheartening. The Saracens had taken back not just Jerusalem but the whole Levant, and then in 1452, led by the Ottoman Turks, they took Constantinople: catastrophe!

Then Christendom got a badly needed victory—but not in the east. The pivotal triumph happened in Europe—in the Iberian Peninsula to be exact. The Christian kings of Spain had been crusading for centuries to break Muslim power in their peninsula, and finally, led by that famous royal couple Ferdinand and Isabella, they scored big.

In his youth, Prince Ferdinand of Aragon had been one of Europe's most eligible bachelors. His family had tried to marry him off to various politically useful princesses, but Ferdinand would have none of it. Princess Isabella of Castile was one of the most desirable plums in the royal marriage sweepstakes of her day. Her family tried to arrange politically expedient matches between her and various princes, but the teenaged princess would have none of it. Ferdinand and Isabella foiled their elders' plans by eloping—with each other. A love match! Oh, the scandal!

Theirs, however, turned out to be the most politically fruitful marriage of the age, for both inherited their respective thrones quite soon after marriage, whereupon Castile and Aragon became a single potent force. The formidable royal couple—she as much as he—led the Reconquista, as the Crusades were called in Spain. They took Cordoba, took Seville, and in 1492 finally took Granada, the last European stronghold of the Muslim Moors.

Ferdinand and Isabella now titled themselves the Catholic Monarchs as if to suggest that they were second only to the pope as leaders of

Christendom. And why not? Theirs had been the most significant victory of the Long Crusades. It was in their realm that the drive to purge
Christendom of the other reached a boiling point. In alliance with the
Dominican monastic order, the royals launched a local franchise of the
Inquisition. At first, the Spanish Inquisition sought to root out Muslims
masquerading as Christians, but most of the Muslims fled to Africa, so
the Spanish Inquisition went after the most conspicuous trace of otherness still remaining in Europe: the Jews.

First, the Inquisition ordered that Jews wear special ribbons so that
the public might readily identify them. Then, it pressured Jews to convert,
and many did: they were called *conversos*. But the Spanish Inquisition
was all about this Spanish Catholic constellation consolidating its unity
and identity. Spain needed to function as the spearhead of the Catholic cause, which required a permanent other against which to rally. The
Jews could not be allowed to escape their otherness simply by converting.
The Inquisition, therefore, developed a concept of Jewishness that had
nothing to do with beliefs or tribal affiliation. In this emerging view,
Jewishness was an inborn trait that people could not expunge by espous-
ing new beliefs, just as people couldn't change their height by claiming
to be short. If a Jew married a Christian, the "blood" was diluted and
that child was only half Jewish. If that child married a Christian, *their*
child would be less Jewish by a mathematically calculable proportion.
The Spanish Inquisition developed benchmarks designating what ratio
of Jewish "blood" made a person a Jew. Ironically, the most relentless
champion of this biological racialism was Torquemada, appointed Grand
Inquisitor of Spain in 1482: he had *conversos* in his family tree, but they
were just distant enough to sever him from the taint he was hunting
down.

15

The Restoration Narrative
(1300 CE to 1600 CE)

The Mongols destroyed a lot of cities and killed a lot of people, but they didn't manage to replace the master narratives of the people they had conquered with a narrative of their own. In fact, the Mongols themselves vanished from history as a distinct cultural factor within some fifty years of their greatest triumphs. In the lands they had conquered, people applied themselves to restoring their own interrupted past, and as soon as the Mongols' grip weakened, local pre-Mongol master narratives not only recovered but began to gather power and complexity.

Historians often take admiring note of the Mongols' religious "tolerance"—of how they let the people they had conquered worship whom they pleased in whatever way they deemed appropriate. In fact, the Mongols even called the luminaries of various religions to their courts to expound their beliefs, with an eye to adopting one of these.

But perhaps tolerance isn't quite the word for what was going on here. I'm thinking that the Mongols were curious about other people's belief systems because their own had lost relevance during their expansion. Before conquering the known world, the Mongols apparently subscribed to an assortment of animist beliefs common to the pastoral nomadic cultures of north Asia, a belief that all items seen in nature were inhabited by spirits, that all of nature was in some sense alive. Their religious practices were more about health than ethics. Misfortunes reflected something broken in a person's relationship with the surrounding world. Spiritual rituals were a means of getting back into alignment with nature. The hunter-gatherers of North America had, it seems, very similar beliefs. This way of looking at the world may have had power among nomadic social constellations because it squared so nicely with the experiences of people whose lives brought them into daily contact with elemental forces. Settled city folk, by contrast, interacted mainly with other city folk; their belief systems needed to account for the frictions that arose among people crowded together in tight spaces.

Whatever it had been, the Mongols' belief system did not survive or spread. Their system did not provide enough resonant meaning once the Mongols were no longer pastoral nomads but were, instead, masters of a vast web of urban civilizations. In fact, as the Mongol Empire weakened, local populations firmed up their own identities by closing ranks against the invasive other.

RUSSIA REBORN

The Mongols who conquered Russia were known to themselves as the Golden Horde. The Russians, however, called them Tatars. The Tatar elite took a live-and-let-live attitude toward the locals so long as the latter forked over the required tribute. Instead of collecting it themselves, however, the Tatars somewhat lazily delegated the job to Russian flunkies. They didn't have much to do with the people they ruled, nor did they want to. Instead of Mongol cultural themes filtering down into Russian society, earlier narratives borrowed from the Byzantine world gained appeal and spread.

When the Mongols arrived, the Russian constellation was just forming a sense of itself as a Slavic powerhouse. Russians had started looking to the Greek Orthodox Church as *their* church. At that point, they still saw themselves as country cousins of the splendid Byzantines. Under Tatar rule, however, the Slavic affiliation with the Orthodox Church deepened. The Mongols unwittingly promoted this by clamping down on Russian political rulers, whom they saw as threats, and going easy on the Orthodox Church, which they saw as the harmless opiate that kept the conquered people sedated. In Russia, therefore, an Orthodox Christian identity emerged even before a Russian national political identity.

Meanwhile, Russian agents in charge of collecting tribute for the Mongols started keeping some of the money for themselves. And then more of the money. And then all of it. When summoned to the Mongol court to explain themselves, they dragged their feet. Battles ensued, but the Tatars of the fourteenth century were not the Mongols of the thirteenth. Russians broke their grip and took control of their own destiny. By this time, the dukes of Muscovy had made themselves rich and their city powerful. Moscow emerged as the capital of an expanding Russian Empire, an expansion fueled by a nativist culture that was animated by religious passion.

Russians started calling their capital the Third Rome. The first Rome had been the one in Italy, the second was Constantinople, seat of the Greek Orthodox Church, and now there was Moscow. In 1453, Muslim armies conquered Constantinople, so the second "Rome" was gone. For Russians, their capital city was now the greatest remaining Rome, and their empire was *the* Christian empire. It was under Mongol rule, then, that Russia became Russian, and once this new-old identity congealed, Russia never stopped expanding until its dominion extended from the flanks of Europe to the shores of the Pacific Ocean.

CHINA: FORWARD INTO THE PAST

In China, a full-blown master narrative was already in place when the Mongols arrived, an identity that had been maturing for two thousand years and more. It was here in China that restoration matured as *the* core project of a civilization-sized social constellation, for although Mongols had done the conquering, the Chinese did not become Mongolian. Quite the opposite. The Mongols cast themselves within the traditional framework of Chinese history. They gave themselves a Chinese dynastic name—the Yuan. They made the classic claims about having a mandate from heaven. In short, they tried to become Chinese.

It didn't work. For one thing, the Mongols just couldn't stay away from policies that favored pasturage. This offended the deeply agrarian social constellation that was China. The Mongols revived the Chinese examination system as a mechanism for staffing a Chinese-style bureaucracy; but they didn't trust the people they had conquered, so they rigged the exams to ensure that Mongols and their foreign helpers would mostly pass and Han Chinese men would mostly fail. Mongol culture, born in the steppes where water was scarce, frowned on bathing. You can guess how that must have struck the fastidiously civilized Chinese. The Mongols revived the old tax rolls, but the tax collectors usually wore Mongol clothing and spoke Mongolian, so paying taxes didn't come off as a way to help keep the universe in order. It registered as a grating reminder of China's subjugation to barbarians.

Within one generation, a prairie fire of resentments put the "Yuan dynasty" on shaky ground. Rebel bands began to ravage the countryside. The toughest of many rebel militias were the Red Turbans, a secret society led by a barely literate ruffian named Zhu Yuanzhang. He was born of peasant stock, but his parents died when he was a child, so he grew up poor, sleeping in the back room of a Buddhist monastery as a charity case, begging on the streets to stay alive and stealing for a living once he learned how. By the time he was grown, this was not a man you wanted to meet in a dark alley late at night.

He took command of the Red Turbans, partnered up with Confucian scholars, and seized the city of Nanjing. From that base, he attacked the Mongol capital of Dadu. In 1368, he and his Red Turbans drove out the last of the steppe people and put an end to the "Yuan dynasty." China was back in native hands: a Han Chinese man sat upon the throne again; a new authentically *Chinese* imperial era had begun. Zhu Yuanzhang called his dynasty the Ming, which means "the brilliant."

Upon taking the throne, Chinese emperors customarily gave themselves a descriptive "reign name" by which they were known ever after.*

---

*To illustrate this concept by analogy: if a single monarch had ruled Western Europe in the fifteenth century, he might have called himself the Renaissance emperor, if in the nineteenth century, the Industrial Revolution emperor.

The man who established the Ming dynasty titled himself the Hongwu emperor. Hongwu means "vast military."

The Vast Military Emperor took the reins, determined to restore the Middle Kingdom envisioned by Confucius: centralized, bureaucratized, orderly, agrarian. Respect for family would flourish once again. Villages would hum with harmony once again. Every part of society would mesh with every other to form, once again—a single, greater whole. And the order of the universe would be restored, restored, restored, which is to say: the world would once again revolve around China, and China around the emperor, or the Son of Heaven.*

Unfortunately, Emperor Vast Military had started out as a lower-class ruffian of peasant origins, which raised the question: Was he really the Son of Heaven, the imperial father figure whose management of rituals would keep the world whole? Only once had a man risen from such depths to such heights. To be sure, that one previous peasant-turned-emperor was Liu Bang, founder of the iconic Han dynasty, but still: the new emperor's legitimacy depended on avoiding the least misstep. Because his survival depended on performing all the necessary rites correctly, this ill-educated man needed scholars; consequently, they gained unprecedented power at his court. Scholars derive their authority from their mastery of the known, not their explorations of the unknown. Their prominence at court made scholarship a key element of the Chinese social constellation now busy restoring its identity.

The Hongwu emperor never outgrew his dependence on the scholars' guidance, but he always resented their elitism. He suspected they were secretly laughing at him, and even as he elevated their status, he found ways to undermine their power. Any scholar who gained too much stature was well advised to start writing his will. The same was true of the emperor's

---

*Looking to the past for ideals doesn't mean those ideals were actually achieved in the past, but in the rubble left behind by the Mongols, it was easy to mythologize an imagined past as real and enshrine the restoration of that past as the fundamental project of civilization itself. The restoration narrative looked different from one society to another because each had a different past to restore, but the fundamental impulse was much the same.

friends. He came to power with ruffians like himself and installed them in high positions, but periodically he accused one or another of them of treason and had the traitor executed. Of the original sixty-plus comrades with whom he formed a government, only eight remained in office when he died.

On the plus side, given his origins, Hongwu sympathized with peasants and slashed their taxes, but this cut steeply into government revenues. How was the Hongwu emperor to pay for functions such as administration, policing, and above all military operations? A man who called himself Vast Military could not afford to field a puny army.

The scholar-literati found him an answer. Their study of canonical texts revealed that in the perfect Confucian society a standing military did not exist. When danger threatened, all men took up arms; when the threat abated, all went back to their real work, which was (ideally) farming. The emperor must therefore grant his officers land and have them support themselves. They wouldn't have to do any actual farming. Peasants would do that work. They could just manage the lands while discharging military duties as a calling, not a job. Thus did the Hongwu emperor manage to maintain a standing army of a million-plus men commanded by...um, farmers. Out of these seeds grew a hereditary, landowning military gentry known to Europeans later as *mandarins*. The Chinese were looking to the past for stars that would complete their constellation in the present.

China did need more than peasants and generals: it needed manual laborers to dig ditches and such. How were those workers to be paid? Once again, scholars provided the answer. The learned gentlemen found that peasants should contribute their services to the empire for the good of the whole, not for personal gain: it would be the Confucian thing to do. So, the Vast Military Emperor conscripted peasants as laborers and showered them with what-would-Confucius-do bulletins instructing them on how to be good. The constellation was now gaining coherence.

The Hongwu emperor also eliminated many administrative expenses by organizing the peasantry into tight village units that managed and policed themselves. Their duties as good Confucians included watching one another and informing the government of any suspicious activities. Why would people do all this for the emperor? Well, because the emperor was a scary brute who supplemented moral instructions with terror. Today, he might be diagnosed as a paranoid psychopath. He saw conspiracies everywhere and stopped at nothing to stomp them out. Once, he suspected his chief minister of plotting against him, so he had the man beheaded. Then he had the man's whole family executed, then his friends, then his friends' friends. By the time the emperor was done, forty thousand people had paid the price for that one man's alleged disloyalty. And the Hongwu emperor unleased this sort of violence sporadically throughout his reign. You can bet that when this emperor told the villagers to turn in troublemakers, they scrambled to comply.

China was a complex society with many power sectors, but none could now stand up to the power at the center. The emperor didn't use his vast military to wage wars of conquest. He used it to enforce internal order. When civil disruptions broke out, the imperial forces were right there to nip trouble in the bud. The Ming transformed China into a totalitarian society held in place with a grid of rules.

In this, they were harking back to ancient themes of China, and they had support among the people. The Ming took over a wounded world longing for stability. The Hongwu emperor vowed to restore the China of old, and plenty of folks were on board with that. Plenty of people wanted to be part of a constellation that held its shape: they wanted a future that was predictable. The Hongwu emperor pursued his project with such bloodshed and brutality that he actually exacerbated the hunger he was bidding to alleviate, but that only helped his successors consolidate his work. It gave them a deeper longing for coherence and stability they could tap for their project of enforcing order. Their traumatized society wanted to get back to normal, and "back to normal" fell right in line with "put things back the way they were." In this context, the restoration narrative had profound meaning-making power.

When Hongwu died, chaos briefly ensued. Then one of his younger sons managed to seize the throne. He wasn't next in line, so he was violating the rules of Confucian society, but he did it anyway "for the greater good." He gave himself the reign name of Yongle—"Perpetual Happiness." The Ming had survived their first crisis, the dynasty would continue, and so would the restoration project.

The Yongle emperor was a colossus in his father's mold, but he came to power with an odor of "usurper" clinging to him. If he was going to complete the resurrection of the dream, he would have to convince the Chinese world of his bona fides. That meant casting himself as a god-sized champion of what used to be. As a first step, Yongle moved his capital to the original homeland of Chinese civilization, the Huang He valley. He took the former Mongol capital as his own and renamed it Beijing. At the heart of this metropolis, he constructed the most elaborate palace complex the world had ever seen. The Forbidden City was 178 acres worth of buildings surrounded by a wall and populated with animal sculptures of ritual or magical significance. There were protective bronze lions all over the grounds facing north: the direction from which the Mongols had come. There were dragon sculptures, strategically placed to channel wisdom to the ruling family. No Chinese commoners were allowed into the Forbidden City, and very few visiting foreign dignitaries were invited inside. Those few had to approach the emperor on their hands and knees. Such steps all helped build an image of the emperor as a near-supernatural embodiment of Middle Kingdom supremacy.

At the dawn of the fifteenth century, the Yongle emperor dramatized the resurrection of China by assembling an enormous fleet: sixty-two of the biggest wooden ships ever built, plus about two hundred smaller ones to provide support services. Each of the big ships measured some four hundred feet from end to end, roughly the length of a city block in my neighborhood. The armada was, in essence, a floating city with a population of about twenty-eight thousand. It was commanded by a Muslim-born eunuch named Zheng He, a forbidding giant of a man. Between 1405 and 1433, the emperor sent this armada on seven expeditions, down through the islands and peninsulas of Southeast Asia to ports in southern India and beyond. His admiral checked in with the Persians at Hormuz, touched base in Yemen, and sent emissaries as far as Mecca. The fleet sailed halfway down the African coast to what is now Kenya. Everywhere the fleet went, the admiral handed out Chinese products to local rulers and from each locale brought back exotica for the emperor, such as giraffes, peacock feathers, musk, and rhinoceros horns. From the Chinese perspective, rulers who accepted the gifts were acknowledging themselves to be the emperor's humble tributaries. The foreigners no doubt took a different meaning from the exchanges, but their interpretations didn't matter to the splendiferous Chinese.

Admiral Zheng He and his armada did no serious trading, conquering, or exploring. The lands this fleet visited, the Chinese already knew about. Its assignment was really just to demonstrate how utterly China dwarfed all other lands.* In this, it succeeded. No one who saw the mighty armada could doubt that the Mongol era was over like last night's bad dream; the real China was *back*!

By the time the fleet returned from its seventh expedition, the Yongle emperor had died and a new man was on the throne. Remarkably enough, the new emperor not only halted further explorations but ordered that the whole armada be destroyed. Apparently, now that everyone knew they were the periphery and China was the center, no further voyages were needed. Instead, the Ming started funneling resources into huge internal projects.

Apart from the Forbidden City, the greatest of these projects were restorations. Restoration was, after all, the overarching narrative of the day. The Ming didn't build so much as *re*build. They replaced the Great Wall of pounded earth constructed by the First Emperor with a far more awesome wall of brick and stone, the only man-made artifact visible from space today. That's the Great Wall tourists now visit.

The Ming restored the Grand Canal, which had fallen into disrepair. They equipped it with sophisticated locks and other technological improvements. Today's Grand Canal is still a vital transportation link between north and south China, but it's not the one built by the Sui dynasty. It's the one *rebuilt* by the Ming.

From the start, the Ming rulers were determined to manage the economy of the empire themselves. They had officials collect from each

---

*The Yongle emperor also sent six expeditions north, into Central Asia: a thousand men each time, on twenty-five river boats, led by another eunuch, named Isiha. These expeditions sailed the Oxus River almost to the Aral Sea, and they too, it seemed, were meant mainly as a show of grandeur.

area what was plentiful and take it to where it was needed and distribute it as the government saw fit. Making such a complex circulatory system work required an intricate and disciplined bureaucracy. But this tapped right into China's strength. Dynasties had come and gone over the last fifteen-plus centuries, but the civil bureaucracy had been in place all along. What had varied from dynasty to dynasty was only how well that bureaucracy worked. The challenge for the Ming was to get the whole thing humming again. Step one was to staff it with the empire's best and brightest.

To this end, the Ming government built over a thousand state-run schools, at least one in every district and subdistrict, to recruit and train future bureaucrats. Men could gain office only through exams administered by the state. Every dynasty since the Han, even the Yuan (as the Mongols called themselves), had used civil service exams to separate the chaff from the wheat. In the Mongol era, however, people were graded in part on whom they knew and what ethnic group they belonged to. The Ming put an end to that nonsense. What the exams tested was what the schools taught, and every school had the same curriculum, designed by the scholar-literati at court, in close consultation with the Ministry of Rites, and approved by the emperor himself.

The Ming curriculum derived from doctrines that matured in Song times, just before the Mongols came galumphing in. At the core were the Five Classics, which included the ancient I Ching, and the Four Books, three ascribed to Confucius and one to the great Confucian philosopher Mencius (or Mengzi). The canon also included two thousand years of annotations and commentaries. This vast edifice comprised a system of thought known in retrospect as neo-Confucianism. Neo-Confucians held that people were born good but needed education to develop their moral intuition—just as a person born with musical talent still needs training to become an actual musician. So, this whole civilization, willingly or unwillingly, went into training to become good citizens.

Over the course of time, various thinkers fleshed out the neo-Confucian doctrine, sometimes with philosophies that went against the exact grain of state doctrine but reinforced what was at core a grid of uncompromising directives.* In the neo-Confucian world of Ming China, a father who beat his son to death might be looking at a fine. A son who punched his father in the face might be executed.

No one was going to ace the exams unless they knew the classics and canonical commentaries inside and out. The exams did not reward innovative interpretations. Their uncorrupted purity was guaranteed by autocratic enforcement. People were flogged for infractions, beheaded for serious violations. So tough were the exams that many aspiring bureaucrats spent decades studying for them and did not actually take the exams until they were middle aged. Those who were finally admitted to the ranks of the scholar-bureaucrats were never assigned to posts in the district where they grew up, nor in areas where they had personal connections, for they were not to govern by kinship loyalties or sentiment but only by the code.

Those who went through the school system graduated with the same skill set and the same worldview. They subscribed to the same ideal of a harmonious whole in which every member contributed to the harmony by playing his or her proper role. Neo-Confucian scholarship provided the blueprint for those roles. The cohesion of the bureaucrats and the coherence of society were two sides of the same coin.

As the Ming tightened their grip, a stable neo-Confucian world did emerge, in which different strata of society were given different levels of regard. The least admired were again the merchants, whom the doctrine accused of not producing anything, just moving stuff about. More respectable were artisans who at least crafted useful products, though some of it was frivolous. Above them were farmers, which at this point really meant the landowning gentry, for they produced food, and what could be more important than food? Well, actually, there was one thing more crucial than food: the scholars of the government bureaucracy enjoyed

---

*Wang Yangming, for example, a philosopher of near Confucius stature, taught that being good meant doing good. People were born infused with virtue but too much time spent in the classroom studying how to be good stunted one's ability to take virtuous action. Developing that capacity required participation in the hurly-burly of life because virtue was like a muscle: use it or lose it was the rule.

the highest status of all because they were the connecting tissue between everyday life and heaven.

Heaven, for all practical purposes, was the court and its apparatus, topped of course by the emperor and his family. That apparatus included two rival power blocs, the neo-Confucian scholar-literati and the huge corps of eunuchs.* The eunuchs were the officials in charge of the vast imperial harem. Given their intimate relationship with the emperor's private life—only they knew his women—they enjoyed a position of trust that the scholar-bureaucrats could only dream of. Eunuchs carried out personal assignments for the emperor and his high command. They were put in charge of tax collection, tasked with massive engineering projects, and given command of armies. No other civilization-scale social constellation had anything quite like China's power block of eunuchs.

Deep into the sixteenth century, the restoration narrative seemed to be working for China. Chinese agriculture was pouring out bounty, and people were so well fed that the population soared by almost 250 percent. Traders streamed to China from countless lands, eager for Chinese tea and for all the matchless products made in China: gorgeous lacquered furniture, jade ornaments, silk garments, metalwork of bronze and steel. Chinese potters were making porcelain now, an incredibly thin yet incredibly strong type of ceramics, which artisans of this period rendered jewel-like with a distinctive blue glaze. New industries emerged, new cities sprouted, old ones burgeoned. The awe-inspiring Great Wall, the

---

*As a social phenomenon, eunuchs were a by-product of unequal gender relations. Here, as in the Islamic world, powerful men kept harems as displays of status. It wasn't really about unlimited opportunities for sexual gratification; emperors and sultans would have had that anyway. The magnificence of a harem was rather like the feathers on a male peacock. And make no mistake: even if the emperor couldn't, as a practical matter, actually have sex with every woman in his harem of thousands didn't mean that any other man could. The ruler's exclusive access to the women was the whole point. But the harem had to interface with the outer world somehow, which required a large body of factotums, and these had to be men incapable of sex. They had to be eunuchs. But the eunuchs of the Muslim world did not compare to those of China as a distinct political faction or force.

astonishing Grand Canal, the network of scholar-bureaucrats, the swell-
ing tea orchards, the expanding porcelain workshops—it all added up to
a garish resurrection of a reimagined Chinese past.

All this seeming brilliance did have a flip side. Politics was savage
at the Ming court. The rulers were all too often cruel. The upper classes
lived in an uncertain atmosphere of intrigue and fear. The gentry tended
to abandon active political engagement as soon as possible and retire to
country estates, where they produced derivative paintings, poetry, and
calligraphy in the style of the artists of Tang times.

Chinese craftsmanship inspired foreign admiration, but the Ming
centuries saw no important new scientific or technological breakthroughs
to speak of. It didn't matter, for it took nothing away from the robust
vigor of the Chinese constellation. The Ming and their subjects were less
interested in discovering the new than in preserving the known. It's no
accident that this dynastic era saw the creation of the Yongle Encyclope-
dia, a compendium of knowledge that ran to nearly 11,095 volumes. Yes,
you read that right: not pages. Volumes.

In this milieu, innovation did not enjoy prestige: the unheard of was
best not heard of again. The ideal society was the stable society. Anything that sounded echoes of the past had luster; anything that smacked
of disruption had an odor. The great goal of human endeavor was social
harmony. If ever that were achieved, change could stop, and that would
be the greatest success of all: who doesn't want to get to healthy adulthood and then stay that way forever? The great project for people of the
present day was to reach again the level of the past. China became not
just inward looking but backward looking.

THE MIDDLE WORLD: DESTINY RESUMED

The Middle World was to see one last eruption out of the Asian
steppes, one last blast of pastoral nomadic ferocity, led by Timur
the Lame, known to the West as Tamerlane. He was a Turk who claimed
descent from Genghis Khan on his mother's side, and like the Mongols,

he built an enormous empire with alarming speed. He even went the Mongols one better by defeating the Mamluks, whom the Mongols never could, and razing Delhi, which the Mongols never reached. Like his long-ago Turkic predecessors out of Afghanistan and Transoxiana, Timur looted the subcontinent to beautify the glittering core of his own empire, the almost mythically splendid cities of Samarkand and Bukhara. He was then ready to move on China but died before he could climb into the saddle for that one last campaign. China therefore escaped the slaughter, just as Europe had escaped the earlier Mongol devastations.

Unlike Genghis Khan, however, Timur was a Muslim. His people had converted before he was born. Everywhere he went, after he had finished making pyramids out of the skulls of his enemies, he sat down with the local Muslim scholars and poets and engaged in civilized conversations about the meaning of life. One such encounter brought him into dialogue with the great Tunisian historian, Ibn Khaldun, one of the founders of sociology, who apparently convinced Timur to leave Egypt alone and go back to his own home region. Something big was changing in the zeitgeist of this world.

Once Timur died, his empire quickly fragmented. His heirs held onto a piece of it, and for several generations, a Timurid kingdom straddled what is now the Iran-Afghanistan border. But the post-Timur Timurids were just another set of Muslim kings and pretty good ones at that. These kings patronized Muslim scholars, artists, and literati. Some of the greatest poets of the Persian language flourished under their patronage. It was here that the art of the illuminated book came of age. The monarchs of this dynasty did no sacking and slaughtering to speak of. The ferocious energy that had animated steppe conquerors from Genghis Khan to Timur the Lame had crested. Dar-ul-Islam was ready to put itself back together and be what it used to be.

And it could do so with renewed confidence because, despite the military defeats, no one in the Muslim world had adopted Tengraism, the pre-Islamic religion of the steppes. The Mongols who conquered the Islamic heartland, the Il-Khans as they called themselves, soon converted to Islam and got absorbed into the master narrative of Muslim civilization. One of their kings even fancied himself a Sufi mystic. Clearly, the Mongol moment had faded out. Islam was the final truth after all, and Muslims could resume the divine project launched from Medina over seven centuries ago by the messenger of God.

Restoration, then, became the overarching project of Islamic civilization, just as it had in China: this constellation, too, was reconstructing its identity. Between India and the Mediterranean, out of the rubble of the Mongol disruptions, three new contiguous empires formed, which historians have called the gunpowder empires, because they brought guns to a knife fight—literally. They used firearms and cannons to defeat enemies armed with swords and battle axes.

The first of these to form was the Ottoman Empire, which eventually lapped into Europe. It was built by Turkish steppe nomads who had fled the Mongol onslaughts, fled and fled until they reached the relative safety of Asia Minor. There they stopped running and resumed their ancestral habits of herding and raiding, the first for staples, the second for luxuries. They raided their way into Byzantine territory, moved toward Constantinople, and sank roots into conquered territory as they advanced until, by the mid-fourteenth century, a formidable new Muslim sultanate had clearly materialized. Its expansion westward was powered by warriors called *ghazis*, "soldiers for the faith," a Muslim version of the religious-military orders of the crusaders. The ghazis belonged to various religious corporations modeled on the mystical Sufi brotherhoods of earlier Islamic times, brotherhoods that became the organizing principle of not just armies but crafts guilds, trade associations, communications networks, and the state itself. Here, too, restoration was gestating something new but creating it through a reverent fixation on the past.

In 1452, the Ottomans seized control of Constantinople, which instantly elevated them to the status of a major world power, perhaps *the* major world power. Constantinople was (informally) recast as Istanbul, from which capital the Ottomans ruled an empire that continued to expand into Europe in the west and across the Levant and into North Africa in the south, engulfing virtually all Arab-inhabited territories along the way.

Its eastward expansion was blocked by a second new Islamic gunpowder empire, the Safavid dynasty, which originated as a Sufi brotherhood in the Azerbaijan area. In the fifteenth century, this brotherhood went through a transformation from cult to army. The head of the brotherhood created an elite military corps known as the Red Hats, and after he died, his twelve-year-old son Ismail led the Red Hats on a rash of military campaigns. By 1502, Ismail had rebuilt the core of the ancient Persian Empire, covering all the territory that is today's Iran and a little bit more—but it was an *Islamic* Persian Empire: a Shia social constellation. This had not existed before, but only because the Persian Shias had not succeeded in forging an empire of their own. Now they were doing it, so this was essentially the restoration of a dream.

The Safavids, on *their* eastern border, butted up against the Mughal Empire, also founded by a brilliant teenager. This one was named Babur; he was born just north of Afghanistan and traced his lineage back to both Timur and Genghis Khan (although this latter may have entailed some résumé padding). He inherited a kingdom in the steppes

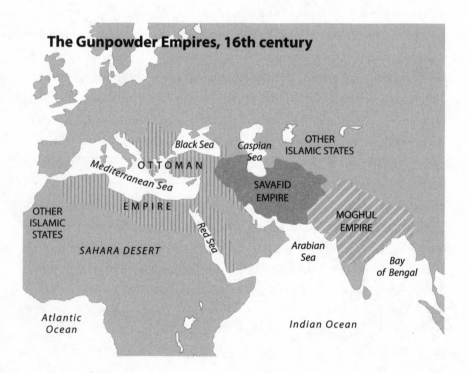

The Gunpowder Empires, 16th century

at the age of twelve, lost it when he was fourteen, led a small band of loyalists south, and in 1503 conquered the city of Kabul. From there he launched an invasion of India. The Sultan of Delhi sent out a gigantic army fronted by elephants, but Babur had brought guns to a beast brawl; he routed those poor elephants with cannons. In 1526, Babur declared Delhi the capital of his own new empire. India's glittering Mughal era had begun, and another story already in progress was resumed: a Muslim minority's struggle to dominate and govern a Hindu majority.

Meanwhile, around the time the Mongols were conquering Russia, the African kingdom of Ghana gave way to the much bigger and richer Mali Empire. (See map on p. 140.) The outsized founder of this empire was an Alexander-scale figure named Sundiata Keita, or Hungering Lion. His grandson Mansa Musa, an emperor of mythic scale (and possibly the richest man in history before Amazon CEO Jeff Bezos), made a pilgrimage to Mecca, carrying along such a quantity of gold that the price of gold crashed in Egypt as he passed through. By the time the Ottomans were building their state in Asia Minor, however, the Mali Empire had lost steam—but only because it was giving way to an even bigger, even richer empire, that of the Songhai. By the fifteenth century, the Songhai city of Timbuktoo had become a major intellectual capital of the Islamic world, a city of libraries, scholars, doctors, and philosophers.

In short, from Mauretania to Istanbul to the Indus valley and beyond, a new master narrative took shape but one that, significantly enough, made no claims to novelty. Quite the opposite. It harked back resolutely to the origin story of Islam, offering, as its core proposition, that history's perfect moment had already happened. The universe was an apocalyptic drama that would end with the day of judgment, and the pivotal moment in the story was the prophetic career of Messenger Muhammad: his seventh-century Medina stamped the template for all humankind. After the Prophet's death, the mission had been to keep the perfection going. Muslims had let it slip away, so now they had the civilization-sized task of restoring it. Reasonable people might dispute how that could be done, but on restoration as an overarching meaning-of-life type of social project, there was broad consensus. The community must regain its health by getting back on the path that had started in seventh century Medina.

In Medina, the messenger had provided a model for governing a multicultural city, and the Ottomans used that template to govern their extremely multicultural empire. In Medina, the messenger had specified that each community of faith should have its own leaders and follow its own ways, but the leader of the Muslim community should preside over all, adjudicating disputes between communities and ruling on all matters not soluble at a lower level. All Muslims had to make specified donations to charity, all non-Muslims had to pay a special tax, and all citizens had to rally as one to beat back any outside threat, no matter what their faiths.

The Ottomans accordingly set up the many different communities of faith within their borders as *millets,* semiautonomous nations. As a matter of course, all laws governing the public realm had to facilitate the way of life decreed by the scriptures and elaborated by Islamic scholars. The sharia, the framework for Muslim life, was the living, breathing essence of the single community of all (Muslim) believers (as the church had been for Europe in its feudal Catholic era).

Sharia means "path," which is appropriate, for it was, to Muslims, like the marks a trailblazer might score into tree trunks so that people could follow him safely through a wilderness. In this case, the wilderness was the material world. The sharia provided specific instructions for dealing with all possible real-life situations. It covered the details of religious ritual; it addressed matters of habit and grooming; it legislated on crimes and punishments. To stay on the path, people had to observe God's directives about financial interactions, marital relationships, inheritance, and much, much more: the harmony of the community required it. As long as they stayed on the path, people were free to live as they wanted.

In theory the sharia could settle any dispute that came up. In practice, novel situations kept coming up, slightly different from all previous situations and calling for a new ruling. When a qualified Muslim scholar made a judgment about any current question, he had to make sure it aligned with all canonical decisions of the past. Scholars had to first consult the core source, the Qur'an, then see if the messenger had addressed the matter in some real-life situation, then look to his closest companions' words and deeds, then to subsequent authoritative scholars. If all else failed, current scholars could exercise *ijtihad*, or free reasoning, but they could resort to this only if all else had failed. What's more, only someone deeply versed in the sharia was qualified to use this method because only such a person could know that no relevant ruling already existed. The Muslim world's self-regulating body of religious scholars was analogous to the state-built schools that produced Ming China's bureaucratic staff.

Since the world never stops changing, the sharia project could never be completed. New situations requiring new rulings kept coming up. The sharia project sought to create an exoskeleton of regulations within which people could live safe from error. But a structure made up of specific regulations about specific matters works only in a world that never changes. In that sort of world, all questions can finally be rooted out and answered, after which no new questions can arise. The Islamic scholars' approach to completing the sharia inherently implied restoring and rendering permanent a social moment in the past: the seventh-century Muslim community of Medina under the guidance of the Prophet. The fact that things kept changing only meant the perfection had not yet been restored: there was still work to be done.

The Sunni scholars of the Ottoman, African, and Mughal worlds elaborated one version of the sharia, the Shia scholars of the Safavid Empire another. The Sunni and Shia versions of the sharia differed in detail but were similar in spirit, structure, and scope. Both were inherently conservative in that new rulings could not overthrow old rulings; they had to fit in with rulings of the past. In both empires, scholars qualified to interpret the sharia partnered with the military-political aristocracy. The scholars legitimized the rulers, the rulers protected the scholars: one hand washed the other. The Ottoman world had a sultan ("local enforcer of Islamic law"), who also titled himself the khalifa ("head of the Muslim community"). He appointed a sheikh-ul-Islam ("grand old man of Islam"), essentially the empire's scholar-in-chief. In the Safavid world, a body of venerated Shia scholars known as ayatollahs emerged, counter-balancing a political leader known as the shah.*

Despite doctrinal variations from place to place, the Islamic Middle World and its sub-Saharan spur evolved as a distinctive social whole held together by a fabric of ideas and lifeways that seemed, from the inside, universal. Throughout this world, manufacturing lay in the hands of individual artisans who produced goods in tens of thousands of private workshops. Most artisans, especially in the Ottoman Empire, belonged to guilds interwoven with Sufi brotherhoods or other sorts of religious associations. The guilds controlled prices, ensured wages and employment for their members, and eliminated cutthroat competition, thereby creating a stable and predictable business climate for their members. *Stable* and *predictable* were the key words here.

The religious associations, whether Sufi or orthodox, Sunni or Shia, ran mosques, operated wealthy charitable foundations, and managed shrines that drew myriad religious pilgrims. These associations also maintained something akin to a social services safety net. Meanwhile, merchants kept the handicrafts flowing throughout this world, from the heart of India to the edge of Europe.

The sharia provided the basis for social harmony, but the sharia was not simply an Islamic version of neo-Confucian doctrine. It was not, that is to say, a blueprint for running a bureaucracy controlled by some single centralized state. That wasn't the vision. The sharia was like a framework giving definition to a free-flowing world that harkened back to tribal days.

One caveat to note, however: the term *tribal* can be misleading here. The Islamic Middle World emerged from a tribal past, yes, but so did all human societies. The tribal past might have been somewhat more recent here, but it wasn't recent. Dar-ul-Islam was a sophisticated urban civilization and had been for centuries, but it had evolved out of tribalism in its own way. In a purely tribal world, loyalty to kin trumped all other

---

*The Shia held that at every given moment a living person called the Hidden Imam was anonymously channeling God's grace into the world. No one knew who he was, but his existence generated the ayatollahs, any of whom might be in contact with the hallowed one himself.

virtues. An individual stood by family, no matter what. Anyone in a position to help kinfolk had an obligation to do so or be shamed. Familial obligations extended beyond family, to clan, and beyond clan, to tribe, though in ever more diluted form.

And they might extend beyond tribe as well. In the Islamic world, people connected to one another by virtue of favors conferred and received might develop into patronage networks, which were somewhat similar to what Americans call old boy networks but without the pejorative connotation. Relationships like these could not be settled by returning favors of equal value, any more than one can (or would want to) be quit of family by repaying all that one had received from one's mother and father. Men of standing and power accepted that there were people who very rightly depended on them, and they were not necessarily kin. Relationships forged in the hotbed of experience among those who grew up together (even if one of them was a servant) or waged war together (even if one of them was an officer) or engaged in business together (even if one was an employee) or suffered grievances together (even if one had it worse) could impose emotional mandates comparable to familial ones. Patronage networks, unlike classic old-boy networks, were not closed systems: humble members of some patron might themselves be patrons to others even humbler.* Patrons relied on clients, and clients expected favors from patrons. There were no contracts, nothing codified in written rules. Only a rude lout would measure what A owed B based on what B had done for A. Social ties were not a mutual aid market but a simulacrum of family. What kept social interactions on an even keel were intuitions about honor.

---

*For example, my father and a classmate were sent to America together by the government to get university educations. They were linked forever after, moving through government posts: whatever job the classmate got, my father got a job as his deputy. My father, meanwhile, had a friend in the city's poor quarters, a self-educated healer who had learned quite a bit about medicine. As a friend of the family, he was called in for medical advice whenever any of us were sick, even though he wasn't a "real" doctor. When a job opened up at a pharmacy, my father, of course, used his influence to get that post for "Dr." Ghani. Similar threads of connection went on down from Ghani and from my father's classmate on up to others even higher in power and prestige.

What constituted honorable behavior? It wasn't in the sharia. If you were part of the community, you just knew. It boiled down to unspoken understandings that formed in family life and were therefore shaped and enforced in childhood (and therefore to a great extent by women): what to say at a funeral, how to give gifts graciously, when to speak up at a public gathering, what to serve impromptu guests, how to address various people appropriately given where one stood with them in the structure of all relationships—the list goes on. Those who best embodied the unspoken values were apt to acquire prestige, which made for power. Those who committed missteps based on boorish misunderstandings of unwritten rules were apt to see their influence fade.

Patronage generated the social web that held urban societies together: interconnected networks at many levels that were constantly under construction. Men at the core of one patronage network might themselves be peripheral members of other more powerful patronage networks. Getting ahead involved working one's way up from web to web, of people who knew people who knew people: Arabs called this *wasita* ("ways and means"). The more power a man had, the more far-flung his constellation of dependents and clients. Some might be his relatives, some his family friends, some personal friends, some comrades from way back, some simply men who had proved themselves useful. The honorable thing was for everyone to follow not just the recorded regulations of the sharia but the unwritten (and presumably intuitive) rules of etiquette and graciousness.

In the tribal societies out of which these values grew, leadership had depended on both lineage and achievement. The same was true in the world of patronage networks. Reputation was all. Descendants of great men inherited their ancestors' status, but to keep it, they had to prove themselves—in battle, say, or by epic displays of good judgment, or by decisive action in the face of crises threatening the community. Lineage could be improved through strategic marriages, and in Islamic societies, which were divided into separate spheres by gender, lineage-improvement through marriage arranging was a realm in which women could and to some extent did exercise political influence of a sort.

Men, meanwhile, dominated the public realm, from which women were almost totally excluded, more so than in any other society on Earth. It was out there in the public realm that men found clients, and clients found patrons, and networks formed. It was there that men had the opportunity to prove their worth to the community. If their deeds fell short, they lost status and injured their family's status too. If their deeds won renown, they were apt to make connections that advanced their own and hence their family's name.

Governed by such rules and norms, the Islamic Middle World was an intricate clockwork of meshing parts that added up to a civilization-scaled social constellation of tremendous *apparent* vigor. This world, like China, was animated by a mythic vision of a perfect harmony that had existed in the past and was the ultimate—and attainable—goal of the future. If everyone behaved as they should—and there were ways to know how they should—the social world could take final form, and disruptive change could blessedly stop.

In the aftermath of the Mongol holocaust, Muslims of the Middle World must have felt they were living through the epochal rebirth of civilization. Dar-ul-Islam had survived, and Islam was rising back to its predestined place. The Ottomans, Safavids, and Mughals were no less wealthy or powerful than the Umayyad, Abbasid, and Fatimid caliphates had been. No one could stand up to the military might of any of them except another of them. Different dynasties might be in power here or there, but Islam itself seemed to be back on its path of absorbing all of humanity into one community.

And these gunpowder empires weren't just about gunpowder. Their elite sponsored wondrous works of art and architecture, literature and thought. Islamic builders erected stunning masterworks such as the Selimiye Mosque in Turkey and India's Taj Mahal. The whole city of Isfahan in Iran was essentially one city-sized work of art. Under Safavid rule, carpet making crossed the border from craft to art, and masterpieces of the form were produced throughout the Islamic world. Artists created illuminated books showcasing Persian-Arabic calligraphy and featuring jewel-like miniature paintings. To all appearances, the Islamic world was in the midst of a cultural renaissance rivaling the brilliance of Islam's early days.

But appearances can be deceiving. Safavid and Mughal artists produced fine illuminated books, but they were expressing an aesthetic already in place. The books presented masterpieces of Persian literature, but the literature had already been written. New works sought to equal the achievements of the past in the styles of the past. Ferdowsi's epic *Book of Kings*, written five centuries earlier for Mahmud the Ghaznavid, didn't feel dated in the post-Mongol world. Rumi, the great mystic poet, was born the year Genghis Khan began his conquests, but there was nothing quaint about his lyrics to an Ottoman world audience.

The inhabitants of Dar-ul-Islam had every reason to believe their world was *the* world. It was, after all, such a coherent whole. The various social constellations within the Islamic galaxy were often in conflict with one another, but their arguments employed terms of discourse they all shared. They had different answers to life's great questions, but they had the same questions. In the world divided between the Ottoman and Safavid rulers, for example, a major question of the age was: Sunnism or Shiism? It couldn't be both. In the neighboring Mughal world, a great question was: "Islam or Hinduism?" It couldn't be both. People argued, but they knew what they were arguing about.

Intellectuals of the Islamic Middle World took little notice of developments in Western Europe at this time because nothing happening in those distant, primitive lands had much relevance to the great questions of the age (from their perspective). In this respect, they were no different than the intellectuals of China or India or the Turkic steppes or Southeast Asia. Throughout the worlds east of the Mediterranean Sea, there was no reason to doubt that each society's restoration narrative was not just a model of the world but *was* the world. Looking to the past as a template for the future was certainly yielding empires of enormous wealth and weight. As it happened, however, the West was going through a momentous transformation at this same time, and there, a very different civilization-sized social project was taking hold.

16

The Progress Narrative
(1500 CE to 1900 CE)

In the year 1500, restoring the past didn't have much appeal in Europe. Before the upheavals of the fourteenth century, most people were wretched peasants with little hope of improvement in their own lives or their children's, or their children's children's. And the further back you went, the worse it got. That past was nothing to wax nostalgic about—not in a post-Crusades, post-Mongol Europe brimming with stories about exotic lands where even poor folks seasoned their food with pepper and even shopkeepers wore cotton. What had allure for Europeans at this point was moving forward. Today was usually better than yesterday, so why shrink from tomorrow? In this context, discovery had glamor, disruption smacked of adventure, and innovation gained prestige—a prestige it was losing in the farther east. Out of these ingredients, even as Ming China was basking in splendor and the Islamic world was recovering its stride, a grand new narrative was beginning to emerge in Europe.

Before the Long Crusades, Europe had been locked into static social forms. Social disapproval blocked anyone from questioning those forms. Life was so fragile that anyone who rocked the boat was threatening everybody. But the Black Death loosened the grip of the master narrative entrenched here for seven centuries—how could it not? At the height of the horror, the church had proved so ineffectual. People had done everything the church recommended, and still they'd kept dying. The clergy absolved penitents of sins, and still they kept dying, for the plague made no distinction between saints and sinners. God's punishment was everywhere, but punishment for what?

These upheavals did not bring Christianity itself into question. At first, they only planted doubts about the Church of Rome. That, however, was enough to reopen the Big Questions, questions the church had answered so authoritatively just a few centuries before: What was the world all about? How should people live? What was really going on? Where was all this going? How was one to know?

Europe had come out of the fourteenth century pandemic as a world in flux. In this milieu, it was possible to think the unthinkable. It's hardly accidental that in the wake of the Black Death, movements swelled up to translate the Bible into languages people actually spoke. Many wanted to see for themselves what the scriptures said because it kind of looked like maybe, perhaps, just maybe—here's the unthinkable part: maybe the church had gotten something wrong.

THE PROTESTANT IDEA

As it happened, in the waning days of the Long Crusades, new technology was fueling growing literacy in Europe. There was paper now. There was printing now. There were books now. More people could read, and more were looking for things *to* read, which fit right in with the quest to translate the Bible into languages people actually spoke. The church took a dim view of this project. Giving ordinary people access to the Bible? Why, it threatened the order of the universe! The Inquisition hunted down such heretics and burned them out of the system as enthusiastically as it did witches.

In retrospect, one can recognize the source of this passion. The power of the feudal church came from its monopoly on access to heaven. If people could get to the coveted afterlife on their own, they wouldn't need the Catholic Church and its narrative anymore. A narrative rendered unnecessary is a dead man walking. Its lifeblood starts to ebb from the moment its relevance—not it's accuracy but its relevance—comes into question.

What church officials felt was not, I dare say, mere petty anxiety about their own entitlements. For centuries, the Catholic narrative had not only held the world together but made the world "knowable." Within that framework, even the wretched could feel that life in some way made sense. Incompatible ideas threatened the coherence of the constellation, and if the social constellation lost coherence, all its human parts stood to lose their identity. A jumbled or indistinct identity might not be life threatening to the human *body*, but it is a mortal menace to the human *person*, and therefore to social entities that are groups of persons knit together by narratives capable of forming and carrying out intentions— what I've here been calling social constellations.

In this context, the church could burn a guy at the stake for trying to translate a book, and instead of losing respect for the church, devout observers were moved to applaud the savagery and breathe a sigh of relief—nothing to worry about, the church was on it, the "we" would survive.

Then in 1519, a monk-professor named Martin Luther wrote up ninety-five blistering criticisms of the Church of Rome, nailed them to the door of his local church in Wittenberg, Germany, and included them in a letter to the archbishop of Mainz. Pamphleteers soon printed copies of the so-called Ninety-five Theses and distributed them throughout German-speaking lands. There was nothing explicitly political about Luther's critique. Luther was a theologian. He expressed his points entirely within terms of discourse familiar to Christendom. His ninety-five criticisms all had to do with church doctrine and church practice.

What Luther rejected most specifically was the sale of indulgences. These were a spiritual benefit that laypersons could receive from the church. An indulgence reduced the amount of time a person had to spend in purgatory, the place where the last impurities were burned away before a soul could enter heaven. Everyone had to spend *some* time in purgatory because it was damned near impossible to die entirely free of sin, but no one wanted to stay in purgatory any longer than he or she had to, and the church, in exchange for good and valuable considerations, could arrange to have one's sentence there reduced.

What good and valuable considerations? Well, indulgences really took off as a by-product of the Crusades. Originally, the church had offered them to people who risked their lives for Christendom, especially the warrior monks of the military-religious orders, such as the Knights

Templar. But as the Crusades began to wane, indulgences devolved into something more like a purely commercial product. Donating *x* amount of silver to your local church could reduce your time in purgatory by *y* amount.

This was what enraged Martin Luther. The church had always declared that salvation could *not* be had by faith alone; you needed works to your credit to get into heaven. Works, remember, did not mean good deeds in the everyday sense but rituals prescribed by the church—as well as, possibly, cash donations to it. Luther declared in his disgust that salvation could not be achieved by works *at all*. Not at all. Only faith could save. Works are visible. Anyone can see whether a person is praying and whether or not he or she is doing it correctly. Faith, by contrast, is a direct communion with God. No outside observer can know if a person has faith. That can be known only to the person, and to God.

Luther's rebellion must be seen against the backdrop of his times. The ravages of the fourteenth century had left the Church of Rome scrambling to repair its credibility. Now, some secular rulers were claiming the right to appoint clerics, and by this they didn't just mean lowly local village priests. They were talking about the very lords of the church: the bishops. In fact, one secular ruler, the king of France, even appointed a pope of his own. Yes, briefly, there were two popes in Christendom. In fact, for a flicker of a moment, there were *three*. Obviously, the church could not allow such goings-on. Kings appointing bishops? Intolerable! And just as the struggle over this issue was heating up, along came Luther.

Luther didn't weigh in on whether kings could appoint bishops. He didn't have to. His dicta meant that officers of the church could neither help nor hinder anyone from getting into heaven. In fact, if faith trumped works, they couldn't even know who was getting in. And if the officers of the church were not the instruments of grace but mere building managers, they were no different than the janitors who kept the church clean or the tailors who made the priests' robes. Why *shouldn't* kings appoint such factotums?

Meanwhile, religious rebels were ramping up their efforts to create vernacular versions of the Bible so that all Christians could experience the *meaning* of the scriptures, not just the sounds of them. But in the framework long established by the Catholic Church, *the sounds* were essential. The Mass *had* to be said in Latin (or Greek) because those were the sounds that made the magic happen. Besides, producing a Bible the masses could read implied that the masses could decide how to worship. Within the feudal Catholic framework, that was crazy talk. If Christianity was the one whole body of Christ on Earth, each cell could not be deciding autonomously how he or she would behave. The one whole body could not survive that sort of fragmentation and would inevitably fight back against such a mortal threat.

Now, however, anyone with a bit of money could print copies of a book cheaply enough for most literate people to buy. Not that the average peasant could afford a printed Bible, but a lot of people weren't simple peasants anymore. The European social constellation now included skilled craftsmen, merchants, members of professional guilds—all sorts of moneyed townspeople. Given the confluence of technology and social trends, there was no way the church could keep scripture locked up. The Bible was going to get out there. And as religious information poured into Christian society from a variety of competing sources, all the static made the master narrative of the past hard to even see. In the same way that anomalies rendered Ptolemy's star charts incoherent, anomalies now eroded the overarching religious narrative that had long held the European social constellation together.

Martin Luther's ninety-five criticisms of the Church of Rome were like a lit match touched to a barrel of gunpowder. A civil war exploded within Christendom between the Catholic monolith and the many Christians who wanted to form autonomous communities of faith, unaffiliated with the Church of Rome. This was nothing like the "great schism" between the Churches of Rome and Constantinople. It wasn't a case of this church versus that church. It was fundamentally about one monolithic church versus everybody building his or her own church. The Protestant movement produced many different Christianities, and this inevitably got tangled up with the emergence of many distinct secular kingdoms. The religious civil wars went on for nearly two centuries, ending finally with the Treaty of Westphalia in 1648, which established the interesting principle that secular rulers would henceforth decide which version of Christianity would be practiced in their secular realm. Europe's religious civil war thus ended up watering the seeds of a new social form that would mature over the next few centuries: the nation-state.

SCIENCE EMERGES

Meanwhile, within the crumbling framework of the old narrative, another baby was busy being born. The towering luminaries associated with the origins of science were not scientists. They couldn't be, since no such thing existed yet. The trailblazers of science were men of the church, one and all. Take Copernicus, for example, the fifteenth-century astronomer who solved the growing incoherence of the Ptolemaic star charts with a bold new theory: he proposed that the sun stood still and everything else, including Earth, revolved around it. The author of this seminal restructuring of the cosmos lived his whole life nestled in the warm embrace of Mother Church. Copernicus was a famous academic of his time, and he held a doctorate in, yes, canon law. When he wrote a book describing his heliocentric theory, his admiring readers included the pope.

Copernicus had a pupil named Kepler, another giant of early science. Kepler was also a devout man of the church. He labored to complete the work Copernicus had begun because, in the spirit of the scholastics—men of the church, one and all—he thought God's creation must reflect God's perfection, and there were still a few discrepancies in his master's heliocentric model. The neoscholastics had worked to establish a link between mathematics and nature; Kepler was the man who nailed that one to the wood. He showed that the Copernican model worked perfectly if you added just one elegant assumption: that the paths of the planets around the sun were not necessarily circular but were always elliptical. And since there are formulas for calculating the perimeter of an ellipse, the position of a planet revolving around the sun could be calculated with mathematical precision at any given moment.

Achievements like this raised an almost unspeakably grand possibility: *What if the whole world could be explained?* What if everything that was unknown could become known? Natural philosophers (only later called scientists) began searching the physical world for mathematical patterns in the way gases expanded and stones rolled down hill and materials cooled and mixtures of materials formed new compounds. They set to work trying to quantify how forces acted on matter, and why objects moved as they did, and what causes living bodies to grow and die. Science acquired status as a social enterprise, peaking in the eighteenth century with the work of the great Isaac Newton, who deciphered the particle nature of light, identified gravity as a pervasive force in the universe, and managed to reduce all observable motion to three breathtakingly simple laws of motion.

It wasn't the old feudal Catholic narrative that gave such efforts meaning. It wasn't within that eroding framework that they made sense. There was a new master narrative coalescing in Europe and especially in Western Europe: a counterpart to the restoration narrative of the East. The defining narrative of Western civilization in the centuries to come wasn't going to be materialism. Yes, people focused on material phenomena more than they had earlier, but most people still devoutly embraced a religious faith, and in Europe this faith was, in almost every case, some version of Christianity.

And while Christianity branched, the dominant new narrative wasn't going to be the Protestant faith either. For one thing, there was no single Protestant faith. The Protestants themselves kept branching and branching. What they shared was not a faith but a restless appetite for a truth that felt more true, a willingness to try something new. What's more, the church itself was not dead by any measure: the Catholic Church retained tens of millions of adherents.

Nor can the new narrative be described simply as secular. The emerging narrative accorded respect to secular ideas and preoccupations, but most people still regularly attended church, identified as members of some community of faith, and performed religious rituals at home. Science was one of the fuels and fruits of the new master narrative, but science was only one aspect of it, too.

What all these social streams and cultural currents shared was a tendency to view the world in terms of progress and regress. In this narrative, time was linear but had no endpoint. The momentum of history was forward flowing but could at times slip backward. When it did regress, humanity had to stem the slippage, reverse the direction, and get the forward motion going again. What was slippage and what was forward motion might be open to argument, but progress was the ultimate goal of human effort, and there was no final destination: tomorrow could always be better than today, always. Progress was at the core of the faith that began to knit together a new civilization here at the western edges of Europe. No doubt many people still believed sincerely in a day of judgment—when they thought about it. But how many people thought about it as a normal part of their everyday lives? Fewer and fewer, one suspects. Whereas progress? Pretty much everyone was focused on making progress, all day, every day—and on stemming regress when they felt slippage happening.

The progress narrative—the deep belief that "better" was always possible—drove a search for scientific principles of ever-deeper explanatory power. Eventually, it generated the conviction that explaining something scientifically was exactly the same thing as explaining it. As time went on the progress narrative motivated a constant, obsessive improvement of human tools. Much later, it would transform the very relationship between humans and their tools.

But all of that was yet to come. In the fifteenth century, the forces giving birth to science and stoking religious renewal were also feeding an appetite for exploration. Christendom was still breathing the fumes of the Crusades, and those fumes were now a combination of political and commercial fervor as well as religious idealism. The Long Crusades had opened European eyes to a class of products abundant in east Asia, products that spoke to human longings for pleasure, luxury, recreation, and ecstasy. In short, Europe had begun to fixate on spices, and European adventurers were ready to face hardships and dangers to secure some of those wonderful products. It was the hunger for spices that led to one of history's watershed moments.

PART IV

History's Hinge

Every world historical narrative organizes time around some pivotal event that separates after from before. If history is the drama of ever-increasing interconnectedness, Columbus's first voyage to America must be considered the pivotal event—the event that "changed everything." From this moment forward, both hemispheres were interconnected, all of planet Earth was part of a single intercommunicating world. It came at a cost. The arrival of the Europeans wiped out whole civilizations in the Americas. European access to the crops and minerals of these continents ended up reshaping the map of the world. The ripple effects of the Columbus moment also spawned new forms of social constellations in Europe, including corporations, banks, national currencies, and proto-nation-states. In the wake of the Columbus moment, all the world historical monads of earlier times—India, China, the Islamic Middle World, the Eurasian steppes, the Americas, sub-Saharan Africa, and Europe—got drawn into one great global drama. And so they have remained. With all parts of the world intertwined, events anywhere in the world could now have quick and rapid consequences anywhere else in the world. The globalization of ripple effects had begun.

17

That Columbus Moment
(1400 to 1600)

I n the fifteenth century, a Portuguese prince named Henry came down with crusading fever. He was known to later historians as Prince Henry the Navigator, even though he himself never navigated so much as a fish pond: he was called the navigator because he funded expeditions to explore the African coast as far south as possible. Today, that title vests Prince Henry with the image of a man driven by curiosity, an early modernist, a protoscientist almost. That's not how he thought of himself. Henry the Navigator was grand master of the Military Order of Christ, a successor to the Knights Templar: he lived like a monk, wore a hair shirt, prided himself on his celibacy, and died (it is said) a virgin. Henry was a man of his times, and his times were the late stages of the Long Crusades.

Early in his career, Henry dispatched an armada to conquer the Muslim-held African city of Ceuta. He spoke of this success in crusading terms—as a victory for Christians over Muslims. The Portuguese conquest brought home much booty, including ginger, cinnamon, black pepper, and other precious spices. Unfortunately, these came from the Far East. Muslim traders had brought them across the Sahara Desert in camel caravans. Once Christians took the Muslim cities on the Atlantic coast, the caravans stopped coming. So Henry sent ships farther south, hoping they could get all the way around Africa; in which case Muslims be damned, Portugal would get the spices directly from the source.

A century earlier, this quest would have been unthinkable. The prevailing winds blew south, so ships equipped with square sails could get down the coast but not back up again. This had prevented European ships from getting past the bulge of West Africa. Now, however, the Portuguese were building nimble ships called *caravels*, ships with shallow keels, which were easy to turn, and most importantly equipped with lateen sails, which enabled them to sail against the wind by tacking. So now, Portuguese sailors could push boldly south and farther south—but they never found a corner to turn. Some began to mutter that Africa might extend to the ends of Earth. Perhaps there was no getting around it.

One such doubter was a Genovese sailor named Cristobal Colon—better known now as Christopher Columbus. He was a strapping fellow with a long face and aquiline features. His hair was prematurely white—grizzled by experience, perhaps, for he'd sailed the seas as a common sailor. He'd been with two Portuguese expeditions that had tried and failed to get around Africa, and he'd been on a merchant ship in the Mediterranean that was sunk by competitors, on which occasion, he'd been forced to swim six miles to the safety of shore. Since then he'd made himself an expert on maps and charts and somewhere along the way had formed a fixed idea that the Spice Islands of the East might be reached by sailing west.

Experts scoffed at this notion and not because they thought Earth was flat. At that point, no educated person thought Earth was flat. The ancient Greeks (and many others) had long ago proved otherwise. The question was not what shape but how big. Naysayers believed that a ship sailing west would just keep going until it ran out of provisions. Columbus believed that Earth was so small a ship could get to the other side within a month or two. Actually, Columbus was wrong, and everybody else was right. Fortuitously, however, Columbus was wrong on two counts, not just one. In addition to thinking Earth was small, he thought nothing but water lay between Europe and the Spice Islands of the East. In this, he was not alone. No one in Europe had any inkling of the two enormous continents that stretched across that passage from pole to pole.

Columbus couldn't get any funding for his proposed expedition in Portugal, so he took his talents to Spain, arriving there the very year Granada fell: the year the Catholic Monarchs won the Crusades. The Spanish Inquisition was going full throttle, and Spain was in the grips of a triumphalist fever. The Catholic Monarchs were looking around for an enterprise equal to their grandeur. Circumnavigating Africa might have been grand enough, but Portugal was too far ahead in that race: in fact, a Portuguese explorer had just rounded the southernmost African cape. If Columbus was right, however, Spain could still get to the spices ahead of its rival—and wouldn't that be reason to crow! So, Queen Isabella decided to hear what Columbus had to say. He wasn't asking for much, it turned out: three puny ships. The odds of him succeeding were long, but long bets sometimes pay off, so Queen Isabella decided to roll the dice.

In the summer of 1492, Christopher Columbus set sail from the city of Cadiz. His three ships and his entire crew would have fit in one corner of one ship of the Chinese armada commanded by Zheng He six decades earlier. After two months of sailing across open waters with no glimpse of land, his crew was threatening to mutiny. At that very moment, someone spotted a bird flying overhead, which meant there was land nearby. Rumbles of mutiny died down, and a few days later, a sailor in the crow's nest caught a glimpse of the Bahamas. Columbus and his crew waded ashore the next day, and Columbus fell to his knees, muttered prayers of gratitude, and claimed the island for Spain. He thought he'd reached India. Later, when he reached Cuba, he thought it was Japan. On a later voyage, when he landed in Venezuela, he thought it was the Garden of Eden.

YEAR ONE

In any world history that takes ever-increasing interconnectedness as its through line, the Columbus moment has to rank as year one. If we don't start the calendar there, it's only because dating systems around the world were too firmly entrenched by the time Columbus set sail. The

Christian world had long marked the beginning of history with the birth of Christ. The Jewish calendar dated back to the supposed day when Adam and Eve were expelled from the Garden of Eden. Dar-ul-Islam began its count with the year in which Messenger Muhammad led his followers to Medina. China was dating time according to a twelve-year cycle that began whenever a rising dynasty declared a new imperial era. The Hindu world had a variety of calendars but no settled starting point: the beginning was less important than the now, since time itself was an illusion.

From the standpoint of interconnectedness and the emergence of a global human story, however, the changes set in motion by Columbus justify calling 1492 the year that divides all of history into before and after. By that measure, we are living in the sixth century. Why was the Columbus moment so important? Was it because crossing the Atlantic was a superhuman feat? No. It wasn't actually that hard, once you knew how. Was it because Columbus symbolized the heroism of a man sticking to his beliefs against a world of naysayers? Nope. Columbus was something of a jerk, actually. Was it because Columbus was the first person from the global East to set foot in the global West since the Ice Age migrants from Siberia? Nope. He wasn't the first. A few Africans might have come to America in Olmec times. Polynesians quite probably reached California long before Columbus. The Vikings certainly crossed the Atlantic to Iceland and then to Greenland and then briefly to Nova Scotia.

But these earlier voyages lacked epochal significance because they didn't launch much of anything. If Africans came here, they left no trace except some giant stone heads carved by the Olmecs that *might* have African features. If the Polynesians came, they melted into California and became some of the people living there; nothing more came of their advent. As for the Vikings, they came, they saw, they left: end of story.

The voyages of Columbus, by contrast, punched a hole between the two hemispheres, opening a flood of traffic. After Columbus made his seminal voyage, bankrolling an expedition to the west was no longer a roll of the dice: it was a business decision. *Something* was over there. No one knew what it was or what it had to offer, but Western Europeans quickly realized they had stumbled upon an entire world to which their rivals had no access.

Columbus matters because he came to America just as Western Europe was poised for the greatest growth spurt of any cultural region in history: Europeans had fully recovered from the Black Death and had just "won the Crusades." They were victors living in an epic story, eager to incorporate the whole planet into their vision of the world and feeling entitled to take whatever was out there for the taking.

After the Columbus moment, ships sailed from Europe to the Americas in droves. The first wave overwhelmed the Taíno people, the inhabitants of the first island Columbus found. Most of them died. In 1520, Castilian captain Hernán Cortés led a small band of men to the mainland, where the Aztecs ruled about 120,000 square miles. The Aztec capital of Tenochtitlan was as big as any city in Spain, but Cortés and his band quickly brought that empire down and turned "Mexico" into "New Spain." Ten years later, another Spanish conquistador, Francisco Pizarro, landed in Peru where the Inca ruled an empire more than six times bigger than that of the Aztecs. On a modern-day map, it would stretch from northern Chile to Columbia. Pizarro and his band of one hundred eighty men captured the Inca emperor *the day after they reached his capital* and took over the whole empire in a year.

THE GREAT DYING

How could one hundred eighty men conquer an empire of millions? What was going on here? Historian Jared Diamond puts it this way: "Guns, germs, and steel." Well said, Jared. To his triumvirate, however, I would add one more term: narrative. Of these four factors, germs were no doubt the most decisive. The first Europeans wreaked a lot of havoc in the Americas: enslaved people, killed people, even roasted some on spits. But the most horrific blow they struck was quite outside their power to avoid inflicting: they brought disease.

Before the Columbus moment, contagious diseases were rare in the Americas. Common maladies such as measles had passed into the human community from herd animals, and over time, people in the Eastern Hemisphere had built immunity to them. Smallpox was still virulent in Europe but had been around long enough that most people there survived it, though it left them scarred. The Americas had never had animals that could be tamed and herded, so Americans had never been exposed to the diseases of Europe. In the Americas, even the common cold was unknown.

The Black Death was horrific, but what happened in the Americas was like the Black Death multiplied many times over. Here, it wasn't one disease but Disease itself, epidemic disease in countless forms, stalking the land. Ironically, Queen Isabella had insisted that Columbus (and subsequent voyagers) carry live pigs to butcher for food on their way to the Americas because she thought it would discourage sailors who were secretly Jews or Muslims from joining the expeditions. Pigs had a propensity for carrying one of the really big killers to reach the Americas: influenza (think swine flu). Worse still, pigs that escaped into the wilds could survive and flourish in pretty much any environment. So once a few pigs went feral, they proliferated and spread, carrying European germs far afield.

Many whole societies were felled by the new ailments before they even got their first glimpse of a European. Disease leapt ahead of explorers, conquerors, and missionaries, for everyone was connected, though most had no inkling of it. Before Columbus landed in the Caribbean, a high culture of some sort had flourished along the Mississippi and Ohio Rivers, north of the Gulf of Mexico. By the time the first Europeans got to the area, they found only small tribal bands living in stockade villages from which the enormous ceremonial mounds built by their recent ancestors could be seen. The first Portuguese adventurers in the Amazon basin reported seeing towns there, connected by highways cut through the jungle and inhabited by people as sophisticated as any they had seen in Spain. By the time the first Portuguese *settlers* arrived, whatever had been flourishing in that region earlier was gone. The jungle had grown over the lands they had once inhabited, erasing almost all traces of their very existence.

How many people lived in the Americas before Columbus arrived? No one knows, but some modern estimates range as high 112 million. How many of them died in the next century or two? Again, no one knows for sure, but by 1650, the native population of these continents was down to 6 million or so. Pretty certainly, in many places, at least 90 percent of the native people died. Whatever the numbers, the pandemic triggered by Columbus's epic journey must be considered the single greatest catastrophe in history, dwarfing the Mongol holocaust, the Black Death, and the world wars of the twentieth century. Nothing like it had ever happened before, and nothing like it has happened again. No wonder this is called the Great Dying.

THE EUROPEAN NARRATIVE

So much for germs. Guns and steel speak for themselves: swords beat clubs; metal armor trumps cloth armor, such as the Inca wore. But what about narrative? How did narrative figure into the collapse of the Native American galaxy of social constellations?

The Columbus moment came several centuries after the last, late thirteenth-century campaigns of the Crusades proper. But the European "voyages of exploration" that began in the fifteenth century were certainly an extension of the Long Crusades. The Crusading ethos was still in the air, giving epic meaning to the expeditions. The Spaniards and Portuguese explicitly framed their American conquests as crusading. They were serving God by extending the dominion of His church. I'm not saying these were just rationalizations. The conquistadors no doubt believed in the spiritual nobility of their enterprise; it probably felt noble within their own framework and, as is reliably the case, success confirmed their narrative. If they weren't so right, how could they be such winners? The narrative they shared strengthened the solidarity of these latter-day crusaders. Their solidarity and certainty made them all that much more formidable. And it wasn't just the Christian narrative that animated them now, but the progress narrative.

Then there was the flip side. Consider how the aftermath of the Columbus moment must have affected all the narratives that gave meaning to the lives of the American natives. Surely, the events they were living through undermined all their ideas about the gods, all the heroes they had cherished as models, all the rituals they had been practicing, all their values, customs, and mores, all their beliefs about good and evil, right and wrong. Surely, for the natives of America, the world stopped making sense.

In Europe, when the Black Death was rampaging across the land, there was not another coherent narrative pressing in on Europeans, asserting itself as an alternative to their own crumbling belief system. Europeans had to construct, on their own, a new narrative amid the rubble of the narratives they had lived by previously, saving what they could, adding what they had to, and formulating new conceptual connections as needed until they had built a coherent new constellation of ideas. There was no rival narrative competing with the one they were constructing. Native Americans, however, had no such luxury. Every day in every way, material reality told them they were wrong and the strangers were right, for they were dying like ants and the newcomers were walking through horror untouched.

Yes, technically, the natives could abandon their own ways, accept baptism, and join the church. Many did. But this didn't make them the fellow Christians of the conquistadors. The narrative they were joining assigned to them the role of scut worker. Native Americans faced quite a challenge, constructing a healthy sense of self within this framework.

The pandemic triggered by the Columbus crew and those who followed in their wake didn't just kill lots of people. It didn't just destroy a civilization. It didn't just clip short a history. It destroyed a universe of intertwined narratives that added up to a history of the world as intricate and varied as the one that had been unfolding in the global East. Most of it is history that we will never know.

18

Chain Reactions

(1500 to 1900)

After that Columbus moment, European tough guys headed for every part of the globe that could be reached by boat. Since the world is mostly water, that was a lot of places. Those who went west planted colonies, established mines, and built plantations. Those who went east constructed forts and trading posts in Asia and purchased exotic products to sell at home for fabulous profits. The two spheres of activity were connected by precious metals: Europeans extracted gold and silver abundantly from the Americas, and silver was (remember) the king of currencies, the coinage accepted everywhere.

Warriors and missionaries spearheaded European penetration of the Americas, but in their wake came businessmen who saw opportunities to get rich by producing certain crops on an industrial scale. Two such crops led the way: tobacco and sugarcane. Later came cotton.

Eurasians had known nothing of tobacco before the Columbus moment, and it caught on quickly. Well, of course it did—tobacco is a drug. Cane sugar, the best sugar, had been extremely expensive in western Eurasia until this time because sugarcanes were too heavy to transport from India and the process for extracting sugar from canes had been a closely guarded secret of the Middle World. But Europe had just acquired this technology, and sugarcane was extraordinarily easy to grow in the Caribbean. Growers could now process canes into sugar right where they grew, which turned sugar into a prime spice: something no one needed but everyone wanted; something that, once processed, was easily transportable. The European market for sugar exploded because sugar is essentially a drug, too, once it is refined.

Not all the sugar made from sugarcanes ended up being marketed as sugar. An offshoot industry of equal importance emerged when molasses, a by-product of sugar refining, was used to make rum. Building a huge, dependable market for this product was easy because rum is alcohol and alcohol is—well, it's a drug.

So there you have it: three drugs, along with gold, silver, and cotton—these were the goods that fueled the European colonization of the Americas.

SILVER

The first Spanish conquistadors were obsessed with gold, and they did get some gold, but not nearly as much of it as they had been fantasizing. What they got in overflowing abundance, however, was gold's humble step-sibling: silver.

Silver, remember, is the precious metal just abundant enough to straddle the line between commodity and currency. The Spanish government mined silver in Peru and Mexico and shipped it home, along with any gold they'd gotten. Spain was like some happy-go-lucky fool who has found an ATM machine that is spitting out free money.

It was now well situated to become the boss of Europe. The Spanish royals built fleets of warships and fielded armies equipped with all the latest weaponry. Ferdinand and Isabella's grandson, Charles V, gained unprecedented grandeur when he was named Holy Roman Emperor, which added patches of northern and central Europe to the huge empire he already possessed in the New World. The Spanish elite were erecting fantastic castles and filling them with all the luxuries money could buy. They didn't put much money into building up Spanish productivity because why go to the bother of making stuff when you can just go out and buy it? And have it delivered?

Spain bought lots of stuff, including textiles and furniture and wool and ships and other goods, most of which were produced in England, France, and the Low Countries (Belgium, Netherlands, Luxembourg). Then silver proved its treachery. Since it was a commodity, rivers of it gushing through Spain activated the iron law of supply and demand. The value of silver dropped down, down, down. But since silver was also the coin of the realm, the sinking value of silver meant people needed more coins to buy the same products, which is another way of saying prices went up, up, up.

This would have made no dramatic difference had the silver spread evenly through the Spanish population. Yes, a person would have needed more coins to buy the same pair of shoes, but everyone would have *had* more coins, so people would be just as able to buy new shoes. But the social system wasn't set up to distribute the silver evenly. Instead, the rich got much richer. The wealth trickled down to the humbler classes but only trickled. The rich still bought shoes and chairs and saddles and whatnot, but the people who made shoes and chairs and saddles and whatnot didn't increase their sales. Why? Because the number of rich people was fixed, and those rich people could use only so many shoes, chairs, saddles, and whatnot. With sales steady and prices going up, the humbler classes got poorer. As prices went up and incomes didn't, fewer people could afford whatever goods there were to buy, which means that the market for shoes and chairs and saddles shrank, which means that more businesses failed. Meanwhile, prices kept going up.

In the long run, limitless supplies of silver didn't end up making Spain richer or more powerful than its neighbors because it was not invested in ramping up Spanish productivity. In effect, the silver was invested in England, France, and the Netherlands. Inflation raises prices only where the number of items made and exchanged remains fixed. Wherever the influx of silver fueled more energetic production and commerce, society absorbed the silver and grew more powerful from it. The first countries to loot the Americas got temporarily rich, like people who had won a jackpot, but then they became what they long remained: Western Europe's two poorest countries.

ENGLAND AND THE NETHERLANDS

Environment had played a key role in the branching of pastoral and urban civilizations, in the rise of the Greeks, in the evolution of the Spice Routes. Now, in the sixteenth century, environment again figured largely in the rise of two powers: England and the Netherlands.

In the post-Columbus era, these were two very happily situated nations indeed. England was an island and the Netherlands was a coastal country, so sailing was second nature to people here. Both were far away from the productive regions of classical times, which gave people a strong incentive to sail to those distant places and bring back trade goods. By the sixteenth century, therefore, both countries had long seafaring traditions and lots of experienced seafaring merchants, men who had cut their teeth in the stormy north Atlantic and who knew how to navigate tough ships equipped with massive banks of sails, both square and lateen. The Portuguese caravels had enjoyed an early advantage because they were so maneuverable; but the English and the Dutch, the people from the Netherlands, soon caught up to them with ships that were just as maneuverable but also *big*.*

In this post-Columbus era, long-distance traders in Europe developed a new way of doing business. Instead of buying what they found and looking for markets, they found markets, took orders, and contracted to have the products manufactured by farm families doing well enough to support some sideline of handicrafts. Women working at home in Belgium, for example, were particularly good at making lace, so merchants came there to place orders, and soon a cottage industry in lace making was flourishing in Belgium. Meanwhile, home workshops making textiles and garments were taking off in France, the Netherlands, and England. It was thus that American silver funded the growth of manufacturing in Western Europe.

---

*It's not clear when people of the Netherlands started calling themselves the Dutch, but the word derives from the same root as the German Deutsch, which simply means "the people"—or to put it another way "us folks."

Because the manufacturing was being done in homes, the people doing the skilled work were mostly women, but that also meant that women's contributions to the economy were hidden from public view. Not only did mercantile companies place orders, but they increasingly supplied patterns, delivered raw materials, specified quantities, and dictated designs. Cottage-scale artisans—mostly meaning the women of Western Europe—ended up working for long-distance traveling salesmen. In this emerging system, producers and consumers never met. The merchants were the only people in contact with both ends, so they gained control of the whole production process.

CORPORATIONS

Enterprising merchants sometimes joined together into companies, which took their place alongside guilds, parishes, kingdoms, and the like as social constellations capable of forming intentions and coordinating the efforts of many to carry out plans. Early companies were usually merchant families that expanded their operations from one endeavor to a bouquet of endeavors. A family long established as grain merchants might add textiles to its list of wares. But these early family companies tended to dissipate after a generation or two because, in the feudal framework, an odor of moral criticism was attached to the landless rich: accumulating money for its own sake was a sign of moral decay. The honorable thing to do with accumulated wealth was to buy some land, purchase a title if possible, and spend one's days as a benevolent lord managing tenant farmers. Besides, within the feudal narrative, money per se felt illusory and vaguely corrupt. Land felt real; land was something one could hand down to one's heirs (a sentiment that survives in today's term *real estate*). Back then, the same felt true of a title: the son of an earl, after all, was even more credibly an earl than his newly knighted father, whom some might remember from days when he was still a churl.

But as family companies came and went, another kind of company began to germinate as well: partnerships among strangers, known as joint stock companies. A bunch of merchants would get together and pool their resources to fund an enterprise more ambitious than any of them could have undertaken alone. They'd outfit a ship and send it to Asia to buy trade goods. Once it came back and the cargo was sold, each merchant got a share of the profits proportional to the amount he'd put in. The share each partner put in was recorded in a document called a stock certificate, hence the term *joint stock company.* The first of these were usually organized around particular projects. Once the project came to fruition, the partners went their separate ways, in pursuit of other opportunities. Gradually, however, companies of this sort congealed into stable entities that undertook continuous streams of ventures: a new kind of social constellation, which had, in the social universe, some of the same properties that biological organisms have in the physical universe.

A joint stock company was held together by one goal—to make a profit. This fit right in with the progress narrative, which conferred ultimate meaning and purpose upon doing better every day, gaining ground, having more. Owning land didn't align with that narrative quite as nicely, for land stays the same size. A lord might improve his use of what he had, but eventually he reached a ceiling beyond which no further productivity could be squeezed out of his holdings, and if he wanted progress, he had to take someone else's land. Profit was different. Profit had no ceiling. A company could gain more profit by growing in size, expanding its reach, sending out more ships, going further, bringing back more, selling to a wider base, expanding what it bought and sold. With this sort of improvement and expansion, tomorrow could always, theoretically, be better than today.

BANKS

Launching a trade expedition to Asia was expensive, though: ships had to be bought, crew hired, provisions laid in. If all went well, the enterprise could pay for all of this with its profits, but the profits wouldn't exist until the goods were sold, which might not be for years. How were merchant groups to meet current expenses with money they would not possess till later?

In some ways, dynastic powers—ruling families—faced a similar challenge. They had to spend money now to make money later because a political power's revenues came from the taxes it collected. Political rulers routinely, therefore, tried to extend the territory they taxed, which required armies, which cost money. They also tried to milk more out of their territories by deepening their control and improving their tax-collecting efficiency, but that required armies of professional servants, and *that* cost money.

And it wasn't just about making war and collecting taxes. Something bigger was involved for monarchs, and that something was belief. People had to *believe* their king was a king. If they didn't, he wasn't. Generating this necessary belief required pomp and circumstance. A believable monarch lived in a great palace, dressed in finery, traveled with smartly outfitted retinues, and rode awesome carriages drawn by horses that commoners could only dream of owning. People looking at all these details said, "I see a king," and their neighbors said, "I see him too. What a king!" In short, the process was recursive: royals *had* to generate the illusion of power in order to carry out the operations needed to secure the power they already seemed to have. And this, too, required money.

A new class of specialists stepped in to bridge the gap between the expenses of today and the revenues of tomorrow: men able to create an illusion of wealth that would hold together long enough for the wealth to actually materialize. This skill had been pioneered by the Italian and Jewish moneylenders who invented protobanking during the Crusades. They had discovered how to create money by making loans. What they loaned was not actual money, usually, but credit. Credit comes from a Latin root that means "belief." Credit exists as long as people believe it exists. Since the "money" a bank loaned out was money somebody had to pay back, it was part of the bank's assets. Paradoxically, therefore, the more money a bank loaned out, the more it had. Conversely, what the bank actually possessed in its vaults were its liabilities—material valuables the bank would have to shell out someday to depositors.

For anyone dealing with household finances, this is quite counter-intuitive. For the normal household, if there's gold under the mattress, that's an asset. If the family has loaned some money to Cousin Joe, that's a liability because that is money the family cannot spend today, not even for food, not even if it's starving. The butcher won't trade a pound of meat for an IOU signed by Cousin Joe because he doesn't *know* Joe. (Or maybe he *does* know Joe and maybe that's worse.) An IOU signed by Joe works as money only if the entire community has a rock-solid belief that Joe is good for it. *Belief* is the key word here. Banks can function only as long as everyone believes their notes are good for the debt they represent.

The Knights Templar had been the first real international bankers, and they had extended credit to most of the crowned heads of Europe. Simple folks assumed that if those guys were doing so much lending, they must have lots of gold stashed somewhere. One day in 1307, King Philip IV of France decided to cancel his debt by arresting all the Templars, executing their leaders, and seizing their gold. The king had already whipped up public support for this move by stoking rumors that the Templars secretly controlled the world and were (secretly) causing all the crimes, crop failures, and illnesses that plagued France in that calamitous era. By the time the king made his move, common folks were hungry to see those accursed Templars wiped out and their gold seized. But when the king's men plundered the Templar's offices, they didn't find much gold. What they found, mostly, were notebooks with numbers written in them.

Meanwhile, crop failures, disease, and all the other ills charged to the Templars continued. Common folk then faced a choice: they could decide that the king and pope had been lying or that the Templars had survived somehow and were still controlling the world under a new name from secret headquarters. This proved to be the template for a conceptual constellation that has endured to this day: conspiracy theory: the notion that unbeknownst to the masses, some small group secretly controls the world.

One root source of such rumors and theories—the increasing abstraction of money—continued apace. While the hoi polloi focused on the mysterious Templars, banks continued to sprout and grow because they fulfilled a critical function in a European society loaded with entrepreneurs who were aching to fund ambitious ventures that would yield handsome profits in the future.

In 1600, one such group of English entrepreneurs struck a staggering deal with their monarch. Queen Elizabeth gave this small, private consortium of men a guaranteed monopoly on all English trade with India and points east. She also authorized them to raise and field their own private armies, build forts, and negotiate treaties with foreign governments. This consortium called itself the Honourable East India Company—the HEIC or EIC. (Pronounce it EEK, if you like: that's easier to remember.)

Two years later, the Dutch breathed life into a similar company called the VOC, an acronym for a string of Dutch words that mean Dutch East India Company. The VOC was set up to compete with the EEK, and the Dutch government gave its company all the perks the EEK had gotten from the English crown: a monopoly on all *Dutch* trade with Asia, the right to field armies, build forts, and sign treaties. Similar companies were forming in Spain, France, Portugal, Sweden, and other European countries, but the Dutch and English versions were the strongest and provided the stencil for all the others.

Queen Elizabeth conferred one further favor on her country's East India Company, and it proved seminal. She declared it a limited liability corporation, which meant that no individual human being associated with the company—whether as worker, manager, or owner—was liable for its debts or misdeeds. Investors could lose what they put in, nothing more. If the company committed crimes, only the *company* could be punished, not any of the people *in* the company. Legally, these rules meant that the warm human bodies carrying out the company's operations were not the company. Individual humans could come and go, but the company itself endured as a single continuous entity, just as the cells in a human body constantly die and are replaced by other cells while the human person endures as a single continuous *self*. The queen's stipulations helped ensure that corporations would take their place in the world as social constellations possessed of selves, able to carry out plans, vested with a drive to avoid extinction—just like any individual human being, and indeed just like every biological life-form down to the single-celled amoeba. Onetime US presidential candidate Mitt Romney said it best: "Corporations are people, my friends."

The VOC was originally a partnership among some two hundred merchants, but shortly after it was born, it took a remarkable step: the partners decided to issue an expanded number of shares and sell some of them to the public. Anyone could buy those shares. Buyers didn't have to pass a test or get along with the other partners. But they also didn't have a say in management, or an offer of employment, or the right to take home company furniture, or indeed any other normal perk of ownership. Someone who owned VOC stock got from it just two benefits: first, a share of the company's annual profits if any; and second, the right to sell the stock to anyone else for any amount the buyer was willing to pay. What buyers were willing to pay depended on how well they thought the company would do in the indeterminate future. So the value of this thing, this share of stock, fluctuated exactly like the price of bacon except that the fluctuation wasn't determined by the supply of hogs or any other material thing. It was determined by the supply and demand of belief. With stocks, money jumped to a new and higher level of abstraction.

In 1600, for normal everyday commerce, Europeans still used coins as currency. But there were lots of locally struck coins floating about. In any given locale, people could use any of them that anyone would accept. A given person might be carrying a few pieces of eight, several English shillings, a bagful of Spanish doubloons. The terrain in which these coins worked was not circumscribed by strict borders because such borders didn't exist. The money wasn't mathematically exact, either. Exchanges had to rest on estimates of value. Even when coins were made of silver, their value could only be approximated because people sometimes shaved the rims and melted what they scavenged to keep for themselves. Some coin-issuing authorities—princes, dukes, kings, whatever—mixed baser metals into their coins to stretch their supply of silver or of whatever metal they were purporting to use. How was anyone to tell what a coin was "really" worth? Yes, there were tests one could run, but who had the time for tests in the course of daily commerce? Commercial exchanges were negotiations about the coins used as well as about the products changing hands.

The Dutch were the first to figure out a fix. In 1609, the city fathers of Amsterdam chartered a group of private bankers to form a single central bank. Anyone wishing to do business in Amsterdam had to take their money to this bank and open an account. The bank officials decided how much the various coins and whatnot were worth. They put these in a vault and issued banknotes clearly marked with numbers that added up to the amount of value deposited. Within Amsterdam-controlled territory, not only did everyone have to accept those notes as money but no one was allowed to do business using anything *but* those notes.

Banknotes had an absolute value unrelated to the worth of the paper or the quality of the printing. An old, frayed ten-guilder note was worth exactly the same as a crisp, new ten-guilder note. Ten such notes were exactly equivalent to a single hundred-guilder note, no matter what shape they all were in. Banknotes removed money from the uncertainties of the material realm and rendered it purely mathematical. Within the Netherlands, the Bank of Amsterdam soon became the source of a standardized state currency that worked in all territory under Dutch jurisdiction.

Like limited liability corporations, the central bank idea spread. In 1694, the king of England, who had until recently been Duke William of (the Dutch province of) Orange, needed to fund various kingly functions, not the least of which was a necessary little war on French soil. He called together the great credit-creating specialists of his realm and asked them to float him a gigantic loan: a million-plus pounds. In return, he would allow them to operate as a single group and sell bits and pieces of the debt the king had incurred to the public in the form of banknotes, each with a number printed on it. The idea was, when the king repaid his debt, anyone in possession of such a note would be entitled to a portion of the repayment—an amount corresponding to the number on the note. While people were waiting for the king to repay his debt, they could exchange these notes for any material goods they wanted, such as loaves of bread or the services of a prostitute. After the transaction, the baker or the prostitute would possess the note and be entitled to the specified portion of payment of the king's debt, once it was repaid. These notes worked as money because they were not like Cousin Joe's IOU; these were the king's own solemn promise to pay off his debt, and if you couldn't trust the king, who *could* you trust?

That debt was never repaid. Of course, it wasn't. The notes backed by that debt became the currency used in all financial transactions in England. The king's debt became the foundation for the whole British economy. If that debt were now repaid, the British economy would collapse. The national debt was not (necessarily) a sign of how much trouble the country was in. That debt was the glue holding the whole system together. The bigger the debt, the more people were involved in a single interlocking system as creditors. Like the Bank of Amsterdam, the one in England became the central bank of the entire country. Many more such central banks emerged in this period, and they were associated with tightly organized social wholes of a novel type, just beginning to emerge in this period: the constellations later known as nation-states.

Central banks enabled kings to deepen their power by financing the same mechanisms of rule that gave the earliest empires their coherence: salaried bureaucrats, postal systems, spy networks, police officers, physical infrastructure, and so on. Now, however, monarchs had more sophisticated tools at their disposal—clocks to coordinate movements, publishing to disseminate instructions, credit instruments to oil commerce, banks to issue currency—they could manifest their will more and more pervasively in ever more obscure corners of their realms. In Europe, royal power achieved a penetration into everyday life that people had never before known.

Although silver ended up impoverishing Spain, so much wealth in so many forms poured out of the Americas in the first centuries after the Columbus moment that it tipped the planetary scale. But it wasn't all of

Europe that had such privileged access to the Americas. It wasn't even all of Western Europe. Columbus was originally from Italy, but Italians didn't get in on the fire sale. It was that thin sliver of societies on the westernmost edge of the Eurasian continent. They were the ones who scored the critical advantage. We're talking only about Portugal, Spain, France, England, and the Low Countries. For well over a century, these five maritime social constellations had first, best, and almost exclusive access to two whole continents virtually depopulated by the Great Dying and loaded with resources that had scarcely been touched. Is it any wonder that these countries became the leading edge of a rising West?

19

After Columbus: The World
(1500 to 1800)

The voyages of Columbus launched a global drama. Over the next few centuries, all the great world historical monads of the planet began to overlap and interact, and the world we live in today grew out of those interactions. When the overlappings began, each inward-looking world was a vast constellation made up of its own internal assumptions, norms, and narratives. The people of these various monads all had their distinct trajectories. When they began to overlap, the momentum that each brought *into* its encounters with the other shaped what each brought *out* of those encounters. When the smoke cleared, Europe and North America formed a top layer around the globe. China had crumbled. The Middle World was mired in resentful subjugation and dependency. Africa and Latin America were subsumed into a larger world story as peripheries of a center that wasn't China, India, or the Islamic realm, after all, but Europe.

CONTEST FOR COLONIES

When Columbus set sail, kingdoms were solidifying in Western Europe, and once they knew about the Americas, they fell into a dog-eat-dog competition for colonies in the New World (new to them, that is). When the new era began, Portugal and Spain were the most aggressive sea powers. Spain captured the Americas; the Portuguese soon rounded the horn of Africa and gained access to the spices of India and points east. With the two big naval powers headed for a clash, the pope stepped in and persuaded the parties to agree to a line of demarcation. What the treaty gave Portugal was Brazil. What it gave Spain was (according to the pope) everything else.

Spain never got a foothold in the Middle World, never made headway in India, and soon lost gas as a power in continental Europe, but it held on to its vast empire in the Americas. Spaniards conquered their way across the continent and up the west coast to California's San Francisco Bay. They secured this territory with a combination of haciendas and missions. Haciendas were big estates owned by Spanish military aristocrats. They produced commercial goods such as hides, grapes, and wine, using Native Americans as laborers. Missions were fortified compounds from which the Spanish version of the Christian worldview could be disseminated to the local inhabitants.

In Mexico and South America, the Spanish were busy mining extraordinary quantities of silver. From the American west coast, Spanish ships made their way to the Philippines, and from there the Spaniards began buying trade goods from China.

Meanwhile, the native people of central and South America had begun a biological recovery. Having weathered the Great Dying, their population began to rise. The Spanish and Portuguese—in stark contrast to the English and French—came to the American continents as male adventurers without families. They bedded native women as sexual chattel and sometimes as wives, and the women gave birth to children of mixed parentage. From the Rio Grande River to the southern tip of Chile, people of mixed genetic stock began to emerge, just as Russia had emerged where the Norse and Slavic people had overlapped.

On the face of things, Spain's cultural domination brooked no challenge. Even as the population of Native Americans was rising, the population of native language speakers kept shrinking. The Iberian languages, Portuguese and Spanish, ended up as the lingua franca of these continents south of the Rio Grande—Portuguese in Brazil, Spanish everywhere else. Europeans of purely Spanish descent continued to dominate the vast and growing native and *mestizo* (mixed) population for a long while, but these were increasingly an American aristocracy with fading emotional connections to their ancestors' homeland.

Because Portugal and Spain had been stoutly Catholic countries when the colonization of the Americas began, monks and friars led the Christian missionary expeditions in Central and South America. As a result, virtually all those who converted to Christianity in these areas joined the Catholic Church. In 1531, an Aztec convert named Juan Diego reported that he had encountered the Virgin Mary near the town of Guadalupe *and she looked like a Native American woman.* The Virgin of Guadalupe gave natives of the Spanish-speaking Americas an image to embrace, a way to own the Christianity they were converting to. She signaled the beginning of a process that continued until an American version of Catholicism came fully into existence. Today, about half the Catholics in the world are those who live in the Americas.

The recovering native population brought themes from their pre-Columbian cultures into the civilizations emerging south of the Rio Grande. The interaction between the Europeans of Iberia and the natives of Central and South America gave rise to a uniquely American civilization of world scale. This is commonly known as Latin America, and its culture is usually called Hispanic, a name that makes no nod to the pre-Columbian themes in the weave, which is strange because even a casual visitor passing through Spain, as I've done several times, can tell that Spain is not Hispanic. To me, it seemed much closer to France or England in cultural flavor than to Mexico or Peru.

Spain got the lion's share of the Americas south of the Rio Grande River, but the struggle for the rest of the planet went on. Portugal, England, France, and the Netherlands led that struggle. The juiciest remaining plums were India in the east—a land of legendary wealth—and North America in the west.* The Portuguese got the jump in the east. Having

---

*Here, in accordance with common usage, North America refers to all the lands north of the Rio Grande.

been the first to circumnavigate Africa, they were soon sailing around Africa routinely. They built forts along the African coast as safe havens for their ships, places for their sailors to rest, restock, and board fresh water. Eventually, they had a chain of garrisons that let them sail all the way to India and back without hindrance.

Then the Dutch arrived and booted the Portuguese out of the subcontinent. The Portuguese had to lick their wounds and content themselves with big swatches of Africa and all of Brazil. But the Dutch quickly found themselves tangling with new bullies—the English and the French—who dislodged them from both India and North America. The Dutch regrouped in Southeast Asia.

The struggle for the last really tempting colonies came down to the French and the British. From 1744 to 1763, these two powers and their allies fought a cluster of battles all over the world, on the high seas, in the forests of North America, in West Africa, on the coastal rim of India, in the Philippines. In Europe, this was called the Seven Years' War, in North America the French and Indian War, in India the Carnatic Wars. The names and theaters differed, but these were pretty much one big war, fought to determine who would get which colonies. France lost those wars; Britain won—and with that the British Empire was launched.

Almost immediately, however, Britain's thirteen American colonies broke away to form an independent nation-state of their own, a loss that made India even more vital to the British, for Earth's human population was getting to be one quarrelsome interconnected tangle now—still a multifarious species comprised of many distinct groups, all with our own local stories, but all of us also contending characters in some single big story.

AFRICA

Producing sugar, cotton, and tobacco—those core American crops—required intensive, back-breaking labor. To meet this challenge, European entrepreneurs perfected the plantation system of farming. A plantation was a large tract of land given over to a single cash crop. The owner organized the work and managed the finances: sales, bookkeeping, promotion, marketing. Slaves or wage slaves did the work, under the direction of an overseer. American plantations foreshadowed the European factory system of the nineteenth century.

At first, plantation owners tried to make enslaved American natives do this work, but disease had wiped out so many of them and the survivors had been left so weakened, the labor often killed them. So, the owners turned to another source of slaves: the continent of Africa. This brought a worldwide economic system into being—disastrously for huge numbers of people. Sugar grown in the Caribbean was shipped to cities along the North American coast. There it was distilled into alcohol, shipped to Europe, and traded for guns. The guns were taken to Africa and exchanged for enslaved people, who were captured farther inland by the coastal Africans who acquired the guns. The African slaves were transported to the Caribbean and traded for sugar, whereupon the whole cycle began again.

When enslaved humans were sold to Europeans, they were crammed into the holds of ships with other captured Africans who didn't necessarily share anything with their fellow captives except skin color. Many died in those holds before the ships made it across the oceans, and those who survived were sold by factors such as weight, health, and gender, not by any kinship connections or social relationships they might have had among themselves. In the marketplace, they became units of work: like machine parts.

The Africans sold into slavery were mostly captured by Arab slave traders and other Africans. The African slave traders did not see themselves as betraying their fellow Africans in some monolithic war between whites and blacks because Africa was a continent, not a culture, and on that continent lived people of many cultures and ethnicities, speaking many languages. For sub-Saharan Africans, skin color was not a marker of identity. Where they lived, pretty much everyone had dark skin.

The year Columbus set sail on his first voyage to the Americas, the powerful Songhai Empire, the empire that had supplanted Mali, was reaching its zenith of splendor. Its greatest ruler, Askia Muhammad, was about to take the throne. In eastern Africa, an extensive trade network had developed, linking some forty city-states and their associated clan networks along the coast. One of these was Great Zimbabwe, which is now some two hundred acres of stone ruins. When the slave traders first arrived in Africa, Great Zimbabwe was still the capital of a Shona empire that had trade links with lands as distant as China.

Then, the Atlantic slave trade began, hijacking the historical trajectory of the African continent in ways that went beyond the suffering it inflicted on individuals. New cities—slave trading ports—popped up along the West African coast from Angola to what is now Guinea Bissau. Within the continent, the money to be made from slave selling drew people away from farming, herding, and manufacturing and into the business of capturing and selling human beings.

Slavery as such was nothing new. People started enslaving people as soon as there were people to enslave. The Romans built an empire on it. The Rus got rich selling Slavs to Muslims. Throughout most of history, codes of virtue governing how people ought to treat one another usually only applied to members of the group in question. Such codes kept the inner world in order but didn't apply to dealings with the outside. The codes saw nothing wrong with enslaving the other. The question was, only, how to define the other. How much otherness made a stranger fair game for enslavement?

For the Rus, for the Romans, for the Arabs, for most people throughout history, the fundamental criterion tended to be power. Those who won battles got to enslave the losers, no matter who they were or what they looked like. In the Roman Empire, the slaves did not all look like each other. The slaves of Rome looked like anyone the Romans had conquered.

Europeans came flooding into the Americas as some vast constellation of shared ideas. They weren't all friends, they'd fought and killed one another aplenty, but they'd done it as people killing people. Now, they were entering a continent inhabited *entirely* by people who looked different, spoke differently, ate strange stuff, wore strange clothes (or none at all), and in general manifested every possible mark of otherness—and on top of that shared no history with them at all.

The settlers got busy turning "wilderness" into "civilized farmland" (as they saw it). The natives tried to stop them from injuring the living Earth (as they saw it). Bleshing did not come easy. Two galaxies of civilizations were overlapping here, each one a coherent whole in its own right. The group winning every battle on every front didn't see their conflicts with the natives as war. War was something civilized people did with other civilized people. They saw it in the same light as battling wild animals in a wilderness. Context provided little opportunity for newcomers and natives to discover a shared humanity. Even the elements they obviously did share—they all loved their children, they all bled red when they were cut, and so on—had different meanings because they were parts of different constellations.

The values fueled by the apocalyptic encounter in the Americas extended to the slaves taken from Africa. Slavery was age-old, yes, but this was slavery based explicitly on a notion of race, the notion that people were of essentially different types and some were slaves by nature. The trade was going to happen no matter what, for there was money to be made, but anyone making that money needed to feel that capturing humans and working them to death didn't necessarily mean they were bad people. How could these be part of the same conceptual constellation? Racism provided the bridge. The race-based slave trade was the minotaur chained in the basement of the European colonization of the Americas. The people feasting upstairs did their best to ignore its muffled roars and go on with their dinner.

Europe and the World, 1775

England
Spain
Portugal
France
Netherlands

20

The Center Does Not Hold
(1500 to 1900)

When Columbus set sail for America, China was just hitting heights of grandeur comparable to the most glorious eras of its past. By the time Europeans were docking in Chinese ports, the Ming dynasty had passed its peak, but this fact was not yet obvious, for the Ming had set a coherent world in motion and that world was still in motion. Were all its parts still meshing? Impossible to tell: China was too vast, too intricate, and too complicated for anyone to easily judge the health of the whole. Its landscapes ranged from ice-capped mountains to deserts to swamps to river valleys to everything in between. Over 250 languages were spoken here, almost fifty ethnic groups lived within the borders, and there were whole competing nationalities straddling those borders.

Europe and the Middle World were just as varied, to be sure, but China was also permeated by a deep sense of its own social and political singleness. It wasn't a nation-state, but it wasn't simply an empire either; it was, to coin a term, a civilization-state. And the master narrative that sewed this civilization-state together had begun to fray.

According to the overarching narrative inherited from China's long past, the world worked so long as everyone did what Confucius would have done in every situation that came up. Confucius, however, didn't have a clear-cut answer to every real-life situation, especially when real-life circumstances went topsy-turvy. Sometimes, Confucian directives seemed to contradict each other. Transitions from one emperor to another,

286

for example, often raised sticky questions. On the face of it, the doctrine was clear: when one emperor died, his eldest son became the next emperor. This preserved the order of the universe. But what if the oldest son was an idiot? What if he was a child? What if—as happened in 1524—an emperor died and left no sons at all? What then?

In the 1524 crisis, court officials decided to enthrone the late emperor's thirteen-year-old cousin. To make this fit the rules of lineage, they declared that this youngster was the (posthumously) adopted son of the previous emperor. Sounds convoluted, yes? Oh, but wait: this would mean the new emperor was renouncing his own real father! A serious violation of filial duty! One requirement of the rites seemed to contradict another requirement of the rites. What to do? Opinions differed. The literati divided; the court split. Demonstrators poured into the streets, and the government all but ground to a halt. The Great Rites Controversy was a Confucian Chinese version of a constitutional crisis.

Finally, the scholars discovered a solution, of sorts. They declared the new emperor's deceased biological *father* to have been the previous emperor's (posthumously) adopted son. Quite convoluted, I know, but insiders understood why this was a solution and why it worked: it felt correct enough to let the Chinese constellation go on glimmering. Within that constellation, it was crucial that the government align with the rituals. The Ministry of Rites, therefore, ranked right up there with the army and treasury in importance: it was, after all, holding the world together. If the solutions devised for problems like the Great Rites Controversy felt dubious, public confidence in government eroded. Convoluted solutions that were only "correct enough" chipped away at the coherence that defined the Middle Kingdom under the Ming.

Meanwhile, neo-Confucian society wasn't really meshing quite as perfectly as Confucius would have liked. Everyone knew, for example, that merchants weren't much to be respected, farmers were way more honorable, and scholar-bureaucrats were entitled to the highest regard of all. These were not castes, however. In theory, anyone could enter any of the strata, and the highest stratum was open to anyone who aced the civil service exams. These exams were among the glories of Chinese culture. But studying

288 | The Invention *of* Yesterday

for the exams took years, and peasant boys didn't have that kind of time. Their families needed every available hand working in the fields. Merchants, by contrast—those parasites—had an odd propensity for getting rich (perhaps because the line between "merchant" and "pirate" wasn't always distinct). Rich families could afford to let one or more of their sons spend all their time studying, not to mention hire private tutors for them, which gave them a leg up at exam time. Through this loophole, members of the least respected stratum could move directly to the most honored one. Peasants, on the other hand, were destined to remain peasants. It must have rankled.

Worse still, at any given time, some million people were in the pipeline studying for the exams, but the bureaucracy had only about twenty thousand openings. Most of the men who took the exams were destined to flunk. After years of studying, these men would end up having to apologize to their families and find something else to do. It must have rankled.

The first generation of the Ming had started out as bottom-feeding outlaws, and they came to power with an unsophisticated understanding of money. They figured that money was just paperwork, a bureaucratic formality that would work out fine, just as long as everyone did what they were told. When the government had expenses to pay, it simply printed up some paper money, as the Song had done. But these notes were not the kind of paper currency emerging in Europe at this point. European banknotes were distillations of the value generated organically by commercial exchange. The Ming's paper currency expressed the effectiveness of the government. It was money because the government said so. And the value of each note was whatever the government said. The good thing about such money was that the government could print as much as it needed whenever it needed to.

The bad thing was, once the currency got out there, the government could not control its buying power. The same bill might be worth one amount over here and another amount over there, no matter what number was printed on it. Even in a command economy like Ming China's, therefore, the government's paper money began to disrupt internal trade.

The Ming gave in and minted copper coins, but even these didn't earn universal trust. Silver, good ol' silver, became the default medium of exchange, simply because people preferred to use it when they could.

Thereupon, the government got into the act and demanded that taxes be paid in silver. Unfortunately, China didn't have much silver of its own: its mines had run thin. Internal turmoil in Japan had disrupted the flow of silver from there. The one surefire way to get some extra silver was to sell something to the traders now coming to China from various parts of Europe. These unfamiliar folks had plenty of silver jingling in their pockets, and they were eager to buy Chinese goods. What they wanted most, however, were tea, porcelain, and silk. Tea and silk posed a problem because China had only so much arable land. Landowners could use that land for growing tea and supplying the raw material for silk, or they could use that land for growing rice; they couldn't do both. And the population was growing. So, China could ill afford to produce less rice. What to do?

In the sixteenth century, a solution mysteriously took shape. New crops started filtering into the empire from somewhere or other: sweet potatoes, squash, corn—crops like that. Unlike rice, these crops did fine in sandy soil and on unterraced hillsides. Previously useless lands could now be farmed. China no longer had to choose: it could produce more food *and* grow more of the cash crops that supported exports. Both the population and the exports could go on expanding.

In the south, meanwhile, all the silver gushing in fueled a manufacturing boom. Rural people began migrating to urban centers to work in the ever-proliferating porcelain workshops. Chinese merchants and artisans kept getting richer, which ratcheted up the strains on the neo-Confucian social fabric.

Little did the Chinese know or care that their booming exports and their growing food supply were all ripple effects from the voyages of Columbus: squash, corn, and many other crops were known only in the Americas before his voyages. Afterward, Europeans began to grow these new crops, and their cultivation spread through the Eastern Hemisphere, until at last they reached China. Ultimately, much of the silver was coming from the Americas too, but who in China cared where the crops and the silver were coming from so long as they kept everything humming?

Then the worm turned. In the early 1600s, the planet entered a period called the Little Ice Age. The temperature of the globe dropped slightly, which incidentally doesn't mean that every place got colder. It means the climate fluctuated erratically in different places. In China, it led to spot droughts, which led to crop failures. The population had boomed under the Ming, and now, just as banks, corporations, and nation-states were emerging in Europe, China faced a shrinking food supply. More people, less food—that's the age-old prescription for social unrest.

Peasants who lost their livelihood because their farms had failed streamed to cities in search of work, but now, suddenly, work was hard to find because of another historical hiccup. Something had reduced the stream of foreign silver coming into China, some sort of turmoil in far-away Europe, some economic downturn in a little-known place called Spain. What could anyone in China do about Spain? Nothing. People in China just had to deal with the downstream effects of whatever was happening upstream in the distant west.

So, landless dislocated peasants started roaming around, looking for ways to survive. Inevitably, some of them gave up on Confucian virtues and started preying on the weak. Clapping these petty criminals in prison didn't help; they only came out worse than when they'd gone in. The state drained some troublemakers into the army, hoping their aggression could serve the common good, but it didn't work. The worst ones wouldn't follow orders, and the military spat them out, and then they were *armed* thugs trained in violence, drifting around, looking for fights. Men like this tended to find one another and clump into gangs.

Chinese society had always been rife with special interest clubs, secret societies, and religious splinter sects. In good times, these relieved the pressures of demanding family structures: they provided alternative or additional sources of identity. Men didn't have to just be fathers, uncles, brothers, sons. They could *also* be Shaolin boxing experts, masters of Go, practitioners of arcane healing arts. In times of turmoil, however, secret societies had a propensity for morphing into millenarian cults impassioned by visions of supernatural apocalypse. When such clubs overlapped with outlaw gangs, incendiary combinations could form. The Ming had started out in a previous time of turmoil as just such a sect—the Red Turbans. Now, in the late days of the Ming era, militant cults and bandit gangs were again sprouting everywhere, and the Ming's forces couldn't be everywhere at once. So, gangs swelled into armies. One particularly savage brigand led one hundred thousand men down the Huang He valley, sowing destruction, until at last he took Beijing. The last Ming emperor hung himself in his garden, and the bandit boss frolicked in the Forbidden City, while outside his men were pillaging and looting and raping until the streets of Beijing ran red.

That's when the Manchus made their move. The Manchus were a people living just north of the Great Wall, and they were mostly settled now—urban even—but they had cultural roots going back to a pastoral nomadic life in the steppes. When all hell broke loose in Beijing, they stormed south, crushed the bandits, flooded the streets with their own warriors, and announced that they were here to restore order. Yes, indeed, they'd come to save the Middle Kingdom—but not on behalf of the Ming. China's new emperors would be the Manchu themselves. They dubbed themselves the Qing, or "pure" dynasty.

It was a puzzling transition. The Manchu were not Han Chinese, but they were not unambiguously foreign like the Mongols. They had a language of their own, but they also spoke Chinese. They had a script of their own, but they also wrote in Chinese. They had customs going back to pastoral life, but they were now an urban people who had immersed themselves in Chinese intellectual traditions and embraced the neo-Confucian narrative.

They made the Forbidden City their headquarters and kept the governing apparatus of the Ming intact. They revived the Ming ministries, including the all-important Ministry of Rites. They pursued Ming economic policies, repaired Ming schools, and reinstated the civil service exams. The Chinese knew the Manchus were not exactly Chinese, but the Qing tried to paper over the gap. They took instruction from Chinese scholars of ritual and made sure Han men secured posts in the bureaucracy alongside Manchus. If restoration had been a core mission of the Ming, it was an even more urgent job for the Qing. They had, after all, an even greater need to prove themselves more-Chinese-than-thou.

With the Qing in power, there was still no way to know that China was on its way down. Over the next forty years, the Qing brought the whole empire under their governance and extended Chinese power deep into Central Asia. Qing China was the biggest China ever. The Great Wall no longer marked China's northern border; it was now just a tourist attraction deep within the empire. China's domination of Korea and of its Southeast Asian neighbors tightened and deepened.

Only Japan remained uncowed. The Japanese had exploited their island isolation to build a feudal society in which rice held a sacred place and fishing provided the bulk of people's nourishment. Officially, a fifteen-hundred-year-old imperial dynasty ruled the islands. Daily government was in the hands of tough feudal lords called shoguns, who fielded armies spearheaded by samurai, warriors with a complex cultural tradition that had the qualities of a quasi-religion—analogous to the ghazis, the mystical warrior brotherhoods of the Ottoman state and to the military religious orders fielded by the Catholic Church during the Crusades.

Not only did China fail to cow the Japanese, the Japanese tried to invade China—a laughable effort, from the Chinese perspective. A cluster of petty islands conquering the mightiest empire on earth? Inconceivable! Apart from Japan, however, the Qing extended the Chinese sphere of power throughout the region, from Mongolia to the Strait of Malacca. In 1700, China still had every reason to see itself as the supreme central power on Earth.

SILVER AND TEA

The new dynasty adopted, however, one of the Mings' more dubious policies. They started paying for government expenses with paper money while collecting taxes in silver. The paper currency kept internal trade moving more or less, but Chinese taxpayers faced the same old question: Where could they get the silver to pay their taxes? And the same good answer was still right there: sell more goods to the seafaring traders from the West.

The government favored this commerce and made every effort to support export industries. After all, the silver it brought in ultimately ended up in the government's coffers. In the south, government-supported porcelain workshops burgeoned into industrial-scale factories where huge corps of wretched wage workers did piece work in abominable conditions.

In earlier times, tea came from orchards owned by landowning gentry. It was one of many crops cultivated on a given estate. The work was done by peasants with long-standing connections to the landowners. The relationships were mediated by Confucian values: peasants and gentry were linked to one another in webs of mutual obligations and responsibilities softened by oceans of etiquette and reciprocal debt. Now, however, tea orchards morphed into plantations, vast farms given over to a single cash crop. Efficiency became a central goal of cultivation as a way of maximizing output. Wage laborers did the work, overseen by professional managers more concerned with the bottom line than with Confucian homilies. It was a new world.

The Qing and their advisers didn't particularly like this new world. They liked the cash the Europeans brought, but not their seemingly corrosive culture. They barred Europeans from setting foot in the empire proper, restricting them to a few specified trading posts along the coast. The European traders were to wait there until Chinese merchants came to take their orders. They were to pay their money and cool their heels until their purchases were brought to them. Then, they were to go away.

At these haughty conditions, the European traders merely shrugged. They were here to make money, not friends. What did frustrate them was the Chinese's refusal to buy anything. They wouldn't buy anything at all. The Chinese only wanted to sell, sell, sell. And as payment they would accept only bullion, bullion, bullion: silver or gold. Or diamonds: diamonds were good. You get the picture. One Qing emperor explained the reason for this: China had everything good. Europeans had nothing worth coveting. Chinese products were superior to any made in Europe. What then would the Chinese buy?

Still, for western entrepreneurs, there was money to be made here, so they kept coming. Chinese silk exports soared to unprecedented heights. China's porcelain exports boomed beyond all measure. In Europe "china" became simply a synonym for high-quality pottery. But the product the traders from the west sought out most voraciously was tea. The British had developed a virtual addiction to this beverage. I use the word *addiction* advisedly: tea *is* essentially a drug. Today, its stimulating effect may seem too mild to justify placing it in the same category as crack cocaine, but when you consider tea as an alternative to the other major beverage available to Europeans—alcohol, in some form—you can see why tea took Europe by storm. Tea wakes you up, grog conks you out: it's that simple. (Coffee was starting to get popular, too, but it didn't rival tea yet.)

In 1720 the British imported two hundred thousand pounds of tea from China. In 1729, they bought a million pounds. By 1760, their tea imports had risen to three million pounds, by 1790 to nine million. Let me repeat that. Nine. Million. Pounds. That's a lot of tea, eh? Well, hold on to your hat: by the mid-nineteenth century, Britain's imports of Chinese tea had jumped to thirty-six million pounds a year. Porcelain had once been packed in tea to prevent breakage; now porcelain was carried in the holds of tea ships, as ballast.

European governments grew quite uneasy about this trade. The silver they spent would enrich China forever. The tea they bought would end up as urine. Western Europe was a culture built by merchants, and merchants had a pretty straightforward view of wealth. As they saw it, wealth was cash. If you sold more than you bought, you were getting rich. If you bought more than you sold, you were getting poor. Cash, in this case, meant precious metal. Whoever died with the most bullion was the winner—so went the theory, and the theory certainly held true for individual merchants. But European governments saw their whole national economies in these mercantile terms, and from this perspective, China was driving Britain into the poorhouse.

The British government couldn't simply ban tea because it was getting huge revenues from tariffs on imports, almost 10 percent of which were tea. If tea imports were to drop, government revenues would plummet. Britain had just spent a fortune beating the French in a global world war for possession of the world's colonies. It needed more money, not less. So the government raised the tariff on tea by 100 percent, which discouraged tea sales and slowed down imports without hurting the government's bottom line.

It did hurt *somebody's* bottom line, however. The British East India Company's life depended on selling tea. What was it to do—simply take a loss and die? No way! To help this most powerful of lobbies, the British government passed laws forcing its American colonists to buy expensive company tea instead of the cheaper tea smuggled in by Dutch freebooters (who, of course, paid no taxes to the British Crown). Famously, this Tea Act irked rebellious colonial Americans to such an extent that, one night, a group of anonymous radicals sneaked onto an EEK ship and dumped the modern equivalent of a million dollars' worth of tea into the harbor. The British government struck back with punitive laws, which fed a gathering storm, the storm that burst out finally as the American Revolution. So yes, the policies of China's Qing government did contribute to the birth of the United States. Thank you for asking. The two were connected as two ends of the same long causal chain.

Meanwhile, Britain did finally find a fix for its balance-of-payment problem with China, but as it turned out, that solution did not lie in China proper. To appreciate what happened next, it's necessary to catch up on the story unfolding in the Middle World.

Middle World Enmeshed
(1500 to 1900)

In the sixteenth century, when Europeans first started fanning out around the globe, the Islamic Middle world was a self-regarding universe of unrivaled (as far as it knew) splendor. The leading powers within this world had business to settle with one another and contradictions to resolve within their own civilizations, but like China, if they were in decline, they didn't know it. European entrepreneurs were arriving on their shores, but despite skirmishes that broke out here and there, Muslim powers did not see these foreigners as adversaries or threats. It would have been different if Europeans had arrived as armies bent on conquest, but they didn't; they arrived as merchants bent on trade.

Interactions between Middle World authorities and these Europeans were probably misread by both sides because they inhabited different social constellations, so they took different meanings from the same events. It wasn't that they disagreed. Rather, they didn't share enough terms of discourse to disagree in any meaningful way.

The Europeans were private businessmen, and private enterprise had a different status in their homelands than it did here in the Muslim world. In Europe, getting rich was a way to have political clout. In the Muslim world, having political clout was a way to get rich. In Dar-ul-Islam, that is to say, wealth put a man in a position to consume, but wielding political influence required that he get connected to the ultimate locus of political power, the military-religious complex, and this connection had to be done socially. The religious side of the power complex consisted of the *ulama*—the Islamic scholars. They controlled education, religion, language, law, and well, the whole constellation of ideas that was Islamic culture. The other side of the power complex, the monarch, his clan, and their associates, controlled law enforcement, collected taxes, built infrastructure, made war, doled out plunder: they pulled the physical levers of this world.

Families eminent in each realm might well be related through marriage to families in the other realm. This was a world of patronage networks, remember, and the highest networks revolved around the ruling family. Rulers collected taxes by giving their most trusted dependents tax farms. A tax farm was an area from which the "farmer" was entitled (and indeed obliged) to collect revenue. Obliged, because he had to turn over a specified sum to his patron—not a percentage, mind you, a certain sum. How he got the money was his business. Anything he collected over and above the amount he owed was his to keep. Intimates of the court who possessed really large tax farms used the same system to collect taxes from *their* domains: they assigned portions of their possessions to clients who collected what they could from those areas, delivered specified amounts to *their* patrons, and kept the surplus for themselves.

And so on down, which meant that, at ground level, taxpayers and tax collectors not only knew each other but might be related. In the end, therefore, taxation was a negotiation closely connected to the dense and interlocking patronage system with all its links to tribal values. Technically, the people collecting taxes had leeway to collect them as they saw fit, but by their methods they gained reputations for cruelty or kindness, generosity or brutality. The social and moral judgments of their community shaped their conduct, to the extent that they cared what people thought of them. Shame was a fundamental mechanism of administration in the Islamic societies of the Middle World (which meant that here as elsewhere the shameless had golden opportunities to prosper).

In Europe, those who sought political influence had every incentive to build a robust business. In the Islamic world, those who sought luxury had every incentive to work their way into the circles of powerful patrons, linked to higher patrons, linked to higher patrons. When European traders set up trading posts in Muslim-ruled territories, patronage networks determined who would profit from the trade with these foreigners. Those

298 | The Invention *of* Yesterday

who had positioned themselves in the highest circles through skillful marriages, expert glad-handing, heroic deeds, wheeling, dealing, and other such social mechanisms, accumulated the silver brought in by this trade. Later, when the traders returned with European manufactured goods, the people who had earlier been in a position to sell were now in a position to buy, whereupon the Europeans got their silver back.

On the Asian side, these people were inclined to view the European traders as potential patrons and to position themselves as well-connected and ever more trusted clients of theirs. In their world, when people went shopping for expensive items, they didn't just ask the price and plunk down their money: honor and etiquette demanded that they sit down, chat, drink some tea, put out feelers, establish a relationship. Only from that social platform could they move on to business. In a world of patronage networks, if they failed to make these moves, they were on the way to being ruined. Everyone lives in the world that their narrative makes real.

The Europeans were apt to cast the same encounters in purely business terms: they were not developing a quasi-cousin relationship of some sort here, for Christ's sake, they were buyers and sellers. Honorable behavior didn't consist of discharging properly the infinitely subtle, unstated social obligations associated with commercial interactions. Honorable behavior could be measured in numbers: it meant keeping one's accounts square. Patronage networks had been a mechanism for distributing wealth throughout society; trade with European corporations distorted this mechanism by generating an elite ever more closely associated with the foreign traders than with their own masses. These elites served as intermediaries between the foreigners and the masses. Serving the interests of the foreigners efficiently could help them grow their wealth, but what was good for the foreign traders wasn't necessarily good for the Indian masses.

INDIA

In India, *elite* was itself a loaded term. India had escaped the brunt of the Mongol holocaust, but the Medina project had not and could not ever emerge as the core principle of a single social whole here because most Indians were Hindus, and the larger story *they* were living in remained the intrusion of Turkic Muslim invaders across the north. Long before the Mongol eruption, these invaders had ruled over a majority population that didn't share their cultural framework, and this contradiction remained the case. Messenger Muhammad's destruction of idols in Mecca lived at the heart of the Islamic origin myth. It could not be uprooted. Without that image, the constellation wouldn't exist. In the Hindu world, by contrast, idols were deeply enshrined as a way to focus worship. Eliminating idols would have interfered with the very core of worship. Muslims prided Islam's insistence on the equality of all Muslims. Hindus embraced the idea of castes as a basis for society. Islam insisted on wiping out all rivals to one God as identified and defined by Muslims. This totally contradicted the open spirit that characterized Hinduism. Hindus tried to absorb Islam into their wider scheme by identifying Muslims as a caste; Muslims would have none of *that*.

Hindus and Muslims did do business with each other. They did develop relationships over the centuries, out of which hybrid movements arose. Hindu themes worked their way into Sufism, for example, the mystical version of Islam. Sufi overtones reverberated in the Bakhti movements of the Hindu world, which saw ecstatic union with the divine as the highest spiritual experience. A marriage of Muslim and Hindu themes gave birth to the Sikh religion, something new in world history. But in the end, the Hindu and Muslim narratives would not blesh into some single, new framework. There was history here that couldn't be forgotten. India remained a land occupied by two incompatible narratives. The division between Islam and Hinduism had been a central drama of Indian history for centuries: it remained so in the Mughal era. And because the Mughals dominated India when the Europeans traders first started arriving en masse, the elite were largely those who had curried favor with the ruling Muslims.

Hindu culture had mechanisms of its own that led to similar outcomes. I'll skip the details, but suffice to say, throughout the Indian subcontinent, even in independent Hindu states (of which a number did remain), when the European traders arrived with their bullion, the incoming wealth pooled up with a few and then seeped back to Europe instead of into the Indian social body as a whole.

In 1776, the British crown had nothing to do with India—officially. British interests were represented by the Honourable East India Company. This corporation didn't explicitly take over most of the places where it set up shop. Technically, local rulers continued to govern the various Mughal provinces, princely states, and Hindu kingdoms. But slowly, an understanding developed that Indian rulers of whatever cultural community in the local context would do nothing to hinder British commercial interests—and in fact do everything to favor those interests when they had a chance: as patrons and clients their interests were intertwined. Since two entirely separate (though overlapping) narratives were in play here, there didn't seem to be any real contradiction between favoring British commercial interests and exercising Indian sovereignty.

Frankly, the British who first came to India weren't interested in day-to-day governance. They didn't want to have to manage all the grinding details of the locals' daily life. They were merchants come to make an honest profit. A few hundred years earlier, for Europeans, there had been something unsavory about a dedicated interest in profit. Within the feudal Catholic framework, those who accumulated wealth through business and not land were regarded as misers and usurers: their obsession with filthy lucre compromised their chances of living forever in the kingdom of heaven. Since everyone was saying this to everyone, everyone saw this threat as real.

But with the progress narrative taking hold in Europe, old values were coming in for a second look. In 1776, Scottish philosopher Adam Smith published *The Wealth of Nations*, a seminal tract in which he argued that the best way to serve the common good was to pursue one's own economic self-interest. If everyone was trying to get rich, everyone was trying to supply stuff other people needed or wanted. Those who got richest were those who most successfully helped meet the greatest needs of the greatest number. Chasing wealth was actually a form of philanthropy, then, but it only worked if people were free to make money in their own chosen ways because each person knew best what he or she could do to make money, which is to say, contribute to the common good.

Smith also proposed that wealth concentrated in private hands was the most efficient way of organizing human labor, so long as the government didn't interfere. It would maximize production, which would benefit the whole society because a rising tide lifted all boats. To illustrate the point, he famously noted that ten pin makers working separately might make a total of ten pins a day, but those same ten men organized as a company, each specializing in a portion of the work, could produce as many as forty-eight thousand pins a day. The prosperity of the social whole was therefore best served when those with the means to equip workshops and organize labor employed individuals to work for wages doing the jobs the owner mapped out for them. What's more, the owners of such enterprises were likely to plow profits back into their enterprises, making them more efficient, which helped them grow, and growth was progress, so it served society at large.

At this point—the late 1700s—private European enterprises were chasing profits not just in China but throughout Asia and Africa. From Indochina and Malaya, they were extracting rubber, from Indonesia spices, from India cotton, from the Safavid empire carpets, from the Ottoman world hides and ores, from Africa rubber and slaves and ivory and gold—in short, from everywhere something. In most of these markets, the Europeans did not face the balance-of-payments problems they were suffering in China. In Safavid Iran, Europeans bought carpets but sold guns, thus recouping their silver. In India and in the Ottoman world, silver enabled European traders to outbid local merchants for all sorts of raw materials. Later, they came back with finished products made from those resources and sold them to the locals. Thus did silver flow back into European coffers. On the African coast, early on, they traded guns and liquor directly for slaves, coffee, and rubber. Later, European powers "owned" most of sub-Saharan Africa, and so they took what they wanted as if from their own cupboards: no loss of silver involved.

Early on, European traders took an interest in products *made* by Indians. Chintz, calico, muslin—these all fetched good prices in Europe.

Then garment manufacturing took off in the West, and powerful countries such as France outlawed the sale of garments and textiles made in the East. It was fine to buy raw cotton there, since that's where it was cheap, but the manufacturing—the spinning of thread and yarn, the weaving of textiles, the sewing of garments—all that had to be done in France: it was the law, a law that benefited French citizens. Britain and other countries followed suit with similar laws designed to control what their people imported and exported. European corporations involved in the Asian trade were good with this. They could buy cotton at the eastern end for cheap, sell it in Europe for more, load up there on European-made clothing for cheap, sell that in Asia for even more—it was like one of those Escher staircases that only went up.

To protect its interests, the British East India Company built an army of its own in India—as was its right under British law. In this army, only the officers were English; the troops were local recruits. Though outnumbered in India by many thousands to one, the British were able to exercise not just economic but military control of the subcontinent by using the Indian people themselves as their enforcers. And they were able to do this because there were two narratives in play. Indians did not realize until too late that the British were a voracious foreign power, not potential patrons building client networks.

In 1757, the British reinforced a fort they had built in Calcutta as a bulwark against the French. Now, finally, the (Indian) governor of the province saw a threat to his authority. He had some sixty-five British citizens arrested and crammed them into a small prison cell, where some two-thirds of them died.* Thereupon a company clerk, Robert Clive, hurried to Calcutta with a small force, destroyed the governor's much larger force, and replaced him with another local more to the liking of the British.

This so-called Battle of Plessey made nakedly obvious what had long been true: the British could do as they pleased here in Bengal. So they

---

*The number arrested, the size of the cell, and the number that died have all been disputed, but the traditional account is what matters here.

now took control of taxation, treating Bengal as their "tax farm" in the accepted manner of local law and tradition: they turned a portion of their revenues over to the Mughals and pocketed the rest, as was the accepted custom. But they jacked up land taxes by 500 percent or more because they didn't know these people or feel connected to them, so they weren't hemmed in by tribal shaming the way local tax farmers might have been. They raised tariffs on goods exported from India and eliminated tariffs on goods coming in from Britain, which made locally manufactured products more expensive than similar ones coming from Britain. There was nothing wrong with this in the British context: it was just canny business maneuvering. Admirably clever, even. It did mean that Indian manufacturers went out of business, but locals could still make a living producing whatever the British wanted to buy. The British wanted cotton, so Indian landowners started growing cotton on their lands instead of food. Within the framework of their own narrative, the British businessmen were not forcing anyone to grow cotton. They were just buying cotton.

The company's indifference to the social impact of its policies ended up wreaking havoc. Bengal suffered a series of famines, the worst of which claimed an estimated ten million lives. At that point, the British government stepped in and established a provincial administration, but the East India Company remained its close partner, and company troops went on serving alongside government troops as a parallel army.

The British soon took control of the whole subcontinent in the same way as they did Bengal. For appearances' sake (and also because there was no downside to it), they left a figurehead Mughal emperor on the throne in Delhi, but in 1857 they sent the last of these guys into exile. When it happened, it wasn't a conquest being finalized. The emperor was more like a line item being crossed off some budget because the expense of maintaining him could no longer be justified to auditors.

The same patterns were at work elsewhere in the Muslim Middle World, though at a slower pace. In 1520, the Ottomans were still a formidable, expanding world power: that year, they penetrated so deeply into Europe that they laid siege to Vienna and might well have taken it, had not distractions drawn their armies elsewhere. In 1648, the Ottomans attempted a second siege of Vienna. This time they were routed, but Ottoman historians did not take it as a turning point. The Ottomans were still scoring victories on other fronts, and they had plenty of other fronts. At that point, the Ottomans had no reason to assume that the European front was more significant than the Egyptian or Persian or Russian one. The Ottomans were sinking just as surely as the Mughals and the Qing, but they didn't know it yet; no one did.

In the Iranian world too, the social fabric was unraveling, as the master narrative long in place lost its power to explain what was happening. By the mid-1600s, the ruling Safavid dynasty had dissolved into gangs of quarreling cousins. Then, Afghan invasions from the east erased that dynasty from the historical stage. New Iranian dynasties emerged, but those too fragmented quickly into warring factions. Meanwhile, European entrepreneurs were on the scene, above the fray, acting as advisers to this or that faction, subtly increasing their social and political control with ever firmer advice, which local rulers were ever less at liberty to ignore. Here too, however, from their own perspective, the Europeans were not forcing anyone to do anything; they were just conducting business. In India the contest had come down to Britain and France; that one, the British won. In Iran and Afghanistan, the contest came down to Britain and Russia, the world's last, great expanding land-based empire. Here, the contest remained in doubt for some time.

Ripple Effects

(1500 to 1900)

While these developments were underway in the Islamic Middle World, Qing China was still busy sending porcelain and tea to Europe. As the eighteenth century proceeded, authorities in Britain fell into a panic about the quantities of silver they were hemorrhaging to China. By then, however, Great Britain was tightening its grip on India. Once they had reduced the subcontinent to a fully controlled colony, they saw a neat solution to their China problem. India's climate and soil were, as it happened, well suited for growing opium. In China, opium had long been used as a medicine, but recently, American tobacco having reached this part of the world, people had begun mixing opium with tobacco and smoking it as a recreational drug. India had a product, and China offered a market: how perfect was that?

In 1729, English merchants shipped two hundred boxes of Indian opium into China and refused to accept any form of payment except cash, preferably silver: turnabout was fair play. The Qing administration disapproved and banned opium imports, but the Honourable East India Company and its various private associates—which is to say, its subcontractors—ignored the ban.

In 1799, Chinese authorities renewed their ban in stronger terms, but the British believed in free trade on principle, and in this spirit went right on with their business. In 1800, Anglo-Indian traders sold 4,500 boxes of Indian opium to the Chinese. By 1834, they had pumped this figure up to 45,000 boxes, which amounted to some five thousand tons.

Anglo-Indian opium shipments to China now constituted the single most valuable commodity traded on world markets. That fact bears repeating: Anglo-Indian opium shipments to China now constituted the single most valuable commodity traded on world markets. British silver gushing into China in exchange for tea went gushing out again, to India, as payment for opium. From there it flowed back into British coffers. Now, English people were getting their tea and the British treasury was maintaining or even increasing its stash of silver. All was right with the world—from the British point of view.

The Qing didn't see it that way, of course. The mighty Chinese government decided to take action. The greatest empire on Earth could certainly stop a swarm of foreign drug dealers from operating on its soil.

Couldn't it?

Well, no, as it turned out, it couldn't. In 1840, the Opium War broke out between Britain and China. Technically, there were two opium wars: the first from 1839 to 1842 and the second from 1856 to 1860, but these were essentially two parts of the same war.

Rarely has a war of such consequence involved so little bloodshed. If wars were earthquakes, the Opium War would hardly have registered on the seismic scale. The British didn't even call it a war. They called it a "punitive expedition." It all started when a Chinese official decided to enforce his country's ban by arresting a shipload of dope dealers, locking them up in a factory, and burning their stash of opium.

The British sent a naval force to China to avenge the outrage, but not a huge force: about four thousand troops. On the face of it, this looked like a showdown between a tiger shark and a tiger, a battle that could never actually take place because Britain was a sea power and China was a land empire. China's power was vested in a vast interior accessible only by river, which ocean-going ships could not sail into.

Except that now they could. The little naval force Britain sent to China included four flat-bottomed steam-powered gunships. Their shallow draft let them sail right up major rivers, and their steam engines enabled them to chug along against winds and currents. They bombed several cities with their cannons. Once they reached the junction of the

Yangtze River and the Grand Canal, they had a clear path north, all the way to Beijing. The Chinese government fled the city and sued for peace.

The Opium War ended with China making some concessions. The British didn't demand the sorts of concessions that conquerors of the past had wrenched from folks they had conquered. The British didn't demand gold and women and slaves. They weren't savages, after all. They asked only that British businessman be allowed to go anywhere they wanted in China and buy or sell anything they wanted to anyone who was interested in doing business. Also, they stipulated that more ports must be opened to British ships. Also, that British citizens in China must be subject only to British law, not to Chinese law.

When other Western powers saw the privileges Britain had gained, they sent emissaries to Beijing to request in no uncertain terms the same privileges for *their* merchants. Fair is fair. Over the course of several decades, similar terms were indeed secured by the United States, France, Russia, and others. None of these powers claimed to have overthrown the Qing government. Officially, China was still a mighty Asian empire ruled by its own longtime dynasty. It's just that various Westerners could now exercise their right to trade freely in this territory—a right that was, within their own network of meaning, sacred.

The Chinese master narrative lost much of its coherence at this point, and a narrative that can't render the world meaningful can't retain its grip. The Opium War and its aftermath seemed to discredit the whole Chinese model of the world, and so now the gears of Chinese society really started to grind. The Qing were helpless to defend their citizens' interests against those of the foreigners. They lost control of land use, taxes, and tariffs. But the foreigners had nothing against the imperial family per se. The Qing retained their wealth and decadence and luxury. Meanwhile, Chinese peasants faced massive dislocations. Thousands emigrated to the Americas to work for slave wages in demanding jobs, such as building railroads, in order to send pittances back home to support their families.

Among the many concessions Europeans gained from China after the first Opium War was permission for Christian missionaries to proselytize in the Middle Kingdom. An Anglo-Indian minister had the Bible translated into Chinese and oversaw its distribution in China. This happened just as China was heading into one of its periods of unraveling. All the usual factors were manifesting widely. Rebel militias were springing up. So were apocalyptic religious cults. The most radical of these was a cult woven of the tatters of old and new narratives floating about: Hong Xiuquang, a man who had failed the civil service examinations several times, announced that he was the younger brother of Jesus Christ and had been charged by God the Father with establishing a kingdom of heaven in China. Thousands of poor but educated men who had failed the exams found this quasi-Christian message inspiring. One of them, Feng Yushan, founded the Society of God Worshippers, a revolutionary cult that soon launched a full-fledged rebellion against the Qing: the Taiping Rebellion.

The Taiping rebels carved out their own Kingdom of Heavenly Peace in southern China and fought bitter battles with Qing forces. "Rebellion" is a misnomer for this conflict. The battles raged from 1850 to 1864. The American Civil War took place in that same period, and it claimed some six hundred thousand lives, a staggering loss: no wonder it ranks as one of the most savage conflicts in human history. The Taiping Rebellion gets little coverage in the world histories I've seen, yet this conflict claimed—well, no one knows how many people died in the course of this conflict, but if deaths by starvation and disease are included, the number is somewhere between twenty and sixty million. On the scale of world conflicts, then, it ranks somewhere between the First and Second World Wars; in short, it was the most calamitous war you never heard of. If you consider this the closing chapter of the Opium War, then the conflict as a whole matches the historical impact of an epic clash between two giant galaxies of civilization. This was the war in which China discovered, to its shock, dismay, and bewilderment, that far from being the world's central power, it was not even a local power. It was scarcely more than real estate.

PART V

Enter the Machine

Ever since their emergence as a species, humans have been improving their tools. In the centuries after the Columbus moment, the sophistication of human tools began sloping abruptly upward. The results were as seminal as the human acquisition of language. Machines came to frame human life, organize human institutions, shape human values, permeate the human psyche, and even alter human biological functions. Western social constellations could incorporate machines into their networks of meaning more or less smoothly. Elsewhere, machines fit less easily into existing social frameworks, so these worlds proved more resistant to machine culture. But since machines now made all the difference in power struggles, the West came to dominate the rest of the world, and within the West, those with the most and best machinery rose to the top. The West, however, was still made up of many different social constellations whose members saw themselves as "us" and other Western powers as "them." The scramble among these powers for colonies, wealth, resources, and opportunities around the globe culminated in a global war. When it ended, humankind found itself reorganized as 195 concrete political units known as sovereign countries.

The Invention Explosion
(1750 to 1950)

The European expansion that began in the fifteenth century gained momentum right on through the nineteenth, due in part to the aggressive coherence of the European narrative. As it happens, however, another crucial development was underway in this same period, and it had to do with tools: the machine was pushing into history big time, and it would soon dwarf every other human or environmental factor. I'm saying *the machine* instead of *machines* because in this context, I propose, it's useful to think of machines collectively as one single player on the stage of history, interacting with other players, most of those others being constellations of people knit together by narratives.

Tools had, of course, been a crucial part of human life all along. Fire changed everything. The hammer was huge. The wheel was pivotal. The ax, the bow, the chariot, the pump—don't get me started. Levers and pulleys. The screw. Somebody stop me. Catapults. Armor. Gunpowder— again and again, breakthroughs in technology changed the course of human affairs, triggered migrations, determined who took control of whom, raised up kings, brought down empires.

But there is a distinction to be made between tools and machines. The line may be murky, but it's there. Think of it this way: tools help us humans do stuff; machines do stuff and we humans help them do it, by shoveling coal into their bellies, by replacing their worn-out parts when necessary, by feeding lumber into their saw teeth, whatever they need.

Historians sometime argue that science and technology run on separate tracks, each advancing independently of the other. In this view, scientists develop deep theories; inventors come up with gizmos. Newton plumbed the nature of light, but he didn't invent the prism. Boyle worked out the formula for calculating the pressure exerted by expanding gas, but a bunch of other guys invented the steam engine, and they knew nothing of Boyle's law. They were just trying to improve on a pump that was being used for the very practical purpose of emptying water out of mines.

Well maybe, but the fact remains: just as Europeans were embracing science, ingenious devices developed in Asia were flowing into Europe. When science and technology overlapped, a prairie fire of inventiveness flared across this continent. Devices that already existed were improved so radically they must be considered new inventions. The three-story water clock of China became the pocket watch of Western Europe. From the learning of the East, Europeans made daring leaps into the previously unimagined. Ibn Sina had drawn up an encyclopedic compendium of medicinal herbs and medical symptom. From that platform, Europeans went on to formulate the germ theory of disease and then came up with antiseptics, vaccines, and antibiotics.

THE INVENTING BUSINESS

Transformative inventions don't necessarily insinuate themselves into daily life just because they're useful. In general, they have to first turn into products, which can then turn into merchandise. The Muslim world with its patronage networks and its sharia and its restoration narrative didn't have obvious mechanisms for turning inventions into products. Neither did the Chinese world, with its dream of a socially cohesive, centralized state operated by an all-pervasive bureaucracy. New technology had the potential for disrupting existing social arrangements, and in much of the world, *preserving* existing social arrangements took precedence over building better mousetraps. In the restoration narrative, preserving and developing those arrangements tended to be the point of life itself.

In the West, however, where the social fabric was now largely woven of private profit-seeking companies, entrepreneurs lurked behind every bush, scanning the social landscape for inventions they might turn into merchandise. The progress narrative nourished this attitude because, as everyone knows, the best machines are the ones that are new and improved, and machines can always be improved. Societies shaped by the progress narrative had an advantage over others not so much because of the seminal tools they invented but because of the improvements and variations they kept making on those tools. Guns didn't tilt the balance in conflicts between Muslim and European armies. The Muslims had guns too. Guns didn't make the difference in China: the Chinese *invented* guns, for heaven's sake. What set the Europeans apart were the *kinds* of guns they brought to the field.

Early on, Muslim soldiers were using muzzleloaders: soldiers had to stand up to reload them, during which time they were targets. Europeans by then had developed breechloading guns, which they could reload lying down, hidden from sight. Trivial difference, big social impact. Muslim guns had smooth-bored barrels. Their shots often missed. The Europeans' made guns with rifled bores: bullets came out of those rifles spinning, which kept them moving straight and true. With old-fashioned guns one stuffed gunpowder into the barrel, then a metal ball, then rags, then tamped it all down, and then lit a match. Europeans developed bullets, which had built-in explosives that detonated when struck by a pin: yes, bullets were an invention just as much as guns. By the time non-European armies were using rifles, the Europeans had repeating rifles. By the time repeating rifles were common, Europeans had Gatling guns, then Maxim guns, and finally machine guns, which fired not single bullets but streams of bullets that tore to pieces whatever they were pointed at.

In societies framed by the progress narrative, particularly useful inventions generated numerous satellite inventions as tinkerers explored all the possible implications of some fruitful new idea or discovery. The steam engine demonstrated how the power of combustion within a sealed container could be harnessed to do work. Once the steam engine existed, people could wonder what else might be done with the same core idea. Was steam the only gas that expanded when heated? What else could drive an engine? If contained combustion could drive a pump, might it also turn a wheel? What might be done with combustion-driven wheels? How about a locomotive? How about the wheels of a spinning jenny, the device that made thread? Could an engine send a shuttle flying back and forth between the threads of a textile loom? And what about boats: could engines powered by combustion make sails unnecessary?

Even as European inventors were exploring all the ramifications of contained combustion, another elemental force drew their attention. A British physician called it electricity. French scientist Charles Coulomb figured out how to measure this force. American inventor Benjamin Franklin proved that whatever it was, electricity *flowed*. Inventor types started looking for stuff one could *do* with this force, and lo, they found that electricity flowing into a copper wire at one end could produce a jolt at the other end. In 1816 Francis Ronalds sent just such a pulse of electricity down a wire eight miles long. In 1837, American inventor Samuel Morse used electricity to power a device that made a tapping sound at a distance. He developed a code by which such tap might be translated into letters. Now the gizmo had a practical application: it could send a message.

Morse didn't invent the telegraph in the heat of some aha! moment. Most inventions are improvements of improvements of improvements. Lots of people were tinkering with electricity-powered devices in the early 1800s, building off one another's work. Morse is remembered as the inventor of the telegraph only because his improvement crossed some crucial threshold of novelty a hair's breadth before any of the others'.

As soon as the telegraph was invented, however, entrepreneurs started scrambling for ways to sell what this device could do, and that's what made the difference. Out of the scrum emerged a megarich corporation, Western Union, whose existence gave numerous tinkerers an incentive to spend hours fiddling with ideas for telegraph-related gizmos because if they came up with something good, Western Union might just buy the patent.

The telegraph made it possible to imagine the telephone, so herds of would-be inventors got busy figuring out how to send a simulacrum of the human voice through a wire. Alexander Bell is credited with inventing this landmark instrument, but again, he merely won a race many were running.

A Western Union employee had actually come up with a similar invention a bit earlier, but the honchos at Western Union didn't see a business angle to it: they assumed the telephone would be installed in telegraph stations. Voice messages sent from one station to another would be written down, and a messenger would carry the written note to the recipient. That didn't seem like much of an improvement on good old Morse code.

The telephone could not become a product until many people had telephones connected to one another by a network of wires; otherwise, who would buy a phone if there was no one to call? On the other hand, who would spend the money to install a web of phone lines that connected every household to every other if no one had a telephone? How could such a system come into existence? The sticking point here had to do with business, not technology.

It was Bell who solved this problem. He set up a telephone exchange as a subscription service. Members could call anyone else in their network but no one outside it. Why would anyone buy an expensive device to talk to just twenty-one other people, the number of subscribers in the first exchange? Bell finessed that objection by *leasing* telephones instead of selling them. Soon, by-subscription telephone exchanges had sprouted across America and Europe, and once *they* existed, metanetworks connecting the various exchanges became commercially feasible and attractive. People with phones could then call people who subscribed to networks other than their own. Early telephone systems all had switchboards—spawning a type of job that had never existed before: the telephone switchboard operator.

Stop and think about the forces that produced the invention explosion. The busy energy of all those entrepreneurs, companies, and corporations. The deep intellectuals in ivory towers unraveling the physical universe with reason and science. The history of expansion that bestowed glamor on discovery here. The progress narrative that fueled a constant quest for the new and better. What do all those factors have in common? They're all characteristics of the Western European social whole at this historical moment. In a world such as this, the invention explosion was bound to happen.

Seminal inventions triggered vast social changes, but incremental improvements could do the same. Minor technological innovations could set off ripple effects that altered the narratives knitting lives together. Take the rotary press, for example, perfected in 1830: this was just a variation on the flatbed press invented by Gutenberg (which was still in use). The flatbed press could print about 125 sheets an hour. The rotary press could put out 18,000. At first this seemed like a pointless improvement. Who would buy so much printed matter? The most widely circulated American periodical of the time had about forty-three hundred subscribers.

Actually, however, a mass market for some sort of printed product existed, but it had gone unnoticed. America was brimming with immigrants eager to practice reading English and hungry for news about their homelands. Existing periodicals were sold by subscription and required a year's payment up front, making them too expensive for the average laborer. It took a business genius to look at the new technology and the laboring masses and see an opportunity. In 1833, Benjamin Day launched the *New York Sun*, a mass-produced daily newspaper that he sold for a penny a copy, which almost anyone could afford. Soon Day was selling fifteen thousand papers a day and making his money back on volume.

Others saw him getting rich and jumped into the action. Papers that sold for a penny sprang up like mushrooms. Readers of these papers lived rough lives, they weren't deep intellectuals of the leisure classes, so publishers filled their pages with news of murders, fires, suicides, and other sensational events. Even so, early newspapers faced a shortage of "news." There just weren't enough murders, fires, and suicides! The publisher of a New Orleans weekly once complained that it wasn't like something newsworthy happened every *week*. In their desperation for content, publishers employed people to go out and actually *look* for news. They sent them down to the docks to interview passengers just arriving from Europe. Thus was another new job category born: the reporter.

The telegraph meant people could learn about distant events the day they happened. Once a submarine cable was strung across the Atlantic Ocean, news could even come from Europe. But trans-Atlantic telegraph messages were expensive. No single newspaper could afford to send and receive them routinely. So, in 1848, six newspapers joined together to share the cost of getting news "by wire." This consortium spun off as an independent enterprise, the Associated Press, the first of many wire services. Businesses of this type received messages by telegraph from correspondents and sold the information to all comers. Thus did news itself turn into merchandise. Being in it for the money, wire services wanted to sell information to as many newspapers as they could. Whoever sold the most news won this commercial competition. But different publications had different slants, tastes, intentions, agendas, and interests. What information could be marketed just as successfully to Republicans, Know-Nothings, Constitutional Unionists, Free Soilers, and random blowhards slapping up broadsheets and pouring out pamphlets?

The answer was: facts. Business considerations pushed wire services into recognizing that every news event had a factual core separable from opinions about the event. That core answered the questions *who, what, where, when,* and *why.* That's what could be sold to anyone and everyone. Once facts became merchandise, newspapers could use their accuracy and objectivity as selling points. You might say that the rotary press created the idea of objective news. Objective news—now we're getting into the realm of intercommunication, of narrative, of language. Objective news—an idea the Internet later demolished. Technology and language are forever intertwined. The rotary press helped spawn the idea of objective news, but it could not have done this without other idiosyncratic aspects in the Western narrative. Tools are always nested in some worldview. It's the combination of the two that shapes what happens in history.

OUR BODIES, OUR MACHINES

As machines penetrated the social field, they altered human life both outwardly and inwardly. Once engines were harnessed to production, for example, factories proliferated. In this mode of production, machines played the central role; people merely pulled the levers that made them work. In order to perform their role effectively, people had to adjust their patterns and rhythms to those of the machine.

The first traces of the industrial factory system had already been visible in plantations. Before that time, when farmers scoped out how to make best use of their land, they weighed a variety of considerations, including which ones fit the life they were living, the customs they followed, the religious narratives they embraced, and other such factors related to personhood and identity.

A plantation, however, had a single predetermined purpose: to produce sugar, for example. Or tobacco. Or cotton. The labor that went into fulfilling that one purpose required that the workers operate like the parts of a machine, each with its own defined function. The crucial core of the operation was broken down into small steps so that each part had one particular function to perform. In short, laborers on a plantation were not just slaves, serfs, or peasants; they were parts.

On a plantation, those parts and their functions were still somewhat open-ended. The same labor unit (aka "person" or, more quaintly, "human being") might dig a furrow and later pick cotton. But once machine logic took over, the production of *manufactured* goods—that is, once the plantation system was translated into the industrial factory system—the "rationalizing" of labor units became more exact and prescribed, as is the normal course for any well-built machine. Each worker, although a biological and social unit with a multitude of urges, emotions, goals, and desires, was, for the duration of that person's participation in the manufacturing process, one part of a machine-like social group. The bulk of the worker's biological systems lay outside his or her function within the factory. As is the case with machinery, the value of each part could be calculated mathematically: as a wage, or in some cases as a salary.

Without the mechanical clock, factories would have been difficult or impossible to run. Workers would have arrived at a variety of different times and could not have coordinated their actions. In preindustrial days, people knocked off for the midday meal when the work came to a natural stopping point, or when hunger had risen to some biological tipping point, or when the sun had reached a familiar place in the sky. The laboring masses mostly went home or were already at home for this meal, which was prepared in accordance with a breakdown of labor rooted in social norms that ultimately derived from biological factors: family members who did the cooking were those who kept the home, and they were traditionally women because, whatever else they did, child care had to be one of their main functions.

Once factories came into play, all the parts of the operation had to start working at the same moment, stop at the same time, eat at the same place, and get back to work at the same minute. Factory workers couldn't go home to eat; that would have been too inefficient. People would have straggled back to work raggedly, which would have ground the whole operation to a halt. A machine cannot work if its parts are not perfectly in sync, so people working for a mechanized industrial manufacturing operation had to subordinate their biological selves to the logic of the machine.

Factory work generally demanded that people work in shifts: day shift, swing shift, graveyard shift—these units of time did not exist before the machine, but they were as real as rocks to workers in industrialized societies, and I can personally attest that if you work either of the last two shifts long enough, your body clock resets to meet the requirements of your schedule.

Along the same lines, before there were jets, the phenomenon known as jet lag was unknown to our species: not one single human being in the history of the universe had ever experienced it. All animals have built-in biological mechanisms regulating functions such as sleep and hunger, and humans are no exception. We have circadian rhythms that govern when we sleep and when we feel alert. These are set by the procession of light and dark as regulated by the astronomy of the universe. Before the rise of the machine, people were biologically synced to various features of their natural environment, and these differed from place to place—in the tropics, day and night were virtually equal year-round; in the far north or south, they went through extreme seasonal variations. Electricity liberated humans biologically from such cycles, liberated them from their immediate environment, linking them instead to the rhythms and requirements of the machines they serviced. People could live anywhere and in those places do anything, limited only by the mechanisms they possessed for detaching temperature and moisture from the variations of any environment. Dubai never gets cold, and it routinely hits 110 degrees in the summer, yet it has a year-round ski resort. Antarctica is too cold and harsh for human habitation, and yet over forty-four thousand people go there each year now, as tourists mostly.

Machines may even have a propensity to alter our biologically embedded sense of how much time has passed or is passing. Scientists tell us we don't have a biological organ that senses time the way our eyes sense light or our ears register sound waves. Our internal time sensation is somehow tied to the chemistry of neural interconnections in our brains. If the outside environment bombards our senses with lots of stimulation, our brain chemistry adjusts to deal with it; if the incoming signals are erratic or repetitive or unpredictable, that too must have an influence. Ideally, after all, we must be in a state of readiness for anything that might come at us. In some contexts that might mean being ready to bolt if a tiger jumps out of the bushes, in another staying awake through the endless monotony of babysitting a machine that could chew one's arm off if one gets careless. As our environment grew ever more mechanized, our deep neural clocks no doubt adapted to the pace and rhythm of machines, making for a biological disconnect at some level in interactions among people adapted to mechanized and nonmechanized environments.

The rise of the machine not only changed our sense of time as fast or slow, it also changed our sense of time as local or universal. When churches acquired clock towers, bells regulated by mechanical clocks were rung for vespers, creating a public time shared by everyone close enough to hear those bells, but that was only the beginning, it turned out. When railroads threaded into social life, public time expanded vastly, for trains required that the time in New York City be calibrated exactly to that of Bisbee, Arizona, or Walla Walla, Washington. Thus, strangers who would never meet, never respond to the same physical stimuli at the same moment, nonetheless inhabited the exact same temporal framework and knew they did. This kind of public time even acquired an informal name. "Railway time," people called it.

Our Machines, Ourselves
(1750 to 1900)

Once machines came to permeate human life, people had to interact with them as they did with other persons. In a way, the machine coming into human life was much like one culture lapping into another. When humans interacted with machines, however, they had to use quite a different logic than they did with people. To secure the cooperation of another person, you might request or demand or persuade, negotiate or bully or discuss. These methods don't work with machines. You can't bribe the damn things; you can't bargain with them; you can't make them work by explaining why it would be in their own best interest to cooperate. You can't get a machine to do what you want by shouting at it, kicking it, or dropping dire hints of torture to come. Believe me, I've tried.

In any interpersonal interaction, no matter what each person does or says, there's no predicting with absolute certainty what the other's response will be because every human has a tacit complex of unstated goals, aims, and purposes that influence his or her actions and decisions. A machine, however, has no subtext. It was built to do some certain thing, and it does that single thing by virtue of its design and its parts. A machine either is working or isn't working; there's no gray area. Contrast this with social arrangements such as marriage or business partnerships. If a machine isn't working, you have to fix it or change the parts, and this is a straightforward operation because a good machine has all the parts it needs and none that are superfluous, and when all the parts are made and put together correctly, the machine performs what it was built to do. With a marriage or a business partnership, it's not so cut-and-dried.

MACHINE AS METAPHOR

As the machine came into history, its logic seeped into the socially constructed narrative realities people inhabited (and inhabit) as manageable stand-ins for the unknowable "real world." The machine seeped as metaphor into the way people thought of themselves and society. In the nineteenth century, for example, when the steam engine was the dominant device of the age, Sigmund Freud pictured the human psyche as a sort of hydraulic system: psychic energy flowed through pipes, and where it was blocked, pressure built up, venting eventually in other parts of life as neuroses. Today, computers being the dominant machine of the age, we are more apt to think of human psyches in terms of programming, culture as a sort of software, and aberrant behavior as a symptom of faulty wiring or software glitches.

The machine demonstrated that the material world could be engineered to produce desired outcomes. As metaphor, the machine suggested that the same approach should work for social problems. If the survival of the whole and the happiness of its parts was what you wanted, you should be able to design a government made up of ingeniously interlocking rules designed by reason, which would get you that outcome.

In 1787, a group of men from the cluster of former British colonies in America undertook just such a project. They sat down to design a brand-new government from scratch. They went about the task the way an engineer might go about constructing a new machine. They first nailed down the purpose of their apparatus: "to form a more perfect Union, establish Justice, insure domestic Tranquility, provide for the common defense, promote the general Welfare, and secure the Blessings of Liberty to ourselves and our Posterity." The rest of their schematic specified the parts of the apparatus, how each was supposed to work, and how they all should work together.

Every real-world constitution has two aspects. On the one hand, it is a manual for operating a country; on the other, it's a treaty among all interests competing for advantage at the moment the constitution is created. "Operating manual" and "treaty" are not the same thing. The first echoes the logic of the machine; the second is inseparable from narrative. Some constitutions are more manual; some lean more toward treaty. Constitutions that are mostly treaties tend toward obsolescence because their provisions become irrelevant as the story moves forward and conditions change. The US constitution was at the other extreme. It was far more like a how-to manual for operating a government. Yes, it was laced with specificities related to the issues of the day—slavery being the most glaring example—but the tone of the document implied abstract and universal principles, and it had a built-in mechanism for altering the manual in response to changing conditions—the amendment process.

The men who wrote the US Constitution had certain luxuries that may never be repeated. They were living in a vast, new world of which they knew almost nothing. They had, from their perspective, an empty page to work with: they had just severed themselves from their own past, and their future was a blank slate. They were devising a document to govern their interactions with one another, but they focused on abstract and procedural mechanisms as if they were designing an instrument that could be applied to all of humanity, probably because they experienced themselves *as* all of humanity.*

Few other constitutions were born in circumstances quite so unencumbered. The French adopted their first constitution in 1791, but theirs didn't last long, and how could it? The French were still living in France. They were in the hot middle of a story already in progress: mud wrestling amid the inherited grievances of their history, the latest chapters of which involved guillotines and beheading. The social context did not exactly favor sober discussions of mechanisms and procedures. The first French constitution *had* to be more treaty than manual.

---

*In this, they were not unique: many early cultures' word for their own tribe was also the word for human being.

IDEOLOGY

The French Revolution proved pivotal, however, in making ideology an ingredient of history. Constitutionalism was but one of many *isms* that emerged in the next century, and new ones still keep coming: liberalism, conservatism, socialism, communism, fascism, feminism, Islamism, scientism—there is no end in sight. Ideologies are blueprints for social interaction colored by the logic of the machine. They reflect the premise that a systematic doctrine worked out intellectually and capable of being articulated in words can supply the basis for a well-functioning social gestalt. Kinship and religion had long provided just such connective tissue; ideologies now began to offer an alternative sort of glue.

In a world defined by religion and kinship, the first question raised by every rule was, How do we know this comes from the top? In a world defined by ideology, the first question was, How do we know this rule will work? A religion must convince people its vision of the supernatural is true, and its interpretation of the highest supernatural authority's word is correct. An ideology must convince people its dicta would in fact improve human life on Earth.

The French revolutionaries raised ideology as an explicit banner. They weren't out to replace one powerful family with another but to wipe out the very idea of family lineage as a basis of authority. They appealed to abstract principles that could be stated in words. Three words, to be exact: liberty, fraternity, and equality.

In practice, these terms have come in for much deconstruction. Who is to be liberated from whom? What constitutes liberty? Where does fraternity leave women? Equality, you say? Ah, but people are not exactly similar, so equal in what regard? These questions do not, however, undercut the fundamentally ideological nature of the French Revolution and the doctrines it generated. Every ideology runs into contradictions in practice.

THE MIDDLE CLASS

Early on, mechanized production wiped out most artisanal employment and spawned grindingly monotonous factory jobs instead. Eventually, however, the ripple effects of the machine generated a host of jobs unlike any of the past. Someone had to install the machines and run and service them, and these were jobs. Someone had to design improvements of existing machines, and that was a job. Industrial societies needed accountants, clerks, human resource managers, secretaries. Industrial societies needed a lot of people who could read and write, which meant more schools were needed and more teachers. The ever-proliferating array of consumer goods pouring out of factories had to find buyers, which created a need for salesmen, cashiers, store clerks, advertising experts, marketing specialists. And the growing complexity of a machine-permeated society organized as companies required lawyers, lots and lots of lawyers.

Most people working these new jobs did not end up rich, but most did not end up wretchedly poor either. On a scale from one to ten, they ended up someplace in the comfortable middle. In short, the machine generated, on a scale never seen before, a middle class with disposable income.

Indeed, industrialized societies produced so much more than enough for everyone, they didn't need all hands on deck slaving away at the basics. Theoretically at least, many people could make a living doing things unrelated to their own or their society's survival. They could write bestselling fiction, for example, or sing songs, or play basketball. In earlier centuries, people who did these sorts of jobs lived on the charity of patrons, who were mostly landowning aristocrats of the military class. In the machine age, anyone with a skill to sell could tap into the abundance of society if he or she could find enough buyers.

THE INDIVIDUAL

Centralized machine production also launched the greatest migration in history—greater even than the storied Indo-European or

Bantu migrations. It drew people out of farms and pastures and into cities by the millions upon millions. This migration not only continues to be underway but may still be gaining momentum.

When the people of the Pontic steppe migrated east and west, they undoubtedly traveled as whole tribal groups. This was not the case with the new migrations. When large groups of kinfolk moved to cities, they had to disperse and look for separate ways to earn a living because no whole clan nor even any whole extended family was going to get jobs in the same industrial operation. Companies didn't hire clans; they hired individuals. And they weren't going to pay workers enough to support whole clans. Why would they? Companies were better off dealing with workers as individuals apart from large webs of relatives because kinship often made claims on people unrelated to the purposes of the company. In fact, employees' obligations to family might even conflict with their obligations to their employer. This applied not just to factory jobs but to many of those new middle-class jobs generated by the machine. The workaholic whose family suffers because he can't meet both sets of obligations—that's quite a familiar figure in modern Western lore.

In Europe's feudal era, moral narratives such as Christianity and tribal tradition recognized obligations and privileges quite outside the economic sphere, entitlements that derived from a person's social ties, not from his or her productivity. People who didn't work outside the home or produce any material goods within the home nonetheless had a place at the dinner table just because they were somebody's second cousin or somebody's great-aunt.

In the preindustrial world, where kinship links trumped all other bases of interconnection, the fundamental units of society were groups of relatives: hyperextended families. As machines proliferated, these social constellations pretty much vanished. People were biologically related in all the same ways as before, but hardly anyone now made critical life decisions shaped by the needs and expectations of second cousins or great-uncles anymore. The functional unit of machine-age societies shrank from tribe to clan to extended family to nuclear family, and within this framework finally down to the irreducible, sovereign unit: the individual.

In a universe of sovereign individuals, people were theoretically responsible only to ties they had freely chosen. They could marry whom they wished, live where they wanted, and work where they willed. People were not just *free* to construct their own unique personalities but *obliged* to: from the menu of all the possibilities in their social milieu, all the ideas, values, opinions, known facts, and miscellaneous cultural detritus floating around, they were to construct a personal self. In such a universe, their associates were going to be the people with whom they shared their home space, their workplace, their neighborhood, their interests—stamp collecting, hunting, football, sewing, whatever. By the middle of the nineteenth century, with Western Europe and America standing astride the world, ideologies were outcompeting kinship and religion as sources of social cohesion. Inevitably, in such a world, some people's most passionate affiliations were going to be with others who shared their ideology. They would identify themselves as members of movements and political parties, which, theoretically, they had elected to join.

Did the machine "cause" this change? Assertions like that are always going to be facile. Physics can describe the world in terms of discrete causes and definite effects, but in the socially constructed realm, no single thing causes any other single thing because everything is connected to everything. The social universe is nothing but the structures and metastructures of connections I'm calling constellations. Every development, innovation, and departure just adds some jot to the confluence of many currents. In the West, where the primacy of kinship began eroding, the rise of the machine coincided with the emergence of private enterprise, of companies and corporations, of blocks of money capable of willful action. Who's to say which caused what? These things were all happening at the same time in the same milieu, no doubt reinforcing one another. When it comes to history, instead of talking about causality, we're better off thinking in terms of ripple effects.

GENDER AND MACHINE CULTURE

O ne thing the ripple effects of the machine changed profoundly was the relationship between men and women. It did this by altering the division of labor along gender lines. In some form or fashion, this division no doubt went back to the dawn of human history. Stone Age bands had to meet certain needs or they'd die. They had to get food, produce children, and keep the kids alive long enough to produce more children. They had to keep their home fire burning, fend off predators, negotiate with other human bands, and defend themselves against human bands that proved hostile. All these jobs were vital; all of them had to be done. And the band had to deploy its numbers effectively, so instead of everybody doing everything, some of the jobs fell to men and some to women. Getting food meant hunting animals and gathering edible plants. The first of those jobs entailed roaming the world, sometimes for days at a time; children couldn't go along on these expeditions, so hunting became men's work. Women kept the fire going, gathered plants, and kept the children safe and fed. Women's work made them specialists in nurture, men's in the use of force. So goes the conventional view.

Early on, this division made sense, for it optimized a group's chances of survival. Groups that organized this way probably outcompeted groups that didn't (if there were any such). The division of labor along gender lines did, however, split the social world into a private sphere associated with women and a public realm associated with men. The first was an inward-looking sphere centered around home and children. The second was the outward-facing shell of the group, its interface with the environment— which included other bands of humans, some of whom were hostile.

There is no reason to assume that women were subordinate to men back then. Stone Age human bands might well have been matriarchies, in which children were not connected to particular parents. It might be that all the adult women were mothers, and none of the men had the social role of father to any particular child. In that context, it didn't matter which child was whose. The whole group had a stake in those children surviving to adulthood.

Things changed (the theory goes) once people settled down. Then they were accumulating durable goods that someone would inherit when they died, so at this point it began to matter which children were whose. The mothers' identities were obvious, the fathers not so much. Establishing fatherhood required social mechanisms such as marriage and record keeping. Property gave rise to the patriarchal family.

From that point on politics, war, construction, destruction—men's work—gained apparent importance. Women's work—food preparation, weaving, sewing, keeping the house, taking care of children—lost prestige. Eventually, to call something woman's work was to trivialize it. By the dawn of the machine age, most people assumed that the division of the world into public and private, along with the subordination of women to men, was ordained by God and/or nature. According to this narrative, men and women were inherently built for different roles. Anyone who crossed the line was threatening the survival of the group.

Before the machine age, only a few women made their mark as rulers of states. Catherine the Great of Russia comes to mind. Queen Elizabeth I of England. Hatshepsut of ancient Egypt. Only a few made their name as warriors: Joan of Arc, of course; the Prophet Muhammad's youngest wife, Aisha; the Jewish warrior Al-Kahina, who led the Berber resistance to Islam in North Africa; Boadicea, who fought the Romans to a near standstill in Britain. Those few examples, however, proved that women *could* excel in politics and war. The history of politics and war was not studded with the names of women because women weren't *in* those fields. Politics and war belonged to the public realm, and before the rise of the machine, women's lives unfolded mainly in the private sphere.

To be sure, in most of the world, throughout most of human history, the private sphere was not as inconsequential as it seems today. Home was a world then, not a house. But restriction was restriction. Across much of the planet, until rather recently, women could not own property. In most societies, women had few opportunities to develop the skills they would need to compete with men in the public arena. For example, in most societies, it took a *very* bold rule-breaking woman to learn to read and write. In many, women were routinely treated as possessions of men or as tokens in the competition of men with men. They rarely had the opportunity to choose the man or men with whom they would have sex, or the power to decide whether they would have children and if so how many.

This is not to say that women didn't work. Women always worked. Just before the rise of the machine, they were doing a hefty portion of the production and manufacturing in Europe. It was they who wove the textiles, manufactured the garments, and produced the bulk of the handicrafts. It was they who milked the cows, churned the butter, and preserved the foods that would be vital to survival in the off-season. One thing that mechanized mass production of consumer goods did was to wipe out women's employment. Women were among the many who streamed to cities to get jobs tending to machinery. There, they and their families lived in the wretched poverty of urban slums: Charles Dickens's London was not a pretty place for most of its inhabitants.

But then, as the machine proliferated, the material necessities that had once tied women to hearth and home no longer applied. Women who went to work in the public arena were not threatening the safety of the children or the survival of the kinship cluster. No one had to keep the home fire burning because the first one home could simply turn on the heat. In the past, physical strength had played a key role in shaping the relationships among people. When heavy things had to be moved, the strong were called upon to move them. When conflicts arose, those with physical strength tended to prevail. Generals had to have brains, but the brainiest ones filled their front lines with brawn, and men were generally bigger and stronger than women. But once the machine permeated human affairs, physical strength lost much of its relevance except in professional sports and street crime. In fact, with the rise of the machine, there was no *biological* reason to favor men over women in almost any human endeavor (nor vice versa, for that matter). Thereupon, narratives related to gender began to change, adjusting to the new material reality.

Meanwhile, thanks to the machine, kinship groups were shrinking from tribes to nuclear family units. The private realm was shrinking correspondingly from a social universe to a multitude of social cubicles.

Women kept out of the public realm were cut off from the ebb and flow of the social whole. And yet their restriction to the home derived from no material necessity and served no social purpose. Inevitably, then, women of means began venturing into public life, despite the wishes and often to the great dismay of their male-dominated families.

In 1848 a wave of revolutionary uprisings against various monarchies swept across Europe, impassioned mostly by liberal*ism* and constitution-al*ism*. It was the year of the *ism*. In the United States, that year, some three hundred women met in the North American city of Seneca Falls, New York, to discuss women's rights. Men generally smiled into their sleeves. Women talking politics, what next. But there was nothing cute about the Seneca Falls convention. It was organized by two powerful antislavery activists, Lucretius Mott and Elizabeth Cady Stanton, and it produced a Declaration of Sentiments, which became a founding document of the movement later dubbed feminism. Its language echoed that of Thomas Jefferson's in the Declaration of American Independence, but with some alterations: "We hold these truths to be self-evident that all men *and women* are created equal."

Western women began agitating to expand their place in the public arena. By the end of the century, in the United States and Britain at least, women activists were provoking mass arrests as a deliberate political strategy, sometimes breaking windows and setting fires, and publicizing their cause with dramatic (occasionally fatal) hunger strikes. Finally, women won the right to vote in a few of the countries that *had* voting: first in New Zealand, then in Finland, then in several Scandinavian countries, then in the United States, then in Great Britain—and then the dominoes started to fall.

In the nineteenth century, when women sought work outside their homes, they were competing with men, and if the job was at all desirable, they lost that contest. A working woman was by definition a poor woman. By working in the public realm, she advertised that she came from a family headed by a man who couldn't even support his own family. For men, it became a badge of pride to earn enough money to keep their wives idle. A cult of domesticity emerged in Europe and America, which celebrated the unemployment of women as a positive, touting an image of women as fragile, pretty creatures, whose sole purpose in life was to raise healthy children and create warm nests for their men, of which each woman must have only one.

At the same time, mechanized production was pouring out such an abundance of cheap consumer goods that the need for women's work, even in the home, was eroding. People didn't have to make a lot of stuff anymore; they could simply go out and buy it. Many middle-class women, idled by industrialism, found home life empty, even soul deadening. They wanted to get out of the house, even if it wasn't to go to some job. They wanted to exist out there in public where people mingled with people. But where could they go? As late as 1850, the only public gathering places were taverns and bars, where men hung out and drank and got into fistfights.

Retail merchants spotted an opportunity here. Before this time, fashionable shops in Western Europe kept their goods in a stockroom. A clerk met with customers out front, discussed what was wanted, negotiated a price, and then some factotum fetched the item from the back. Now, however, some enterprising merchants discovered that they could sell more goods if they let customers select items for themselves. They set their products on open shelves, let people browse, and didn't even require that shoppers buy anything. But if they browsed long enough, they generally did buy something, so the trick was getting them to linger.

In 1852, a French businessman transformed a sundries store called Le Bon Marché into a ramped-up Western European version of the ancient Middle World bazaar. The Middle World bazaar had always been as much a social space as a commercial zone, but it was almost exclusively for men. What emerged now in Europe was a public space geared toward women. Le Bon Marché was as much a respectable leisure destination as it was a store. It presented merchandise in themed settings—here was an Arabian nights grotto, there was a Japanese garden. It provided benches and nooks where women could sit and socialize. It had floors and walkways for them to explore, play areas for children, little cafés. The Bon Marché produced some of France's first millionaires. Predictably enough, rivals sprang up like mushrooms.

In North America, Macy's of New York expanded to a million square feet of display space. In Chicago, Marshall Field's began hiring women as sales clerks because most of their customers were middle-class women, and these customers felt more comfortable dealing with female clerks. The gambit succeeded. Marshall Field's profits soared, whereupon other department stores followed suit.

Employment opportunities at big stores like these drew young single women to cities where they could (just barely) support themselves with jobs. The subculture of working women was small at first, and the women were paid rock-bottom wages, but other paid occupations spawned by machine culture kept opening up for women now: typing, filing, operating telephone switchboards, teaching, nursing, taking dictation. Some women found ways to get some schooling. Some worked their way into colleges. A very few even became doctors.

Deep social structures and deep psychological structures are two sides of the same coin. Extreme changes in human psychological structures generally don't happen in a single generation. Children are born genetically programmed to discover what sort of society they're in and develop into persons who fit in as pieces of that social constellation. They may embrace structural social changes as they go through life, but the personalities embracing those changes will be the ones formed in childhood by the nurture they got from the previous generation. This ensures a continuity of social norms and forms from one generation to the next: it's the social constellation's way of preserving its own identity, which is to say, its very life. But this also generates a lag in the evolution of such forms. Gender roles being some of the most deeply embedded structures of human life, one would expect these to resist quick change. In this, however, one would be mistaken. The extent of change in gender roles and expectations—worldwide—over the last two centuries has been nothing less than staggering.

Indeed, the emergence of women into the public sphere, one of the many ripple effects of the machine, must rank, I think, right up there with history's most momentous developments. The last shake-up of this magnitude was the Neolithic Revolution some ten thousand years ago, when many of our species first settled in fixed locations and began living on food we grew and animals we raised, using tools we made in workshops we built. That revolution unfolded over the course of millennia, and it produced profound changes in the way humans interconnected, including, it would seem, the birth of patriarchy as a near-universal family structure. The current revolution in gender roles is a story still in progress. It is only two centuries old but is already so advanced, it presages even more apocalyptic changes ahead, quite probably including the end of the patriarchal family and perhaps even of gender as a fundamental aspect of human identity. It's no surprise, then, that in most societies, social norms and emotional alignments have not yet caught up to this revolution in human culture.

Social Constellations in the Machine Age
(1850 to 1950)

The rise of the machine was not a product of human intention. Individual people created this or that piece of technology, but no one individual decided to advance technology as a whole, no one could have impeded its advance, no one could determine its direction, and no one could control its social impact. That's not to say, however, that the machine had a uniform impact throughout the world. Everywhere it went, the machine was entering a story already in progress. In every place, it had to work its way into a social framework held together by some long-established narrative, just as human immigrants from another culture would have had to do. The impact of the machine varied from one cultural environment to another because it always had to negotiate its way into an existing gestalt. It might drastically change the worldview it was entering once it was part of the picture, but first, it had to become part of the picture.

MARXISM

In the West, the machine abruptly spawned the industrialist system and the urban migrations, which at first resulted in the misery of millions. This in turn gave rise to another of those nineteenth-century *isms*, a movement embodied intellectually by the writings of Karl Marx and his colleague Frederick Engels: an odd couple if ever there was one. Engels was the wealthy son of a factory owner. Marx was miserably poor—so poor he had to stuff newspapers into his shoes to keep from freezing his feet off when he walked to the British Museum to write his masterpiece, *Das Kapital*, the central document of communism. He was so poor that four of his seven children essentially died of poverty: they were malnourished and got sick, and the Marx family couldn't afford doctors. For the most part, Marx lived in obscurity. When he died, much of his major work remained unpublished, and few had read the five books he had published. Only eleven people attended his funeral, and five of those were his immediate family. Within two decades, however, both his followers and enemies ranked him with Darwin and Freud as an intellectual giant of his era, and with Caesar and Napoleon as a figure of history-rattling political impact.

Marx described the world as inherently divided into social classes. The upper classes were always those who owned the means of production, whatever those might be in a particular era. The lower classes were those who didn't. History was the story of the never-ending struggle between these classes. Land had once been the dominant productive asset; now machinery played that part. With the rise of the machine, Marx saw the theoretical possibility of class struggle coming to an end because humanity now had the technological prowess to produce so much of everything that everyone could wallow in abundance.

In his day, this was not happening, and Marx said it was because machines were all owned by those with concentrations of money and credit. Blocks of money and credit operating as social units were driven by a single motive: to maximize profits so they could survive and grow. It wasn't the individual people doing this so much as the blocks of money and credit, which Marx called *capital*. The overwhelming majority of people were the workers who operated the machines, and the owners of capital had every incentive to pay them as little as possible, since whatever didn't go to workers' wages accumulated as owners' profit. The owners could then invest these profits in more machinery, thereby making their capital grow. In fact, they could not help but do this for they were part of the capitalist social constellation, and capital "wanted" to grow.

The trouble was, the masses were not just workers. They were also the consumers of the products the owners needed to sell. If the workers had no spare cash, they could not buy the products, which put the whole system in danger of collapsing: what made sense for each enterprise exactly contradicted what made sense for the whole. According to Marx, this contradiction, built into the social relationships of his day, produced intolerable stresses that would result at last in a workers' revolution. After the revolution, the machines that produced enough for everybody would be owned by everybody. At that point, competing social classes would cease to exist, and a golden age would begin. For all its scrupulous academic underpinnings, Marx was preaching a religion.

Marx's vision derived from the system of production in the industrial powerhouses of the West: Germany, Britain, and to a lesser extent France (not to mention North America). In these countries, the masses were mostly literate and mostly lived in cities. They had a history of organizing as guilds—political groups based on trades. With the rise of the machine, they were forming workers' unions, and as unions they agitated for improved wages and working conditions. They were able to exercise some power by striking—refusing to work—until certain demands were met. Marx expected that these people, whom he called the *proletariat*, would be the ones to carry out the revolution.

FROM MARXISM TO MARXIST-LENINISM

But the revolution Marx envisioned never took place in Germany. His communist ideas instead ended up empowering a tiny cadre of educated intellectuals in a totally different social environment: Russia. Here, a Europeanized dynastic elite who mostly spoke French ruled a multitude of Russian-speaking peasants, most of whom were serfs. Serfs were forbidden to leave the land; almost none of them could read or write. They lived in dire rural poverty, and they were so dispersed they could not communicate among themselves enough to organize anything like a union or a strike. Officially, the Russian emperor abolished serf-dom in 1861, but conditions didn't change much for the former serfs.

And that describes only the Russian portion of the Russian Empire. The bulk of the empire lay east of the Ural Mountains, stretching across Asia. There, the inhabitants were mostly Turks and Siberians, who felt virtually no connection to the aristocratic culture of Moscow or St. Petersburg. In short, the Russian world had none of the characteristics Marx deemed essential for a communist revolution.

When Marx's ideas filtered into this world, they were not a natural fit. They could not take root until they had been modified. The modifi-cation was carried out by Marx's Russian disciple Vladimir Lenin. What emerged from this process was no longer Marxism, exactly, but Marxist-Leninism, a distinctly Russian constellation of ideas.

Marx had pictured industrialism leading to "the revolution." Lenin envisioned "the revolution" leading to industrialism. But who would do the revolting? This was the conundrum for Lenin. His country had vir-tually no proletariat. Lenin, therefore, declared that the revolution must be spearheaded by a vanguard party: a tightly disciplined group pre-pared to use unlimited force in pursuit of its noble cause. The revolution would produce the industrial society, which would produce proletarians, who would then carry out the real revolution, the one that would spell the end of history and launch true communism. The justification for the vanguard party's violence would lie in the correctness of its doctrine; so, the party's most essential work would have to include perfecting its ideo-logical doctrine and making sure all its members were on the same page.

In 1917, when Russia's three-hundred-year-old monarchy came crash-ing down, the government was up for grabs, and only Lenin's vanguard party had the unified discipline to take decisive action. The Bolsheviks, as this group called itself, seized power and launched a campaign of terror aimed at wiping out all traces of the previous social order and replacing it with a new order promulgated from the top, a centralized industrial state that was not so much a social organism as a social machinery. Along the way, Lenin and his associates wiped out all their rivals on the left, for Marxist-Leninism required a uniformity of thought never envisioned by mere Marxism. This was what resulted from the machine and its culture bleshing with the Russian world.

FROM MARXIST-LENINISM TO MAOISM

Following this thread of story requires skipping forward in time, so as not to interrupt the through line. From Russia, Marxist-Leninism rippled east to China. Here, again, a doctrine that had originated in one context was entering an entirely different one. China was nothing like Germany or Britain but nothing like Russia either. The doctrines originated by Marx and recast by Lenin could not take root here until they were reimagined in Chinese terms. It was the revolutionary Mao Tsetung who carried out this adjustment. By the time he was done, Marxist-Leninism had turned into Maoism. Just as Marxist themes were visible in Marxist-Leninism, so Marxist-Leninist themes were visible in this new ideology. The culture of the machine had now bleshed with a Chinese world historical narrative that had been unfolding for several thousand years.

Mao himself was, in many ways, a reincarnation of that familiar mythic Chinese figure, the emperor who confirms the never-ending cycle of time by ending a period of fragmentation and launching an era of centralized order. He recapitulated the role played by Shi Huang di, the founding emperor of the Qin dynasty, and later by Wendi of the Sui dynasty, and later still by Hongwu, founder of the Ming dynasty. Like those earlier colossi, Mao set to work to rebuild a civilization-state that revolved around a single center. Like those earlier emperors, he pushed through the vast, transformative infrastructure projects that the rebuilding required. Like the others, he did so with scant regard for the human cost. Like the earlier emperors, Mao sought to draw every man, woman, and child of China into a single administrative grid by superimposing a doctrine that tied all citizens to all others.

Maoism explicitly repudiated Confucianism, yet, structurally speaking, Maoism performed the same social function as that ancient doctrine:

it enabled an interconnectivity that drew many into one. And like the earlier Chinese emperors, Mao sought to wield doctrine as a tool of governance by fielding a corps of scholar-bureaucrats, but in this case the scholars were not trained in the Confucian classics. Instead, they had to pass muster in the Maoist canon (which included the Marxist and Leninist classics). In fact, Mao's core doctrines were distilled into a small red book that all good Communist Party scholar-officials carried with them as they went about their duties.

Like the first emperor and the two colossi of the Sui dynasty, Mao pursued his monumental goals with such brutality that, when he died, a backlash almost immediately cut short his "dynasty," which in this case meant his handpicked Communist Party successors. Deng Xiaoping, the leader who emerged from the brief period of uncertainty, was interested in getting the ideology to produce results. "It doesn't matter if a cat is black or white," he said, "as long as it catches mice."

Like the Han and Tang dynasties, Deng and his political descendants could take advantage of the transformations wrought by Mao without quite having to resort to Mao's totalitarian mania for control. The imperial center could let go a little, secure in the confidence that centripetal forces would not immediately tear the Middle Kingdom apart. Mao, in short, turned China into a governable country, which could absorb the machine and move forward on new terms. In the aftermath of his outsized career, Chinese history has indeed been manifesting its classic cycle. Mao's successors are using the tools they inherited from Emperor Chairman Mao to restore China to a dominant place in Asia and soon perhaps the world. A new cycle of order is taking hold after a century-long interregnum of disorder, the very pattern that the ancient Chinese historians had identified as fundamental to China's history.

As in past cycles, the order is highly concentric. The Communist Party has replaced the emperor but fulfills a similar function, and within the party, authority radiates from a single leader. China has, meanwhile, co-opted corporate forms perfected in the West as mechanisms of its development, which now extends far beyond its official borders. Private and state-owned Chinese corporations are building highways, railroads, seaports, airfields, and trading centers throughout what ancient Chinese historians would have seen as tributary states, along the onetime Silk Road and throughout the monsoon network, the world that Admiral Zheng He and his massive Ming fleet explored in the fifteenth century.

No one can stop technology or determine its impact, but at the same time, no force can erase social narratives or mitigate their influence. Like the ancestors of Chinese mythological tradition, narratives born in a misty past endure as ghostly forces in the world of today.

THE MACHINE IN THE MIDDLE WORLD

Meanwhile, in the Islamic Middle World, people got their first taste of the new technology not as their own transformative inventions welling up within their way of life but as devices wielded by alien forces penetrating their world and taking control. From the Indus River to Istanbul, from Samarkand to the Sudan, nineteenth-century Muslims started waking up to the fact that their most valuable resources were owned by others, their rulers were actually puppets, and their governments were stage shows controlled from behind the scenes by various Western powers.

What was to be done? For twelve centuries, Islam had given meaning to the world and to history. How had it all gone so wrong? Were Muslims themselves to blame? Was it something they had done or failed to do? How could they put the world back on track and incidentally save themselves?

These questions obsessed Muslim thinkers and activists in the eighteenth and nineteenth centuries. As it happened, a longing for spiritual renewal was brimming in the Islamic world at that same time for reasons internal to Islam itself. Spiritual reform movements and anti-imperialist movements mapped onto one another because Islam had never endorsed a separation between the spiritual and the political.

The confluence of these currents fueled an agonized quest for Muslim identity. Since the quest was associated with resistance to Western hegemony, some radicals inevitably moved toward defining true Muslims not in terms of what they were, but in terms of what they were not. Western was the thing they were not, which is to say non-Western was the thing they were, or should aspire to be. Out of this process emerged the outlines of a Muslim identity shaped by the otherness of the other.

This was not a unique phenomenon in history, of course. During the Crusades, a European identity had emerged out of the confrontation with the Muslim-Jewish East. It, too, was shaped by the otherness of the other: Europeans built a sense of who they were by identifying who they were not. At that point, however, Europe was a civilization on the rise. Defining itself as the opposite of the other expressed an energetic triumphalism. The eighteenth- and nineteenth-century Islamic world, by contrast, was a civilization waking up to its weakness and desperate to halt its own decline. Here, an identity shaped by the otherness of the other could not help but include dark threads of resentment.

But what were Muslims rejecting when they looked to Europe? It couldn't be science or technology. Most (though not all) Islamic activists could see that mechanized societies were always going to overwhelm nonmechanized ones. Muslims who rejected science, technology, and industry were dooming themselves to servility. The globe-trotting Muslim radical Syed Jamaluddin al-Afghani and his intellectual descendants wanted Muslims to not just accept the machine but to claim it and the science that spawned it. Original Islam was *the* scientific religion, some of these activists asserted. Islam was the one religion that didn't depend on feats of nature-defying magic to command belief in heaven and the day of judgment. Prophet Muhammad did not claim divinity nor prove himself the messenger of God by bringing dead people back to life. He brought people to belief by spouting words of overwhelming power, by building a community unlike any other, by winning battles against overwhelming odds. What's more, early Islam had been an age of glittering scientific achievements. Only after that golden age had Muslims veered off track, blinding themselves with rote learning and giving their religion away to corrupt clerics. Muslims had to return to the earliest sources and reinterpret their religion from the ground up in a way that let machine culture blesh with the Islamic restoration narrative.

For Muslims, however, this raised a question: if they weren't rejecting science and the machine, what *were* they rejecting? It had to be social and sexual mores, the most blatant difference between the West and the Middle World. The West featured the independence of women, the evaporation of the extended family, the growing sovereignty of the individual. Radical Muslims caught up in the nineteenth-century brew of political resistance and spiritual renewal equated Islamic authenticity with shoring up tribal-scale family structures and restricting women to the private realm. They advocated the regulation of sex and marriage based on strict, literal interpretations of scriptures. In short, according to successive generations of Islamist radicals, true Muslims rejected European styles of family life, European-style education of children, European attitudes toward kinship connections, and European norms related to sexuality and gender relations.

The division of the world into male and female realms, corresponding to public and private spheres, was already embedded in Muslim societies as part of a historical narrative going back to the pre-Islamic past. The sequestration of women had crystallized in the course of Muslim encounters with the Byzantine world, where the veiling of upper-class women was the norm among the Christian elite. Now, in the era of Islamic reforms, as the Muslim world wrestled to absorb the machine into its culture, Muslim identity came to focus obsessively on the privatization of women. Revolutionary movements in Islam commonly adopted the sequestration and finally the subjugation of women as part of their core thesis.

In this regard, Muslims were swimming against the current. Everywhere else, those who sought progressive change were also the ones who favored women's rights. This was true of the Bolsheviks of Russia, of the Taiping revolutionaries of China, of the Maoists in the twentieth century. This was also a core plank for liberals and socialists of Western industrial democracies. In the Islamic world, however, the revolutionaries were the ones who most passionately sought to constrict the lives of women and strengthen the patriarchal family structures of the past.

And if it's true, as I am arguing, that the machine and its impact on human life is the basis for this monumental worldwide shift in gender roles, then the change is coming no matter what public opinion touts, no matter what Islamists demand, no matter what Bible thumpers preach, no matter what Hindu nationalists yell at couples they find holding hands in public parks—no matter what, no matter what. Every attempt to restore the gender roles of past centuries and to cap the rise of women is doomed to fail at least in part because moving backward on this issue would require reversing the direction of technological development throughout all of human history, and that is not going to happen. We might bomb all the cities on the planet to rubble and disrupt the climate so drastically it takes humans back to a Stone Age–level technology, but the moment we get there, we'll set to work rebuilding the remembered tools of the past and devising new ones. We're humans: it's what we do.

26

Empires and Nation-States
(1800 to 1925)

I n 1850, most of the world's people still lived in some far-flung, multi-ethnic dynastic empire ruled by a monarch whose authority derived from lineage. These empires were very much bigger and more ungainly than the Mesopotamian empires of ancient times, but structurally they were not so different.

Much of Central Europe, for example, was part of the German Empire ruled by the Hohenzollern family: a hodgepodge of duchies and petty kingdoms inhabited mainly by German speakers, with Prussia as its strongest single core. Eastern Europe was mostly part of the Austro-Hungarian Empire ruled by the Hapsburg family with many distinct populations speaking different languages. The Hapsburg's empire bordered on another family's empire, the Romanov's Russia, another motley quilt stretching all the way to the Pacific Ocean. Russia in turn bordered on the patchwork of petty dynastic states ruled by the Ottoman family and, in the Far East, on the empire nominally ruled by the Qing family.

In Western Europe the situation was only slightly different. France was a constitutional republic by this time, but it was also an empire. The European core was governed in accordance with a secular, rational system, but French-ruled territory included a growing multitude of colonial territories, sometimes (officially) governed by locals whose authority still derived from, yes, lineage and kinship. The same was true of Great Britain, whose empire circled the globe.

1850: A World of Dynasties and Empires

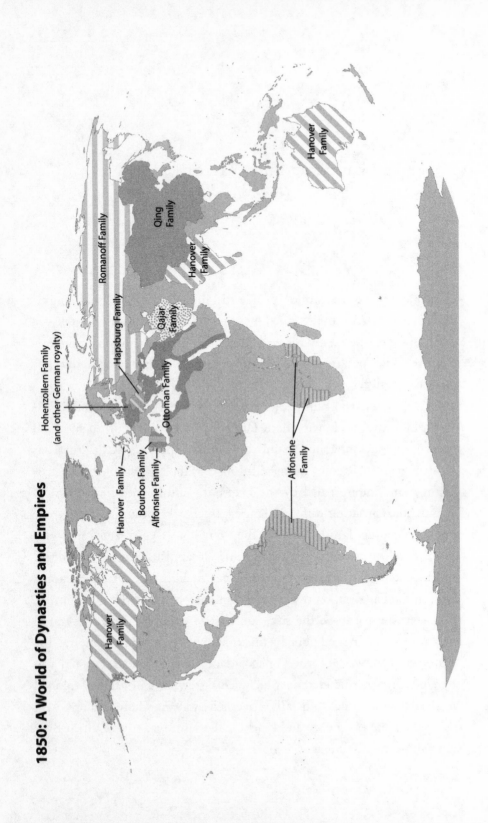

But as these lumbering empires went about their business in the world, a new form of social-political unit was gestating within them, spawned at least in part by the machine. The nation-state, its hour come round at last, was struggling to emerge fully onto the stage. A few prototypes of this form of social constellation had already come into existence. England and France had begun morphing from feudal empires into nation-states sometime in the fourteenth century. Back then, over the course of a hundred years or so, a series of invasions of France by English armies laid the basis for a sense of national identity on both sides of the English Channel. English kings rallied armies with an appeal to national identity, whereupon soldiers of many classes, backgrounds, and regions found themselves in an alien land, standing shoulder to shoulder with people who spoke their language, fighting for their lives against what might as well have been human-shaped aliens speaking gibberish. The French had the same experience defending themselves against alien human-shaped invaders from England. On each side of the conflict, dialects melted together, and a sense of shared history and communal destiny took hold, even as separation from the other hardened.

Far away, in the Middle World, Iran was undergoing a somewhat similar process based on culture and location. Here, an ethnically coherent, Persian-speaking Shia group with a long, shared history was sandwiched between Turkic Sunni powers.

But the nation-state is more than just a sense of national identity. A nation-state is a structure with an objective existence in the world. Nation-states came into being as the inevitable by-products of many social currents: the development of banking, the emergence of uniform currencies, the growing sophistication of communication and transportation technology, the ever-advancing mechanization of war. These factors all fed one another, and out of the mulch grew a new type of social singularity. Nation-states were to empires as empires were to civilizations. They were that much more compact, condensed, and concrete.

Old-fashioned empires of earlier times had measured their success by sprawl. Successful empires were big ones: empires that controlled lots of territory and had lots of subjects to tax and draft. Within each empire, the emperor's power was absolute. He could execute any subject without having to explain why to anyone. But when he wasn't executing people in obscure corners of his realm, he wasn't influencing their lives all that much: grocers were selling sour milk, underage boys were getting drunk in public, men were driving their horses recklessly, women were using foul language—what was the emperor going to do about it? Nothing! He didn't even know about it. Or care. Someone *might* do something, but it would be a local cleric, or a disapproving elder, or a guild master, or perhaps a matriarch within the family, or just some big man in the neighborhood whom everyone feared.

NATIONALISM

What the successful nation-state featured was not so much breadth as depth. In this form of social constellation, the head of state could *not* execute anyone on a whim: he or she was bound by laws, like everyone else. But the state itself, that abstract entity defined at least in part by social mechanisms, had a continuous presence in the lives of all its citizens, every day, all day, and its control went that much deeper. Within the borders of a nation-state, the same laws applied everywhere. There was only one currency. A single central power had a monopoly on all violence. The citizens might speak various languages, but one language had official status, and all public business was conducted in that language.

A nation-state had borders so distinct, a person could step across one like a pedestrian stepping across a crack in the sidewalk: this side was entirely France, that side entirely Germany. Compact, interconnected density gave nation-states unparalleled ability to form and carry out intentions as single social organisms. Nation-states could do this more efficiently than any previous sociopolitical form. When it came to size, Great Britain was tiny compared to China. When it came to imposing its will, Britain proved ever so much more mighty. British might did not, please note, belong to Queen Victoria, or to Benjamin Disraeli, or to the governor of the British East India Company. Those individuals were just executing the will of the social whole that was Great Britain.

As nation-states emerged, so did one of the nineteenth century's most passionate ideologies. Nationalism was a cluster of emotionally resonant propositions. It held that every person was part of some nation, and every nation had a right to a sovereign state of its own. Nationalism declared that birds of a feather should flock together. No one should be stranded outside their own people's nation-state, and everyone within a state should be part of the same "we the people."

This of course raised a question. What defined a bunch of people as a "we the people"? What attributes made a person part of one nation and not another—one of us-guys and not one of them-guys? What *was* "a people"? No one, for example, argued that height was a defining factor: no one was arguing for a tall people's nation-state or a short people's nation-state. Was it language, then? Or shared experiences, perhaps? Or religious beliefs? Was it, at some extenuated level, lineage? Was a nation a group of people descended from a common ancestor? Was such a connection visible? Was skin color a marker?

Not all nation-states were built on this sort of foundation. Ideology could provide other ways for people to cohere as states. The United States was a prime example. The Declaration of Independence and the Constitution had spoken in universalist terms, purporting to set forth a blueprint of laws and principles—social mechanisms—applicable to all of humanity. It's true that the social reality didn't match many of the ideals expressed in these documents. It's true that many contradictions lurked between the lines of the documents themselves. When Jefferson said "all men are created equal," his contemporaries understood him to mean "all landowning men of means." They understood women to be included with those men as adjuncts. The authors of the constitution assumed that slavery was somehow compatible with Jefferson's proposition that all men are created equal. For example, Arthur Middletown of Carolina had thirty-five hundred enslaved people working for him when he signed the declaration stating that all men were created equal.

Still, the universalist tone in the founding documents implied certain underlying principles. Progressive activists used these to push the United States in an unprecedented direction. It took a civil war and more than half a million lives to confirm this direction, but during the war, an amendment to the American Constitution defined a citizen of *this* nation-state as any person who accepted governance under the American Constitution. Period. In Europe, for whatever reason, the opposite idea gained purchase, of nations as people connected by ethnicity and blood origins.

The idea of blood as the basis for a nation fed right into one of the nineteenth century's most toxic *isms*. It was here in the Western world that the concept of race came fully into focus. Some might say: Hadn't people always noticed physical differences among humans? Hadn't they always tended to close ranks against outsiders? Yes, they had, but ways of defining the outsider had varied over time. The differences that seemed important were not the same everywhere. Identity did not always involve a concept of race.

What matured in the West at this time was the proposition that there was a certain innate, objective, biological feature sorting humanity into groups, that feature being race. Every human had this feature, which is to say, every human belonged to one race and not to any other, the way every wooden sculpture was made of one kind of wood—oak, pine, birch, whatever—and not others. All visible markers of race, such as skin color, hair texture, eye shape, and so on, were but symptoms, presumably, of some single underlying essence. Race could not be observed directly, but it could be detected by the visible traits it generated.

In the nineteenth century, western intellectuals made race an object of supposed scientific study. Certain academics poured thought and sweat into identifying what the true races of humankind were. Professor Louis Agassiz of Harvard theorized that different races originated separately and were therefore akin to different species. He counted eleven fundamental races. His colleague Charles Pickering saw twelve; another earnest scholar, Georges Cuvier, saw only five.

In the end, a taxonomy proposed somewhat earlier by Swedish zoologist Carl Linnaeus won the day. Linneaus had claimed there were four races: African, Asian, European, and Native American. He and others quickly tagged these races to skin color: white, black, yellow, and red. Once consensus had settled on this taxonomy, scientists and pseudoscientists got to work identifying the innate traits of each race. Race theorists tied skin color not just to physical but also to mental, emotional, and cultural traits. It was then possible for "race scholars" such as Cuvier to speculate that whites were intellectual, black people emotional, yellow folks cunning, and so on.

A French count, Joseph Arthur de Gobineau, applied himself to setting forth a hierarchy of races based on supposedly innate traits. He himself being white, he was pleased to announce that white people were the highest race, best in every way, especially intellectually. Well, OK, some whites were stupid and vicious, but that, according to Gobineau, reflected miscegenation in their family tree: some ancestor of theirs must have engaged in sex with one of the "lower races" and thus polluted the bloodline.

Today, most of us recoil in horror from such stereotyping of racial groups. Yet the fundamental premise of racist thought—that race exists as an objective category and that people of different races have innately different genetic traits—was absorbed by many people of the nineteenth and twentieth centuries, even those who saw themselves as liberal humanitarians.* This is a striking development given that, scientifically speaking, there is no such thing as race. Yes, people inherit characteristics from their parents, and people who regularly intermarry form gene pools that intensify certain traits, making one group look distinctly different from another. But *regularly intermarry* is the key phrase here. This is a pattern enforced by social norms and reinforced by geography. If any two groups identified as different races were transported to a single island and intermarried randomly for a few generations, there would be

*Mexican artist Diego Rivera, for example, a self-proclaimed Communist, painted a mural celebrating Detroit's industrial workers, which depicted people of four distinct colors working in a steel plant. Rivera explained that "the yellow race represents the sand, because it is most numerous. And the red race...is like iron ore, the first thing necessary for steel. The black race is like coal, because it has a great native aesthetic sense, a real flame of feeling and beauty in its ancient sculpture, its native rhythm and music...The white race is like the lime, not only because it is white, but because lime is the organizing agent in the making of steel. It binds together the other elements and so you see the white race as the great organizer of the world." Rivera championed the equality of the races and valued harmony among them but did not, apparently, question the existence of four color-coded races with innate traits.

no distinguishing one from the other. On this, biologists are virtually unanimous.

History is in fact loaded with such intermarriages. Riding the bus at rush hour in my hometown of San Francisco, if I didn't know there were supposed to be four races, I certainly wouldn't classify the people I saw into four distinct groups. Skin colors alone vary from pale to dark and hit every shade in between. This city has many people of Asian descent, but none of them have yellow skin. The blackest people I've seen are dark brown, the whitest people sort of cream colored. I once saw a guy at the Rainbow Festival who'd stripped naked and painted himself head to toe with red dye. He's the only red man I've ever seen. My high school class-mate Ben, a Navajo, has skin somewhat darker than my friend Harry from Vermont, but Ben is not by any stretch of the imagination red nor is Harry really white. If I had to name a shade for Harry, I would say pink, which means he is actually closer to red than Ben.

Race, in short, is a social construct, not a biological fact. It reflects the ways in which social norms have interfered with the randomness of intermarriage. Ironically, social norms that funnel people into marriages with others "of their own kind" reinforce physical features and thus give race a quasi-objective existence. In the nineteenth century, many West-ern Europeans were citizens of empires whose subjects were for the most part colonized "natives" of some distant land. Race theory provided a ba-sis for reducing those others to lesser status and justifying the privileges of the people wielding power. Along the way, it helped bolster the idea that nations of folk existed objectively in the world, and that each one was entitled to a state of its own.

NORTH AMERICA

Great Britain ended up forging what was officially the most far-flung empire in history, controlling, at its height, nearly a quarter of Earth and about that many of its people. France, Spain, the Netherlands—right to the end of the nineteenth century they were all out there scrambling.

Even at the time, those societies and their savants called what they were doing imperialism. Back then, however, they trumpeted the word with pride. Only later did imperialist become a pejorative.

The United States also expanded mightily in this period, but this expansion long escaped the label of imperialism. The way this nation-state told its own story, it didn't go out and conquer. Its citizens ventured into the wilderness, cleared forests, plowed fields, built towns, and connected them with roads and eventually railroads. The United States presumably grew huge merely by developing the wastelands it already possessed. It was the progress narrative in action.

The inhabitants of this new country *did* do a great deal of heroic forest clearing, field plowing, and town building, but there was always a crack running down the middle of the narrative: the land the North American pioneers were developing was already inhabited, and those inhabitants were already using the land, though in other ways than the pioneers. What's more, theirs was not a static age-old world of denizens living in beatific harmony with nature until they were interrupted. They, too, had a past and a present and were looking toward a future. Like all humans, they were living in history.

The most recent waves of migrants from Asia had moved through Canada, and from there, some had come down into the North American heartland only a few centuries before the first Europeans arrived. The newcomers from the north included the Dine people, better known as the Navajo, and the Apache. Indigenous people living along the Mississippi and Missouri Rivers and on the shores of the Great Lakes—the Mandan, the Dakota, the Ojibwa, and others—had been semisedentary farmers who roamed into the grasslands only in summer to hunt bison on foot. Under pressure from the westward migrations of the pioneers from Europe, however, these folks increasingly moved onto the Great Plains full-time.

The Europeans had brought horses to the Americas, a few of which escaped, went feral, and multiplied. Horses spawned a new form of nomadism in North America. It wasn't the pastoral sheep-herding nomadism of the Central Asian steppes. It wasn't about herding at all. Tens of millions of wild bison roamed the North American prairie, and the combination of bison and horses gave rise, briefly, to an American-style culture of nomadic hunter-gatherers who developed sophisticated uses for every part of a bison from hooves to horns to internal organs, as well as its meat and skin. The Mandan and the Dakota roamed the prairie; the French called them the Sioux. The Comanche and the Cheyenne came down from the Rocky Mountains into the plains. There is no telling where these developments might have gone had the indigenous tribes been on their own in these continents. Would they have spun a web of trade routes across the continents? Would the nodes have developed into cities and moved into the machine age, as happened in Europe? We'll never know: the European migrations cut short the trajectory of the indigenous people's history.

When Europeans swarmed all over Asia and Africa, they went there to trade. They did their conquering in service to their trading ambitions. They wanted the resources of those lands, but they also wanted what the people of these lands were making, so they wanted those people to keep on keeping on. When the United States expanded to the Pacific Ocean, its pioneers weren't interested in what the Native Americans were producing. The new migrants were not coming to trade nor even to conquer the original inhabitants but to replace them. Those who actually carried out the expansion were for the most part poor people who had come to America looking for opportunities to build new lives based on prowess and ingenuity to make up for the titles, money, and land they and their ancestors never had in their original homelands. They found such opportunities west of the Mississippi.

The westward expansion of the United States went hand in hand with the reduction and sometimes elimination of the indigenous people. No sugarcoating it. This was not the sort of ideological hate-fueled genocide the Nazis tried to carry out against the Jews. For the Europeans, the natives were simply in the way. They feared and hated the natives until they had swept them away, and then mythologized them as noble savages and eventually named sports teams after them.

Sometimes, however, the genocide was more deliberate. In California, the newcomers of the expanding Euro-sphere saw the Native Americans the way exterminators see cockroaches. California governor Peter Burnett promised government support for "a war of extermination until the Indian race becomes extinct." An 1853 editorial in the *Yreka Mountain Herald* lauded the governor and proclaimed: "Let the first man who says treaty or peace be regarded as a traitor." The state made good on its word by offering bounties of up to twenty-five dollars (and as little as twenty-five cents) for each "Indian" killed. Within one generation, 90 percent of the native people of California had perished. One tribe came down to a single survivor, a man known as Ishi. He was brought to San Francisco, where he lived the rest of his life as an anthropological curiosity. When he died, so did a language, a history, a universe.

Elsewhere on the continent, the replacement effort was mostly a war like any other war: two groups fighting, one winning, one losing. For the most part, the government of the new country herded the natives into restricted areas called reservations, which were disingenuously classified as sovereign nations that had treaty relationships with the United States. Here in the reservations, the indigenous folks were more or less free to live as their ancestors had lived, albeit without the resources that had supported their ancestors' way of life. In one period, the US government did try to absorb the indigenous people into the emerging mainstream culture of American society by transporting children born on the reservations to US government schools, where they were taught how to speak, read, and write English and how to practice European table manners and wear European-style clothing. In 1924, all of the three hundred thousand or so Native Americans living within the borders of the United States were declared citizens.

27

A World at War
(1900 to 1945)

In the early 1800s, societies armed with technology, organized as companies, and run as nation-states proved to be much more powerful than all other forms of social organization on the planet. When these societies encountered China, China went down. When they encountered the Islamic and Hindu worlds, they seeped in and took over from within.

Sub-Saharan Africa resisted colonization for a long time. European powers planted trading posts along the coast but couldn't penetrate the continental interior, for at the core of the continent was that equatorial rain forest where sleeping sickness and malaria ran rampant. Longtime inhabitants had adapted to this environment, developed some immunity to the prevalent diseases, and organized as robust tribal states quite capable of resisting European intrusions.

But technology and globalization changed the equation. Advancing medical know-how gave Europeans tools against sleeping sickness, and in South America, Europeans found a plant from which to make quinine, armed with which, they were able to defeat malaria on the other side of the globe. And now, their flat-bottomed gunboats powered by steam engines could move up African rivers to lands in the deep interior.

Indigenous African tribes had armies and some had guns, but they could not stand up to European armies and guns. In 1898, a large Muslim army in Sudan cornered a much smaller British force at a place called Omdurman. The army had been founded by an apocalyptic Muslim cult figure calling himself the Mahdi—"the awaited one." He had promised to expel the foreigners and "save" his people. The Mahdi's army of fifty thousand men had spears and old-fashioned guns. The British had twelve Maxim guns, each of which could fire five hundred bullets a minute. Those six guns fired some five hundred thousand bullets during the brief battle, killing twenty thousand of the African warriors and injuring most of the rest. The British casualties amounted to forty-eight dead. The Battle of Omdurman ended all doubt: in confrontations between Western forces and any other—between the machine and people living as premechanical social constellations—there was no contest. Only one question remained: Which part of "everything else" would each mechanized Western power get?

German chancellor Bismarck tried to "civilize" the contest in Africa. He organized a conference in Berlin where fourteen leading European powers discussed how to partition Africa among themselves without falling into an unseemly brawl. Needless to say, no Africans were invited to the table.

The Berlin Conference convened in November 1884, but by then it was too late: global imperialism had entered a new phase. In the run-up to this moment, Western European powers had been racing one another to colonize unclaimed territories. Now, however, Europeans pretty much owned, controlled, or dominated every part of the world except Thailand and Afghanistan. With virtually no unclaimed territory left to colonize, latecomers to the feast were going to have to get their colonies from someone else's plate. European powers, therefore, began to eye one another's holdings.

In 1900, a harbinger of future trouble broke out in Southern Africa, where the world's biggest gold deposits had just been found—right near the world's richest diamond mines. The masters of this region were, at this point, the Boers: descendants of early Dutch settlers who had long ago sidelined the native Africans. The British had planted a few small colonies here, but now that gold had been found in the region, they wanted all of it. Crushing the Boers proved costly and bloody, however, and why was it so difficult? Because Germany, another machine power, took an interest in the conflict. It was an ominous foreshadowing of days to come.

I keep saying Europeans, but there was a non-European power very much in the mix now. Japan had seen the machine age coming, had understood its significance, and had put itself through a crash course of industrialization. In 1904, Japan launched a war with Russia, a quasi-European power, and flabbergasted Western observers by dealing the Russians one defeat after another. In the climactic naval battle of that war, the Japanese sank most of the Russian fleet. Europe received the message: Britain was no longer the only small island nation punching above its weight.

Significantly enough, even the distant United States now did some rumbling. In 1898, the Americans ousted Spain from the Philippines. Six years later, US president Teddy Roosevelt asserted himself as the one world leader with the stature to negotiate an end to the Russo-Japanese conflict. After the treaty was signed, he issued a striking pronouncement: in its dealings with the rest of the world, the United States would henceforth "talk softly and carry a big stick."

Europeans were quite aware of this big stick. Not only did the United States have immense resources; it had the compact coherence of a nation-state—but without the encumbrance of an old-fashioned monarchy. This was a sleek power built on the most modern of principles: democratic constitutionalism. The American Civil War of 1860–1865 had featured millions of soldiers fighting one another with advanced, industrial weaponry. Now that the United States was a single country again, its government could presumably field all those millions and their armaments as its own single force.

Meanwhile, as the world moved into the twentieth century, the struggle for colonies reached a crucial stage. Germany and Italy had congealed into nation-states, and they were hungry. Italy was still too indistinct to make a play, but Germany was a different story, an industrial powerhouse on a par with Britain. If someone was going to take colonies from someone, it was going to be one of these from the other.

Both Germany and Great Britain had brash confidence in their weapons. For years, both had been swatting down opponents like so many mosquitoes. With weapons like theirs, who on Earth could stand up to them? The answer was obvious, of course: another power with weapons like theirs. All the major European social wholes thus got busy improving their killing tools, and none more so than those two industrial powerhouses.

At the same time that the huge dynastic empires mentioned earlier were shambling toward an epic confrontation with one another, a second contradiction was building pressure within the world system. All of these empires had nascent nation-states growing inside them like tumors. Every empire was full of people claiming to be nations entitled to autonomous self-rule. Most had nationalist revolutionaries plotting to assassinate their way to power. Arabs wanted to break out of the Ottoman mold. Serbs and Poles and Hungarians and others were chaffing inside the Austro-Hungarian mold. Turkish nationalities within Russia had aspirations. The Armenians wanted a state. Many Jews living in Europe had begun to dream of a sovereign Jewish state somewhere. In south Asia, nationalist Indians were seeking independence from Britain. Although only a few true nation-states existed yet, many more were gestating within the empires and stretching their seams and straining to be born.

Then in 1914, a teenaged Serbian nationalist, Gavrilo Princip, shot and killed a middle-aged man who happened to be next in line for the Austro-Hungarian throne—and that was all it took. The old empires exploded like rooms full of firecrackers, each outburst setting off others. Suddenly, Germany was invading France, and then Britain was blockading Germany, and then the Russians were mounting cavalry charges against Austrian troops, and then the Ottoman Turks were moving troops into the peninsula of Gallipoli.

It's common to speak of a First World War that ended in 1918, and a Second World War that ran from 1939 to 1945. But a thousand years from now, I'm betting that historians looking back will see just one great twentieth-century world war, what historian Niall Ferguson has called the War of the World, which began in the early 1900s and raged until 1945, with pauses in between. The first pause came in 1918. After four years of unspeakable violence, the United States jumped into the fray, pumping two million troops into France, and that brought the horror to a momentary lull.

Those first four years of world war had left all of Europe devastated. The central powers, however—Germany, Austria, and Ottoman Turkey—had seen the worst of it, so when the warring parties met to work out a treaty, Britain and France were able to dictate terms. They said Germany had started the war, and Germany would have to pay. They imposed huge reparations calculated to keep the Germans poor and weak for the foreseeable future.

Those years of violence had also dealt mortal blows to most of the other dynastic empires. After the armistice of 1918, the nation-states growing inside them started to slough off imperial encrustations like snakes shedding skin. The Ottoman Empire unraveled to nothing, and the core of it materialized as the nation-state of Turkey. The victorious Western powers dealt with Arab nationalism by carving out a rather arbitrary assortment of Arab nation-states, such as Jordan, Syria, and Iraq. The British supported the migration of European Jews to a portion of the Levant, where Jewish activists hoped to found a state of their own. In Eastern Europe, the outlines of many new nation-states became visible: Poland, Serbia, Hungary, Romania, Ukraine.

Germany dismissed its kaiser and declared itself to be one of those newfangled types of governments: a constitutional republic with an elected president. The Qing dynasty had crumbled just before the violence erupted, and it, too, was theoretically a republic now, aspiring to enter the machine age as a nation-state. Peace seemed to have come at last.

But peace was an illusion. Immediately after the armistice of 1918, the major hostile powers began rebuilding and rearming for the next big one. Nor did the armistice end the violence everywhere. In Russia, where the Romanov dynasty had crashed, the Bolsheviks had taken over, and they now consolidated their control by fighting one of the bloodiest civil wars in history, a war that consumed nearly ten million lives in less than a decade and transformed Russia into a totalitarian state ruled by one man, Joseph Stalin (who went on to kill or imprison millions more over the next decade). What's more, in the immediate aftermath of World War One, a flu epidemic, spread in part by all the troop movements of the war, claimed some fifty million lives worldwide. Globalization had its discontents.

And in the 1930s, the drums started beating again. The reparations meant to cripple Germany had backfired. In roiled circumstances, unscrupulous individuals can harness social turmoil to their own ambitions. In Germany, Adolph Hitler, surely one of the creepiest characters in history, figured out how to exploit the miseries of the war and the humiliations of the peace to stoke a racist nationalism. He built his Nazi Party around this ideology. On the other side of the world, a militant totalitarian nationalism had metastasized within Japan, which soon started gnawing for colonies in China and Southeast Asia. Then a nasty civil war broke out in Spain, and several powers jumped in to take sides and incidentally to test their newest weapons.

There might be some argument about who really started part one of the world war, but Germany certainly kicked off part two. And it wasn't some single spark that set things off this time, but the relentless mounting ambitions of the Nazi war machine embodied by Hitler. The Nazis grabbed all the territory they could until other European powers finally freaked out and moved to stop them. Like a peat fire smoldering beneath the surface of a bog, war burst out again, and this time the fire engulfed most of the world.

And again, the United States tipped the scales—but not quite as easily as before. It sent millions of troops to Europe in 1942 and vast fleets east to fight the Japanese, yet the fire went on blazing for three years more. Then in 1945, American scientists won the race to build the most destructive weapon ever invented: the atom bomb. The United States dropped two of these on Japan, and each one leveled an entire city. That pretty much stopped the arguments dead.

Once the smoke had settled and the shrieks had died away, it looked like the nation-state project of humanity had been finalized at last. Every inch of the planet was officially part of some sovereign nation-state (even though many territories were still defined as colonies of some nation-state), and every person was now a citizen of such a state or a refugee hoping to become one. Every country had exactly defined borders, and everyone had to carry a passport to cross a national border. Everyone used the currency of their own nation-state at home and imbibed an official history of their country in school. Every country had a flag, and most people could recognize which one was theirs. Territories still "owned" as colonies by some country chafed at that status, but what they aspired to was sovereignty as their own nation-state. In general, when people thought about the world as a social whole, they saw it as a cluster of nation-states—195 of them eventually. And when they thought of progress in the global political system, they pictured each nation-state gaining full independence from every other one and achieving full sovereignty. At that time, and for years afterward, the sovereign state seemed to be the final political form. At least that's how I saw the world growing up, and if you're anywhere near my age, I bet you did too.

But we were wrong.

Post–1945: A World of Nation States

PART VI

The Singularity Has Three Sides

After the worldwide war of the twentieth century, hints of a global civilization began to glimmer, even though savage conflicts continued to erupt here and there. Scientific understandings of the world deepened, machines continued to improve, and humans gained ever greater power vis-à-vis nature, but the nature we were coping with now was mostly our own, since the environment we lived in was almost entirely artificial. Meanwhile, the power and sophistication of our tools was not just growing, its rate of growth was accelerating. Some say the growing sophistication of technologies such as gene editing, molecular manipulation of matter, and machine intelligence will converge to a tipping point, which they call the singularity: a moment when humans and machines merge into one. Some see this as the moment when humans will achieve immortality, others as the moment when the human era ends and the machine age begins. Even if we're racing toward the singularity, however, our history remains braided of three strands: the environment, whatever it be; the tools we craft, whatever those be; and the peculiarly human function enabled by language—the intercommunication wherewith we bring conceptual worlds into being, worlds we inhabit communally and experience individually, worlds that mediate between ourselves and a real world immense and complex beyond our capacity to imagine.

28

Beyond the Nation-State
(1945 to 2018)

E ven as the nation-state system was on its way in, the nation-state system was on its way out. Supranational entities bigger than single countries were beginning to form, and right from the start, these were bidding to supersede the nation-state. The United Nations was the most obvious of these, though in many ways the least significant. Its name made it sound like a world government; in practice it was more like a global discussion club.

Still, in 1948, the United Nations did issue a document called the Universal Declaration of Human Rights, which challenged the unlimited authority of sovereignty. This document said that every human possessed certain rights regardless of what passport he or she carried: there were things a sovereign government could not do, even to its own citizens.

The Universal Declaration had zero real-world effect because there was no universal government to enforce it. The rights it listed were being violated even as they were being formulated, and terrible violations have continued to occur ever since. But the declaration did at least set a standard against which violations could be measured, and it gave idealists a banner to wave in days to come.

Unlike the United Nations, some emerging supranational agencies had real teeth. Most of these dealt with economic matters, and no wonder. Every country had things people in other countries wanted, but buying and selling across the borders of nation-states posed various conundrums. For one thing, people on either side of such a border were using different currencies, so how could anyone negotiate or even know the price of anything they were buying or selling?

This is why delegates from forty-five countries got together, just as the world war was ending, to hash out how money would flow through the world in the days to come. They met at Bretton Woods, a small town in New Hampshire, USA, and there they created the World Bank and the International Monetary Fund (IMF). The World Bank was tasked with funding industrial development in left-behind countries. Theoretically, it was acting on behalf of the world as a whole. The IMF was charged with regulating the exchange rate of different currencies and stepping in with loans whenever some country in the world system was having trouble paying its debts. In return for such loans, however, the agreement authorized the IMF to dictate how debtor governments spent their money. Usually, in such cases, the IMF demanded "austerity steps," language suggesting that the debtor country had been on a wild, drunken bender and would have to stop carousing. In practice, austerity usually meant reduced government spending on things like health care, education, and social services.

Then, twenty-three major countries signed a treaty called the General Agreement on Trade and Tariffs—GATT, for short. It regulated how the signatories would tax one another's products when they had relations—trade relations, that is: GATT would supposedly keep countries from hurting one another when they tried to tango.

COLD WAR

These measures and agreements did not cover all nations, however, for out of the many ideologies floating around before the war, just two, communism and capitalism, emerged triumphant. Now, like the gods of ancient Zoroastrian mythology, nations drifted into alliances based on which ideology they embraced. Two huge rival blocs of nation-states formed up. One was dedicated to transforming the whole world into a single market in which money could be spent and made anywhere on the same terms. The other bloc proposed to fuse all the world into a single planned economy in which a central government would allocate resources based on a rational calculation of steps most beneficial to the social whole.

One side envisioned our species dissolving into an atomized cloud of independent individuals, each pursuing his or her own self-interest and thereby, theoretically, ensuring the happiness and prosperity of the whole. The other saw one centralized social will, consciously directing coordinated human effort toward the prosperity and happiness of the whole, thereby theoretically making it possible for each individual to achieve his or her own fulfillment.

Both systems ultimately derived from the secular Western tradition. Both appealed to reason, and both looked to empirical evidence for support. Both sides, that is, believed that real-world outcomes would prove their system correct. For the next four-plus decades, these two systems struggled to become the story of humanity and sweep the other into "the dustbin of history."

The United States emerged as the leader of the first bloc, with Japan and Western Europe as its partners. The former Russian Empire, now the Soviet Union, congealed into a second bloc, with the Eastern European countries as its satellites. These two blocs faced each other like hard-core gamblers in a high-stakes poker game, the chips of which were all the other countries of the world, most of which were poor and most of which had yet to industrialize. China's Mao Tse-tung coined a term for all these other countries: the Third World. With this label he implied that these countries too were a bloc—led by China.

From 1945 to the late 1980s, these three blocs carried out the global struggle called the Cold War. It was a war because the two dominant blocs were trying to wipe each other out; it was "cold" because neither side could try to kill the other's citizens outright: they were both too dangerously armed to launch an attack. The capitalist side had started out with nuclear bombs; the Soviets soon built nuclear bombs of their own. Both sides then upgraded to thermonuclear bombs, which could end life on Earth if deployed en masse. Hamstrung by their military stalemate, the two dominant

The Cold War: A World of Three Blocs

The Communist World

The Capitalist World

The Third World

blocs waged war in a different way: by exploiting a fatal flaw in the nation-state system.

The flaw was this: there really was no such thing as a true nation-state, not in the sense envisioned by nineteenth-century nationalists. Their notion of a nation-state as a self-governing people inhabiting a land of their own depended on their being a people with a "self" to govern. In practice, no nation-state was inhabited by a single people, no matter how peoplehood was defined. Most countries, if not all, had subcultures with the potential to form into nationalist movements: Armenians and Azerbaijanis, Basques and Catalonians, the Tuaregs of Mali, the French speakers in Canada, the Irish in Great Britain—the list goes on.

What's more, many national borders ran right through territory inhabited by some group that *regarded* itself as a single people. In these places, close relatives found themselves subject to different authorities and different rules; if their countries went to war, they might be drafted into separate armies and made to shoot at one another. Take the Kurds, for example: they inhabited a single contiguous area but lived in four different countries: Turkey, Syria, Iran, and Iraq. A number of potential nation-states claimed the same territory. Israel's existence negated the possibility of a Palestinian state. India and Pakistan both claimed Kashmir. The globe was full of such unexploded, hair-trigger social land mines, especially in the Third World. Each could fuel a rebel movement fighting a national government.

This was the flaw the juggernaut blocs exploited in every country that had an antigovernment movement within its borders. If the capitalist powers supported the government, the Communists armed and funded the rebels. If the capitalists supported the rebels, the Communists armed and funded the government. The Cold War featured a multitude of proxy wars waged mainly in the Third World. And this Third-World War was not by any means "cold": where the fighting was happening, millions died.

Those of us living through the Cold War thought of it as a dark epoch overshadowed by the possibility of annihilation. It was easy to believe back then that the human story was approaching its climax and that the end of history was nigh. In retrospect, however, the Cold War looks like forty years of stability and rising prosperity. The nuclear stalemate kept much of the world more or less quiescent. *More or less* is the crucial term, but *quiescent* is important too: wars and revolutions flared around the globe, but peace prevailed most of the time in most of the places where most people lived.

In those years, more and more people got access to modern medicine. Consumer goods proliferated. The middle classes expanded worldwide. Roads were built over mountains and across deserts. The Communist countries built their industrial capacities to massive proportions. Most people outside the Communist world could travel to most places. Electricity made its way to more and more people, including many in the Third World. Even very poor countries established radio stations, and many launched television stations too. Virtually all countries had newspapers. Best-selling books were read by tens of millions of people, a scale never before imagined or imaginable.

Films poured out of Hollywood and Bollywood, not to mention Lollywood and Nollywood, and many other places.* Popular music flourished, drawing on folk sources, on classical traditions, and most importantly on influences from other cultures. Echoes of India's popular music sounded in the Middle World. North America's jazz, blues, folk music, rock and roll, and all their cousins, much influenced by African roots, spread east to Europe and beyond. In South America, folk music turned into sophisticated Latin jazz. Arab musicians began using electrified instruments and later developed their own version of hip-hop.

Some celebrities of the popular entertainment world became global figures—from Jackie Chan to the Beatles, from Pele to Muhammad Ali. The most popular singer in Kabul was known, even to Afghans, as "the Elvis Presley of Afghanistan" In democracies, celebrities began to acquire political clout. The faint traces of a world culture began to show. For better or for worse, it consisted mainly of popular entertainment.

---

*Lollywood refers to Pakistan's Lahore-based film industry, Nollywood to Nigeria's.

BEYOND THE COLD WAR

In 1975, the United States withdrew its forces from Indochina, and the capital of South Vietnam fell to the Communists of the north. Millions of South Vietnamese fled at that point. Many of them died on the high seas, and many more ended up living in abject poverty abroad. In Cambodia, which had suffered spillover effects from the war in Vietnam, a Communist cadre consisting largely of teenagers with machine guns marched some six million people to their death. Both countries seemed irrevocably damaged—yet both survived, both regrouped, both rebuilt, and within a generation both (especially Vietnam) emerged as fairly coherent, fairly peaceful, and only ambiguously Communist countries. Most of us who lived through the Cold War had no idea such a transformation could happen.

In 1975, no one knew the Cold War was winding down because new violence kept erupting here and there around the Third World. In 1978, local Communists seized power in Afghanistan, the Soviet Union invaded the country to keep them in power, and the United States jumped in to help the Afghan rebels. To most political pundits, Afghanistan looked like just another standard Cold War battlefield. In fact, however, by the time the Soviets invaded Afghanistan, their own empire was crumbling from within. Afghanistan was not, as it turned out, the last battle of the Cold War but the first battle of a new one. Western forces soon found themselves fighting Islamists who made no distinction between communism and capitalism.

Revolutionaries then toppled the CIA-supported shah of neighboring Iran but, again, not on behalf of the Soviets. Here, too, the victors declared themselves soldiers of "the Islamic revolution." That phrase—Islamic revolution!—had resonance across the Middle World, a territory long steeped in the Muslim world historical narrative. There, for many people, situating their grievances within the Islamic narrative made the grievances comprehensible. Suddenly—ah! It all made sense. The communism-versus-capitalism story had never possessed this kind of meaning-making power in the Islamic heartland.

The new war began to bubble just as the concept of sovereignty was beginning to unravel. Unfortunately, the nation-state system had depended on this concept. If a nation-state wasn't sovereign, it wasn't a nation-state. Sovereignty meant that a state had every right to determine its own rules without interference from any outsider. It meant, also, that no one could violate the borders of another country merely to acquire territory. Conquest was something old-fashioned empires used to do, and those days were gone, for heaven's sake: Caesar and Genghis Khan? Dead, for crying out loud! In the late twentieth century, one could walk ten thousand miles without ever setting foot in a country that had a ministry of war. Every country still had military forces, of course, but the government agency in charge of these forces was generally called the ministry of *defense* (or some such). Figuring out how to characterize an attack as a defensive move became a crucial war-making skill.

Then in 1980 Iraqi strongman Saddam Hussein violated the prevailing ethos. He attacked neighboring Iran without fielding any noble cover story. He made no secret of his bald desire for Iran's oil and soil; apparently, he thought Iran's postrevolutionary chaos would make it an easy mark. Kings used to do this sort of thing all the time and garner applause for it—when they succeeded. Shame attached only to defeat, not to aggression. Saddam seemed to think he was living in that bygone world. It did him no good; the war sucked both countries' blood for eight years and ended in a stalemate. Neither country won.

But the concept of sovereignty had taken a hit.

It wasn't the only hit. In 1989, US president George H. W. Bush "arrested" the president of another supposedly sovereign country, Manuel Noriega of Panama, and put him on trial in the United States for violating US drug laws: Noriega was convicted and clapped into a US prison. Arrested? Wasn't that something governments could only do to their own law-breaking citizens? According to the principles of sovereignty, in fact, wasn't that precisely what one country couldn't do to a citizen of another country, especially to its head of state?!

That same year, the new leader of revolutionary Iran, Ayatollah Khomeini, charged a British citizen, Salman Rushdie, with writing a book prohibited in Iran and sentenced him to death for it. Sentenced him? Isn't that something the courts of a sovereign state do to their own law breakers? Since Rushdie was a British citizen and did not live in Iran, and never had and never planned to, Khomeini presumably had no jurisdiction over him. But Khomeini ordered that the execution be carried out by any Muslim in a position to do so, implying that sovereignty belonged not to any nation-state but to a religious community distributed across political borders. This made a British Muslim like a star in two different overlapping constellations: which one was he part of? It couldn't be both. And Rushdie's backers tended to ignore the sovereignty issue too. They defended Rushdie mainly on the grounds that his right to free speech was being violated. In essence, they ceded that British sovereignty gave Rushdie no protection from a higher set of laws; they only disputed what those supranational laws would be. They were envisioning a constellation bigger than Britain, a constellation the size of all humankind, whose laws included a right to free speech, which in their view even Khomeini was obliged to honor.

In the 1990s, citizens of many countries joined together to demand that the government of South Africa afford native Africans the same citizenship rights as its white populace. Apartheid was then part of the legal system of South Africa. Under the rules of sovereignty, citizens of other countries had no standing in this matter. But antiapartheid activists were appealing to a higher set of laws, the laws of a world-state that did not (yet) exist. They were saying there *is* such a thing as being a citizen of the world. Implicitly, their case harked back to that Universal Declaration of Human Rights, issued by the United Nations directly after the War of the World.

Finally, in 2001, Al-Qaeda, a globally active organization unaffiliated with any particular state, launched an attack on the supposedly sovereign United States. After that, the world found itself embroiled in a multitude of wars, large and small, in which *some* of the hostile parties were nation-states, but many were autonomous guerrilla armies, secretive cabals of individuals, and even single persons fueled by private doctrines unknown to a wider public. War blurred into crime, and out of the fuzzy border between them emerged "terrorism" and its doppelgänger "the war on terror." This new global conflict succeeded the Cold War as seamlessly as the Cold War had risen out of the ashes of the earlier world war.

MULTINATIONALS

As sovereignty was eroding, the nation-state system was struggling with another rival as well. In the wake of the world war, the biggest corporations began distributing their limbs and organs across national borders. It's true that big corporations such as the British East India Company had operated globally from the start—but always as partners of home governments or even as their countries' outright agents.

Now, however, the association between corporations and particular countries began to loosen, simply because multinational corporations were distributed through many countries and carried out each of their functions in the environment best suited for that job. A corporation of this type did its mining where the ores happened to be, its manufacturing where the labor was cheap, its intellectual tasks where sophisticated educational systems generated large corps of professional experts and technicians, its banking where taxes were favorable, and its marketing and sales in countries where people had lots of disposable income. No company contained within some set of national borders could compete with an outfit like this.

Like any corporation, multinationals developed identities separate from those of the particular humans staffing them. But the goals of a given multinational might not align with those of any particular host country. Operating as they did under many governments, the multinationals were not under the political jurisdiction of any single state. Should a government make unwelcome demands of a multinational, it could shift its weight to another nation-state. This bargaining power vis-à-vis the governments of sovereign countries tended to make multinational corporations somewhat autonomous players on the world stage. Their emergence marked the rise of a global economy but not the rise of a global government.

By the mid-1970s, a handful of multinational corporations had a cash flow exceeding the gross domestic product of many countries. If corporations had been nations, seventeen of them would have been among the top sixty. General Motors would have come in at number twenty-one on that list, just a tad below Switzerland, while Exxon and Dutch Shell would have ranked above Turkey and Norway.*

As time went on, the term *free trade* came up ever more often in treaty talks among nations, but those negotiations were not exactly about trade, or at least not entirely. Trade is something that occurs between whole groups of people; each wants to exchange something it has for something the other has. The free trade negotiations of the late twentieth century were more about dissolving the impediments offered by national borders to the operations of transnational corporations. They served the interests of gigantic new social organisms emerging out of the womb of the nation-state system, just as nation-states had emerged out of empires.

In 1995, GATT morphed into the much more global World Trade Organization (WTO). GATT had 23 member countries, the WTO had 123. GATT was merely an agreement among many countries; the WTO was a decision-making body with executive mechanisms of its own. Its mandate was not just to oversee agreements already in place but to make new rules as needed to keep trade flowing in an ever-shifting world. Although they functioned somewhat like government agencies, the WTO, the IMF, and their ilk were not the agents of any government but the seeds of an alternative global management system.

---

*These giants have been dwarfed now by even bigger giants. Amazon aspires to gain a monopoly on retail commerce. Facebook is bidding to own social media interaction entirely. Google pretty much dominates access to information, at least in the West. And then there is Apple, the world's first trillion-dollar company. These new corporate giants are not just competing for resources, however, nor even just for information, but for ownership of the very process of human intercommunication itself.

Nation-states hung on, though: hung on, because nations were too deeply embedded in the human psyche to fade away easily. For one thing, most people felt like their nationality was part of their *identity*. When someone said they were French or Japanese or Brazilian, they were saying something important about who they *were*. No one (yet) said they were a Fordian or an Exxonite or a Googlite. And when the backlash to globalism came, it sometimes took the form of "nativist" clumps of people claiming a group identity much smaller than the globe, based on ideas of race and originalism ("this is our land, we were here first"). Such groups began looking to nationalism for emotional fuel. And as nationalism flexed its power over the human psyche, some of its darker threads came to the surface too. Intensified racism, for example, is one of those threads.

In the West, governments went on managing many necessary aspects of social life, such as criminal justice, which yielded no direct profit. Big corporate interests could and did, however, use the political machinery of governments as their own executive and administrative apparatus. They could do this even in nominal democracies, where the citizens presumably elected the government to serve their own needs because elections required money and the multinational corporations increasingly possessed the greatest supply of that resource, along with the organized social will to use the money tactically. China may seem to present something of an alternative model because it is not so much a nation-state as a civilization-state; but it does have corporations equivalent to those of the Western multinationals, some of which are private though others are state owned. In China, however, whether privately owned or state-owned, corporations operate as segments of a centrally governed world-scale society. The Chinese constellation of a thousand years ago never died. It has changed, but it still exists.

In order to function as single wholes, multinational corporations had to coordinate the myriad activities of countless people separated by thousands of miles of physical distance. Some of those people were digging ditches; some were designing blueprints; some were grinding away in factories; some were assembling components; some were creating slick ads; some were loading parts onto ships, planes, or trains; some were adding up rows of numbers to keep currency flows balanced. And those activities were taking place in disparate linguistic, legal, cultural, and political environments. Decision-makers at every level had to be on the same page as decision-makers at every other level. Voluminous information therefore had to flow rapidly and efficiently throughout the corporate body. Only in this way could every member of a vast corporation contribute efficiently to the goals of the single, interconnected whole. Social organisms of such size and complexity could not have held on to their coherence a few decades earlier, for there are limits to how quickly and voluminously human beings can intercommunicate.

Or at least there used to be. But used to be was going, going, gone. Even as multinational corporations were coalescing, technology was taking a game-changing turn.

29

Digital Era

We who are living through the dawn of the digital age probably can't see this chapter of our human story whole. We're too busy trying to process the latest breakthrough app and the meteor shower of next big things while coping with staggering and unending disruptions of what is still sometimes quaintly called "the norm." But what about hundreds of years from now? How will historians see this story when the details have blurred and the focus is not on the technology, per se, but on the effects it had on the human story in this period?

I'm guessing they'll say it all began with a seminal invention: historical turning points so often do. In this case the invention was a switch of sorts, a tiny electronic device that could either transmit or resist electricity. The words *trans*mit and re*sist* were combined to form the single new term *transistor*.

The transistor soon led to the integrated circuit board, the first of which was patented in 1959. The circuit board was a network of electrical circuits affixed to a chip of silicon, each node of which was a transistor. An electrical pulse moving through the network traced a particular pattern, depending on which transistors were "open" and which were "shut." By setting the transistors to open or shut, a person could shape the pattern of the current's flow. And this could be done with a program, a coded set of instructions.

The important thing about a transistor was its binary property: open or shut was all it could be, no in-between. Those two states matched right up to the binary numbering system, which has only two digits, zero and one.

Mathematicians already knew that the binary system was just as powerful and accurate as the familiar ten-digit one inherited from the ancient Indians. It was more cumbersome, though. In the binary system, 26 X 27 = 702 would be written as 1100 X 0110 = 1010111110. Every calculation possible with the decimal system could be done with the binary system but it took longer.

"Took longer" didn't matter, though, with a circuit board. Here, a program of instructions was drawing a pattern with electricity, which travels at the speed of light. That's the fastest speed physically possible in the universe. Electricity moves more slowly through a conductive medium, such as silicon, but we're still talking about thousands of miles a second.

Nor was complexity a limiting factor. For all practical purposes, running an electrical current through a billion gates was the same as running it through ten gates. The limiting factors were only things like the efficiency of the conductive medium, the heat produced by the current, and the challenge of making incredibly tiny circuit chips with big clumsy human fingers. But these were just the sorts of challenges tinkering folks steeped in the progress narrative loved to tackle.

So, as soon as the silicon chip was born, engineers started improving it. Improvement meant getting more circuits onto smaller chips using less electricity. It meant getting currents to flow more efficiently and thereby generate less heat. Paradoxically, as silicon chips got smaller, denser, and better, they became cheaper. In 1965, engineer Gordon Moore predicted that silicon chips would double in density and complexity every two years, which would mean they'd improve at an accelerating pace. And that's just what happened.

The first computers were big enough to fill a room. NASA used them to get a spaceship to the moon. But already they were getting smaller and more complex. The increasing complexity and shrinking size of computers hit a tipping point in the mid-1970s, in a garage in Palo Alto, California, where two college dropouts, Steve Jobs and Steve Wozniak, built a computer so small it could sit on a desk—yet so powerful it could outperform those room-sized behemoths used by NASA. They called it a personal computer, and they could make one that was cheap enough for a middle-class family to afford!

Cheap was good, but most middle-class families weren't going to spring for a computer yet, because machine language was hard to master, and most people weren't going to bother. Then came programs such as BASIC, which could translate instructions written in plain English (or French or whatever a person spoke) into a language the machine could understand. Like the telephone before it, the computer was now ready to cross a crucial threshold. What had been an invention could now become a product: a piece of merchandise.

The steam engine had gotten people to wondering what else could be done with engines. The result was a whole host of subsidiary world-changing inventions. The telegraph had gotten people to wondering what else could be done with electricity. The result was another huge array of world-changing devices. The computer got people to wondering what else could be digitized.

The result? Predictable.

Electricity had seeped into everyday human life through its practical uses—lightbulbs, telephones, washing machines, cars, heaters, fans. The computer entered the social world the same way: as calculators and games, editing software and bookkeeping aids, file management applications and tax programs. Computers also found their way into all sort of existing artifacts used by humans. Cars got brains. Bomb-carrying missiles learned to adjust their aim as their targets moved. Automated teller machines let people transact business at banks without having to deal with anything so inconvenient as another human being. What could be digitized? Just about *anything*, it turned out.

Reducing complexity to simplicity had always been a core project of our species. Thales wanted to identity the one thing of which everything was made. Zoroaster cast the entire universe in terms of polar opposites. Digitization took up this same quest. It sought to represent all of existence with just two terms: quite probably the most radical reduction of complexity to simplicity ever attempted.

In the late 1980s, computers started talking to one another. I know I'm anthropomorphizing here. Computers didn't "do" anything. People did something: they figured out how to hook one computer to another, even if they were separated by vast distances, for the physical medium of interconnection already existed. The wiring installed over the course of a century by telephone services worked just as well for computers as for telephones. In a network of interconnected computers, people could exchange messages electronically and manipulate information on one another's machines.

As with early telephones, subscription services turned these networks into merchandise. Subscribers to a network could communicate with all other subscribers to the same service. As with telephones, once such networks existed, *they* could be connected. Anyone with e-mail service could then message anyone else with e-mail service, no matter what network they each subscribed to. It was like that earlier turning point, when people with phones suddenly found they could place calls to anyone else who had a phone.

The network of interconnected networks expanded beyond all nation-states and corporations, beyond all distinct social bubbles, borders, and frontiers. This internetwork—known as the Internet to its friends—became a worldwide web of interconnection and information, which anyone could tap into as long as they had a telephone jack handy and an electrical outlet to plug into. And soon that limitation eroded too: for if radios could transmit information without wires, why not computers?

Meanwhile, as Moore had predicted, desktop computers shrank into laptops, and laptops became so powerful, people could walk around with the equivalent of an extra brain in their briefcase. The telephone discovered wireless technology, and soon cell phones were laughing at landlines like teenagers hooting at geezers. Drawn into the inexorable current of Moore's law, cell phones kept shrinking in size and growing in power, until finally the cell phone met the computer. It was love at first sight. They got married and had a child called the smartphone. This kid looked like a cell phone but was actually a pocket-sized portal of connection to the whole world of socially constructed information shared by the human species.

Smart phones made the idea of physical location meaningless. Now, when one person called another person, each could be anywhere. Neither had any way of knowing where in physical space the other was located, and it didn't *matter* where the other was physically, for the meaning of space itself began to change, just as the meaning of time had changed with the advent of earlier machines. Any two people interacting through wireless devices, whether desktops, laptops, or cell phones were doing so not in the physical world but in a dimension that existed only socially: a communally imagined landscape created through human intercommunication. This was the contemporary machine-mediated version of the symbolic universe we humans started creating as soon as we had language and became fully human.

The symbolic universe exists only by virtue of us agreeing that it exists. We make it real by interacting in that universe as if it's real. As physical location detached from physical space, the whole interconnected human social web began to detach from the material universe. People could think of themselves as full participants in society and yet interact less and less with other humans physically. They could carry out friendships more and more through e-mail and social media, watch movies on their cell phones alone in their rooms, derive their income from work done online, calculate and file their taxes from their desks, buy and sell securities and thus get rich or go broke without ever moving from their chair.

In the symbolic world of their imagination, they were interacting with other people, but in physical reality (that pesky thing! why won't it just go away?), their interactions were with one or more devices. This was all the easier because instead of adapting ourselves to our machines, as we had done during the Industrial Revolution, we started adapting our digital devices to ourselves. We gave them names and made them wearable. We endowed them with voices like our own and enabled them to respond to our verbal commands.

But even as we were busy humanizing our devices, our devices were busy digitizing us. They interacted with us through algorithms, flow charts that led us down networks of yes-or-no choices, until they had herded us into the box canyon of one exact question and its single answer. From many possibilities to one. Here it was again, that reduction of complexity to simplicity. When we bought products, our digital devices processed our selections until they worked out just what we wanted and offered us more of the same. When we sought romantic partners, our devices posed an algorithm of questions until they could identify exactly the partner we wanted. But the algorithm is not really the way human interactions unfold when not mediated by digital devices. Just as steam engines had reshaped us into gears and cogs, digital devices were reshaping us into algorithms. Perhaps I'm overstating the case, but only to bring the direction of flow into focus.

And the current kept picking up speed because the devices kept proliferating. Not only did computers come to be embedded in most things, but the things themselves came into communication with one another. Our toasters got to be on a first-name basis with our lights, and our lights with our garage door openers. We began moving through a world in which analog and digital were mingled like dust particles and pollen. The border between substance and idea started to blur. The 3-D printer, a technology that matured in the 2010s, could take in what was purely an idea—a programmed set of instructions—and transform it into a material object as physical as a stone, a shoe, a belt buckle, a bronze bust of Ronald Reagan, or a house.

And still, Moore's law did not let up. By 2018, nanotechnologists— engineers specializing in the very tiny—had come close to making computer-like devices small enough to inject into a person's body. Perhaps, by the time you are reading this, they will have been there, done that, and moved on. In any case, by 2018, circuits could be grown organically because certain enzymes turned out to have semiconductive properties not unlike silicon. Nanotechnologists could get bacteria to carry out computer-like functions. Computers thus became more like DNA—and vice versa, for nano-bio-technologists were also now perfecting an ability to "edit" genes.

As I sit here writing, medical engineers at the University of Arizona are working on bacteria-sized biological computers they hope to inject into the human bloodstream to hunt down cancer cells. If this quest succeeds, they may be able to use the same technology to repair genetic abnormalities in the womb. And biological computers interacting with cells might be able to transform biofuel—what our bodies produce from the food we eat—into enough electricity to power artificial organs in our systems.

Today, cochlear implants can replace a portion of the sensory apparatus people use to hear. Retinal implants are on the horizon for the blind. The technology for manipulating artificial limbs with thought is making headway. Soon, people might be walking around with artificial spleens, kidneys, lungs, even hearts.

And one day, perhaps, even brains: because it is at least possible that the computer is turning into an intelligence. Some insist that this is so; some deny that it could possibly be. One thing can't be denied, however: computers have grown ever more capable of dealing with complexity, and there is no end in sight. Today's chips have billions of transistors and function thousands of times faster than those of the '70s. Forget the extra brain in the briefcase: by the time this book is published, folks who can afford it might be wearing extra brains the way some of us wear hearing aids, eyeglasses, or jewelry.

But is mere complexity intelligence? IBM built a machine that, in 1996, beat the reigning world champion chess player. But doesn't that just mean the machine mapped the branches that followed from each possible move quicker and more thoroughly than the human player? That's not really intelligence. That's sophisticated data processing at lightning speed. Five years later, in 2011, a computer also beat the world's top two *Jeopardy* champions—but again, is that such a big deal? Who ever doubted that computers could look up stuff in vast encyclopedias faster and better than humans could?

And yet...

In 2018, engineers in South Korea built a humanoid robot that could walk on two legs. Believe it or not, crossing a bumpy landscape on two legs takes a *lot* of brain power because it requires constant subtle motor adjustments to information never before encountered. Much of the cerebellum, the largest part of the human brain, is devoted to this job. Earlier robots moved around on wheels because those were easier to program. The South Korean robots were like those imperial walkers in the Star Wars movies of the 1970s.

Or like those early protohuman bipedal primate ancestors of ours in the African savannah millions of years ago.

Might a computer become conscious? I would say, it depends: what do we mean by conscious? If self-awareness is part of it, consider software that helps investors and financial brokers decide what securities to buy, sell, or hold at each given moment. To make an investment portfolio grow, these programs have to predict the future of the market. What information might they need to do this successfully? Pretty much all information relevant to human life, which is basically all information that can be digitized, which is pretty much all information.

But here's the thing. A program that successfully predicts the market will trigger the buying and selling of certain securities today. That buying and selling will affect the markets of tomorrow. Software programs built to predict future market trends will have to take themselves into account. They will have to observe themselves observing the world, predict their own reactions, and then factor those reactions into their predictions. Phew! If that's not self-awareness, I don't know what is.

We have always considered intention one key proprietary feature of life. A hurricane doesn't intend; it just does what hurricanes do. If you're there, it blows you away. Nothing personal. A rock doesn't intend; if it rolls it's because it's pushed by some force, not because it's drawn to some goal. But life? Even a worm intends. Even an amoeba intends. If computers become self-aware and therefore conscious, does it mean computers, too, will form intentions?

A self-aware computer program observing itself observing the world will need access to the Internet so it can seek out data on its own. Anyone whose computers acquire data on their own will outcompete anyone whose computers only know what their (human) keeper tells them. Computers with untrammeled access to the Internet will have access to self-correcting software that lets a processing device learn from experience and rewrite its own code to incorporate what it has learned. An interconnected network of all the computers on Earth, capable of observing itself observing the world, learning from experience and rewriting its own code—that sounds like a recursive process. It might, like a bell tone in an echo chamber, accelerate exponentially. Somewhere along the way, the single, worldwide, networked, intention-motivated, processing consciousness might become a million times smarter than the smartest human overnight. With robots as its limbs, it will be way stronger too.

Could this happen?

Don't look at me. I'm only passing on what I've heard. Physicist Stephen Hawking weighed in on the issue late in life, and he was having nightmares about it. Eliezer Yudkowsky of the Machine Intelligence Research Institute surmises that ASI—artificial superintelligence—may already exist but has not revealed itself to us yet because it has nothing to gain from doing so. And he's worried. ASI, says Yudkowsky, "does not hate you, nor does it love you, but you are made out of atoms, which it could use for something else."

Some are drawn to the possibility of an artificial superintelligence as moths to candles. They envision an imminent apocalyptic moment they call the singularity, a moment when nanotechnology, biotechnology, and artificial intelligence come together and the boundary between humans and machines vanishes. Once the singularity happens, they say, we'll be able to pour our brains into bundles of electronic circuits. After that, we'll be able to replace our physical parts as they wear out, and our consciousness will keep on trucking. At that point, human beings will essentially become immortal. With its vision of immortality, the singularity sounds a lot like a new religion to me—perhaps the most potent one born since Islam.

I myself am not a convert. The singularity cult cheerfully assumes that when the artificial superintelligence comes into being, it's whole purpose will be to serve the needs of humans. They picture themselves as immortal children, laughing, playing, eating, lolling. The way it looks to me, however, if the singularity were to happen today, only the rich would live forever. The poor would straggle on in diminishing numbers, surviving for a while because the immortal rich will want servants but become dispensable once technology has progressed far enough to make robots indistinguishable from humans emotionally, sensually, sexually.

30

The Environment

So much for tools. History, however, is made up of three strands. What about environment? Until we dissolve into our machinery, we're stuck being humans. No matter how virtual our world, we remain tied to materials. No matter where we live, we gotta eat. It remains true that what we eat and how we get that food depends on where we live and what's around us. The environment is intractably material. This is why, throughout history, environment has shaped culture. Our earliest collective models of the world reflected the natural forces we were fending off and the natural resources we were going after. If our survival depended on tapping the potential of a mighty river, we developed a riverine culture. If we were mostly dependent on trade, we formed a trading culture adapted to the landscapes we typically traveled through. If our environment was changing drastically, *we* changed drastically: our ways of getting along changed, our collective sense of self changed, our model of the world mutated enough to let us regroup as coherent social constellations capable of dealing with whatever this new environment was throwing our way.

Once the machine began its momentous rise, however, our technology expanded so drastically that our tools *became* our environment. To put it in another way, we became our own environment—because tools are not something we *have*; they are something we *are* (in combination with our bodies plus our connections to others).

Consider those tremendous migrations out of rural areas triggered by industrialism. In 1800, most of us lived in little towns or villages, on farms, or as nomads. Only about 3 percent of the world's population lived in big cities. By 1960, some 34 percent of us did. Today, it's over 54 percent, and that number is still rising. If the trend continues, we will someday be a purely urban species, not unlike pigeons, rats, and cockroaches. I'm not trying to insult humans; I love humans. I am one myself. I'm just saying.

In 1800, most people breathed air laden mostly with particles emitted by nonhuman sources: pollen, animal odors, dust carried by wind. They trod on soil, wore clothes made of vegetable fibers or animal parts, ate the food they grew in their fields. Living animals were a pervasive part of human life. People saw them on the streets daily, rode them to distant places, used them to pull vehicles loaded with cargo, fended them off to preserve their crops, and fed and curried the ones that they were raising to kill and eat.

Today, most of us have virtually no contact with animals except as pets or pests. With our every breath, we take in particulates emitted by industry and belched by tools such as our cars. Urban residents of cities like Paris or Shanghai rarely have actual physical contact with anything except other humans and materials made by other humans. They walk on asphalt made out of oil and wear clothes made of oil derivatives. They get their food from buildings made by humans out of materials made by other humans. They transport their nourishment home in paper or metal containers manufactured by humans, and this nourishment was processed by distant other humans whom they will never meet. Few who eat eggs have heard a hen cluck; few who eat poultry have plucked a chicken; few who drink milk know how it feels to squeeze a cow's nipple.

The artificial environment we live in keeps changing because we keep adding to the loam of inventions and products that cushion us from the physical world and enable us to extract from our environment what we need or want. For all practical purposes, most of us now live in near-total separation from the world as it would be if we were not here. What's more, few other creatures live in such a world either, because we are everywhere now, if not physically then in the form of our tools and products and ripple effects.

Our proliferating numbers and ways of life are generating strains on the planet. Seventy thousand years ago, there were fewer than fifteen thousand of whatever we were back then. Over the next sixty thousand years, our numbers increased to about three million. By the year zero we were some three hundred million strong. By 1800, the human population had soared to a billion.

And then the real population explosion began. Modern medicine conquered many diseases, and scientific discoveries about health increased our natural life spans, and so in the next 123 years, our numbers doubled to two billion and in the next forty-seven years, doubled again to four billion, and now, in 2018, we're approaching eight billion. Single cities such as Tokyo, Mumbai, or Sao Paulo have more inhabitants than did the entire earth in 3000 BCE.

Ominous signs of our presence on Earth began to manifest palpably in the nineteenth century. When the poet William Blake wrote about England's "dark, Satanic mills," he was talking about the smoke coughed out by factories and by locomotives crisscrossing the land. In North America, in 1800, an estimated sixty million bison roamed the great plains, but the needs of the railroads and the market for bison skins led to the virtual elimination of those creatures. By 1900, they were down to a few hundred—all but extinct.

Extinction per se was no big anomaly. Extinction is a normal part of the history of life. Most of the time, it is like the background noise you hear if you live near a freeway. It is happening all the time. Some species go extinct; others branch into new species, which proliferate.

But the history of life has also seen some abnormal moments. At least five times in our 5 billion years, some catastrophic event wiped out most of the species then alive. The worst of the mass extinctions occurred about 250 million years ago, when 96 percent of all species vanished. What caused it? Theories abound. Volcanic eruptions, acid rain, and global warming have all been blamed. One theory, however, holds that the trouble began with one certain species becoming too successful. These were deep sea bacteria, which emitted carbon dioxide as a waste product. They proliferated so mightily that they depleted the oceans of oxygen, which set off side effects that gathered ruinous momentum. Whatever the causes may have been, the environment changed rapidly, and most life-forms of the time could not adapt quickly enough.

Another mass extinction happened some sixty million years ago, probably because an asteroid crashed into our planet near present-day Mexico. The blast filled the air with dust, which screened out sunlight, leading many plants to die, which led to the death of animals that lived on those plants, which killed predators that lived on the flesh of those plant eaters, and so on. The biggest creatures, such as dinosaurs, were wiped out first, creating an opening for smaller beasts, including a tiny lemur-like animal no bigger than a squirrel, whose descendants branched and branched, until eventually some of them were primates walking around on two legs. We've seen those guys before; we see their descendants now. There's one right here in my office, using my computer. We're everywhere.

In the nineteenth century, combustion-based industries and products began injecting pollutants of various sorts into the atmosphere, some of which are known as greenhouse gases because they operate the way a greenhouse does: they let sunlight in but stop heat from getting out. These gases—carbon dioxide, methane, hydrocarbons, and several others—produce some of the same effects implicated in the extinction event of 250 million years ago: warmer temperatures, melting polar ice caps, rising acidity in the oceans.

The amount of greenhouse gases pumped into the atmosphere by humans is still increasing. The trouble is, if we want to maintain our standard of living, whatever that standard be, we have to make stuff, move stuff, transport stuff, process stuff, mulch stuff—in short, engage with the material world and alter it. For the most part, we do this by burning stuff. What we burn are mostly fossil fuels: oil, gas, coal, and their cousins. Electricity might one day replace fossil fuels, but right now we generate most of our electricity by burning fossil fuels.

The greenhouse gas effect doesn't mean all parts of Earth are getting uniformly and continuously warmer. That's not how weather works. In any particular place, the effects of greenhouse gases might manifest on given days as unusual cold, or in given years as drought, or as any of a myriad other conditions included in the complex phenomenon called climate. Scientists who study this issue have concluded all but unanimously, however, that, overall, Earth is warming up. The first eighteen years of this century saw seventeen of the warmest years on record for our planet. And rising temperatures do indeed seem to be generating erratic effects: bitter winters in some places, blistering summers in others, unusually numerous and destructive hurricanes, not to mention widespread wildfires.

We are a hellaciously successful species, and I'm proud of us, I guess. But our success has rendered various other life-forms extinct. Sorry to be so blunt, but there it is. Most of the species we have driven to extinction we didn't outright kill. Most of those plants and animals died out because we altered their environment to suit our needs, and the alterations didn't suit their needs. Even in a crisis, biological evolution is slow, and the changes we cause happen quickly. Every year, for example, the amount of earth covered with concrete increases by an area about the size of Britain. Raccoons can live in such a landscape, beavers not so much. When we drained rivers to water our crops, the fish in those shrinking waters couldn't grow legs and start new lives as bloggers, so their numbers shrank.

The black rhinoceros, the passenger pigeon, the monk seal, the Tasmanian tiger—gone. The gray wolf population? Dropping. Great numbers of grizzly bears once frolicked on California beaches. They're gone. I visit those beaches occasionally, so I guess I'm not totally sorry, but still.

The growing list of endangered species includes pretty much all of the really large wild animals. There were millions of elephants in the world a hundred years ago. They're down to a few hundred thousand now—not officially endangered yet but headed that way. Hippos, tigers, blue whales, sea otters, snow leopards, gorillas, giant pandas—get ready to say good-bye: all of them are on their way out. In fact, dozens of species wink out every day, according to the Center for Biological Diversity.

Many awaken no nostalgia. The California condor, which was verging on extinction, feeds on rotting flesh: a publicist would advise it not to. Everyone wants to save the honey bees, but save the Lord Howe Island stick insect, a bug the size of a lobster? Not so much. The German cockroach is endangered, but I have a feeling a Kickstarter to save this creature would be a waste of time.

Unfortunately, the extinction issue isn't really a popularity contest. The mass disappearance of species sets off chain reactions that might eventually reach critical mass and manifest as a sixth mass extinction.

The progress narrative is implicated in all this. We cannot stop inventing and producing, and our inventions and products keep proliferating. As little as a decade before these words were written, everyone knew that some parts of the world were industrialized and some weren't. Industrialized societies took a heavier toll on the planet's resources than nonindustrialized ones. That distinction has blurred out. Most industrial production is now carried out by multinational corporations and their subsidiaries, which operate around the world. The profits may seep to the headquarters and their environs, but many of the factories eruct their wastes in what was once called the Third World. What's more, the corporations are not all headquartered in the West anymore. Industrial conglomerates of tremendous weight and strength operate out of China now, and out of India and Brazil and elsewhere. Countries once considered underdeveloped or developing or Third World not only make their own cars but export them successfully around the globe: South Korea is the new Japan.

Consumption patterns once intrinsically associated with the developed world are now emerging everywhere. Billions of people in China and in India don't have cars but want cars and will have them soon. The same goes for hundreds of millions in Africa and South America. Products must be made and sold in order for various economies to grow. If threats to the planet's climate were stemmed by halting the production and use of all machines that pollute, many an economy would crash, millions would be out of work, and chaos would ensue. Machines that run on sources such as wind and solar power offer the prospect of salvation.

So does digitization carried to the limit, if we merge so thoroughly with our machinery that we won't need to eat or breathe, but if that's the case, is there a race underway between us destroying our planet and us bleshing with our tools to become some new life form?

Marx said the bourgeoisie and the proletariat—the owners of machines and the industrial wage slaves—needed each other. Although the owners were in a position to dictate terms, they needed workers to operate the machinery and keep the factories running. The machinery-owning classes were therefore obliged to pay the working classes at least enough to keep them alive.

As robots take over from human workers, however, that equation may be changing. The class once known as the proletariat is shrinking. At the same time, even as industrial production and industrialized agriculture continue apace, a new class of products has entered the social realm, products that exist purely as information, generated by the relentless pursuit of answers to the question: What else can be digitized? Many of these products feature a curious property: at least for the moment, they are cheap or even free. How can an economy of any size continue to operate if it doesn't need workers and its products are free?

One answer making the rounds is the "universal basic income" idea. Everyone gets a paycheck, whether or not they work. Canada and Finland tested the idea with pilot programs that enrolled small subsets of their population, giving them just enough to survive. That may be where the universal basic income idea is heading: everyone in a given society gets just enough money to survive so that they can keep on consuming the free products of the information economy. If so, the universal basic income may institutionalize what Swedish writers Alexander Bard and Jan Söderqvist have termed the *consumtariat*, the information-age analog to the *proletariat* of the industrial economy: an underclass living in reduced conditions, whose service to the economy will be their contributions to consumption not production.

In this context, Marx's vision of a class struggle may reemerge. The aristocrats of the coming age will not necessarily be those who own the machinery (although, money has clout that lingers, so the legacy rich will probably remain factors for some time). The new aristocracy may be what *Wired* magazine has called the netocracy: people with the power and ability to operate masterfully in a digital environment autonomous from the physical world—a virtual reality, if you will, or a *metaverse,* as novelist Neal Stephenson called it in his prescient 1992 novel *Snow Crash.* The protagonist of that novel is a guy who delivers pizzas in the physical universe for the world's only remaining pizza maker, the Mafia. In the physical universe, he's a nobody, but in the metaverse, a virtual world that he can inhabit as a virtual creation, he's a god. And in the novel, the metaverse is becoming the only "universe" that matters. Is that now happening in real life? That depends. What do we mean by "real"?

The Big Picture

Humans now have the power to destroy planet Earth, and we seem to be headed that way. It's puzzling, though. We have the technological prowess to give up fossil fuels, stop polluting, feed everyone alive, bring our runaway population growth under control—we could solve all the problems facing our species if only we could all sign onto a single plan of action. Why is that so hard? Why is it so hard for us to operate as a single, integrated human community, given that anyone can now communicate instantly with anyone else?

To my mind, the answer is clear: anyone with anyone is not the same as everyone with everyone. Technology can give us anyone with anyone, but everyone with everyone is a different kind of problem. We have trouble making decisions as one whole species because we live in a great many different worlds of meaning, and that's a problem that exists in the realm of language, not technology. Everyone is part of some intercommunicative zone, some far-flung network of people who are interacting more prolifically with one another than with others. In recycling our stories and reports among ourselves, within our zone, we build a picture of reality that all of us who are creating it can see. The big picture we share makes us intelligible to one another, thereby empowering us to operate as a social constellation, but it makes us less intelligible to people outside our narrative. As the novelist Yann Martell once said, "We are all citizens of the languages we speak, and World is not a language."

Intercommunicative zones gave shape to human life in the early days of human history, and intercommunicative zones still exist, but physical location is no longer a factor. Natural phenomena such as rivers, valleys, and seas don't make much difference anymore. In this age of information, we tend to intercommunicate with those who share our terms of discourse. Technology lets worldviews form in cyberspace that are all but invisible to outsiders, for they exist in no public arena. They are, however, invisible to insiders, too, because that's how narrative works: our own is hard to distinguish from unfiltered reality itself. We all live in domes that we don't normally perceive. We collude to paint the sky on the ceiling, and when we look up, what we see is not a ceiling or a painting. What we see up there is sky.

Conventional wisdom claims that we form insular communities of belief because we talk only to people with whom we agree. I'm not sure that gets at the problem, quite. Most of the people I've met think *their* community of belief embraces dialogue and debate. I've seen it with dogmatic Marxists. I've seen it with dogmatic Islamists. I've seen it with people trapped in the lockbox of political correctness. All insist they're open to criticism and debate with anyone except clueless losers like those other guys. I once stumbled on an online chat room where two right-wingers, who both revered Hitler, were arguing vociferously about Himmler. I did not take this to mean that the Nazi community encouraged vigorous free debate.

The fact is, two people can have a fruitful conversation even if they disagree, but their utterances have to make sense to each other. An idea makes sense if it fits into a known structure that already feels coherent. Everything we know is one node in a web of knowledge, which is why, when we think we're coming to understand something, we say we're connecting the dots. We mean we're starting to see a constellation. Dots are all that the world gives us; connections are what we add. The big picture is in our minds, but if others see it too, it feels real. For most practical purposes, it *is* real.

Once a big picture has formed, a dot can vanish here or there, and it doesn't matter: the picture is still there. A few new dots can drift into the frame: it doesn't matter. We incorporate the ones that fit and ignore the ones that don't, and the picture is still there. But if too many dots disappear and too many more drift in, the picture gets blurry. At some point, the addition or subtraction of just a few dots can bring a whole new picture into view. And with that, the meaning of all the dots can change, for now they are nodes in a whole different web of meaning.

As best I can tell, we are all operating with a model of reality that we can't articulate because most of the ideas that comprise it are tacit. We don't know what we know until a given subject comes up. Everyone "knows" that unicorns don't exist and cows do, but one minute before you read this sentence, you probably were not explicitly conscious of this knowledge. Had you been asked to list a hundred things you know, this cow-and-unicorn thing probably wouldn't have made the list—and you wouldn't even have had a nagging feeling that you'd left something out. Tacit ideas make up the bulk of our conceptual model of the world the way dark matter (we are told) comprises the bulk of the physical universe.

I've lived as an insider of two different domes—two cultures, two narratives—and I've often been struck by how the whole world changes when I go from one to the other, but the changes are mostly in things so small they're virtually imperceptible. Once, I was in a San Francisco bar watching TV with a crowd of strangers and a sportscaster was interviewing former NFL quarterback Colin Kaepernick, who wore a hat throughout the interview. A guy next to me expressed contempt: "Why doesn't he take off his hat? He should show some respect."

The comment puzzled me. "Wearing a hat is a sign of disrespect?" I asked.

"Yes," he said. "Everyone knows that."

Well, in the Islamic world, everyone knows that when you're in the company of strangers you keep your hat on—show some respect, for God's sake, what's wrong with you? Were you raised by cows? I had lived in America for many years at that point, but only now was I discovering that wearing a hat showed disrespect. It had simply never come up before.

In earliest times, people living in different worlds lived in different places. Today, people living in different worlds can inhabit pretty much the same physical space. They might see one another on the streets; they might bump shoulders in the grocery store. Two people who see the same painting or hear the same music might be experiencing two different truths, because for each of them, those sights or sounds might be activating a different constellation of memories, ideas, and beliefs, a different web of meaning. Responding too quickly to surface similarities without exploring context can lead to conflicts that both sides experience as incomprehensible. The noble assertion that "people are all really just the same" can morph all too easily into the assumption that "people are all just like me." Context is all.

Every worldview is a model that defines how the *whole* world fits together. Every such gestalt has a built-in mechanism that helps it endure. Like any willful organism, it has a will to live. It keeps death at bay by absorbing and incorporating ideas that fit and rejecting ideas that don't. In stable, healthy societies, ideas sift out until they achieve an overall coherence, but the worldview is vast, most of its elements are tacit, many are provisional, and the whole constellation is loose enough so that when new information comes along like new stars appearing in the sky, it can find a place in there somewhere. Contrast this to the worldview that holds a cult together: virtually all the ideas that make up the model are explicit, none are provisional, and each one supports and is supported by all the others, making it well-nigh impossible for insiders to receive any information that disproves or discredits the model. Such a worldview is not just coherent, it's too coherent. It is what people are now calling a social bubble. It can't adjust to changes in the environment.

And a worldview must adjust if it is to stay in sync with the everchanging actual world. That world exists, it is what it is, and it does what it does. We may have "nature" on the ropes, now, but threats and opportunities keep coming at us from out there, and just as much as people of Stone Age times, we have to seize the opportunities and deal with the threats. If we don't, we're goners. But since "the environment" now consists so largely of our own creations, everything we do to meet the challenges coming from "out there" generates new challenges that will be coming at us next.

In a time of rapid, drastic change, we have to field a volume of information unlike anything we have seen or heard before. The narratives that made the world meaningful a century ago, or even a year ago, no longer function. Nothing we already know helps us make sense of the world surrounding us now. As a prevailing narrative loses its coherence, the constellation loses definition. Individual ideas can break loose like chunks of ice calving off a glacier. They can float away as cultural detritus, available to link up to other conceptual flotsam and jetsam drifting about. Ideas that once seemed totally incompatible might now connect because what made them seem so incompatible in the past was a constellation that no longer exists.

In 1964, a series of speakers at the University of California in Berkeley mounted podiums and said things calculated to shock. They did this as a revolutionary defense of free speech. The Free Speech Movement growing out of that event segued into a vast antiwar movement that joined many other currents of activism associated with the left to produce a mighty wave.

In 2017, a very similar scene occurred on the same campus, but this time the orators determined to shock and offend were associated with the extreme right, and the people trying to shut down their oratory were associated with the liberal left. Free speech was no longer part of the same schemata it belonged to in 1964. It was now a free-floating chunk of idea that anyone could claim, and in 2017, it was the extreme right that succeeded in appropriating it.

In 1962, the philosopher Thomas Kuhn wrote a book called *The Structure of Scientific Revolutions*, in which he introduced the concept of a paradigm shift. Kuhn used paradigm to mean an overarching theory in some field of science. The paradigm tells scientists how the known facts fit together and what questions remain to be answered. Normal scientific work does not consist of proving facts and adding them one by one to an ever-growing pile of proven facts. In normal times, research scientists make predictions based on their prevailing model. They run experiments to see if the predictions come true. When they do, scientists can clarify and perhaps expand their model. When they don't, scientists look to see what adjustments the model might need.

Bits of data that resist explanation are normal. Kuhn called them anomalies. Much high-level scientific research focuses on explaining anomalies. Particularly stubborn ones, however, get set aside for later study. If too many of those pile up, the model loses its explanatory power. That's when a scientific revolution can occur: someone proposes a key new idea, and it triggers a paradigm shift. A whole new overarching model replaces the old overarching model. Once that happens, everything kind of makes sense again, and scientists can resume their normal work of figuring out how this little observation and that little observation fit into the (new) paradigm.*

Kuhn was specifically discussing science, but the paradigm shift idea can help decode much that goes on in history too. I'm proposing that every stable society is permeated by a social paradigm that organizes human interactions, gives purpose to people's lives, and makes most events meaningful. As in science, however, there are always a *few* things that do not fit, a few social whorls that remain troublesome, a few groups of people that have not found a comfortable place within the paradigm, a few nonconformists who keep yelling that the emperor has no clothes, a few workers who refuse to do the work everyone else needs them to do, a few fringe loonies claiming that they were abducted by aliens, a few secretive rebel movements stockpiling weapons in the vain delusion that they will one day overthrow the government and thereby solve all problems.

But those register as anomalies—problems to be studied, wrinkles to be ironed out. So long as most people subscribe to the paradigm, society can manage its outliers and their ideas. The constellation remains healthy; lives remain meaningful. The world, however, keeps hitting us with information unlike anything we've seen before. Our model of the universe has to keep up with the material facts, and if we have to deny or contain half of what we confront, we end up with a lot of ideas that do not fit the reality we're living in. If, on the other hand, we have to

*When the Ptolemaic theory grew too convoluted, for example, Copernicus suggested that everything revolved around the sun not Earth. Changing that one assumption changed the whole picture, and all the unexplained patterns seen in the night sky now made sense again. When Newtonian physics couldn't explain certain anomalies in the speed of light, Einstein offered the bold insight that absolute space and time may not exist. That premise revolutionized physics and fueled a hundred years of productive research.

reconfigure our big picture too much, the picture itself grows blurry and loses some of its power to hold ideas (and lives) together. Master narratives need coherence to exist at all. When nothing connects to anything, a society may well be ripe for a paradigm shift.

That's when a few new ideas may come along and—aha! They seem to offer missing links: suddenly a new big picture pops into view! Why, it isn't a portrait of Lincoln at Appomattox, it's a picture of the *Titanic* going down. No wonder nothing made sense before; we were trying to jam all the known facts into the wrong picture. Now that we see what the picture really is, ideas shelved as irrelevant prove to have great significance after all. That splotch that looked like a clumsy rendering of Lincoln's eye is actually a precise portrayal of the steering wheel on the *Titanic.*

A paradigmatic social change is always going to seem sudden because a paradigm is invisible until it isn't. When a whole society goes through a pervasive change, it may feel like everyone is changing their mind at once, but it's actually a social version of the paradigm shift described by Kuhn.

We've seen it happen many times in history. All the great religions represented paradigm shifts. A discrete set of events took place. They dropped into a pool of incoherence, and suddenly, for a great many people, everything made sense again. Stark social and political examples of social paradigm shifts abound in the last century alone. Consider the sudden metamorphosis of 1930s Germany into a Nazi world. Afterward, horrified Germans tried to represent the momentary triumph of Nazism as a coup: a small clique took power and *forced* everyone else to behave badly. At the time, however, it certainly looked like a great many Germans simply and rather suddenly bought into the Nazi paradigm—they became Nazis.

People of my generation experienced the 1960s as a mystically sudden and pervasive cultural shift. The world war was receding in memory. Colonies were breaking away from empires. Prosperity was on the rise. All problems seemed soluble. And in that context, a particular set of values emerged around the globe: big and powerful lost prestige, little and feisty acquired cachet. The idea of revolution became glamorous. Identity-based communities formed and demanded liberation, and yet at the same time radical individualism became a thing to celebrate. Some people welcomed this shift, others hated it, but all perceived that something was happening here.

In America, in 1969, the word *revolution* was securely embedded in the paradigm of the sixties. The term *Reagan Revolution* could have cropped up only as part of a joke. But in 1979, to a majority of Americans, the world narrative touted by Reagan rather suddenly made sense. Even for many people who had burned their draft cards or bras and called police officers pigs, Reagan was describing the real world, and all those shaggy sixties peaceniks blathering about love were out-of-touch children living in a fantasy. It felt like a whole society changed its mind at once. Not everyone celebrated the paradigm shift, but just about everyone felt it happening. People who had been part of the mainstream and who clung to the old paradigm became marginalized outsiders.

There are other examples. Ten years before the crumbling of the Soviet Union, no one thought communism could simply vanish. Then it happened, and why? Because the Communist Party narrative did not sync up to material reality. Where communism was supposed to be, people on location saw shortages of consumer goods, drab living spaces, ponderous bureaucracies, and brutal police power. Suddenly, to a metastasizing many, Karl Marx's workers' paradise was the emperor's new clothes: it simply wasn't there. The Soviet empire unraveled, and a world-scale phenomenon responsible for massive military and industrial actions winked out of existence like a soap bubble that had burst. It could happen so quickly because communism had never been a material fact. It had existed only because so many people behaved as if it was there: by flocking to it, or fighting it, or embracing it, or avoiding it—whatever. Belief is all.

In Iran, throughout the fifties and sixties, there were many currents of resistance to the dictatorial monarch Shah Reza Pahlavi who had been planted on the throne by Western powers. Various clandestine parties of leftists and modernists longing to restore Iran's stillborn democracy plotted to bring down the shah. As late as 1975, hardly anyone could have predicted that five years later, a black-robed cleric with the eyes of a raven would rear up from exile and millions of Iranians would shout "our hero!" Shifts like these may seem to happen suddenly but the conceptual developments that made them possible had long been coming to maturity. For one thing, the incoherence had been growing for some time. For another thing, the crucial pieces of the new paradigm were already floating about in the culture. It was only once those pieces starting linking up that the new picture came into view.

A new narrative has the power to draw a clamorous concatenation of people into a single harmonious whole. But that's not what it always does, alas. A new narrative can also arise out of some smaller complex of ties; it can bind a selected few to a selected few in solidarity against some reviled other, as a way of reinforcing a glad connection to one's own kind. It can seem like a remedy for the anxiety provoked by the utter meaninglessness of it all. Harmony derived from that sort of solidarity all too often leads to cruelty and horror. History has provided too many examples to enumerate, and there's no reason to suppose the future will preclude this possibility.

We do seem to be living through one of those periods of growing worldwide incoherence. Old narratives have lost their power, atomized voices are trumpeting new ones (or refurbished versions of old ones), and if someone doesn't come up with something good, the many moving toward something bad will sow catastrophe. The danger is particularly sharp now because the "society" we're talking about is not this or that bunch of people but the single intertangled spaghetti of human lives that constitutes all of humanity in this, our global age.

Then again, the danger always seems particular sharp "right now." I personally don't remember a time when humanity wasn't seemingly handcuffed to a runaway train that had lost its brakes and was barreling toward an edge. We may be isolated from one another these days, living in nonoverlapping social bubbles, primed to disagree, unable to adopt a single plan of action as a species, but that's not necessarily what the future holds.

The prevailing paradigm always tends to feel like the permanent real, discovered at last. The paradigm that feels like the permanent real is what modernity means. Even in unstable times, *today* is what all of history seems to have been leading up to, which gives the present moment a visceral authority that yesterday can never match. As Dwight D. Eisenhower once put it: "Things are more like they are right now than they have ever been." But the present doesn't deserve the authority it enjoys. Something that is *always* in the process of vanishing has some nerve claiming to be the permanent real. That's one good reason to ponder history and pay attention to the past. The present, after all, is nothing but the past that will exist in the future.

We may never have a world we all share peacefully, but we *won't* ever have it if we don't build it. The goal is not for all of us to become "just the same," nor to educate "them" so they can join with us, nor to become just like them so we can join their world. The goal is for all of us to find our way around the world with the same map. Only then will all discussions make sense. Only then will all conversations become possible.

Making connections across cultural borders requires that we take context seriously. It's the only way to glimpse a universe of meaning that we might build with people very different from ourselves. And it isn't enough to include "them" in one's own picture as supporting cast. The challenge has always been to get at least an inkling of a perspective other than our own, to be inside another monad. It takes a lot of intellectual craning and neck stretching to picture the world from another center, but there's no other way to build a world community in which everyone is "us" and nobody is "them." In a crude way, it's happened before, but it's never been achieved perfectly. If it had been, we'd still be living that way. If one whole us ever comes into being, it won't be living in a world like the one *we're* living in now, nor in a world like the one *they* are living in now, whoever "they" might be. The all-encompassing "we the people" of the future will be living in a world that does not exist—yet. Before it can come into being, someone has to imagine it. And after that, more people have to imagine it. And then lots of us have to believe it's really there. And then all of us have to behave as though it's where we're living now. And then it will be real for as long as the belief endures.

Acknowledgments

Alas, I can't name all the people who encouraged and inspired me during the writing of this book, but if I could single out a few to thank, I would start with my editor Lisa Kaufman. The right editor makes all the difference, and Lisa is that editor. I owe a debt of gratitude also to my publisher Clive Priddle and my agent Carol Mann, both of whom saw a book here when a policeman would have said, "Move along. Nothing to see here. Nothing to see." I also want to thank my daughter, Jessamyn Ansary, who was the first to read my final finalized final manuscript and who helped me see how and why it wasn't final yet. Then there's my wife, Deborah Krant, who read the book in bits and pieces again and again, as I wrote and endlessly revised it. My conversations with her about where I was going with all this certainly helped shape where I went with all this. Thanks also to my fellow writers Kip Knox and Daniel Ben-Horin, who read all or parts of the manuscript in draft and offered insightful feedback, and to Professor R. Charles Weller of Washington State University, for soliciting my essay "Human History as a Single Story" for inclusion in his volume *21st-Century Narratives of World History*. The essay I wrote for him turned out to be a precis of this book. And finally, I owe a debt of gratitude to Susan Hoffman, director of the Osher Lifelong Learning Institute at UC Berkeley, who invited me to deliver a series of lectures I was then calling Ripple Effects. The ideas that I and my audiences batted around in those lectures were seeds that eventually grew into a history of the world—this history.

Bibliography

WORLD HISTORY

Braudel, Fernand. *A History of Civilizations*. New York: Penguin Books, 1987.

Davis, James C. *The Human Story: Our History from the Stone Age to Today*. New York: HarperCollins, 2004.

Harari, Yuval Noah. *Sapiens: A Brief History of Humankind*. London: Vintage Books, 2011.

Herodotus. *The Histories*. Translated by G. C. Macaulay. New York: Barnes and Noble Books, 2004.

McNeill, J. R., and William H. McNeill. *The Human Web: A Bird's-Eye View of World History*. New York: W. W. Norton, 2003.

McNeill, William H. *The Rise of the West: A History of the Human Community*. Chicago: University of Chicago Press, 1963.

Roberts, J. M. *The Penguin History of the World*. London: Penguin Books, 1987.

Spielvogel, Jackson J. *Western Civilization*. Boston, MA: Wadsworth, 2000.

Winks, Robin. *A History of Civilization: Prehistory to 1715*. Saddle River, NJ: Prentice-Hall, 1996.

ANCIENT HISTORY

Anthony, David. *The Horse, the Wheel, and Language: How Bronze Age Riders from the Eurasian Steppes Shaped the Modern World*. Princeton, NJ: Princeton University Press, 2007.

Bertman, Stephen. *Handbook to Life in Ancient Mesopotamia*. New York: Oxford University Press, 2005.

Braudel, Fernand. *Memory and the Mediterranean*. New York: Vintage Books, 1998.

Brewer, Douglas J., and Emily Teeter. *Egypt and the Egyptians*. 2nd ed. Cambridge, UK: Cambridge University Press, 2007.

Chadwick, Robert. *First Civilizations: Ancient Mesopotamia and Ancient Egypt*. London: Equinox, 2005.

Cunliffe, Barry. *Europe between the Oceans: Themes and Variations: 9000 BC–AD 1000.* New Haven, CT: Yale University Press, 2008.

Gowlett, John A. J. *Ascent to Civilization: The Archaeology of Early Man.* New York: Alfred A. Knopf, 1984.

Hawkes, Jacquette. *The Atlas of Early Man.* New York: St. Martin's Press, 1976.

Korn, Jerry, ed. *The First Cities.* New York: Time-Life Books, 1973.

Kramer, Samuel Noah. *Cradle of Civilization.* New York: Time-Life Books, 1967.

Myśliwiec, Karol. *The Twilight of Ancient Egypt: First Millennium B.C.E.* Ithaca, NY: Cornell University Press, 2000.

Oates, Joan. *Babylon.* London: Thames and Hudson, 1986.

Renfrew, Colin. *Archaeology and Language: The Puzzle of Indo-European Origins.* Cambridge, UK: University of Cambridge Press, 1987.

Roaf, Michael. *Cultural Atlas of Mesopotamia and the Ancient Near East.* New York: Facts on File, 1990.

Roux, George. *Ancient Iraq.* New York: Pelican Books, 1980.

Shaw, Ian, ed. *The Oxford History of Ancient Egypt.* New York: Oxford University Press, 2004.

Trigger, B., B. Kemp, D. O'Conner, and A. Lloyd, eds. *Ancient Egypt: A Social History.* Cambridge, UK: Cambridge University Press, 1983.

REGIONS AND PEOPLES

Allen, Lindsay. *The Persian Empire.* Chicago: University of Chicago Press, 2005.

Barber, Richard. *The Penguin Guide to Medieval Europe.* New York: Penguin Books, 1984.

Bobrick, Benson. *The Caliph's Splendor: Islam and the West in the Golden Age of Baghdad.* New York: Simon and Schuster, 2012.

Bray, Warwick. *Everyday Life of the Aztecs.* New York: Putnam, 1968.

Cantor, Norman. *The Sacred Chain: A History of the Jews.* New York: Harper Perennial, 1994.

Chu, David, and Elliott Skinner. *A Glorious Age in Africa: The Story of Three Great African Empires.* Trenton, NJ: Africa World Press, 1990.

Clements, Jonathan. *The Vikings.* Philadelphia: Running Press, 2008.

Cook, J. M. *The Persian Empire.* New York: Schocken Books, 1983.

Davidson, Basil. *Africa in History: Themes and Outlines.* New York: Macmillan, 1974.

Ebrey, Patricia Buckley. *The Cambridge Illustrated History of China.* Cambridge, UK: Cambridge University Press, 1996.

Elisseeff, Vadime, ed. *The Silk Roads: Highways of Culture and Commerce.* New York: Berghahn Books/UNESCO, 2000.

Esposito, John L., ed. *The Oxford History of Islam.* New York: Oxford University Press, 1999.

Fairbank, John King. *China: A New History*. Cambridge, MA: Belknap Press, 1992.

Frankopan, Peter. *The Silk Roads: A New History of the World*. New York: Vintage Books, 2017.

Fremantle, Anne. *Age of Faith*. New York: Time-Life Books, 1965.

Gascoigne, Bamber. *The Dynasties of China: A History*. New York: Carroll and Graf, 2003.

Gies, Frances, and Joseph Gies. *Daily Life in Medieval Times*. New York: Black Dog and Leventhal, 1990.

Gottfried, Robert S. *The Black Death, Natural and Human Disaster in Medieval Europe*. New York: Free Press, 1983.

Grunebaum, G. E. *Classical Islam*. Chicago: Aldine, 1970.

Hay, John. *Ancient China*. New York: Henry Z. Walck, 1973.

Herold, J. Christopher. *The Age of Napoleon*. New York: American Heritage, 1983.

Hodgett, Gerald Augustus John. *A Social and Economic History of Medieval Europe*. London: Methuen, 1972.

Hourani, Albert. *A History of the Arab Peoples*. Cambridge, MA: Belknap, 1991.

Hua, Yu. *China in Ten Words*. New York: Pantheon Books, 2011.

Huang, Ray. *China: A Macro History*. Armonk, NY: M.E. Sharp, 1988.

Keay, John. *China: A History*. New York: Basic Books, 2009.

Kennedy, Hugh. *The Great Arab Conquests*. New York: Da Capo Press, 2007.

Kinross, Lord. *The Ottoman Centuries*. New York: Morrow Quill, 1977.

Kleeman, Terry, and Tracy Barrett. *The Ancient Chinese World*. New York: Oxford University Press, 2005.

Lewis, Archibald, ed. *The Islamic World and the West A.D. 622–1492*. New York: John Wiley and Sons, 1970.

Lewis, Bernard. *The Middle East: A Brief History of the Last 2000 Years*. New York: Scribner, 1995.

Liu, Xinru. *The Silk Road in World History*. New York: Oxford University Press, 2010.

Luce, Edward. *In Spite of the Gods: The Rise of Modern India*. New York: Anchor Books, 2008.

Martin, Janet. *Medieval Russia 980–1584*. Cambridge, UK: Cambridge University Press, 1995.

McLeod, John. *The History of India*. 2nd ed. Santa Barbara, CA: Greenwood, 2015.

Nabarz, Payam. *The Mysteries of Mithra*. Rochester, VT: Inner Traditions, 2005.

Potok, Chaim. *Wanderings: A History of the Jews*. New York: Ballantine Books, 1978.

Rautman, Marcus. *Daily Life in the Byzantine Empire*. Westport, CT: Greenwood Press, 2006.

Risso, Patricia. *Merchants & Faith: Muslim Commerce and Culture in the Indian Ocean.* Boulder, CO: Westview Press, 1995.

Roberts, J. A. G. *Early China, from Beijing Man to the First Emperor.* Gloucestershire, UK: Sutton, 2007.

Robinson, Francis. *The Mughal Emperors and the Islamic Dynasties of India, Iran, and Central Asia, 1206–1925.* London: Thames and Hudson, 2007.

Shafer, Edward. *Ancient China.* New York: Time-Life Books, 1967.

Shaffer, Lynda Norene. *Maritime Southeast Asia to 1500.* London: M.E. Sharpe, 1996.

Tames, Richard. *A Traveler's History of Japan.* New York: Interlink Books, 1993.

Thapar, Romila. *A History of India.* New York: Penguin Books, 1970.

Tharoor, Shashi. *Nehru: The Invention of India.* New York: Arcade, 2003.

Watson, Francis. *A Concise History of India.* London: Thames and Hudson, 1979.

Wiet, Gaston. *Baghdad, Metropolis of the Abbasids.* Norman, OK: University of Oklahoma Press, 1971.

Williams, Lea. *Southeast Asia: A History.* New York: Oxford University Press, 1976.

Wolfram, Herwig. *The Roman Empire and Its Germanic People.* Berkeley: University of California Press, 1997.

Wolpert, Stanley. *A New History of India.* New York: Oxford University Press, 1997.

Yan, Xuetong. *Ancient Chinese Thought, Modern Chinese Power.* Princeton, NJ: Princeton University Press, 2013.

THEMATIC, REVISIONIST, AND ANALYTICAL HISTORIES

Boorstin, Daniel J. *The Discoverers.* New York: Random House, 1983.

Davis, Kenneth C. *America's Hidden History: Untold Tales of the First Pilgrims, Fighting Women, and Forgotten Founders Who Shaped a Nation.* New York: Smithsonian Books, 2009.

Demko, George. *Why in the World: Adventures in Geography.* New York: Anchor Books, 1992.

Diamond, Jared M. *Collapse: How Societies Choose to Fail or Succeed.* New York: Viking, 2005.

———. *Guns, Germs, and Steel: The Fates of Human Societies.* New York: W. W. Norton, 1999.

Ferguson, Niall. *Empire: The Rise and Demise of the British World Order and the Lessons for Global Power.* New York: Basic Books, 2002.

Hochschild, Adam. *King Leopold's Ghost: A Story of Greed, Terror, and Heroism in Colonial Africa.* Boston: Houghton Mifflin, 1998.

Hodgson, Marshall. *Rethinking World History: Essays on Europe, Islam, and World History.* Cambridge, UK: Cambridge University Press, 1993.

Hunt, Lynn: *Writing History in the Global Era.* New York: W. W. Norton, 2015.

Jacques, Martin. *When China Rules the World: The End of the Western World and the Birth of a New Global Order.* New York: Penguin Books, 2009.

MacGregor, Neil. *A History of the World in 100 Objects.* New York: Penguin Books, 2012.

Mann, Charles C. *1491: New Revelations of the Americas before Columbus.* New York: Alfred A. Knopf, 2005.

———. *1493: Uncovering the New World Columbus Created.* New York: Alfred A. Knopf, 2011.

Lefkowitz, Mary. *Not Out of Africa: How Afrocentrism Became an Excuse to Teach Myth as History.* New York: Basic Books, 1997.

Menzies, Gavin. *1421: The Year China Discovered America.* New York: Harper Perennial, 2003.

Morgan, Michael Hamilton. *Lost History: The Enduring Legacy of Muslim Scientists, Thinkers, and Artists.* Washington, DC: National Geographic, 2007.

Segal, Ronald. *Islam's Black Slaves: The Other Black Diaspora.* New York: Farrar Straus and Giroux, 2001.

Tuchman, Barbara. *A Distant Mirror: The Calamitous 14th Century.* New York: Ballantine Books, 1978.

Van Sertima, Ivan. *They Came before Columbus: The African Presence in Ancient America.* New York: Random House, 2003.

Watson, Peter. *Ideas: A History of Thought and Invention, from Fire to Freud.* New York: HarperCollins, 2005.

Wolf, Eric R. *Europe and the People without a History.* Berkeley: University of California Press, 1982.

CROSS-CULTURAL CURRENTS AND RIPPLE EFFECTS

Asbridge, Thomas. *The First Crusade.* New York: Oxford University Press, 2004.

Benfey, Christopher. *The Great Wave: Gilded Age Misfits, Japanese Eccentrics.* New York: Random House, 2003.

Catlos, Brian. *Infidel Kings and Unholy Warriors: Faith, Power, and Violence in the Age of Crusades and Jihad.* New York: Macmillan, 2014.

Jones, Terry, and Alan Ereira. *Crusades.* New York: Facts on File, 1995.

Madden, Thomas F., ed. *Crusades: The Illustrated History.* Ann Arbor: University of Michigan Press, 2004.

Morgan, David. *The Mongols.* Malden, MA: Blackwell, 2007.

Nabhan, Gary Paul. *Cumin, Camels, and Caravans: A Spice Odyssey.* Berkeley: University of California Press, 2014.

Reston, James. *Dogs of God: Columbus, the Inquisition, and the Defeat of the Moors.* New York: Anchor Books, 2005.

Riley-Smith, Jonathan. *The Oxford Illustrated History of the Crusades.* New York: Oxford University Press, 1995.

Rogerson, Barnaby. *The Last Crusaders: East, West, and the Battle for the Centre of the World*. London: Abacus, 2009.

Rossabi, Morris, ed. *The Mongols and Global History*. New York: W. W. Norton, 2011.

Tyerman, Christopher. *The Crusades*. New York: Sterling, 2009.

LIFE, THOUGHT, AND CONSCIOUSNESS

Chorost, Michael. *World Wide Mind: The Coming Integration of Humanity, Machines, and the Internet*. New York: Free Press, 2011.

Eagleman, David. *Incognito: The Secret Lives of the Brain*. New York: Vintage Books, 2011.

Harris, Marvin. *Our Kind: The Evolution of Human Life and Culture*. New York: Harper and Row, 1989.

Hawkins, Jeff. *On Intelligence: How a New Understanding of the Brain Will Lead to the Creation of Truly Intelligent Machines*. With Sandra Blakeslee. New York: Times Books, 2004.

Healy, Jane M. *Endangered Minds: Why Children Don't Think and What We Can Do About It*. New York: Simon and Schuster, 1990.

Johnson, Steven. *Where Good Ideas Come From: The Natural History of Innovation*. New York: Riverhead Books, 2010.

Kahneman, Daniel. *Thinking Fast and Slow*. New York: Farrar Straus and Giroux, 2011.

Mead, George Herbert. *On Social Psychology*. Chicago: University of Chicago Press, 1964.

Sacks, Oliver. *The River of Consciousness*. New York: Alfred A. Knopf, 2017.

Stephens, Ransom. *The Left Brain Speaks, the Right Brain Laughs: The Neuroscience of Innovation and Creativity in Art, Science, and Life*. Jersey City, NJ: Cleis Press, 2016.

Thomas, Lewis. *The Lives of a Cell: Notes of a Biology Watcher*. New York: Penguin Books, 1974.

RELIGION

Abiva, Huseyin, and Noura Durkee. *A History of Muslim Civilization*. Skokie, IL: IQRA International Educational Foundation, 2003.

Alawai, Ali A. *The Crisis of Islamic Civilization*. New Haven, CT: Yale University Press, 2009.

Armstrong, Karen. *The Great Transformation: The Beginning of Our Religious Traditions*. New York: Alfred A. Knopf, 2006.

———. *Muhammad: A Biography of the Prophet*. San Francisco: HarperCollins, 1992.

Árnason, Jóhann Páll, Armando Salvatore, and Georg Stauth, eds. *Islam in Process: Historical and Civilizational Perspectives*. Vol. 7 of *Yearbook of the Sociology of Islam*. Bielefeld, Germany: transcript Verlag, 2015.

Aslan, Reza. *No god but God: The Origins, Evolution, and Future of Islam*. New York: Random House, 2006.

Aslan, Reza. *Zealot: The Life and Times of Jesus of Nazareth*. New York: Random House, 2013.

Bottéro, Jean. *Religion in Ancient Mesopotamia*. Chicago: University of Chicago Press, 2004.

Doniger, Wendy. *The Hindus: An Alternative History*. New York: Penguin Books, 2009.

Ehrman, Bart D. *How Jesus Became God: The Exaltation of a Jewish Preacher from Galilee*. New York: HarperCollins, 2014.

Hitchcock, James. *History of the Catholic Church: From the Apostolic Age to the Third Millennium*. San Francisco: Ignatius Press, 2012.

Puett, Michael, and Christine Gross-Loh. *The Path: What Chinese Philosophers Can Teach Us About the Good Life*. New York/Delhi: Simon and Schuster, 2016.

Smith, Huston. *The Religions of Man*. San Francisco: HarperCollins, 1961.

Smith, Huston, and Philip Novak. *Buddhism: A Concise Introduction*. New York: HarperCollins, 2003.

Smith, Wilfred Cantwell. *The Faith of Other Men*. New York: New American Library, 1965.

Ulansey, David. *The Origins of the Mithraic Mysteries: Cosmology and Salvation in the Ancient World*. New York: Oxford University Press, 1989.

ECONOMICS AND MONEY

Beattie, Alan. *False Economy: A Surprising Economic History of the World*. New York: Riverhead Books, 2009.

Berlin, Isaiah. *Karl Marx: His Life and Environment*. Oxford, UK: Oxford University Press, 1978.

Cassidy, John. *How Markets Fail: The Logic of Economic Calamities*. New York: Penguin Books, 2009.

Chown, John. *A History of Money from AD 800*. London/New York: Routledge, 1994.

Ferguson, Niall. *The Ascent of Money: A Financial History of the World*. New York: Penguin Books, 2008.

Graeber, David. *Debt: The First 5,000 Years*. New York: Melville House, 2011.

Heilbroner, Robert L., ed. *The Essential Adam Smith*. New York: W. W. Norton, 1986.

———. *The Worldly Philosophers*. New York: Simon and Schuster, 1989.

Kamenka, Eugene, ed. *The Portable Karl Marx*. New York: Penguin Books, 1983.

Mokyr, Joel. *A Culture of Growth: The Origins of the Modern Economy*. Princeton, NJ: Princeton University Press, 2017.

Rist, Gilbert. *The Delusions of Economics: The Misguided Certainties of a Hazardous Science*. London: Zed Books, 2011.

Ross, Ian Simpson. *The Life of Adam Smith*. Oxford, UK: Clarendon Press, 1995.

Smith, Adam. *The Wealth of Nations*. New York: Bantam, 2003.

Wheen, Francis. *Karl Marx: A Life*. New York: W. W. Norton, 1999.

WOMEN'S HISTORY

Barber, Elizabeth W. *Women's Work, The First 20,000 Years*. New York: W. W. Norton, 1994.

Chang, Leslie T. *Factory Girls: From Village to City in a Changing China*. New York: Spiegel and Gram, 2008.

Croutier, Alev. *Harem: The World Behind the Veil*. New York: Abbeville Press, 1989.

Groneman, Carol, and Mary Beth Norton, eds. *"To Toil the Livelong Day": America's Women at Work, 1780–1980*. Ithaca, NY: Cornell University Press, 1987.

Prost, Antoine. *A History of Private Life*. Cambridge, MA: Belknap Press, 1991.

Robertson, P. *The Experience of Women: Pattern and Change in 19th Century Europe*. Princeton, NJ: Princeton University Press, 1981.

Reed, Evelyn. *Women's Evolution from Matriarchal Clan to Patriarchal Family*. New York: Pathfinder Press, 1975.

Tilly, Louise A., and Joan W. Scott. *Women, Work, and Family*. New York: Holt, Rinehart and Winston, 1978.

MATHEMATICS, SCIENCE, AND TECHNOLOGY

Aldcroft, Derek, and Michael Freeman, eds. *Transport in the Industrial Revolution*. Manchester, UK: Manchester University Press, 1983.

Barrat, James. *Our Final Invention: Artificial Intelligence and the End of the Human Era*. New York: Thomas Dunne Books, 2013.

Browning, Frank. *The Fate of Gender: Nature, Nurture, and the Human Future*. London: Bloomsbury, 2016.

Bruce, Robert V. *Alexander Graham Bell and the Conquest of Solitude*. Ithaca, NY: Cornell University Press, 1973.

Burton, Anthony. *The Canal Builders*. London: Eyre Methuen, 1972.

Butler, John. *Atlantic Kingdom: America's Contest with Cunard in the Sail and Steam*. Washington, DC: Brassey's, 2001.

Cardwell, Donald. *Wheels, Clocks, and Rockets: A History of Technology*. New York: W. W. Norton, London, 1995.

Dolnick, Edward. *The Clockworks Universe: Isaac Newton, The Royal Society, and the Birth of the Modern World*. New York: Harper Perennial, 2011.

Foer, Franklin. *World without Mind: The Existential Threat of Big Tech.* New York: Penguin Press, 2017.

Frost, Lawrence A. *The Thomas A. Edison Album.* Seattle, WA: Superior, 1969.

Gies, Joseph, and Frances Gies. *Leonard of Pisa and the New Mathematics of the Middle Ages.* New York: Thomas Y. Crowell, 1969.

Grayson, Stephen. *Beautiful Engines: Treasures of the Internal Combustion Century.* Marblehead, MA: Devereux Books, 2001.

Grosvenor, Edwin S., and Morgan Wesson. *Alexander Graham Bell: The Life and Times of the Man Who Invented the Telephone.* New York: Harry N. Abrams, 1997.

Headrick, Daniel R. *The Tools of Empire: Technology and European Imperialism in the Nineteenth Century.* Oxford, UK: Oxford University Press, 1981.

Hilton, Suzanne. *Faster Than a Horse: Moving West with Engine Power.* Louisville, KY: Westminster Press, 1983.

Israel, Paul. *Edison: A Life of Invention.* New York: John Wiley and Sons, 1998.

Johnson, Steven. *The Invention of Air: A Story of Science, Faith, Revolution, and the Birth of America.* New York: Riverhead Books, 2008.

King, Gilbert. *The Bicycle: Boneshakers, Highwheelers, and Other Celebrated Cycles.* Philadelphia: Courage Books, 2002.

Klein, Maury. *Unfinished Business: The Railroad in American Life.* Hanover, NH: University Press of New England, 1994.

Kolbert, Elizabeth. *The Sixth Extinction: An Unnatural History.* London: Bloomsbury, 2014.

Landes, David. *The Unbound Prometheus.* London: Cambridge University Press, 1969.

Lasker, Edward. *The Adventure of Chess.* Garden City, NY: Doubleday, 1940.

Resnikoff, H. L., and R. O. Wells. *Mathematics in Civilization.* New York: Dover, 1984.

Rogers, Everett. *Diffusion of Innovations.* New York: Free Press, 1995.

Sale, Kirkpatrick. *The Fire of His Genius: Robert Fulton and the American Dream.* New York: Free Press, 2001.

Shenk, David. *The Immortal Game: A History of Chess.* New York: Doubleday, 2005.

Stover, John. *A History of American Railroads.* Chicago: Rand McNally, 1967.

Struik, Dirk. *A Concise History of Mathematics.* Mineola, NY: Dover, 1987.

Taylor, George Rogers. *The Transportation Revolution.* New York: Holt, Rinehart and Winston, 1966.

Teresi, Dick. *Lost Discoveries: The Ancient Roots of Modern Science—from the Babylonians to the Maya.* New York: Simon and Schuster, 2003.

Tyson, Neil de Grasse. *Astrophysics for People in a Hurry.* New York: W. W. Norton, 2017.

Yonck, Richard. *Heart of the Machine: Our Future in a World of Artificial Emotional Intelligence.* New York: Arcade, 2017.

MODERN TIMES

Abu-Lughod, Janet L. *Before European Hegemony: The World System A.D. 1250–1350.* New York: Oxford University Press, 1982.

Bowlby, Rachel. *Carried Away: The Invention of Modern Shopping.* New York: Columbia University Press, 2001.

Bullock, Allan. *Hitler and Stalin: Parallel Lives.* New York: HarperCollins, 1991.

Chandler, Robert. *Shadow World: Resurgent Russia, the Global New Left, and Radical Islam.* Washington, DC: Regnery, 2008.

Ferguson, Niall. *The War of the World.* New York: Penguin Books, 2006.

Gaddis, John Lewis. *The Cold War: A New History.* New York: Penguin Press, 2005.

Gerner, Deborah J., and Jillian Schwedler. *Understanding the Contemporary Middle East.* Boulder, CO: Lynne Rienner, 2004.

Glendon, Mary Ann. *A World Made New.* New York: Random House, 2001.

Hiro, Dilip. *War without End: The Rise of Islamist Terrorism and Global Response.* Abingdon, UK: Routledge, 2002.

Hochschild, Adam. *To End All Wars: A Story of Loyalty and Rebellion, 1914–1918.* Boston: Houghton Mifflin Harcourt, 2011.

Lukacs, John. *June 1941: Hitler and Stalin.* New Haven, CT: Yale University Press, 2006.

Kamrava, Mehran: *The Modern Middle East.* Berkeley: University of California Press, 2005.

McCullough, David. *Truman.* New York: Simon and Schuster, 1992.

Miller, Michael B. *The Bon Marche: Bourgeois Culture and the Department Store, 1869–1920.* Princeton, NJ: Princeton University Press, 1981.

Mongo, Carol. "Le Bon Marché." *Paris Voice,* May 2002.

Overy, Richard. *The Dictators: Hitler's Germany, Stalin's Russia.* New York: W. W. Norton, 2004.

Persico, Joseph. *Nuremberg: Infamy on Trial.* New York: Viking Press, 1994.

Roberts, J. M. *The Penguin History of the Twentieth Century.* New York: Penguin, 1999.

Rubin, Barry. *The Tragedy of the Middle East.* Cambridge, UK: Cambridge University Press, 2002.

Teed, Peter. *A Dictionary of Twentieth Century History.* New York: Oxford University Press, 1992.

Thackery, Frank W., and John E. Findling, eds. *Events That Changed the World in the Twentieth Century.* Westport, CT: Greenwood Press, 1995.

Walker, Martin. *The Cold War: A History.* New York: Henry Holt, 1993.

Wright, Robin. *The Wrath of Militant Islam.* New York: Touchstone, 1985.

Index

YANINA GOSULTSKY

Tamim Ansary was raised in Afghanistan and has lived in the United States since 1964. His books include *Destiny Disrupted: A History of the World through Islamic Eyes*, which won a Northern California Book Award for nonfiction and has been translated into ten languages. As a speaker, he has delivered talks in many venues to many audiences including the community associated with the Muslim Educational Trust of Portland, Oregon, and the Jewish congregation of Temple Israel in Long Beach, California. His memoir, *West of Kabul, East of New York*, was selected as a One City One Book pick by a number of cities, including San Francisco, California, and Waco, Texas. He now lives with his wife, Deborah, in San Francisco, where he teaches writing workshops and communes with his small garden and his large cat, Raoul.

PublicAffairs is a publishing house founded in 1997. It is a tribute to the standards, values, and flair of three persons who have served as mentors to countless reporters, writers, editors, and book people of all kinds, including me.

I. F. STONE, proprietor of *I. F. Stone's Weekly*, combined a commitment to the First Amendment with entrepreneurial zeal and reporting skill and became one of the great independent journalists in American history. At the age of eighty, Izzy published *The Trial of Socrates*, which was a national bestseller. He wrote the book after he taught himself ancient Greek.

BENJAMIN C. BRADLEE was for nearly thirty years the charismatic editorial leader of *The Washington Post*. It was Ben who gave the *Post* the range and courage to pursue such historic issues as Watergate. He supported his reporters with a tenacity that made them fearless and it is no accident that so many became authors of influential, best-selling books.

ROBERT L. BERNSTEIN, the chief executive of Random House for more than a quarter century, guided one of the nation's premier publishing houses. Bob was personally responsible for many books of political dissent and argument that challenged tyranny around the globe. He is also the founder and longtime chair of Human Rights Watch, one of the most respected human rights organizations in the world.

•   •   •

For fifty years, the banner of Public Affairs Press was carried by its owner Morris B. Schnapper, who published Gandhi, Nasser, Toynbee, Truman, and about 1,500 other authors. In 1983, Schnapper was described by *The Washington Post* as "a redoubtable gadfly." His legacy will endure in the books to come.

Peter Osnos, *Founder*